Formal Philosophy

FORMAL PHILOSOPHY

Selected Papers of Richard Montague

Edited and with an introduction by   Richmond H. Thomason

New Haven and London, Yale University Press, 1974

Copyright © 1974 by Yale University.
All rights reserved. This book may not be
reproduced, in whole or in part, in any form
(except by reviewers for the public press),
without written permission from the publishers.
Library of Congress catalog card number: 73-77159.
International standard book number: 0-300-01527-5.

Designed by Sally Sullivan
and set in Times Roman type.
Printed in the United States of America by
The Murray Printing Company,
Forge Village, Massachusetts.

Published in Great Britain, Europe, and Africa by
Yale University Press, Ltd., London.
Distributed in Latin America by Kaiman & Polon,
Inc., New York City; in Australasia and Southeast
Asia by John Wiley & Sons Australasia Pty. Ltd.,
Sydney; in India by UBS Publishers' Distributors Pvt.,
Ltd., Delhi; in Japan by John Weatherhill, Inc., Tokyo.

Contents

Introduction[1]

A. MONTAGUE'S SEMIOTIC PROGRAM

This posthumous volume contains all of Richard Montague's papers that were felt to have application to philosophical and linguistic problems. Over the period between the 1955 lecture that appears below as Chapter 1 and his last paper, Chapter 8, written in 1970, Montague's views on language developed into a comprehensive framework for the semiotic study of natural languages such as English.[2] This introduction is confined to the papers that develop this program and provide a mature statement of it, Chapters 3, 4, 5, 6, 7, and 8.[3] Its purpose is to show in some detail how Montague adapted metamathematical materials for application to the syntactic, semantic, and pragmatic study of natural languages.[4]

Montague's framework will seem much less familar to linguists than to logicians; though many of its logical elements are novel, they are natural developments of standard logical theories. The linguistic elements, however, were developed quite independently of current grammatical theories. As a result, though it is easy to discuss Montague's work without making reference to

[1] In drafting this introduction, I have benefited from the helpful comments of many colleagues, including Anil Gupta, J. A. W. Kamp, David Kaplan, David Lewis, Zane Parks, Terence Parsons, Barbara Partee, Robert Stalnaker, and Sarah Thomason.

[2] For a brief account of semiotic and its three branches—syntax, semantics, and pragmatics—see the opening paragraphs of Chapter 3.

[3] See van Fraassen [20] for an expository discussion of Chapter 11 and its application to the philosophy of science.

[4] There is a very careful and full description of the concepts and methodology of metamathematics in Church [2], pp. 1–68. Also see Church [1] for more material on semantics, and Kalish [6].

material from linguistics, it is quite impossible to do so without presupposing familiarity with symbolic logic. This introduction is directed to readers who are acquainted with the rudiments of set theory, and whose knowledge of symbolic logic includes at least the first-order predicate calculus and its semantic interpretation.

Many linguists may not realize at first glance how fundamentally Montague's approach differs from current linguistic conceptions. Before turning to syntactic theory, it may therefore be helpful to make a methodological point. According to Montague the syntax, semantics, and pragmatics of natural languages are branches of mathematics, not of psychology. The syntax of English, for example, is just as much a part of mathematics as number theory or geometry. This view is a corollary of Montague's strategy of studying natural languages by means of the same techniques used in metamathematics to study formal languages. Metamathematics is a branch of mathematics, and generalizing it to comprehend natural languages does not render it any less a mathematical discipline.

This mathematical conception of semiotic does not imply that data are irrelevant to, for instance, the syntax of English. Just as mathematicians refer to intuitions about points and lines in establishing a geometrical theory, we may refer to intuitions about sentences, noun phrases, subordinate clauses, and the like in establishing a grammar of English. But this conception does presuppose agreement among theoreticians on the intuitions, and it renders statistical evidence about, say, the reactions of a sample of native speakers to 'Mary is been by my mother' just as irrelevant to syntax as evidence about their reactions to '7 + 5 = 22' would be to number theory.

Even though most transformationalists regard syntax as a branch of psychology, this methodological reorientation is not as drastic in practice as it seems at first. Contemporary grammarians do not in general make essential use of statistical data. They appeal to introspective evidence and tend to discount data on which they are not able to agree with their colleagues.

But the reorientation does affect one point: the nature of "linguistic universals." For contemporary linguists such universals are psychological in nature, and there is a presupposition that features found to hold good for all known human languages will be universal in this psychological sense. Such universals have no interest for Montague. They are mentioned nowhere in his papers, nor does he ever suggest that his work should be applied to topics such as the psychology of language acquisition. Where the term 'universal' appears in his writings, as in "Universal Grammar," the title of Chapter 7, it has reference to the mathematician's natural tendency to generalize. A theory that is intuitive and mathematically elegant, and that comprehends all special cases of a certain topic, can be termed a universal theory of the topic. In this sense topology is a universal theory of geometry, and Montague's theory of universal grammar is a universal theory of grammar. So little attention is given in "Universal Grammar" to the task of presenting an account that is merely psychologically universal that languages with expressions that are infinitely long are comprehended by the theory of that paper.

B. SYNTAX

1. Disambiguated languages in general

Montague not only regarded syntax as a branch of mathematics, but was uncompromising in presenting his syntactic theories as such, with great attention to generality and rigor and little concern for the uninitiated reader. Though he gave several illustrations of the application of his program to what he called 'fragments of English', these examples themselves are presented with a notational sophistication that makes them forbidding to non-mathematicians. Probably nothing can be done to make easy reading of Montague's writings; they must be studied slowly and with care. But, though this may not seem evident at first glance, they are accessible to any patient reader acquainted with symbolic logic and set theoretic notation. In what follows I will try to make this process easier by providing some examples that link Montague's work to more familiar logical material.

Chapter 7 begins with a general account of the syntax of "disambiguated languages," languages without syntactic ambiguities such as that of the English sentence 'John told someone he would be awarded the prize', where the pronoun 'he' can have 'John' as its antecedent, or have 'someone' as its antecedent, or can be a demonstrative pronoun referring to someone indicated by the context of use of the sentence. Human languages are rich in syntactic ambiguities, and disambiguated languages must be regarded as theoretical constructs. But both logicians and linguists have been interested in such languages: logicians because logical consequence can only be defined as a relation among syntactically disambiguated sentences,[5] linguists because one of the traditional tasks of syntax is the exposure of syntactic ambiguity.

Any familar logical calculus will serve as an example of a disambiguated language, for example the following version $\mathfrak{A}^0$ of the propositional calculus. The individual constants of this language are 'a', 'b', and 'c', the one-place predicates (or, as we will call them to stress relations with English grammar, the *one-place verbs* or *intransitive verbs*) are 'P' and 'Q', the only one-place connective is '$\neg$', and the two-place connectives are '$\wedge$' and '$\vee$'. The set of formulas of $\mathfrak{A}^0$ is defined recursively,[6] as the smallest set K such that (0) if ξ is a one-place verb and α an individual constant, then $\ulcorner \xi(\alpha) \urcorner \in K$,[7] (1) if ζ is a one-place connective and $\varphi \in K$, then $\ulcorner \zeta \dashv \varphi \vdash \urcorner \in K$, and (2) if ζ is a two-place connective and $\varphi, \psi \in K$, then $\ulcorner \dashv \varphi \vdash \zeta \dashv \psi \vdash \urcorner \in K$. This

---

[5] At least, this is what logicians have presupposed. A by-product of Montague's work, however, is a theory of how logical consequence can be defined for languages admitting syntactic ambiguity. For those logicians concerned only with artificial languages this generalization will be of little interest, since there is no serious point to constructing an artificial language that is not disambiguated. (In the literal sense of Montague's definition, some of the formalized languages presented in the logical literature have been syntactically ambiguous. But in all such cases the ambiguity has no semantic effect.)

[6] See van Fraassen [19], pp. 18–24, and Thomason [17], pp. 309–20 for accounts of definition by recursion (or, as it is sometimes called, 'definition by induction').

[7] See Note 7 of Chapter 6 for an explanation of the policy concerning quotation that we will follow in this introduction. The symbol '$\in$' is set theoretic notation. Readers to whom such notation is unfamiliar should consult an introduction to set theory, such as Suppes [16], before turning to Montague's papers.

generates formulas such as '$P(a)$', '$\neg + \neg + P(a) + +$', '$+ P(a) + \lor + Q(a) +$', and '$+ \neg + \neg + P(a) + + + \land + \neg + Q(b) + +$'.[8]

Five syntactic categories figure in this formulation: individual constants, one-place verbs, one-place connectives, two-place connectives, and formulas. All categories but the last were defined by enumerating their members. The three pairs of parentheses '(' and ')', '$+$' and '$+$', and '$+$' and '$+$' belong to no syntactic category; they are introduced *syncategorematically* in the recursive definition of the set of formulas. Their syncategorematic character is borne out by the fact that the standard semantic interpretation of this language (the truth-functional one) assigns no independent meaning to parentheses. The semantic purpose of parentheses is not to bear meanings, but to disambiguate; they ensure that the formulas of $\mathfrak{A}^0$ are syntactically unambiguous.[9] Had they been omitted from any clause of the recursion, the resulting language would not have conformed to Montague's definition of disambiguation.

To illustrate this point, let L^1 be the language that results from replacing clause 2 above by the following clause: (2') if ζ is a two-place connective and $\varphi, \psi \in K$ then $\varphi \zeta \psi \in K$.[10] The language L^1 is ambiguous, as is shown by the fact that '$P(a) \lor Q(a) \land Q(b)$', a formula of L^1, is assigned the following two syntactic structures.[11]

---

[8] This way of introducing parentheses into formulas gives them an awkward appearance, but ensures that the parentheses introduced with each clause serve to disambiguate the formulas produced by that clause. If, for instance, parentheses are omitted from clause 1 then negations become ambiguous.

[9] In the propositional calculus, at least, syntactic disambiguation will ensure semantic disambiguation. In natural languages there is another source of semantic ambiguity: lexical items can be assigned more than one semantic value.

[10] The letter 'L' is used here rather than '$\mathfrak{A}$' because L^1 is not a disambiguated language. Montague's treatment of languages that are not disambiguated will be discussed below.

[11] As Barbara Partee points out in Partee [11], trees such as these ("M-trees") are analogous to Katz and Postal's "T-markers" rather than to the phrase structure trees commonly found in transformational grammar. Analyses give the pedigree of a phrase, the history of how it was built up by syntactic rules. When a language is disambiguated, each of its phrases has only one analysis tree.

(B-1)

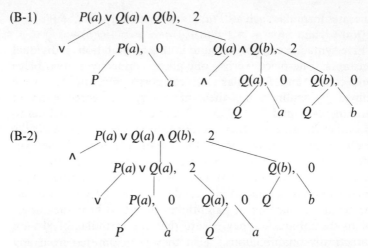

(B-2)

If '$P(a) \lor Q(a) \land Q(b)$' is likened to the English 'John will telephone or John will write and Mary will write', then the first analysis tree gives a reading synonymous with 'John will telephone, or Mary and John will write' and the second analysis tree a reading synonymous with 'John will telephone or write, and Mary will write'.

Analysis trees trace the manner in which particular expressions are generated by the recursion that determines a language. To the right of those expressions not at the tips of the tree, separated by a comma, is an index indicating the clause of the recursion according to which the expression was constructed from the sequence of expressions appearing below it. See Chapter 6, Section 7, for a discussion of such trees, called 'analyses' there. In Chapter 7, as we will see, the concept of an analysis is placed in a more general setting.

Characterized as it was above, much as formalized languages usually are presented, it is not immediately clear how $\mathfrak{A}^0$ can be fitted to Montague's general account of a disambiguated language, in "Universal Grammar." This account exploits the fact that all formalized languages share a syntactic structure: the structure imposed by a recursive definition. The syntactic categories that figure in such recursions constitute one of the most significant features of a language; they provide the means of classifying its expressions. Now, whenever two expressions are assigned to the same syntactic category they will combine with other expressions in exactly the same way—they associate according to the same modes of combination. This is exemplified by the recursive definition of the formulas of $\mathfrak{A}^0$; for instance, if φ and ψ are both formulas, then $\ulcorner \neg + \varphi + \urcorner$ and $\ulcorner \neg + \psi + \urcorner$ are both formulas. These modes of syntactic combination comprise another of the features that, according to Montague, characterize a language. Modes of combination are functions taking expressions (or, to be precise, sequences of expressions) into expressions.

As an exercise, let's define these functions for $\mathfrak{A}^0$, letting F_0^0 be the mode of combining one-place verbs with individual constants to make formulas, F_1^0 be the mode of combining one-place connectives with formulas to make formulas, and F_2^0 be the mode of combining two-place connectives with two-place sequences of formulas to make formulas. Here are the equations defining these functions.

$$F_0^0(\delta, \alpha) = \ulcorner \delta(\alpha) \urcorner$$
$$F_1^0(\zeta, \varphi) = \ulcorner \zeta + \varphi + \urcorner$$
$$F_2^0(\zeta, \varphi, \psi) = \ulcorner \dotplus \varphi \dotplus \zeta \dotplus \psi \dotplus \urcorner$$

Notice that these three functions merely are operations defined for all expressions of the language; for instance, $F_1^0(\text{'}\neg (P_\wedge \text{'}, \text{'})a\text{'}) = \text{'} \neg (P_\wedge +)a + \text{'}$. These functions, called the *structural operations* of $\mathfrak{A}^0$, are used in stating syntactic rules, but in themselves are not syntactic rules. It is such a rule, for instance, that tells us that F_0^0 is the syntactic operation that is used to make a formula out of a one-place verb and an individual constant. To state the syntactic rules of $\mathfrak{A}^0$ in the special form required by Montague's definition (Chapter 7, Section 2) we must first name the syntactic categories of $\mathfrak{A}^0$; let them be ICST, 1V, 1C, 2C, and FOR.[12] Let Δ^0 be the set $\{$ICST, 1V, 1C, 2C, FOR$\}$. This set, which serves to index the syntactic categories of $\mathfrak{A}^0$, is

---

[12] Strictly speaking, 'ICST', '1V', and so forth are names of the category indices. We need not inquire what the indices are; they can be anything, say the first five natural numbers, as long as they differ from one another.

according to Montague's formal definition one of the components of a disambiguated language.

A syntactic rule must contain three pieces of information: the structural operation F that serves as the mode of combination of the rule, the respective syntactic categories of the various input expressions that are to serve as arguments of F, and the syntactic category that the rule assigns to the resulting output expression, the value of F. The first rule of $\mathfrak{A}^0$, for instance, states that if ξ is a 1V and α an ICST then $\xi(\alpha)$ is a FOR. Thus, Montague conceives of syntactic rules as ordered triples whose first component is a structural operation, whose second component is a sequence consisting of as many category indices as the first component has argument places, and whose third component is a category index. The following three triples constitute the set S^0 of syntactic rules of $\mathfrak{A}^0$.

$$\langle F_0^0, \langle 1V, ICST \rangle, FOR \rangle$$
$$\langle F_1^0, \langle 1C, FOR \rangle, FOR \rangle$$
$$\langle F_2^0, \langle 2C, FOR, FOR \rangle, FOR \rangle$$

These rules correspond respectively to clauses 0, 1, and 2 of the recursive definition given above.

In $\mathfrak{A}^0$, the category of formulas is especially prominent in the syntactic rules; in fact, it is the only syntactic category that figures recursively in these rules.[13] This, however, is from Montague's general point of view a purely accidental feature; sentences[14] are given no privileged place in his syntax. There is no reason why syntactic rules may not lead from any categories to any category, and in Montague's fragments of English, recursions are carried through many syntactic categories besides that of sentences. However, it is useful to distinguish the category of sentences from the other syntactic categories of a language—not for any syntactic reason, but because according to the semantic theory sentences must denote truth values. Therefore a dis-

---

[13] This means it is the only category having unlimited self-embedding. A formula can occur as a constituent phrase of another formula, but a one-place verb phrase cannot be embedded in another one-place verb phrase.

[14] Sentences differ from formulas only in that the latter may have occurrences of free variables.

ambiguated language must include, besides a specification of Δ and of the set S of its syntactic rules, a particular member of Δ that is identified as the category of sentences of the language. In the case of $\mathfrak{A}^0$, this category is of course FOR.

The sets Δ^0 and S^0 provide a structural characterization of the language $\mathfrak{A}^0$; in a transformational syntax their task would be performed by phrase structure rules and transformations, rather than by the lexicon. It is the basis clauses of the recursion that contain lexical rather than structural information; these clauses serve to enumerate the various "basic expressions" assigned to each syntactic category. In Montague's definition of a disambiguated language, the lexicon enters as the family of sets X_δ, where $\delta \in \Delta$. The set X_δ contains the basic expressions of the category δ. For $\mathfrak{A}^0$, these sets are constituted as follows.

$$X^0_{\text{ICST}} = \{`a`, `b`, `c`\}$$
$$X^0_{1V} = \{`P`, `Q`\}$$
$$X^0_{1C} = \{`\neg`\}$$
$$X^0_{2C} = \{`\wedge`, `\vee`\}$$
$$X^0_{\text{FOR}} = \Lambda$$

The fact that X^0_{FOR} is the empty set does not prevent $\mathfrak{A}^0$ from having formulas; this signifies only that all its formulas will be syntactically complex.

Let C^0_δ be the set of all *phrases* of the category δ of $\mathfrak{A}^0$—that is, the set of all expressions (basic or complex) assigned to δ. Thus, for instance, C_{FOR} is the set of all formulas of $\mathfrak{A}^0$. The indexed family $C^0 = \langle C^0_\delta \rangle_{\delta \in \Delta^0}$, listing all the sets of phrases of the various syntactic categories of $\mathfrak{A}^0$, can be defined in terms of the set S^0 of syntactic rules and the operations F^0_i and sets X^0_δ, for $i \in \{0, 1, 2\}$ and $\delta \in \Delta^0$. In other words, once these things have been specified the set C^0_δ is uniquely determined for each category δ of $\mathfrak{A}^0$. The recursive definition that accomplishes this task has the same form for all disambiguated languages; the general version is set forth in Section 2 of Chapter 7. As applied to $\mathfrak{A}^0$ the definition takes on the following appearance:

The indexed family C^0 of all syntactic categories of $\mathfrak{A}^0$ is the smallest family C of sets indexed by Δ^0 such that

(1) $X_\delta^0 \subseteq C_\delta$ for all $\delta \in \Delta^0$; (2.0) for all $\zeta \in C_{1V}$ and $\alpha \in C_{ICST}$, $F_0^0(\zeta, \alpha) \in C_{FOR}$; (2.1) for all $\zeta \in C_{1C}$ and $\varphi \in C_{FOR}$, $F_1^0(\zeta, \varphi) \in C_{FOR}$; and (2.2) for all $\zeta \in C_{2C}$ and $\varphi, \psi \in C_{FOR}$, $F_2^0(\zeta, \varphi, \psi) \in C_{FOR}$.[15]

The set A^0 of *proper expressions* of $\mathfrak{A}^0$ consists of the basic expressions of $\mathfrak{A}^0$ together with those expressions that can be obtained from these by repeated applications of the structural operations of $\mathfrak{A}^0$. This set will in general contain many expressions of little syntactic interest, such as '$\wedge(P)$' and '$\neg(a(\vee))$', the former being $F_0^0('\wedge', 'P')$ and the latter being $F_0^0('\neg', F_0^0('a', '\vee'))$. The set has some mathematical usefulness, however, since it is the field of the algebra whose operations are the structural operations of $\mathfrak{A}^0$. By invoking this algebra Montague is able to appeal to mathematical concepts such as that of a homomorphism in making definitions and proving metatheorems. Of more syntactic interest, however, is the set of *phrases* of $\mathfrak{A}^0$, which consists of those proper expressions of $\mathfrak{A}^0$ that, for some category δ of $\mathfrak{A}^0$, belong to the set C_δ^0 of phrases of δ.

Where A^0 is the set of proper expressions of $\mathfrak{A}^0$, Montague's general definition of a disambiguated language identifies $\mathfrak{A}^0$ with the indexed family $\langle A^0, F_i^0, X_\delta^0, S^0, FOR \rangle_{i \in \{0,1,2\}, \delta \in \Delta^0}$.[16] To qualify as a disambiguated language, however, $\mathfrak{A}^0$ must meet two conditions: no expression produced as a value of one of the structural operations of $\mathfrak{A}^0$ can also be a basic expression of $\mathfrak{A}^0$ (i.e. a member of one of the sets X_δ^0), and furthermore every complex proper expression must be producible from one and only one structural operation, and from a unique assignment of arguments to that operation.

Thus, for example, '$\nvdash P(a) \nvdash \wedge \nvdash Q(a) \nvdash$' can only have the form $F_0^1('P(a)', 'Q(a)')$ in $\mathfrak{A}^0$. There are no other structural operation and arguments (the arguments being proper expressions) that produce '$\nvdash P(a) \nvdash \wedge \nvdash Q(a) \nvdash$' in $\mathfrak{A}^0$. The conditions defining

[15] To obtain a more explicit special case of the general definition, clauses 2.0 to 2.2 of this example should be replaced by a general statement that the structural operations of $\mathfrak{A}^0$ take phrases of $\mathfrak{A}^0$ of the appropriate categories into phrases of $\mathfrak{A}^{0'}$ of the appropriate category, in accordance with the syntactic rules of $\mathfrak{A}^0$.

[16] The set A^0 and operations $\langle F_i^0 \rangle_{i \in \{0,1,2\}}$ are redundant here; they can be reconstructed from the other components of the structure.

a disambiguated language guarantee that every phrase of the language will have exactly one analysis tree. Since analysis trees serve to specify the syntactic structure of complex phrases, this means that every complex phrase of a disambiguated language will have just one syntactic structure.[17]

The parentheses that figure in the structural operations of $\mathfrak{A}^0$ ensure that $\mathfrak{A}^0$ is disambiguated; they are inserted into the mechanism of F_2^0, for instance, in such a way that given any expression having the form $F_2^0(\zeta, \varphi, \psi)$ it is possible to recover ζ, φ, and ψ; there is a unique triple $\langle \eta, \chi_1, \chi_2 \rangle$ of proper expressions of $\mathfrak{A}^0$ such that $F_2^0(\eta, \chi_1, \chi_2) = \ulcorner \nleftarrow \varphi \nrightarrow \zeta \nleftarrow \psi \nrightarrow \urcorner$, and in fact if $F_2^0(\eta, \chi_1, \chi_2) = \ulcorner \nleftarrow \varphi \nrightarrow \zeta \nleftarrow \psi \nrightarrow \urcorner$ then $\eta = \zeta$, $\chi_1 = \varphi$, and $\chi_2 = \psi$. Moreover, no proper expression $\ulcorner \nleftarrow \varphi \nrightarrow \zeta \nleftarrow \psi \nrightarrow \urcorner$ of $\mathfrak{A}^0$ can be either a basic expression of $\mathfrak{A}^0$ or a value of either of the structural operations F_0^0 and F_1^0. (It is to make good this last claim that three styles of parentheses were introduced into $\mathfrak{A}^0$.)

2. Syntactic ambiguity

The language L^1 that we discussed briefly in the previous section is a good example of a language that is not disambiguated, and—like English—nontrivially so. To put it roughly, L^1 is just like $\mathfrak{A}^0$ except that F_2^0 is replaced by an operation that neglects to insert parentheses.

$$F_2^1(\zeta, \varphi, \psi) = \varphi \zeta \psi$$

We have pointed out that formulas such as '$P(a) \vee Q(a) \wedge Q(b)$' can be produced in L^1, having the same ambiguity that is found in the English 'John will telephone or John will write and Mary

---

[17] Though in an intuitive sense a language is not ambiguous if each of its phrases has only one analysis tree, Montague's definition exceeds this requirement in stringency. For example, if F_0^0 were concatenation, so that $F_0^0(\zeta, \alpha) = \zeta\alpha$, $\mathfrak{A}^0$ would not qualify as a disambiguated language according to Montague's definition. (The reason is that different arguments of F_0^0 can yield the same value; for instance, $F_0^0('a', 'bc') = 'abc' = F_0^0('ab', 'c')$. But this modification would not render any of the phrases of the language syntactically ambiguous. In another respect, Montague's definition is perhaps less stringent than intuition would require; it permits a disambiguated language to have basic expressions belonging to more than one syntactic category.

will write'. Ambiguous formulas of L^1 such as

$$P(a) \vee Q(a) \wedge Q(b)$$
$$\neg + P(a) \wedge \neg + Q(b) + \vee P(c) +$$
and $\quad \neg + P(a) + \vee P(b) \vee P(c)$

contrast with disambiguated formulas of $\mathfrak{A}^0$ like

$$\pm P(a) \pm \vee \pm \pm Q(a) \pm \wedge \pm Q(b) \pm \pm,$$
$$\neg \pm \pm \pm P(a) \pm \wedge \pm \neg + Q(b) + \pm \pm \vee \pm P(c) \pm +,$$
and $\quad \pm \neg + P(a) + \pm \vee \pm \pm P(b) \pm \vee \pm P(c) \pm \pm.$[18]

It is natural to think of the language L^1 as an indexed family like $\mathfrak{A}^0$, with F_2^1 in place of F_2^0. In general, a disambiguated language would then be a language (where a language is a structure $\langle A, F_\gamma, X_\delta, S, \delta_0 \rangle_{\gamma \in \Gamma, \delta \in \Delta}$) that also meets the two conditions guaranteeing disambiguity; languages in general, however, need not meet these conditions. But in Chapter 7 Montague adopts a different and more general approach to syntactic ambiguity. There he gave primacy to disambiguated languages such as $\mathfrak{A}^0$, these being the only structures in which we are to think of phrases as being generated recursively. According to this policy, syntactic rules are never allowed to produce syntactically ambiguous expressions. The definition of Chapter 7, Section 2, identifies a language L with a pair $\langle \mathfrak{A}, R \rangle$, where $\mathfrak{A}$ is a disambiguated language and R is a relation between certain of the proper expressions of $\mathfrak{A}$ and syntactic objects called the *proper expressions* of L. The proper expressions of L may be syntactically ambiguous; their correlates with respect to R are their syntactic analyses, and there is nothing to prevent a proper expression of L from having more than one syntactic analysis.[19] The relation R can be conceived of as the disambiguating relation

---

[18] There is a sense in which '$\neg + P(a) + \vee P(b) \vee P(c)$' is not ambiguous, since any way of inserting parentheses will yield an expression with the same meaning. But in the present context we have in mind only *syntactic ambiguity*, not semantic ambiguity with respect to a given (in this case, the standard truth functional) interpretation. In general, many syntactically ambiguous expressions will not be semantically ambiguous.

[19] In an abstract sense of 'analysis'. It is not required here that analyses take the form of trees tracing the generation of the expression by certain recursive rules.

linking the various possible syntactic analyses of a syntactically ambiguous expression with the expression itself, or conversely as a "blurring relation" giving various syntactically ambiguous forms of an unambiguous expression.

If we choose to use expressions of $\mathfrak{A}^0$ as analyses of expressions of L^1 it is easy enough to define the appropriate relation R^1—and hence to define L^1, since $L^1 = \langle \mathfrak{A}^0, R^1 \rangle$. For phrases ζ of $\mathfrak{A}^0$ in any of the categories ICST, 1V, 1C, and 2C, $\zeta R^1 \zeta$. And for $\varphi \in C^0_{\text{FOR}}$, the ψ such that $\varphi R^1 \psi$ are obtained by deleting any parentheses '$\nleftarrow$' and '$\nrightarrow$' in φ. Thus, we have

'$P(a)$'R^1'$P(a)$',
'$\nleftarrow \neg \nleftarrow P(a) \nrightarrow \nrightarrow \vee \nleftarrow P(b) \nrightarrow$'$R^1$'$\neg \nleftarrow P(a) \nrightarrow \vee P(b)$',
'$\nleftarrow \nleftarrow P(a) \nrightarrow \vee \nleftarrow P(b) \nrightarrow \nrightarrow \wedge \nleftarrow P(c) \nrightarrow$'$R^1$'$P(a) \vee P(b) \wedge P(c)$',
'$\nleftarrow P(a) \nrightarrow \vee \nleftarrow \nleftarrow P(b) \nrightarrow \wedge \nleftarrow P(c) \nrightarrow \nrightarrow$'$R^1$'$P(a) \vee P(b) \wedge P(c)$'.

The syntactic ambiguity of formulas of L^1 like '$P(a) \vee P(b) \wedge P(c)$' has semantic consequences. Notions that presuppose a unique syntactic structure, like the semantic relation of logical consequence discussed below, can only be defined relative to *analyzed expressions* of L^1: pairs of the form $\langle \zeta, \zeta' \rangle$, where ζ is an expression of L^1 and $\zeta R^1 \zeta'$. On one analysis of '$P(a) \vee P(b) \wedge P(c)$', for example—the analysis '$\nleftarrow P(a) \nrightarrow \vee \nleftarrow \nleftarrow P(b) \nrightarrow \wedge \nleftarrow P(c) \nrightarrow \nrightarrow$'—this formula is implied by '$P(a)$' but does not imply '$P(a)$'. On another analysis—the analysis '$\nleftarrow \nleftarrow P(a) \nrightarrow \vee \nleftarrow P(b) \nrightarrow \nrightarrow \wedge \nleftarrow P(c) \nrightarrow$'— the formula implies '$P(c)$' but is not implied by '$P(c)$'. It would make no sense to speak of '$P(a) \vee P(b) \wedge P(c)$' itself as standing in "absolute" relations of logical consequence, independently of any particular analysis. Thus, the relation R plays a prominent role in Section 4 of Chapter 7, where notions such as logical consequence are characterized.

Montague uses the relational method to define the (syntactically ambiguous) fragment of English he presents in Chapter 7. Just as we used $\mathfrak{A}^0$ to disambiguate L^1, he first defines an English-like language that is disambiguated by means of parentheses, and then introduces a relation of parentheses-deletion to obtain his fragment. But in his other syntactic work on natural languages, he uses a different approach to syntactic ambiguity, and generates ambiguous expressions directly by recursive processes. On this recursive approach to syntactic ambiguity a language (ambiguous or not) would be defined as a system $\langle A, F_\gamma, X_\delta, S, \delta_0 \rangle_{\gamma \in \Gamma, \delta \in \Delta}$ meeting the specifications laid down in Chapter 7, Section 2, except for those ensuring syntactic univocity. On the recursive approach, then, the ambiguous language L^1 would be identified with the system $\langle A^1, F_\gamma^1, X_\delta^1, S^1, \delta_0^1 \rangle_{\gamma \in \Gamma, \delta \in \Delta}$, where $F_0^1 = F_0^0$, $F_1^1 = F_1^0$, and $F_2^1(\zeta, \varphi, \psi) = \varphi \zeta \psi$; and where S^1 consists of the three syntactic rules

$$\langle F_0^1, \langle 1V, ICST \rangle, FOR \rangle,$$
$$\langle F_1^1, \langle 1C, FOR \rangle, FOR \rangle,$$
and $\quad \langle F_2^1, \langle 2C, FOR, FOR \rangle, FOR \rangle.$

The syntactic ambiguity of '$P(a) \vee Q(a) \wedge Q(b)$' is demonstrated on this approach by its having two distinct analysis trees, the trees B-1 and B-2.

The recursive account of syntactic ambiguity can be thought of as a special case of the relational definition given in Chapter 7, since a recursively characterized language L can easily be transformed into an isomorphic relationally characterized language L'. The analysis trees of L constitute a disambiguated language $\mathfrak{A}'$, and L' is defined as $\langle \mathfrak{A}', R' \rangle$, where R' relates an analysis tree to the phrase it generates. In other words, L is disambiguated by the relation that links analysis trees with the expressions they analyze, and so L can be regarded as falling under the definition of Chapter 7. But, on the other hand, the relational definition is nontrivially more general than the recursive one, because it does not forbid different expressions of an ambiguous language to share the same analysis, something that cannot occur in recursively defined ambiguous languages.

The opportunity that this generalization affords is suggestive; it leads one to think of the relation R as containing a meaning-preserving mechanism that generates ambiguous "surface structures" from unambiguous "deep structures." This in fact was Montague's intention. But though he thus introduced a place into his framework for devices like transformational rules (according to the conception of these rules whereby they preserve meaning and generate surface structures from underlying logical structures), he nevertheless was reluctant to make use of it. Only in the fragment of English presented in Chapter 7 does he make use of the relation R, and here R is a one-many relation of parentheses deletion. Thus, even this fragment can be represented as a recursively generated ambiguous language.

Montague's policy, then, seems to have been to avoid as much as possible the use of a level at which syntactic rules become intrinsically meaning-preserving and to explain synonymy by means of semantic rules. Though, for instance, he published no theory of passive voice, the treatment suggested by this methodology would be to provide different analysis trees for 'John kisses Mary' and 'Mary is kissed by John', exhibiting these sentences as being built up from their constituent phrases according to different patterns. Just as the standard semantic theory of $\mathfrak{A}^0$ renders '$\nvdash P(a) \nvdash \wedge \nvdash P(a) \nvdash$' equivalent to '$P(a)$', the semantic theory of a fragment of English permitting formation of these sentences should render 'John kisses Mary' and 'Mary is kissed by John' equivalent.

3. Human languages

The abstract notion of a language that is developed with such generality in Chapter 7 is not of great interest in metamathematics. Its importance lies in the bridge it affords between formal languages of the sort studied by logicians and human languages. Montague's case for the claim that human languages are instances of his general theory rests on his development of certain fragments of English in the form required by his framework for semiotic; these are the fragments found in Chapters 6, 7, and 8. Some of the constructions emphasized in the formulation of these languages are awkward; for instance, 'boy such that he loves a woman' replaces the more natural 'boy who loves a woman'. But it is evident that the phrases generated in these fragments belong to English and that, though there are many types of grammatical English phrases they cannot produce, they are far from trivial. They permit the formation of many highly complex constructions and constitute more powerful and comprehensive fragments of English than have ever been put forward with precise grammars and full model theoretic interpretations. And there is good reason to think that the fragments can be significantly enlarged without any major changes in the framework of Chapter 7 (in this connection, see Rodman [13]).

A paper by Barbara Partee, Partee [11], contains detailed comparisons of the grammar of Chapter 8 with transformational grammar, and her work in Rodman [13] contains, as well as syntactic extensions of Montague's fragments, further material helping to make Montague's work accessible to linguists. In this introduction we will therefore try to illuminate Montague's work on English in another way, which may help to make it understandable to those familiar with logic. We will present an artificial language containing many of the constructions treated in Chapter 6. This plan of exposition introduces the syntactic material in the way it occurred to Montague, who was influenced very little by existing syntactic theories of English. Instead, having worked with formal languages of increasing complexity and power, he came to realize that by having a lexicon of English words and a list of structural operations consisting of English constructions, English itself could be regarded as one of these formal languages. It would be possible to construct a series of formal languages, each differing very little from the next, with familiar logical calculi at one end and Montague's fragments of English at the other. Our artificial language L^2 would stand near the middle of such a series.

We will formulate L^2, an ambiguous language, according to the recursive pattern of Chapter 6 rather than the relational pattern of Chapter 7. Thus, L^2 can be treated as a syntactic system $\langle A^2, F_\gamma^2, X_\delta^2, S^2, \delta_0^2 \rangle_{\gamma \in \Gamma^2, \delta \in \Delta^2}$ that generates phrases directly. No parentheses figure in the structural operations of L^2 and many of its phrases are ambiguous, but they are disambiguated by analysis trees. L^2 is an outgrowth of logical languages like L^1, differing primarily in the number of its syntactic categories and the complexity of its structural operations. The rationale of these differences, of course, is that unlike L^1, L^2 is to be an approximation of English.

Like L^1, the language L^2 will have syntactic categories of intransitive verbs and formulas; we will retain the old indices, 1V and FOR, for these. For purposes of simplicity, negation will be omitted from L^2; but there will be many new syntactic categories, most of them corresponding to ones from the traditional grammar of English. The following table summarizes the most important data about these categories. In particular, the category index and set of basic expressions are presented in the table. The category designation serves as a generic name of the category. The terminology from which these designations are taken is adapted from Montague, and comes from both traditional grammar and logic.

(B-3)

Category Designation	Category Index	Nearest Equivalent in Traditional Grammar	Set of Basic Expressions
Name	N	Proper name or pronoun	$\{`b`, `c`, `John`, `x_0`, `x_1`, `x_2`, \ldots\}$
Two-place connective	2C	Conjunction	$\{`\wedge`, `\vee`\}$
One-place verb	1V	Intransitive verb	$\{`P`, `Q`, `walks`, `talks`\}$
Common noun	CN	Common noun	$\{`f`, `man`, `picture`, `town`\}$
Ad-verb	A1V	(Verb modifying) adverb	$\{`quickly`\}$
Ad-common noun	ACN	Adjective	$\{`old`, `heavy`\}$
Adformula	AFOR	(Sentence modifying) adverb	$\{`frequently`\}$
Ad-verb forming preposition	PRA1V	Preposition	$\{`with`, `to`\}$
Ad-common noun forming preposition	PRACN	Preposition	$\{`of`\}$
Propositional attitude	PA	Sentential complement-taking verb	$\{`believes`\}$
Formula	FOR	Sentence	$\wedge$

Some of the basic expressions of L^2 are letters or special logical symbols, some are words from English. I have used both to stress the intermediate character of L^2; though some of the formulas of L^2, for instance, are actual sentences of English, many are a kind of pidgin mixture of elements from artificial and human language. As artificial elements are dropped and English vocabulary is added to modifications of L^2 they will begin to resemble the fragment of Chapter 6, which recognizably belongs to English, though relying on various stilted turns of phrase. But even at this stage it will have become clear that the study of such formal languages is in fact a branch of English syntax, not merely an exercise in devising peculiar logical calculi.

Before turning to the syntactic rules of L^2, I will explain informally the roles played by its various syntactic categories. Several of the new features of L^2 relate to quantification. In the formal languages designed by logicians it is customary, and indeed essential, to have infinitely many symbols called *individual variables*;[20] it is common to liken their syntactic role to that of pronouns. Montague's use of such variables is a striking feature of his grammars for English. The individual variables of L^2 are the symbols 'x_0', 'x_1', 'x_2', ... They are classified as names together with the symbols 'b', 'c', and 'John'. If we had used only English words instead of letters as our basic expressions it might have been better to have used 'he$_0$', 'he$_1$', 'he$_2$', . . . or 'one$_0$', 'one$_1$', 'one$_2$', . . . as individual variables.

In formulating a logical calculus it is usual to use a formula like '$(\wedge x_0)(P(x_0) \rightarrow Q(x_0))$' to stand for the universal quantification (with respect to 'x_0') of the conditional formula '$P(x_0) \rightarrow Q(x_0)$'. By letting '$P$', say, represent 'French policeman' and 'Q' represent 'speaks French', this universal quantification is made to stand for the English sentence 'Every French policeman speaks French'. This device gives quantification a very different appearance from the one it takes in English, and moreover obscures the difference between common noun phrases like 'French policeman' and intransitive verb phrases like 'speaks French'.

To make a grammar that is closer to English in its repre-

---

[20] Infinitely many are required in logical calculi because otherwise axiomatizations of the valid formulas of first-order logic would be incomplete. We use infinitely many in our fragment of English because otherwise it would not be possible to introduce common noun phrases freely into formulas.

sentation of quantification, a syntactic category of common nouns has been incorporated in L^2. Universal formulas will now be constructed by replacing a variable in a formula, say 'x_0' in '$x_0 P$',[21] by an expression having the form $\ulcorner$every $\zeta\urcorner$, where ζ is a common noun phrase. The expression 'every' is introduced syncategorematically here.[22] This rule yields formulas such as 'every $f P$', which differs from English sentences only in having letters in place of English words. And indeed, the same rule also yields 'every man walks' as a formula of L^2. We will also introduce existential quantification into L^2 and have formulas such as '$a f P$' and 'a man walks'.

This description of the quantifier rule is incomplete in one respect: it needs to be elaborated to cope with cases in which the variable that is replaced has more than one occurrence in the formula to be quantified. We would lose contact with English if we treated 'every $f Q$ with every f', for instance, as a universal quantification of '$x_0 Q$ with x_0'. Notice, for instance, that 'Every man votes for every man' is not to be considered a result of universally quantifying 'x_0 votes for x_0'. The proper universalization of this is 'Every man votes for himself' or, alternatively, 'Every man votes for that man'.

To deal with such cases we will use the pattern set by this last sentence and adopt the rule of Chapter 6, which has the advantage of being simple, even if the sentences it produces are stylistically awkward. The structural operation of this rule inserts $\ulcorner$every $\zeta\urcorner$ only for the first occurrence of a fixed variable, say $\ulcorner x_n\urcorner$, in a formula φ, and then replaces every subsequent occurrence of $\ulcorner x_n\urcorner$ in φ by occurrences of $\ulcorner$that $\zeta'\urcorner$, where ζ' is the head noun of the common noun phrase ζ, i.e. is the leftmost basic common noun to occur in ζ. This rule yields formulas like 'every $f P$ or that $f Q$', 'every man walks or that man is old', and 'every man such that every picture of that man is old is old'.

[21] To obtain a closer approximation of English word-order we will place subject before predicate in the rule combining intransitive verb phrases with names.
[22] This is an important difference between the approach of Chapter 6 and that of Chapter 8. In the latter paper, 'every' is treated as an expression that forms terms (or noun phrases) from common noun phrases, and so phrases like 'every man' are treated as proper expressions rather than as syncategorematic fragments of universal formulas. In this regard, see Section C.6, below.

The 'such that' construction figuring in this last sentence is another form that is prominent in the grammar of Chapter 6. Like the more natural construction involving 'who', as in 'man who is old', 'such that' permits the formation of relative clauses. A phrase like 'f such that $x_0 Q$ with that f' is clearly a common noun phrase. We can, for example, apply a quantifier rule to it and the formula '$x_1 Q$ quickly' to construct a formula like 'every f such that $x_0 Q$ with that $f Q$ quickly'. Like Montague in Chapter 6 we will treat 'f such that $x_0 Q$ with that f' as a common noun phrase and construct it from the basic common noun 'f' and the formula '$x_0 Q$ with x_1'. Notice that variable binding occurs in this rule, and takes a form like the one it assumes in the quantifier rules; 'x_0' is replaced in the above example by 'that f'. The rule for relative clauses takes the following general form: if ζ is a common noun phrase and φ is a sentence, then $\ulcorner \zeta$ such that $\varphi' \urcorner$ is a common noun phrase, where φ' is the result of replacing every occurrence of $\ulcorner x_n \urcorner$ in φ by an occurrence of $\ulcorner$ that $\zeta' \urcorner$, where ζ' is the first basic common noun phrase to occur in ζ.

Adjectives are another type of English expression that classical logical calculi do not distinguish from intransitive verbs or common nouns.[23] Adjectives play at least two major roles in English grammar: they combine with common noun phrases to form common noun phrases ('French' plus 'policeman' yields 'French policeman'), as well as with the copula and names to form sentences ('John' plus 'French' yields 'John is French'). Both of these roles can be mirrored in L^2. Where ξ is an adjective and ζ a common noun phrase, then the syntactic rule for adjectives in *attributive position* will stipulate that $\xi \zeta$ is a common noun

---

[23] That is, they are not distinguished according to the informal correspondences of formalization between first-order logic and English that are found in logic textbooks. The fact that syntactic categories of English are collapsed by these practices of formalization has often been noted, and can be construed to the detriment of the syntax of first-order logic, or of the usual practices of formalization, or of the traditional grammar of English. Accordingly, a cure can be sought by enriching the formal language, by altering the practices of formalization, or by modifying the traditional grammar of English. Montague chose the first approach; the other two are adopted by Donald Davidson and his students and by the generative semanticists.

phrase. And where α is a name and ξ is an adjective the syntactic rule for adjectives in *predicative position* will stipulate that $\ulcorner \alpha$ is $\xi \urcorner$ is a formula.[24]

In Chapter 6 Montague is quick to note a semantic advantage of his approach to adjectives. The standard formalization of 'He is a French policeman', '$P(x_0) \wedge Q(x_0)$', makes this sentence logically imply both 'He is French' and 'He is a policeman'. But 'He is a deposed king' and 'He is a short basketball player' provide counterexamples to these alleged implications. Montague's semantic framework leads to the conclusion that adjectives should be interpreted as functions taking properties into properties, and there is no necessity that such functions should always yield the conjunction of the argument property with some other fixed property determined by the adjective. Adjectives such as 'deposed' and 'short' are therefore not exceptions to the theory.

L^2 also contains adverbs, but to deal with all the types of English expressions that are called 'adverbs' it is necessary to distinguish between those (called 'adverbs' by Montague, and 'ad-verbs' in this introduction) that modify intransitive verbs and those (called 'adformulas') that modify sentences. Ad-verbs stand to intransitive verbs as adjectives (in attributive position) stand to common nouns. In 'x_1 walks quickly', for instance, 'walks quickly' is an intransitive verb phrase, constructed from the basic intransitive verb 'walks' and the ad-verb 'quickly'.[25] Our syntactic rule for ad-verbs will then be that where ξ is an ad-verb and ζ an intransitive verb phrase then $\zeta \, \xi$ is an intransitive verb phrase.[26]

The English 'necessarily' and 'possibly' are treated as adformulas by modal logicians, and like the basic adformula 'frequently'

---

[24] See Rule S17, Chapter 6. This rule neglects the fact that some adjectives, like 'alleged' and 'former', do not occur in predicative position, along with (apparent) adjectives like 'piano' in 'piano player' and 'piano mover'. It might seem more elegant to formulate the rule so that if ξ is an adjective then $\ulcorner$ is $\xi \urcorner$ is an intransitive verb phrase. The rule of predication would then guarantee that $\ulcorner \alpha$ is $\xi \urcorner$ is a formula if α is a name. But then the rule for ad-verbs will generate formulas such as 'John is old quickly'.

[25] Our account of verbs is so simplified that matters of inflection are completely ignored. In a more advanced grammar 'walk' would be a basic intransitive verb, not 'walks'.

[26] See Rule S5, Chapter 6.

should be classified syntactically as such.[27] Montague himself
did not discuss the problem of how one should go about distinguishing these two types of modifiers in English, and his
classification of particular examples is sometimes questionable.
'In a dream', for instance, cited as an ad-verb in Chapter 6,
Section 9, Remark iv, is probably best regarded as an adformula.
See Thomason and Stalnaker [18] for criteria supporting this
point. The syntactic rule for adformulas will be that where ξ is
an adformula and φ a formula, $\xi\varphi$ is also a formula. Thus,
adformulas and ad-verbs will occur in different positions in the
formulas of L^2. 'John walks quickly', for instance, contrasts
with 'frequently John walks'.

Like adverbs, prepositions must be subclassified before being
introduced into L^2. Some English prepositions, like 'of', combine
with names to form adjectives; 'of John', for example, is an
adjective phrase in 'picture of John'. Others, like 'with', combine
with names to form ad-verbs; 'with John' is an ad-verb phrase
in 'walks with John'.[28] Still a third kind of preposition, less
common than the others, combines with names to form adformulas; 'during' is an example. I have not incorporated such
a category in L^2. The syntactic rules for prepositions are simple:
names follow them. Thus, 'of John' is an adjective and 'with
John' an ad-verb.

I have included 'believes' among the basic expressions of L^2
and classified it as a *propositional attitude*. Given a formula φ
and a name α, 'believes' permits the construction of a formula
having the form $\ulcorner\alpha$ believes that $\varphi\urcorner$. There are a number of ways
of parsing such formulas: for instance, $\ulcorner$that $\varphi\urcorner$ can be construed
as a nominalized formula and 'believes' as a transitive verb, or
$\ulcorner$believes that $\varphi\urcorner$ can be construed as an intransitive verb phrase
formed by combining 'believes that' with the formula φ. L^2

---

[27] One reason for this is that if 'necessarily' were an ad-verb then 'The number
of the planets is necessarily the number of the planets' and 'Nine is the number
of the planets' would imply 'Nine is necessarily the number of the planets'.

[28] In fact, most prepositions have both functions, and so would belong to the
sets of basic expressions of both PRA1V and PRACN. We can say both 'Mary
talks of John' and 'man with an overcoat'.

embodies one of the simplest such theories of propositional attitudes; it will have a syntactic rule that generates $\ulcorner \alpha$ believes that $\varphi \urcorner$ directly from 'believes', α, and φ. 'That' is introduced syncategorematically in this rule.

Montague's syntactic framework contains no stipulation that the number of syntactic rules must be finite. In formulating the rules for quantification and relative clauses it simplifies matters somewhat to take advantage of this, treating these rules as rule schemes having instances for each individual variable of L^2. To introduce universal quantification, for example, for each $n \geqslant 0$ there will be a structural operation, $F^2_{n,8}$; this operation will involve substitution for the individual variable $\ulcorner x_n \urcorner$. If desired, this could easily be reformulated to render the number of rules finite.

The structural operations of L^2 are defined as follows.

$$F^2_0(\zeta, \varphi, \psi) = \varphi \, \zeta \, \psi$$
$$F^2_1(\zeta, \alpha) = \alpha \, \zeta$$

$$F^2_2(\xi, \zeta) = \begin{cases} \xi \, \zeta \text{ if } \xi \text{ contains only one basic expression} \\ \zeta \, \xi \text{ if } \xi \text{ contains more than one basic expression} \end{cases}$$

$$F^2_3(\zeta, \varphi) = \zeta \, \varphi$$
$$F^2_4(\xi, \zeta) = \zeta \, \xi$$
$$F^2_5(\zeta, \alpha) = \zeta \, \alpha$$
$$F^2_6(\zeta, \alpha) = \zeta \, \alpha$$
$$F^2_7(\zeta, \alpha, \varphi) = \ulcorner \alpha \, \zeta \text{ that } \varphi \urcorner$$

$$F^2_{n,8}(\zeta, \varphi) = \begin{cases} \psi, \text{ if there are any occurrences of } \ulcorner x_n \urcorner \text{ in } \varphi \\ \text{and any occurrences of a member of } X_{\mathrm{CN}} \text{ in} \\ \zeta, \text{ where } \psi \text{ is the result of replacing the first} \\ \text{occurrence of } \ulcorner x_n \urcorner \text{ in } \varphi \text{ by } \ulcorner \text{every } \zeta \urcorner \text{ and all} \\ \text{subsequent occurrences of } \ulcorner x_n \urcorner \text{ in } \varphi \text{ by} \\ \ulcorner \text{that } \zeta' \urcorner, \text{ where } \zeta' \text{ is the first member of} \\ X_{\mathrm{CN}} \text{ to occur in } \zeta \\ \\ \varphi, \text{ if there are no occurrences of } \ulcorner x_n \urcorner \text{ in} \\ \varphi \text{ or there are no occurrences of any member} \\ \text{of } X_{\mathrm{CN}} \text{ in } \zeta \end{cases}$$

$$F^2_{n,9}(\zeta, \varphi) = \begin{cases} \psi, \text{ if there are any occurrences of } \ulcorner x_n \urcorner \text{ in } \varphi \\ \text{and any occurrences of a member of } X_{CN} \\ \text{in } \zeta, \text{ where } \varphi \text{ is the result of replacing the} \\ \text{first occurrence of } \ulcorner x_n \urcorner \text{ in } \varphi \text{ by } \ulcorner a\,\zeta \urcorner, \text{ and} \\ \text{all subsequent occurrences of } \ulcorner x_n \urcorner \text{ in } \varphi \text{ by} \\ \ulcorner \text{that } \zeta' \urcorner, \text{ where } \zeta' \text{ is the first member of} \\ X_{CN} \text{ to occur in } \zeta \\ \\ \varphi, \text{ if there are no occurrences of } \ulcorner x_n \urcorner \text{ in } \varphi \\ \text{or there are no occurrences of any member} \\ \text{of } X_{CN} \text{ in } \zeta \end{cases}$$

$$F^2_{n,10}(\zeta, \varphi) = \begin{cases} \ulcorner \zeta \text{ such that } \psi \urcorner, \text{ if there are any occurrences} \\ \text{of } \ulcorner x_n \urcorner \text{ in } \varphi \text{ and any occurrences of a} \\ \text{member of } X_{CN} \text{ in } \zeta, \text{ where } \psi \text{ is the result} \\ \text{of replacing every occurrence of } \ulcorner x_n \urcorner \text{ in } \varphi \\ \text{by } \ulcorner \text{that } \zeta' \urcorner, \text{ where } \zeta' \text{ is the first member of} \\ X_{CN} \text{ to occur in } \zeta \\ \\ \ulcorner \zeta \text{ such that } \varphi \urcorner, \text{ if there are no occurrences} \\ \text{of } \ulcorner x_n \urcorner \text{ in } \varphi \text{ or there are no occurrences of} \\ \text{any member of } X_{CN} \text{ in } \zeta \end{cases}$$

$$F^2_{11}(\alpha, \zeta) = \ulcorner \alpha \text{ is } \zeta \urcorner$$

Several instances of these operations are listed below; each of the following examples is a case that actually occurs in the construction of expressions of L^2.

F^2_0('$\wedge$', '$a\,P$', '$a\,Q$') = '$a\,P \wedge a\,Q$'

F^2_0('$\wedge$', 'John is old', 'John walks') = 'John is old $\wedge$ John walks'

F^2_1('Q', 'John') = 'John Q'

F^2_1('walks quickly', 'x_3') = 'x_3 walks quickly'

F^2_2('old', 'man') = 'old man'

F^2_2('of x_0', 'old picture') = 'old picture of x_0'

F^2_3('frequently', 'a man walks with John') = 'frequently a man walks with John'

F^2_4('quickly', 'walks with John') = 'walks with John quickly'

F^2_5('with', 'x_2') = 'with x_2'

F^2_6('of', 'x_1') = 'of x_1'

F_7^2('believes', 'x_2', 'every man is old') = 'x_2 believes that every man is old'

$F_{4,8}^2$('man', 'x_4 believes that x_4 is old') = 'every man believes that that man is old'

$F_{1,8}^2$('man', 'x_4 believes that x_4 is old') = 'x_4 believes that x_4 is old'

$F_{2,8}^2$('old picture of x_3', 'x_2 is of a man') = 'every old picture of x_3 is of a man'

$F_{3,9}^2$('old old man', 'x_3 walks with x_0') = 'a old old man walks with x_0'

$F_{2,9}^2$('man', 'John walks with $x_2 \wedge$ John talks to x_2') = 'John walks with a man $\wedge$ John talks to that man'

$F_{2,9}^2$('man', 'frequently x_2 walks with a man such that that man talks to x_2') = 'frequently a man walks with a man such that that man talks to that man'

$F_{5,10}^2$('man', 'x_5 is old') = 'man such that that man is old'

$F_{2,10}^2$('old picture', 'x_2 is of a man') = 'old picture such that that picture is of a man'

F_{11}^2('John', 'old') = 'John is old'

F_{11}^2('x_5', 'of x_8') = 'x_5 is of x_8'

Finally, the syntactic rules of L^2 are just what our informal discussion would lead us to expect. They are as follows:

$$\langle F_0^2, \langle 2C, FOR, FOR \rangle, FOR \rangle$$
$$\langle F_1^2, \langle 1V, N \rangle, FOR \rangle$$
$$\langle F_2^2, \langle ACN, CN \rangle, CN \rangle$$
$$\langle F_3^2, \langle AFOR, FOR \rangle, FOR \rangle$$
$$\langle F_4^2, \langle A1V, 1V \rangle, 1V \rangle$$
$$\langle F_5^2, \langle PRA1V, N \rangle, A1V \rangle$$
$$\langle F_6^2, \langle PRACN, N \rangle, ACN \rangle$$
$$\langle F_7^2, \langle PA, N, FOR \rangle, FOR \rangle$$

For all $n \geqslant 0$, $\langle F_{n,8}^2, \langle CN, FOR \rangle, FOR \rangle$

For all $n \geqslant 0$, $\langle F_{n,9}^2, \langle CN, FOR \rangle, FOR \rangle$

For all $n \geqslant 0$, $\langle F_{n,10}^2, \langle CN, FOR \rangle, CN \rangle$

$$\langle F_{11}^2, \langle N, ACN \rangle, FOR \rangle$$

According to the third of these rules, for instance, the result of combining an adjective with a common noun by means of F_2^2 will be a common noun, and according to the last the result of inserting 'is' between a name and an adjective will be a formula.

The following two analysis trees show L^2 to be ambiguous. This syntactic ambiguity is a useful one, since (once L^2 has been given a proper semantic interpretation) it serves to explain the semantic ambiguity that speakers of English find in 'every man walks to a town' and similar sentences. If the standard semantic interpretation of quantifiers is applied to L^2, (B-4) and (B-5) will then correspond to different readings of 'every man walks to a town': (B-4) with the reading that would be formalized '$\wedge\, x(P(x) \rightarrow \vee\, y(Q(y) \wedge R(x, y)))$' and (B-5) with the one that would be formalized '$\vee\, y(Q(y) \wedge \wedge\, x(P(x) \rightarrow R(x, y)))$'.

(B-4)

(B-5)

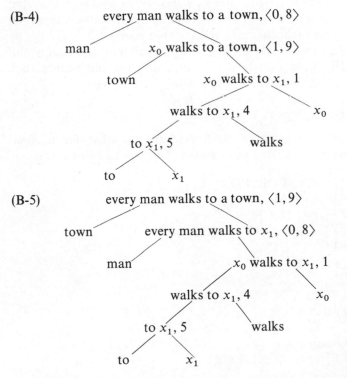

Here the pair $\langle 1, 9 \rangle$, for instance, is used as an index of the syntactic rule involving the structural operation $F^2_{1,9}$.

We will conclude our presentation of L^2 with the following analysis tree, which illustrates many syntactic rules.

(B-6)

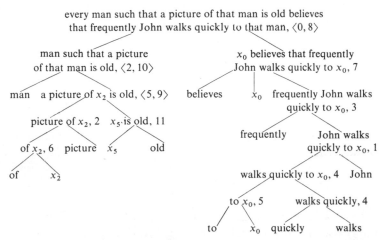

The most important respect in which L^2 wants improvement, of course, is its syntactic rules. Many such improvements can be found in Montague's syntactic papers, especially in Chapter 8. Readers who are interested in working such things out for themselves might begin by adding transitive verbs, following this with a syntactic category to accommodate words like 'very' and a possessive construction yielding common noun phrases like 'x_1's picture'. Adding negation and a more natural quantification rule that will yield sentences like 'Every old man believes that he is old' are more difficult projects, ones requiring attention to matters such as the inflection of verbs, gender of common nouns, and declension of pronouns. Reflexive and relative pronouns, and constructions involving the infinitive are still more advanced phenomena, which are discussed only tentatively in Montague's writings.

There are, of course, a great many syntactic phenomena that are extremely problematic from the standpoint of Montague's framework, and at present it is too early to tell how many of these can be incorporated into extensions of Montague's grammars without sacrificing their theoretical elegance. The only way to find out whether it is practicable to do so for a significant number of English constructions is to try.

C. SEMANTICS

1. Model theory

The strategy that Montague inherited from metamathematical semantics, or *model theory*, consists in assigning semantic values to linguistic expressions by means of *semantic rules*. These rules are formulated in a recursive definition that retraces the syntactic construction of the expressions. Montague's chief generalization of model theory was to make semantic assignments relative to various factors. Before turning to various details of the resulting semiotic program I will first discuss, in this and the next section, these two fundamental points.

The grammar of a language L provides a list of basic expressions and a list of syntactic rules showing how complex expressions are made from simpler ones. For the moment, we will assume both lists to be finite. Then this presentation of the proper expressions of $\mathfrak{A}$, the disambiguated language associated with L, provides us with a natural way of defining properties of these expressions by means of a finite amount of information. Take the disambiguated language $\mathfrak{A}^0$, for example. To define a property $\mathscr{P}$ of the expressions of $\mathfrak{A}^0$, it will suffice if we can stipulate which basic expressions of $\mathfrak{A}^0$ possess $\mathscr{P}$, and whether $\ulcorner \xi(\alpha) \urcorner$, $\ulcorner \zeta + \varphi + \urcorner$, and $\ulcorner \neq \varphi \neq \zeta \neq \psi \neq \urcorner$ possess $\mathscr{P}$, given complete information as to which of α, ξ, ζ, φ, and ψ possess $\mathscr{P}$. For example, take the property of being a proper expression of $\mathfrak{A}^0$ that contains at least one occurrence of a parenthesis '$+$'. This property can be defined by pointing out that no basic expression of $\mathfrak{A}^0$ has the property, that $\ulcorner \xi(\alpha) \urcorner$ has the property if and only if at least one of ξ and α have the property, that $\ulcorner \zeta + \varphi + \urcorner$ invariably has the property, whether or not ζ and φ have it, and that $\ulcorner \neq \varphi \neq \zeta \neq \psi \neq \urcorner$ has the property if and only if at least one of φ, ζ, and ψ has it.

Metamathematical semantics uses definitions of this kind to determine how semantic values are given to the proper expressions of a disambiguated language such as $\mathfrak{A}^0$.[29] (This is what was meant by saying that semantic rules retrace syntactic rules.) To describe the standard semantic theory of $\mathfrak{A}^0$, we first introduce the notion of a *truth function*. Any two mathematical entities can be selected to play the roles of truth and falsity; we will arbitrarily use the numbers 1 and 0, respectively, for this purpose and will call them *truth values*. An *n-place truth function* is an n-place function from truth values to truth values. Among one-place truth functions the function H_1 such that $H_1(0) = 1$ and $H_1(1) = 0$ is of special interest in the interpretation of $\mathfrak{A}^0$, as are the two-place truth functions H_2 and H_3 such that $H_2(0,0) = H_2(0,1) = H_2(1,0) = 0$ and $H_2(1,1) = 1$, and $H_3(0,1) = H_3(1,0) = H_3(1,1) = 1$ and $H_3(0,0) = 0$. Since H_1 reverses truth value, it will correspond to negation; H_2 yields the value 1 (for truth) if and only if both its arguments have this value, so it will correspond to conjunction; and H_3 will correspond to disjunction.

A nonempty set E, together with an assignment f of members $f(\text{'}a\text{'})$, $f(\text{'}b\text{'})$, and $f(\text{'}c\text{'})$ of E to 'a', 'b', and 'c', of subsets $f(\text{'}P\text{'})$ and $f(\text{'}Q\text{'})$ of E to 'P' and 'Q', and of the truth functions $f(\text{'}\neg\text{'}) = H_1$, $f(\text{'}\wedge\text{'}) = H_2$, and $f(\text{'}\vee\text{'}) = H_3$ to '$\neg$', '$\wedge$', and '$\vee$' is called a *model* of $\mathfrak{A}^0$. Thus, a model consists of a set together with an assignment of appropriate entities (members or subsets of this set, or truth functions) to the basic expressions of $\mathfrak{A}^0$; $f(\text{'}a\text{'})$, for instance, is to be thought of as the entity denoted by 'a' and $f(\text{'}P\text{'})$ as the set of entities satisfying 'P'.

The definition of a model, then, stipulates what kinds of things are to be associated with basic expressions as their semantic

---

[29] In the foregoing exposition we have followed the strategy Montague uses in Chapter 7, Sections 3 and 4, and have regarded semantic interpretations as assigning values to proper expressions in general, rather than only to those proper expressions that are phrases. In this case, the generality of Montague's approach is largely spurious. Though it does enable him to treat interpretations algebraically, it leads to much pointlessness. There is no good reason, for instance, for insisting that a proper expression of $\mathfrak{A}^0$ such as '$\nleftarrow \wedge \nleftrightarrow P \nleftarrow \vee \nleftrightarrow$' must be given a semantic value, since this expression has no natural interpretation. From here on in this introduction, therefore, we will think of interpretations as assigning values only to phrases. This does not affect the main point under discussion: that interpretations are determined by a recursive definition that traces the syntactic constitution of phrases.

values. The most important part óf the theoretical business of establishing a semantic theory has been accomplished in performing this task. Even in this very simple case important theoretical decisions and commitments have been made. For instance, the resulting semantic framework renders intensional phenomena anomalous; connectives such as the necessity operator or the subjunctive conditional cannot be interpreted by assigning them truth functions as denotations. We will return to this point below.

The components E and f of a model $\langle E, f \rangle$ play very different roles. The former provides *possible denotations* that could be given to expressions of any language whatsoever; the latter assigns certain of these possible denotations to the expressions of a particular language. We will call E the *model structure* of the model $\langle E, f \rangle$ and f the *model assignment* of $\langle E, f \rangle$. It may seem strange in this simple case to glorify E with the name 'structure', but we are looking forward to generalizations, especially to generalizations directed to intensional constructions. And even in classical model theory there are cases where one must consider more complicated model structures. In many-sorted calculi, for instance—calculi with more than one kind of quantification—the model structure will be a sequence $\langle E_1, \ldots, E_n \rangle$ of domains rather than a single domain E.

It will be helpful in our later discussions to be more explicit in our account of how a model structure E determines a family of possible denotations. The denotations we actually used in the model theory of $\mathfrak{A}^0$ were members of E, subsets of E, and truth functions. The latter are functions built up from the set $\{0, 1\}$ of truth values by means of the process, given two sets X and Y, of taking the set Y^X of functions from X to Y.[30] For instance, the function H_1 denoted by '$\neg$' is in the set $\{0, 1\}^{\{0,1\}}$ and the function H_2 denoted by '$\wedge$' is in the set $(\{0, 1\}^{\{0,1\}})^{\{0,1\}}$. In the case of H_2 we have identified two-place functions from $\{0, 1\}$ to $\{0, 1\}$ with one-place functions from $\{0, 1\}$ to $\{0, 1\}^{\{0,1\}}$. Thus,

---

[30] Montague often uses '2' to signify the set $\{0, 1\}$, a notation that is justified by von Neumann's definition of the natural numbers. We will not use this abbreviation in the introduction.

we write '$H_2(1, 0)$' for '$(H_2(1))(0)$', which signifies the result of applying G to 0, where G is the function obtained by applying H_2 to 1.

By slightly altering the denotations of one-place verbs we can treat all the possible denotations as built up in this same way. Instead of assigning one-place verbs such as 'P' subsets of E we might as well have assigned them functions from E to $\{0, 1\}$. Since a subset X of E can be identified with its characteristic function Ch_X, the function in $\{0, 1\}^E$ such that $Ch_X(x) = 1$ if $x \in X$ and $Ch_X(x) = 0$ if $x \notin X$, this change—which we will now adopt—makes no difference aside from making the theory more easy to generalize.

To formulate precisely our point about the possible denotations relative to a model set E, we now introduce the notion of a *type*. Let e be the type of entities[31] and t be the type of truth values. The set T^0 of classical types is the smallest set such that $e \in T^0$ and $t \in T^0$, and whenever $\sigma, \tau \in T^0$ the pair $\langle \sigma, \tau \rangle \in T^0$. Thus, for instance, e, $\langle e, t \rangle$, $\langle t, t \rangle$, and $\langle t, \langle t, t \rangle \rangle$ are all types. The pair $\langle \sigma, \tau \rangle$ is to be thought of as the type of functions from things of type σ to things of type τ, so that H_1 has type $\langle t, t \rangle$ and H_2 has type $\langle t, \langle t, t \rangle \rangle$. The set of possible denotations of type τ relative to a model structure E is defined recursively: E is the set of possible denotations of type e, $\{0, 1\}$ is the set of possible denotations of type t, and whenever X is the set of possible denotations of type σ and Y the set of possible denotations of type τ, Y^X is the set of possible denotations of type $\langle \sigma, \tau \rangle$. From this it follows, for instance, that $\{0, 1\}^{\{0, 1\}}$ is the set of possible denotations of type $\langle t, t \rangle$.

Types play the role in model theory that syntactic categories play in grammar; they constitute the fundamental classification of the subject. In the model theory of a language such as $\mathfrak{A}^0$, these classifications must be arranged so that each syntactic category can be assigned a type which serves as the type of appropriate denotations for the expressions of that category. The type of individual constants, for instance, is e, that of one-

---

[31] 'Entity' is used as a technical term for 'possible individual' in Chapter 7.

place verbs is $\langle e, t \rangle$ and that of one-place connectives is $\langle t, t \rangle$. And so in a model $\langle E, f \rangle$ of $\mathfrak{A}^0$, $f(`a`) \in E$, $f(`P`) \in \{0, 1\}^E$, and $f(`\neg`) \in \{0, 1\}^{\{0, 1\}}$.

Strictly speaking, a model of a language assigns values only to basic expressions of the language. In order to obtain assignments of values to phrases, we must lay down semantic rules showing how to give values to complex expressions. If the definition of what is to be a model has been carried out properly, this task should be straightforward, for the values given to basic expressions by a model should be structured to contain the information needed to determine the values the model should give to phrases constituted from these parts.

For example, suppose the set E and assignment f comprise a model of $\mathfrak{A}^0$. We wish to extend f to obtain an assignment f' that is defined for all phrases of $\mathfrak{A}^0$. To do so, we first stipulate that if ζ is a basic expression of $\mathfrak{A}^0$ then $f'(\zeta) = f(\zeta)$; second that if ξ is a one-place verb and α an individual constant then $f'(F_0^0(\xi, \alpha)) = (f'(\xi))(f'(\alpha))$; third that if ζ is a one-place connective and φ a formula then $f'(F_1^0(\zeta, \varphi)) = (f'(\zeta))(f'(\varphi))$; fourth that if ζ is a two-place connective and φ and ψ are formulas then $f'(F_2^0(\zeta, \varphi, \psi)) = (f'(\zeta))(f'(\varphi), f'(\psi))$.

It is an important consequence of this approach to semantic rules that the syntactic construction of the language influences their structure. For each syntactic rule there is a corresponding semantic rule. One of the ways in which semantic arguments can legitimately bear on syntax follows from this consideration: only certain of the grammars that generate the phrases of a given language may be compatible with a given semantic interpretation of the language.

For example, let $\mathfrak{A}^3$ be the result of adding to $\mathfrak{A}^0$ a syntactic rule $\langle F_4^3, \langle \text{FOR, FOR, FOR} \rangle, \text{FOR} \rangle$, where $F_4^3(\varphi, \psi, \chi) = ⫢\varphi⫫ \wedge ⫢\psi⫫ \vee ⫢\chi⫫$. Syntactically, $\mathfrak{A}^3$ is a disambiguated language. But this is unacceptable because semantically it is ambiguous, given our preformal understanding of '$\wedge$' and '$\vee$', and of the workings of parentheses. Since there is no way to semantically interpret F_4^3 in accordance with this preformal understanding, we cannot write an acceptable semantic rule for the syntactic rule associated with this structural operation. Our argument shows $\mathfrak{A}^3$ to incorporate an unacceptable grammar; if we wish to give syntactic rules generating the phrases of $\mathfrak{A}^3$, formulas of the sort $\nvDash \varphi \nvDash \wedge \nvDash \psi \nvDash \vee \nvDash \chi \nvDash$ must be treated as syntactically ambiguous.

The interaction between syntax and semantics is systematic and thoroughgoing in Montague's theories. Indeed, the aim of the program is to produce a mathematically elegant semiotic theory of natural language, and in view of examples of influence such as this it would be unwise to allow any phase of the theory to develop in isolation. The methodology of the program, then, should consist in developing stronger and stronger fragments of the language under study, each fragment being furnished with a syntax and a semantic and pragmatic interpretation. Under no circumstances should syntactic research proceed far in advance of such interpretation, since there is great risk that the results of such research might have to be discarded because of semantic inadequacies. There is far less risk of error in semantic research that is unguided by syntactic considerations, but there is some danger of producing theories that will have little or no application to natural languages.

2. Semantic interpretation and syntactic ambiguity

We have described only the interpretation of disambiguated languages, taking our material direct from metamathematical semantics. The interpretation of ambiguous languages is a generalization of Montague's devising, and though the need of such a generalization may have impeded attempts to apply metamathematical semantics to natural languages, the modification it requires is not extensive. Instead of interpreting unambiguous expressions, one interprets analyzed expressions, i.e. one interprets expressions relative to particular syntactic analyses.

To illustrate this procedure, take the ambiguous language $L^1 = \langle \mathfrak{A}^0, R^1 \rangle$ that was discussed in Section B.2, above. The first step in interpreting L^1 is to deal with the disambiguated language $\mathfrak{A}^0$; this we have just done. The models of L^1 are the models of $\mathfrak{A}^0$; where $\langle E, f \rangle$ is such a model, let f' be the associated function that assigns semantic values to phrases of $\mathfrak{A}^0$. Then where φ is a formula of L^1 and $\psi R^1 \varphi$ (so that the formula ψ of $\mathfrak{A}^0$ is an analysis of φ), the formula φ has the truth value $f'(\psi)$ with respect to $\langle E, f \rangle$, according to the analysis ψ. For example, suppose that $f'(\text{'}P(a)\text{'}) = 1$ and $f'(\text{'}Q(b)\text{'}) = 0$, so that $f'(\text{'}{\not\vdash}\,{\not\vdash}P(a){\not\vdash}\, \vee \,{\not\vdash}Q(a{\not\vdash}\,{\not\vdash}\, \wedge \,{\not\vdash}Q(b){\not\vdash}\text{'}) = 0$ and $f'(\text{'}{\not\vdash}P(a){\not\vdash}\, \vee \,{\not\vdash}\,{\not\vdash}Q(a){\not\vdash}\, \wedge \,{\not\vdash}Q(b){\not\vdash}\,{\not\vdash}\text{'}) = 1$. Then according to the analysis '${\not\vdash}\,{\not\vdash}P(a){\not\vdash}\, \vee \,{\not\vdash}Q(a){\not\vdash}\,{\not\vdash}\, \wedge \,{\not\vdash}Q(b){\not\vdash}$' of '$P(a) \vee Q(a) \wedge Q(b)$', which professes the formula to be a conjunction, the model $\langle E, f \rangle$ makes it false. (Recall that 1 is the value representing truth, 0 the value representing falsity.) And according to the analysis '${\not\vdash}P(a){\not\vdash}\, \vee \,{\not\vdash}\,{\not\vdash}Q(a){\not\vdash}\, \wedge \,{\not\vdash}Q(b){\not\vdash}\,{\not\vdash}$' of '$P(a) \vee Q(a) \wedge Q(b)$', which professes the formula to be a disjunction, the model $\langle E, f \rangle$ makes it true.

Semantic relations such as logical consequence are then defined with respect to analyses of expressions; one does not say that φ is a logical consequence of ψ in L^1, but that φ is a logical consequence of ψ in L^1 relative to the analyses φ' of φ and ψ' of ψ. For instance, according to the analysis '$Q(b)$' of '$Q(b)$' and the analysis '${\not\vdash}P(a){\not\vdash}\, \vee \,{\not\vdash}\,{\not\vdash}Q(a){\not\vdash}\, \wedge \,{\not\vdash}Q(b){\not\vdash}\,{\not\vdash}$' of '$P(a) \vee Q(a) \wedge Q(b)$', '$Q(b)$' is not a logical consequence of '$P(a) \vee Q(a) \wedge Q(b)$'.

3. Intensions and the interpretation of tense

In Section C.1 we said that defining the concept of a model of a language $\mathfrak{A}$—stipulating what kinds of semantic values various syntactic categories of expressions of $\mathfrak{A}$ are to take—is the most important thing to be done in setting up a semantic interpretation of $\mathfrak{A}$ along model theoretic lines. We now turn to Montague's solution to this problem for languages with intensional constructions, beginning with a special case that seems to raise fewer philosophical problems than most: tense.

Tense can be added to the language $\mathfrak{A}^0$ by admitting a new one-place connective '$\mathscr{P}$', where '$\mathscr{P}{\not\vdash}\varphi{\not\vdash}$' is read 'It was the case that φ'.[32] The resulting language $\mathfrak{A}^4$ has formulas such as

$$\text{'}\mathscr{P}{\not\vdash}P(a){\not\vdash}\text{'}, \quad \text{'}\neg{\not\vdash}\mathscr{P}{\not\vdash}\neg{\not\vdash}P(a){\not\vdash}\,{\not\vdash}\,{\not\vdash}\text{'},$$

[32] Future tense could also have been added, as well as past tense, but all the points we wish to make can be made with just the latter.

and   '$\mathscr{P} + {\dashv}\!{\vdash} \mathscr{P} + P(a){\dashv} {\dashv} \vee {\dashv}\!{\vdash} Q(a){\dashv} {\dashv}$ '.

It isn't surprising that the interpretation of this language should involve the notion of time and that, in particular, some structure representing time should be introduced into the models of $\mathfrak{A}^4$. In tense logic, in place of systems $\langle E, f \rangle$ we have systems $\langle \langle E, I, < \rangle, f \rangle$ consisting of an *interpretation structure* $\langle E, T, < \rangle$ and an *interpretation assignment f*. Here, as before, E is a nonempty set, the set of entities. I is another nonempty set, linearly ordered by the relation $<$. (In other words, for all $i, i' \in I$, $i < i'$ or $i' < i$ or $i = i'$.) I represents the set of moments of time and $<$ the relation of *being later than*. The insight to be exploited in developing the model theory of $\mathfrak{A}^4$ is that the formulas of this language are to be treated as taking on different truth values at different moments of time, just as the English sentence 'It is Tuesday' is sometimes true and sometimes false.

This point, that formulas will have truth values relative to moments of time, has important consequences in defining the models of $\mathfrak{A}^4$. Let $\mathscr{B}$ be a system $\langle \langle E, I, < \rangle, f \rangle$. Just as we cannot tell whether 'It is Tuesday' is true or false until we have determined the time to which it is to be referred, we can no longer think of a system $\mathscr{B}$ as assigning a truth value to each formula. Instead it gives a truth value to each formula relative to the various moments in I. If, like Montague, we are to think of a model as a device for assigning denotations to expressions—truth values to formulas, for instance—then a model is not a system $\mathscr{B}$, but a pair $\langle \mathscr{B}, i \rangle$, where $i \in I$. This is why $\mathscr{B}$ is called not a 'model' but an 'interpretation'. As we will see, interpretations can be viewed as assigning *intensions* or *senses* to expressions, rather than denotations.[33]

It is natural to generalize our insight about truth values and expect that an interpretation $\mathscr{B}$ will assign the expressions of $\mathfrak{A}^4$ just the kinds of values that the classical model theory of $\mathfrak{A}^0$ would give them—except that these values are now relative to the indices in I. In particular, then, for each $i \in I$, $\mathscr{B}$ will assign 'a' a member $\mathrm{Ext}_{\mathscr{B}, i}('a')$ of E, and will assign 'P' a function

---

[33] In pragmatics, interpretations assign more general functions (called 'meanings' in Chapter 7) to expressions. See Chapter 7, Section 4.

$\text{Ext}_{\mathscr{B},i}(`P')$ from $E$ to $\{0, 1\}$. Intuitively, $\text{Ext}_{\mathscr{B},i}(`a')$ is the individual denoted by 'a' at time i, and $\text{Ext}_{\mathscr{B},i}(`P')$ the characteristic function of the set of entities satisfying '$P$' at time $i$. There is no need for $\text{Ext}_{\mathscr{B},i}(`P')$ to be a constant function of i. If 'P' stands for the English 'is under seven years old', for instance, then $\text{Ext}_{\mathscr{B},i}(`P')$ will change its membership as $i$ varies, for as $i$ increases the age of things will also increase. For the same reason, $\text{Ext}_{\mathscr{B},i}(`a')$ will vary with i if 'a' stands for 'Mary's age', though for many noun phrases, in particular most proper names such as 'Mary', this function will be constant.[34]

This generalization runs into difficulties, however, when the connectives of $\mathfrak{A}^4$ are taken into consideration; it does not permit a uniform treatment of past tense and negation. If one-place connectives are to have the same denotations they are given in the interpretation of $\mathfrak{A}^0$, though relative to members of I, then $\text{Ext}_{\mathscr{B},i}(`\mathscr{P}')$ should be a truth function. But then $\text{Ext}_{\mathscr{B},i}(`\mathscr{P} + P(a) +')$ would depend only on the truth value $\text{Ext}_{\mathscr{B},i}(`P(a)')$ given to '$P(a)$' at $i$, just as $\text{Ext}_{\mathscr{B},i}(`\neg + P(a) +')$ depends only on this truth value. But here we run afoul of counter-examples:

(C-1) Iceland is covered with a glacier

and

(C-2) Africa is covered with a glacier

are both false at the present moment, while

(C-3) Iceland was once covered with a glacier

and

(C-4) Africa was once covered with a glacier

differ in truth value.

Here is another illustration of how syntactic and semantic considerations can interact. If we are to carry through the method of interpretation we have begun, we must discard the grammar of past tense embodied in $\mathfrak{A}^4$ and choose another syntactic formulation that does not assign negation and past tense to

---

[34] The fact that we may at different times use the same proper name to refer to different people or things is irrelevant. This is pragmatic, not semantic variation.

the same syntactic category. On the other hand, if we are to preserve this grammar, we must devise a new strategy of interpretation that will not require us to assign a truth function to '$\mathscr{P}$'.

In this introduction we will follow the second course and modify the semantic strategy. Rather than thinking of past tense as acting on the extensional values of formulas, we will let it act on *intensions* where, like extensions, these intensions are possible denotations constructed from an interpretation structure.[35] Examples (C-1) to (C-4) show that past tense is not truth functional, but reflection on these examples brings the reason to light; the truth values of (C-3) and (C-4) at a moment i depend on the truth values of (C-1) and (C-2) at moments other than i. Thus, if we take into account certain functions from I into truth values— for instance, the function N that for each moment i gives the truth value of the formula φ at i—then $\text{Ext}_{\mathscr{B},i}(\ulcorner\mathscr{P}+\varphi+\urcorner)$ can be characterized in terms of N. We need not say, however, that N is the denotation of φ. Instead we will speak of N as the *intension* or *sense* of φ. The term 'denotation' will continue to be used as it was in the semantics of $\mathfrak{A}^0$—so that the denotation of an individual constant, for instance, will be an entity—but denotation will now be relative to moments of time.

To put this plan into practice we must generalize the notion of a possible denotation so that functions from moments to truth values will be generated as possible denotations. We will think of the set X^I of functions from moments of time to a set X as the set of intensions of members of X. For each semantic type τ there will be a type of intensions of things of type τ; call this the type $\langle s, \tau \rangle$. Our new set T of types is then defined as the smallest set Y such that $e \in Y$ and $t \in Y$, $\langle \sigma, \tau \rangle \in Y$ whenever $\sigma, \tau \in Y$, and $\langle s, \tau \rangle \in Y$ whenever $\tau \in Y$. Relative to an interpretation structure $\langle E, I, < \rangle$ the sets of possible denotations of types e and t are E and $\{0, 1\}$, respectively, and where X is

---

[35] In $\mathfrak{A}^4$, intensions and many other possible denotations will never actually be denoted by any other expressions of the language. But plausible languages can be constructed in which expressions do denote intensions. The 'that' of indirect discourse, for instance, can be interpreted as forming names of intensions. In Chapter 5 there is an extended discussion of this construction.

the set of possible denotations of type σ and Y the set of possible denotations of type τ, Y^X is the set of possible denotations of type $\langle \sigma, \tau \rangle$ and Y^I the set of possible denotations of type τ.

Relative to the interpretation structure $\langle E, I, < \rangle$, then, E^I will be the set of possible denotations that are intensions of entities; such an intension is a rule which, given a moment of time, yields a unique entity. The intension corresponding to 'Mary', for instance, would be the function that yields Mary as its value for all moments of time, while that corresponding to 'Mary's age' will yield for each moment of time i a number n such that Mary is n years old at i.

Now let $\mathscr{B}$ be an interpretation $\langle \langle E, I, < \rangle, f \rangle$ and ζ be a phrase of $\mathfrak{A}^4$. There are two ways in which $\mathscr{B}$ relates a semantic value to ζ. As well as the extension (or denotation) $\text{Ext}_{\mathscr{B},i}(\zeta)$ of ζ at the moment i, where $i \in I$, there is the intension $\text{Int}_{\mathscr{B}}(\zeta)$ of ζ. Montague requires that all intensions be senses, that they have type $\langle s, \tau \rangle$ for some type τ. Given this requirement the notions of intension and extension are interdefinable; in fact, $\text{Ext}_{\mathscr{B},i}(\zeta) = N(i)$, where $N = \text{Int}_{\mathscr{B}}(\zeta)$, and where $\text{Ext}_{\mathscr{B},i}(\zeta)$ has type τ, $\text{Int}_{\mathscr{B}}(\zeta)$ is that function N from I to the set of possible denotations of $\mathscr{B}$ of type τ such that for all $i \in I$, $N(i) = \text{Ext}_{\mathscr{B},i}(\zeta)$. This interdefinability is a great advantage as regards theoretical economy. It means that intensions can be introduced into semantics along natural lines that require no drastic revision of extensional theories. It is quite common in mathematics to generalize a structure by considering the space of functions from some domain to that structure, and intensional semantics stands in just this relation to extensional semantics.

This terminology is reminiscent of the framework of Frege [3], the classical source of semantic research into intensional phenomena. Our problem concerning the connective '$\mathscr{P}$' was that it constitutes an oblique context, in that the denotation of '$\mathscr{P} + P(a) +$'—its truth value—is a function not of the denotation but of the intension of '$P(a)$'. In our technical terminology, $\text{Ext}_{\mathscr{B},i}('\mathscr{P} + P(a) +')$ is linked by a semantic rule not to $\text{Ext}_{\mathscr{B},i}('P(a)')$, but to the function N from I to $\{0, 1\}$ such that $N(i) = \text{Ext}_{\mathscr{B},i}('P(a)')$. That is, $\text{Ext}_{\mathscr{B},i}('\mathscr{P} + P(a) +')$ is linked by a semantic rule to $\text{Int}_{\mathscr{B}}('P(a)')$. It is a remarkable feature of Frege's work that it can be incorporated so readily into a model theoretic account of intensional phenomena.

Since extension and intension are interdefinable, we can choose to define either notion recursively. To do this for intensions, we first stipulate the following assignment of semantic types to the syntactic categories of $\mathfrak{A}^4$.

(C-5) *Syntactic category*   *Semantic type*

IC	$\langle s, e \rangle$
1V	$\langle s, \langle e, t \rangle \rangle$
1C	$\langle \langle s, t \rangle, \langle s, t \rangle \rangle$
2C	$\langle \langle s, t \rangle, \langle \langle s, t \rangle, \langle s, t \rangle \rangle \rangle$
FOR	$\langle s, t \rangle$

Individual constants, one-place verbs, and formulas take semantic values corresponding to senses of the values they were given in extensional model theory. Connectives, however, are not assigned senses as values—and indeed, it is difficult to see what could be meant by the sense of a connective, since unlike noun phrases, verbs, and sentences, connectives do not seem to behave differently in oblique and direct contexts. Types corresponding to functions on certain senses are assigned to connectives by table (C-5). Since they do not have a semantic type of the form $\langle s, \tau \rangle$, the values of connectives will not themselves be senses.

Let $\langle \langle E, I, < \rangle, f \rangle$ be an interpretation of $\mathfrak{A}^4$. The interpretation assignment f is a function on basic expressions of $\mathfrak{A}^4$, such that $f(\zeta)$ is a possible denotation of type τ relative to $\langle E, I, < \rangle$ whenever ζ is a basic expression of semantic type τ, as given in Table (C-5). Furthermore, let M, N_1, and N_2 be members of $\{0, 1\}^I$. Then $f_{\neg}(M) = M'$, where $M'(i) = 0$ if $M(i) = 1$ and $M'(i) = 1$ if $M(i) = 0$. And $f_{\mathscr{P}}(M) = M''$, where $M''(i) = 0$ if $M(i') = 0$ for all $i' < i$ and $M''(i) = 1$ if $M(i') = 1$ for some $i' < i$. Finally, $(f_{\wedge}(N_1))(N_2) = N'$, where $N'(i) = 0$ if $N_1(i) = 0$ or $N_2(i) = 0$, and $N'(i) = 1$ if $N_1(i) = 1$ and $N_2(i) = 1$; and $(F_{\vee}(N_1))(N_2) = N''$, where $N''(i) = 1$ if $N_1(i) = 1$ or $N_2(i) = 1$, and $N''(i) = 0$ if $N_1(i) = 0$ and $N_2(i) = 0$.

This completes the definition of an interpretation of $\mathfrak{A}^4$. The recursive definition of the intension $\text{Int}_{\mathscr{B}}(\zeta)$ assigned to an expression ζ by an interpretation $\mathscr{B}$ is as follows. For basic expressions ζ, $\text{Int}_{\mathscr{B}}(\zeta) = f(\zeta)$. If δ is a one-place verb and α an individual constant then $\text{Int}_{\mathscr{B}}(\delta(\alpha)) = M$, where M is the function from I to $\{0, 1\}$ such that $M(i) = (\text{Int}_{\mathscr{B}}(\delta)(i))(N(i))$, where $N = \text{Int}_{\mathscr{B}}(\alpha)$. If ζ is a one-place connective and φ a formula then $\text{Int}_{\mathscr{B}}(\ulcorner \zeta + \varphi + \urcorner) = M(\text{Int}_{\mathscr{B}}(\varphi))$, where $M = \text{Int}_{\mathscr{B}}(\zeta)$. And if ζ is a two-place connective and φ, ψ are formulas then $\text{Int}_{\mathscr{B}}(\ulcorner + \varphi + \zeta + \psi + \urcorner) = M(\text{Int}_{\mathscr{B}}(\psi))$, where $M = (\text{Int}_{\mathscr{B}}(\zeta))(\text{Int}_{\mathscr{B}}(\varphi))$.

The extension (or denotation) $\text{Ext}_{\mathscr{B}, i}(\zeta)$ of an expression ζ relative to the index i is $N(i)$, where $N = \text{Int}_{\mathscr{B}}(\zeta)$. This definition presupposes that ζ is an expression whose value is a sense, i.e. that $\text{Int}_{\mathscr{B}}(\zeta)$ is a function with domain I. As we pointed out above, Montague's framework in Chapter 7 explicitly requires that this presupposition be met always; but we have violated it in our treatment of connectives. Having abandoned this presupposition, we must either say that negation has an intension but no extension, or, preferably, that the distinction between sense and denotation does not apply to negation. It would be better to think of the assignment $\text{Int}_{\mathscr{B}}$ as giving semantic values to expressions which are not denotations, and which are intensions only when for some type τ they have the type $\langle s, \tau \rangle$. Since the distinction between intension and extension seems rather forced when extended to certain syntactic categories—ad-verbs and determiners, as well as connectives—this may be a worthwhile relaxation of Montague's definition of a Fregean interpretation. On the other hand, it would not be difficult to revise our semantic theory of $\mathfrak{A}^4$ so that connectives would be assigned senses.[36]

4. Possible worlds

One of the chief developments that made it possible to put physics on a rigorous mathematical basis was agreement on the form a system of units should take. Choice of a centimeter-gram-second system of units rather than, say, a foot-pound-hour system is only a matter of convenience. But the decision that

[36] One-place connectives, for instance, would take the semantic type $\langle s, \langle \langle s, t \rangle, \langle s, t \rangle \rangle \rangle$, and negation would be assigned a constant function on I, the function whose value is uniformly the function we originally gave to negation.

every measurable physical quantity should be an arithmetical function of units of distance, mass, and time is vital in determining what is to count as a physical state and what language will be used to describe these states.

Many philosophers seem to have regarded the establishment of a theory of meaning as requiring an analogous foundation in terms of a system of units. Wittgenstein's *Tractatus* is, among other things, an attempt to regard meanings as dependent on just two basic notions: *entity* and *truth value*. Quine, in *Word and Object* and later writings, attempts to lay down behavioral units of stimulus and response for semantics. Montague's framework (adopted not only by him but by many other practitioners of "possible-worlds semantics") is a generalization of the *Tractatus* framework. The type of entities and the type of truth values are retained as basic semantic units, but another basic type is added, that of possible worlds. This type is designed to relieve a particularly painful source of pressure on the simpler framework, for which intensional phenomena were anomalous. The literature of attempts to apply extensional semantics to these phenomena, from Russell's *On Denoting* to the present, illustrates the fact that these phenomena were perceived as anomalous by philosophers of language.

One conclusion we may draw from the work of these philosophers is that if a theory accounting for intensional phenomena can be obtained within the extensional framework it will be at the cost of much regimentation of human languages and will conflict, among other things, with the traditional grammar of these languages. Logical syntax and linguistic syntax will be entirely different subjects, like articulatory and acoustic phonetics. Among the many examples of this regimentation are Russell's view that 'The premier of France speaks French', and Quine's view that 'Quine speaks French' and 'This is hot' do not have subject-predicate form;[37] Carnap's view that 'Empedocles said

---

[37] These are included among devices used to solve intensional puzzles because of the use of the theory of descriptions to resolve certain versions of the problem of opaque contexts. All the devices that are cited here are mentioned because they are ingenious and important. They must be taken seriously as alternatives to theories such as Montague's.

he was a god' involves quotation; and Davidson's view that 'talks' is really a transitive verb.[38]

This regimentation need not be seen as unwelcome. Most extensionalist philosophers of language regarded human language as vague and muddled. Formalization was a process of purification and logical form was severed from syntactic form. But for someone like Montague, who was concerned to develop the theory of human languages on the same basis used to study formal languages, a division between "semantically based syntax" and "natural language syntax" would be intolerable. There remain two ways of dealing with the phenomena that led in the first place to the distinction between logical and syntactic form: one could try to revise the traditional grammar of English to bring it into accord with extensional semantics, or one could try to replace extensional semantics by a more general theory. The former approach is typical of transformationalist linguists of the generative semantics school.[39] Montague, who was interested in assimilating into his fragments of English many of the generalizations of traditional grammar and who seems to have mistrusted the distinction between deep and surface structure, represents the latter approach. For discussion of a case in which Montague altered traditional semantics for the sake of preserving traditional grammar, see Section 6, below.

The difficulties facing extensional semantics can be represented in a more superficial, but also more striking way. (More superficial, because it makes certain presuppositions that were avoided in the above paragraphs.) As Frege pointed out, certain desirable generalizations break down in extensional semantics: in particular, the generalization that meanings can be attached to expressions in such a way that the meanings of complex expressions are functions of the meanings of their components. If, for instance, the meaning of a singular term were the individual it denotes then 'Scott' and 'the author of *Waverley*' would have the same meaning. But 'Scott was necessarily Scott' and 'Scott was necessarily the

----

[38] That is, when logically analyzed it expresses a relation between a person and an action.

[39] See, for instance, Harman [4].

author of *Waverley*' clearly differ in meaning, though syntactically
they differ only in that one has 'the author of *Waverley*' where the
other has 'Scott'. An extensional theory such as the one we gave
of $\mathfrak{A}^0$ in Section 1, which has no way of linking expressions to
semantic values other than the relation of denotation, and which
employs entities as the denotations of singular terms, will
evidently have difficulties with this example.

Similar reasons weigh against treating sets of entities as the
meanings of one-place verbs, since 'is Scott' and 'is the author
of *Waverley*' would then have the same meaning—and therefore,
so would 'Scott is Scott' and 'Scott is the author of *Waverley*'.
Finally, it is even more obvious that the meaning of a sentence
cannot be identified with a truth value; this would imply
that at least two out of every three sentences have the same
meaning.

Reflection on these examples leads naturally enough to the
notion of a possible world. The phrase 'the author of *Waverley*',
like 'the number of the planets' or 'the President of the U.S.',
will have denotations that vary according to circumstances.
If the meanings of these expressions were the denotations they
in fact have (i.e. the denotations they have in the circumstances
in which we find ourselves), it would be necessary to settle all
sorts of factual questions in order to determine matters of meaning
in semantics. Given any matter of fact at all that can be expressed
by means of a sentence, a singular term can be constructed (in a
language which, like English, is sufficiently rich in nominaliza-
tions) whose denotation depends on that matter of fact. This
would render that part of semantics concerned with the description of meanings completely dependent on evidence and
observation—in history, astronomy, etc.—for factual information needed to fix these meanings.

The resulting divergence between such a theory's treatment of
meanings and a speaker's understanding of them is highly implausible. In order for a speaker to understand what 'the author
of *Waverley*' means, for instance, he need not know who wrote
Waverley. Possible-worlds semantics avoids this difficulty by
dealing not just with the denotations that expressions take in a
particular world designated "the actual world," but with rules

that govern their denotations in all possible worlds.[40] The principle of possible-worlds semantics is that such rules can be identified with the intensions of expressions.

Our interpretation of tense in Section 2, above, shows how the notion of a possible world can be incorporated in a model theoretic semantics. A set T of semantic types is defined just as in tense logic, with basic types e and t of entities and truth values; for all types σ and τ a type $\langle \sigma, \tau \rangle$ is postulated of functions from things of type σ to things of type τ. Adding an intensional element, we also postulate for each type τ a type $\langle s, \tau \rangle$ of senses of things of type τ. If X is the set of possible denotations of type τ and I the set of possible worlds of a given model structure, then the set X^I of functions from I to X is the set of all possible denotations of type $\langle s, \tau \rangle$, relative to that model structure. Thus, possible worlds enter into interpretations in the same way as moments of time. This makes it desirable to have a neutral term for the set I of sense-determining indices; however, Montague uses the term 'possible world' in this more general usage as well. In the interpretation of languages involving tense as well as propositional attitudes the set of sense-determining indices will consist of pairs $\langle i, i' \rangle$, where i is a possible world and i' a moment of time.

The theory resulting from this addition to the extensional framework provides for the construction of semantic types corresponding to kinds of intensional entities that have received attention in the philosophical literature. For instance, the type $\langle s, e \rangle$ will correspond to functions that for each possible world determine a unique entity. These can be identified with *individual concepts*, the intensions of singular terms, since they constitute precisely what is needed to provide a denotation for a singular term in each situation. We pointed out in connection with tense that there is no need for such functions to be constant. In particular two of them, N and M, say, can have the same value in some but not all possible worlds. Here is a semantic explanation of how assertions of identity can be contingent, for $\ulcorner \alpha = \beta \urcorner$

----

[40] See Lewis [9], pp. 184–88, for an argument that expressions such as 'actual' should be interpreted in a pragmatic metalanguage that does not discriminate among possible worlds. Relative to a context of use involving a possible world i, 'the actual world' designates i. Relative to a context of use involving a possible world i', 'the actual world' designates i'.

will be true in some but not all possible worlds if the intension of α is N and that of β is M.

In similar fashion propositions can be assigned the type $\langle s, t \rangle$ and properties the type $\langle s, \langle e, t \rangle \rangle$. The property assigned to 'being the author of *Waverley*', for instance, would be the function N such that where i is a possible world, $N(i)$ is that function M from entities to truth values such that $M(x) = 1$ if and only if x is, in i, the author of *Waverley*.

This framework of semantic types enters into the general characterization of the semantic interpretation of languages that is given in Chapter 7. For simplicity, assume we are working with a disambiguated language $\mathfrak{A} = \langle A, F_\gamma, X_\delta, S, \delta_0 \rangle_{\gamma \in \Gamma, \delta \in \Delta}$. To interpret such a language we must first have a *type assignment g* that for each category $\delta \in \Delta$ gives a semantic type $g(\delta)$, to be thought of as the semantic type of the expressions in the syntactic category δ, provided that these expressions have intensions at all. This exposition departs somewhat from the presentation in Chapter 7. There Montague's type assignments associate with δ the semantic type of the *extensions* of expressions in δ, and he assumes that every expression has both an intension and an extension. In terms of the notation just introduced, he requires that for all $\delta \in \Delta$, $g(\delta)$ must be a semantic type of the form $\langle s, \tau \rangle$; we violated this condition in interpreting the connectives of $\mathfrak{A}^4$. Since δ_0 is understood to be the category of formulas, we must require that $g(\delta_0) = \langle s, t \rangle$; formulas must have propositions as their intensions. Otherwise the framework of Chapter 7 places no restrictions on type assignments.[41] The particular semantic type given to a syntactic category will depend on our purposes in constructing the language (if it is artificial) or on our pretheoretic understanding of the language (if it is a human language).

An *interpretation* (Montague calls them 'Fregean interpretations' in Chapter 7, to distinguish them from still more general sorts of interpretations) acts as a semantic lexicon; it determines a function that assigns semantic values to the basic expressions of $\mathfrak{A}$, within the limits set by a fixed type assignment g. In other words, associated with each interpretation of $\mathfrak{A}$ there will be a

[41] This feature is modified in Chapter 8, where category indices are given a structure that determines their semantic role.

function f from basic expressions of $\mathfrak{A}$ to possible denotations (the space of possible denotations will be uniquely determined by the interpretation). This function must be such that if $\zeta \in C_\delta$ then $f(\zeta)$ has the semantic type $g(\delta)$, for all syntactic categories δ of $\mathfrak{A}$. If ζ is a formula, for instance, $\zeta \in C_{\delta_0}$, $f(\zeta)$ will have the semantic type $g(\delta_0)$, i.e. the type $\langle s, t \rangle$.

To secure an interpretation of the phrases of $\mathfrak{A}$, f also must assign a value f_γ to each structural operation F_γ of $\mathfrak{A}$. Since an n-place structural operation F is a function carrying an n-tuple of expressions into another expression, and we must think of these argument and value expressions as themselves having semantic values, n-place structural operations must be assigned n-place functions taking possible denotations into possible denotations. And these functions must meet type restrictions corresponding to the category indices in the semantic rule in which F figures.[42] In precise terms, if $\langle F_\gamma, \langle \delta_1, \ldots, \delta_n \rangle, \varepsilon \rangle$ is a syntactic rule of $\mathfrak{A}$ then whenever for all i, $1 \leqslant i \leqslant n$, N_i is a possible denotation having type $g(\delta_i)$, $f_\gamma(N_1, \ldots, N_n)$ is a possible denotation having type $g(\varepsilon)$.

In the typical and simplest case, the semantic function assigned to a structural operation will simply be an instruction to apply one intension to another. The semantic operation of intensional application is the analogue for intensions of functional application for extensions. For instance, the result of intensionally applying a property to an individual concept is a proposition. In general, let N_1 have the semantic type $\langle s, \langle \sigma, \tau \rangle \rangle$ and N_2 have the type $\langle s, \sigma \rangle$; then where i is a possible world $N_1(i)$ has type $\langle \sigma, \tau \rangle$ and $N_2(i)$ has type σ. Then the result of intensionally applying N_1 to N_2 is the intension M of type $\langle s, \tau \rangle$ such that $M(i) = (N_1(i))(N_2(i))$ for all possible worlds i. The syntactic rule for combining subject and predicate in $\mathfrak{A}^4$, which yields a formula $\ulcorner \zeta(\alpha) \urcorner$ from a one-place verb ζ and individual constant α, calls for intensional application in its semantic interpretation. If ζ is assigned the intension N_1 of type $\langle s, \langle e, t \rangle \rangle$ and α the intension N_2 of type $\langle s, e \rangle$ then $\ulcorner \zeta(\alpha) \urcorner$ will take the intension that results from intensionally applying N_1 to N_2.

[42] Since $\mathfrak{A}$ was supposed to be disambiguated, the operation F cannot figure in more than one syntactic rule.

Many other syntactic rules will also be interpreted by intensional application: for instance the rules for combining an ad-verb with a verb phrase, or connectives with sentences (where connectives are interpreted by senses, as in Chapter 7).

But the rules of Chapter 6 for placing adjectives in predicative position, and for quantifying in formulas, are not applicative. Since an adjective modifies a common noun phrase to obtain another common noun phrase, the denotation of an adjective will be a function from properties to properties. The category of adjectives, then, will have the semantic type $\langle s, \langle \langle s, \langle e, t \rangle \rangle$, $\langle s, \langle e, t \rangle \rangle \rangle \rangle$. This renders the syntactic rule for placing adjectives in attributive position (i.e. for placing them so that the adjective modifies a common noun phrase) applicative in its semantic interpretation. But the semantic theory of Chapter 6 renders $\ulcorner \alpha$ is $\zeta \urcorner$ true in i, where α is a name and ζ an adjective, if and only if $\ulcorner \alpha$ is a ζ entity $\urcorner$ is true in i. This cannot be construed in terms of intensional application.

The case in which all structural operations of a language are assigned intensional application as their interpretation is a particularly elegant one, and—especially in combination with a categorial grammar—it permits a strikingly simple formulation of the semantic framework. This fact is exploited in David Lewis' exposition, Lewis [8]. But in view of cases like predicative adjectives, it is not clear that this special case can be applied to English without invoking a theory of deep structure like that of the generative semantics school of transformationalists.

5. Theory and evidence in semantics

Philosophers and linguists are apt to object to the form taken by Montague's semantic theories, on the ground that content has been sacrificed to generality. Montague himself made no special effort to counteract this impression; his writings are far more devoted to general mathematical formulations than to examples or applications. But this feature of his work is not merely a defect of style. To a considerable extent the rarefied character of his semantic writings is a consequence of his fundamental approach. This line of criticism, then, is not entirely misdirected and deserves to be taken seriously. Nevertheless it is liable to become associated with certain misunderstandings, and these must be brought to light in order to obtain a balanced picture of the issues.

First, the problems of semantic theory should be distinguished from those of lexicography. It is the business of semantics to account for meanings.[43] A central goal of this account is to explain how different kinds of meanings attach to different syntactic categories; another is to explain how the meanings of phrases depend on those of their components. Consider, for example, the meanings of 'walk', 'the', 'He is pale', 'quickly', 'of', and 'Mary's uncle'. No two of these meanings will be alike in kind. How can we account for these generic differences? Clearly, too, given the meanings of the syntactic rules that go into the making of 'man who wants to find a unicorn', the meaning of this phrase will be determined once those of its components ('man', 'want', 'find', 'unicorn', 'who', 'to', 'a', and the third person present singular morpheme) have been fixed.[44] How ought we to describe this determination? We can legitimately expect any semantic theory to provide answers to these questions.

But we should not expect a semantic theory to furnish an account of how any two expressions belonging to the same syntactic category differ in meaning.[45] 'Walk' and 'run', for instance, and 'unicorn' and 'zebra' certainly do differ in meaning, and we require a dictionary of English to tell us how. But the making of a dictionary demands considerable knowledge of the world. The task of explaining the particular meanings of various basic expressions will obviously presuppose, if not factual information, at least a minutely detailed terminology for classifying things of all kinds. Perhaps even pictures or a museum of representative specimens

---

[43] Here, the term 'meaning' is not to be taken in any technical sense that would prejudice the following discussion toward any particular kind of semantic theory.

[44] The last four items may be redundant, since a syntactic theory may well treat them as syncategorematic. In this case their "meanings" will be specified by the interpretation of the syntactic rules through which they are introduced into phrases.

[45] The sentence is italicized because I believe that failure to appreciate this point, and to distinguish lexicography from semantic theory, is a persistent and harmful source of misunderstanding in matters of semantic methodology. The distinction is perhaps the most significant for linguists of the strategies of logical semantics.

would have to be counted as "terminology"—after all, there are words in English such as 'meter' and 'yard'. At any rate, lexicography will have to borrow concepts from all areas of knowledge and practice: astronomy, jurisprudence, cuisine, automotives, pigeon breeding, and so forth. It would be unfair and unproductive to require a theoretician, particularly in the early stages of developing his theory, to focus his attention on questions such as these. These are matters of application, not of theory.[46]

On the other hand, theoretical license should not be abused. A policy of refusing to allow semantic distinctions between basic expressions would be harmful if followed uniformly. For instance, if linguistic evidence shows that 'every' and 'some' are best treated alike syntactically, this should not force us to exclude an account of universal and existential quantification from our semantics. 'Every' and 'some' can be given fixed meanings without our having to do the same for all other words, too. This form of discrimination is familiar from model theory. There are *logical constants*, like '$\wedge$' in $\mathfrak{A}^0$, whose denotation is independent of models, and *logical variables*, like 'P' and 'a' in $\mathfrak{A}^0$, whose denotation is not.[47]

These reflections do not yield general criteria for distinguishing "semantic constants" from "semantic variables," and for languages such as Montague's fragments of English this is not an easy line to draw. Perhaps the best policy is to begin with a fairly abstract approach, making few words semantically constant, and hoping that subsequent work will lead to improvements. But after all, we cannot expect to find anything like a truth function answering to 'walk'. It is fortunate, then, that there are devices making it possible to build content into basic expressions without treating them as logical constants; Montague uses meaning postulates

---

[46] In this connection it is interesting to note that the words that have been studied with the most success in theoretical semantics are, generally, those that are most confounding to lexicographers: words like 'and', 'or', 'not', 'every', 'some', and 'the'. In dealing with such words the common lexicographical practice is to deviate from the normal form of an entry and comment on the grammatical function of the word, following this with examples of sentences in which the word is used.

[47] I confine this distinction to words (in more precise terms, to basic expressions) since it seems natural to require, though this is not built into the framework of Chapter 7, that all syntactic rules be treated as logical constants.

for this purpose. But, as we will point out below, meaning postulates have their drawbacks.

The program we envisage, then, would begin with a highly abstract theory making few intracategorial semantic distinctions, but powerful enough to provide a semantic rule for every syntactic rule of the language under consideration. The theory would then evolve toward the concrete by adding meaning postulates or other devices allowing distinctions in the semantic treatment of expressions belonging to the same syntactic category. But this evolution would no doubt come to a stop long before anything resembling a dictionary were achieved.[48]

There is another respect in which Montague's semantic theory is abstract; it not only allows a multiplicity of interpretation assignments, but a multiplicity of interpretation structures. That is, interpretations can differ in the materials that are used to construct the space of possible denotations, as well as in the particular semantic values they attach to basic expressions. The semantic theory makes no commitment as to which sets of entities or of possible worlds or even (usually) of moments of time are the "correct" or "intended" ones for the interpretation of a given language. What is more to the point (since many of these structures are isomorphic), the semantic theory treats the spaces of entities and possible worlds as bare, undifferentiated sets having no structure whatever, and though the space of moments of time is at least an ordered set, it is common and convenient to impose very few requirements on the ordering relation.

In itself, this is not damaging; one might conclude that it is merely an empirical matter to construct an appropriate set of entities and possible worlds for one of Montague's fragments of English. Very little is known, for instance, about the actual geometry of physical space, but this does not call geometrical theory into question. The theory is applicable, but owing to experimental difficulties we do not know exactly how to apply it. The case in possible worlds semantics, however, is worse. Not only has no one ever constructed anything like a suitable

[48] For supporting arguments concerning this position regarding lexicography and semantic theory, see Putnam [12].

candidate for the set of all possible worlds for a rich fragment of English, but it is extremely unclear what kinds of considerations would be used to guide the construction of possible worlds, or to decide between rival candidates for the set of all possible worlds, once constructed.

Such considerations call into question the applicability of Montague's framework. I believe, however, that there is no need to construe them as discrediting it, particularly when it is viewed as an initial stage of scientific semantics. They do indicate that further developments of the framework are in order. But this is something that everyone can accept.

Though at its present stage of development possible worlds semantics is isolated from practical applications, this does not mean that it is isolated from linguistic evidence. This point is vital, and I will try to show in some detail how Montague's semantic work was guided by data.

First, throughout Montague's semantic writings great emphasis is given to various examples illustrating intensional phenomena, most of them similar to those of Frege [3] or the subsequent literature. This is no accident; these examples themselves and the philosophical literature concerning them constitute a body of data with which any successful semantic theory must deal. Frequently in the initial stages of a science certain puzzles will come to be focal points of theoretical attention, it being generally accepted that they lie at the heart of things. Such is the relation of the Russell paradox to set theory, of the apparent invariance of the velocity of light to frame of reference to relativity theory, and of Frege's puzzles to semantics.

Montague's claim that possible worlds semantics provides a rigorous solution to these puzzles is a serious matter, then, and one that places the theory in relation to a well-known cluster of phenomena and theoretical issues. Much of his explicit discussion of examples is designed to support this claim, though in his later papers, especially in Chapter 5, he attempted to show that the applications of the theory were in fact much wider than the stock examples would seem to indicate.

Second, Montague's predecessors also left a positive legacy of semantic generalizations, and many of these are incorporated in his framework. The principle that meanings of phrases should be determined by the meanings of their components is such a generalization; so is the idea that semantic interpretation is relative to syntactic structure, and that syntactic structure is determined in part by the order in which syntactic rules are applied. Montague was particularly careful to preserve generalizations from model theoretic semantics, and in fact our plan of exposition of his semantic theories has exploited the continuity between classical model theory and his framework.

Third, of course there is a body of semantic evidence that can be consulted independently of the literature. Evidence of this kind bears on Montague's theories in many ways. For one thing, insofar as there are direct intuitions about the validity of inferences[49] these intuitions can be used as data for a semantic theory which, like Montague's, is designed to permit the definition of relations of consequence. When evidence from this quarter counts against a theory it will typically consist of an inference that is intuited as valid but is not established by the theory as an instance of logical consequence. (In case there is an inference that seems invalid but is treated by the theory as valid, it is generally possible to find a more damaging kind of counter-evidence: an inference sanctioned as a logical consequence whose premisses are true and whose conclusion is false.)

There is always a way of saving the theory, however, in these instances. Intuitive certainty that the inference is valid is evidence that in some sense it is necessary; but the necessity need not be logical. Though the inference 'Kim is pregnant; therefore Kim is not a man' for example, is intuited as valid, it would be absurd to require a logical theory to explain this fact. The inference is warranted by a biological, not a logical generalization.

---

[49] By this, we mean intuitions directed to the particular inference itself, that assess its validity independently of the actual truth values of its premisses and conclusion, and the actual truth values of the premisses and conclusions of similar inferences. One can define validity by saying that $\ulcorner\varphi$; therefore $\psi\urcorner$ is valid if and only if for all inferences $\ulcorner\varphi'$; therefore $\psi'\urcorner$ that result from $\ulcorner\varphi$; therefore $\psi\urcorner$ by substituting phrases for basic expressions of the same syntactic category, ψ' is true if φ' is true. But validity, thus defined, cannot be assessed by direct intuitions, since it depends on syntactic theory, as well as on the actual truth values of sentences other than φ and ψ.

Many philosophers have proposed a category of inferences validated by semantic considerations alone, and have supposed this category to include many inferences that are not logically valid: 'This is red; therefore this is colored' is one of the standard modern examples of such an inference.[50] Montague's fragments of English provide many cases of this sort. For example, on the theory of Chapter 8 the inference

(C-6) Every rodent is an animal and some rodents hibernate; therefore some animals hibernate

is not logically valid.[51] To account for examples such as (C-6), Montague made use of meaning postulates to define a kind of validity less strict than logical validity.

The device of meaning postulates makes use of the fact that in natural languages the sets X_δ of basic expressions are finite. Once the interpretations of a natural language L have been defined it may then be possible to select a finite number of conditions involving these basic expressions—the conditions being expressed either in L or in some extension of L—such that all, or at least many, inferences like (C-6) will hold good in every interpretation in which these conditions are satisfied, though they do not hold good in all interpretations whatsoever. These conditions, the meaning postulates for L, will in this way permit the characterization of an appropriate level of validity. For examples of meaning postulates, see Chapter 6, p. 212, Chapter 7, pp. 243–44, and Chapter 8, pp. 263–64.

Ordinarily there will be infinitely many inferences like (C-6), so the meaning postulates cannot merely repeat a conditional corresponding to each inference. The task of laying down meaning postulates for a language is therefore not entirely trivial. But the result of accomplishing it will not be an articulated, organic theory like that used to define logical consequence. Each type of valid inference, as it is discovered, will yield a new meaning

---

[50] For an exhaustive treatment of this topic, with many references to the literature, see Pap [10].

[51] The reason is that Montague regards it as having the same form as 'Every price is a number and some prices are changing; therefore some numbers are changing'. See Chapter 8, Section 4.

postulate and the eventual outcome will be the sum of ad hoc responses to these discoveries. The topic of meaning postulates is one area of possible-worlds semantics that may stand in need of fundamental revisions. Progress in this quarter would go far, too, toward making the overall theory more applicable.

Fourth, semantic intuitions concerning the ambiguity of various expressions of natural language can be used as data. Montague relied on instances of ambiguity in his linguistic work just as heavily as on evidence about validity. Typical sentences that he found ambiguous are 'Every man loves a woman', 'John believes that Bill believes that he loves Mary', and 'John seeks a unicorn'. Part of the task of accounting for these ambiguities is syntactic, since in each case the sentence must be provided with alternative syntactic analyses.[52] But the semantics must then be adjusted to associate different interpretations with these analyses. Montague's semantic theories were modified in the light of such data; the last example, for instance, is one reason why in Chapter 8 singular terms are treated as expressing properties of properties rather than individual concepts.

Fifth, we should not forget the firmest and most irrefragable kind of data with which a semantic theory must cope. The theory must harmonize with the actual denotations taken by the expressions of natural languages, and in particular with the actual truth values of sentences. It may seem banal that a semantic theory ought not to imply that things that are actually false are consequences of things that actually are true. But the problem of constructing a nontrivial semantic interpretation of a sufficiently rich fragment of English while avoiding such disasters is not as easy as it may seem.

In Montague's work there are many instances of appeal to the actual truth values of English sentences. In most cases, however, his use of this evidence is tacit; he assumes that a brief citation will suffice to indicate the examples he has in mind. The following sentences resemble those whose truth

---

[52] Montague gives no criteria for distinguishing cases of semantic ambiguity that must be accounted for by positing an underlying syntactic ambiguity from those that can be explained merely by treating certain basic expressions as semantically ambiguous. However, I believe there are good reasons for classifying the above examples in the first category. See the discussion of (C-11) to (C-13) in Section 6, below, for an argument that offers such reasons.

values are cited as compatible with the theories of Chapters 5, 6, and 8.

While 'This is a big flea' is true for some values of 'this', 'This is big' is false for these values. While 'This is a reputed millionaire' is true for some values of 'this', 'This is a millionaire' is false for these values. While 'This man owes that man a horse' is true for some values of 'this man' and 'that man' and a certain syntactic analysis of the sentence, 'There is a horse which this man owes that man' is false for the same values of 'this man' and 'that man'. While 'The temperature is ninety' and 'The temperature is rising' are true at some time and place, 'Ninety is rising' is false relative to the same time and place. While 'This man seeks a woman who loves him' is true for some value of 'this man' and on one analysis of the sentence, 'There is a woman who loves this man and is such that this man seeks her' is false for the same value of 'this man'.

Attentiveness to such data is of the utmost importance in semantic research, because on the one hand any counterexamples of this sort are bound to be damaging, while on the other hand a semantic theory that is nontrivial in its theoretical structure and that manages to avoid such counterexamples would in virtue of this alone take the lead over all known theories. Data about actual truth and falsity constitute the acid test of semantic theories.

One well known body of such data has proved troublesome for possible worlds semantics: instances concerning propositional attitudes that involve awareness, such as 'believes that' or 'is aware that'. It follows from the possible worlds framework that any sentences true in all possible worlds, such as 'The square root of two is irrational' and 'Two is even', must express the same proposition and so ought to be substitutable *salva veritate* in all contexts obeying Frege's principle that the meaning of a phrase is a function of the meanings of its parts.[53] But whereas

[53] There are some contexts, anyway, that do not satisfy this principle: quotation is one. But where the set of entities of an interpretation of $\mathfrak{A}$ contains all the expressions of $\mathfrak{A}$, it is a trivial matter to write a semantic rule for quotation; quotation marks form names of the expressions they enclose. But the task of finding appropriate semantic values for the clauses embedded in belief contexts and writing semantic rules for constructions involving 'believes that' is not so easy. The strategy of possible worlds semantics leads naturally in such cases to treating embedded sentential clauses as expressing propositions.

'Thales believed that two is even' is true, 'Thales believed that the square root of two is irrational' is false.

In answer to tensions with the evidence, a responsible theoretician must try either to modify his theory or explain away the data. In the present case, the former course would involve experimenting with modified semantic theories that do not imply that one believes all the logical consequences of one's beliefs. The latter course would involve constructing philosophical arguments to the effect that in fact one does believe all the logical consequences of one's beliefs. Montague probed both alternatives, though neither attempt seems to have issued in a result he considered definitive: see Chapter 7, Section 4, for the theoretical modification and Chapter 4, p. 139 for an argument to the effect that one actually does believe the logical consequences of one's beliefs. Theoretical modifications have been explored by logicians other than Montague; see Hintikka [5], for example. Explaining the problem away is a far more original approach and may prove less quixotic than it at first appears. It is hard to see how the apparent falsity of 'Thales was aware that the square root of two is irrational' could be explained away by Montague's line of argument, but even if ultimately unsuccessful this train of thought might well lead to a deeper philosophical understanding of belief and related phenomena.

We have not tried to disguise the fact that difficulties can be found with possible worlds semantics. But the worst of these, far from illustrating an unhealthy isolation from linguistic evidence, consists of a tension with this evidence. Other difficulties I know of, such as the unsystematic character of meaning postulates, merely show that there is reason to seek refinements of the present framework. On the other hand, possible worlds semantics has succeeded in producing solutions to semantic puzzles of long standing, in the form of generalizations of widely accepted mathematical theories. In view of this achievement, and taking into account the theoretical attention the topic is now receiving, the problems arising with awareness cannot be said to justify abandoning the framework, at least until a better one has been proposed.

6. Noun phrases as quantifiers

In Montague's framework, syntactic structure is related to logical consequence. For instance, if according to the semantic theory of $\mathfrak{A}^2$

(C-7) a man is old

is a logical consequence of

(C-8) a man such that that man is old is heavy,

then

(C-9) a picture of John is old

must be a logical consequence of

(C-10) a picture of John such that that picture is old is heavy.

This is so because of purely syntactic considerations: the latter inference comes from substituting 'picture of John' for 'man' in the former inference.[54] If the syntactic theory of a language makes an inference of ψ' from φ' a substitution instance of an inference of ψ from φ, then ψ' will be a logical consequence of φ' if ψ is a logical consequence of φ.

This consideration illustrates the fact that the choice of a syntactic theory for a language will not leave us entirely free in our construction of a semantic theory for that language. Such influence of syntax on semantics does not make itself felt very strongly in artificial languages. Here the syntax is an artifact of convenience and can be adjusted at will to meet the demands of semantics. In human languages, however, syntactic theory is constrained to conform to a body of syntactic data, and it can sometimes happen that the semantic theory must be adjusted to meet syntactic needs.

---

[54] The relation of substitution has to be defined relative to analysis trees. The result of substituting ξ' for a basic expression ξ in an analysis tree of ζ is produced by putting ξ' for ξ at the topmost nodes of the tree and adjusting expressions lower in the tree according to the syntactic rules used to produce them.

Montague's treatment of noun phrases in Chapter 8 is an instructive example of this. The expressions classified by English grammar as noun phrases include examples, such as 'a man', 'every woman' and 'no one', that logicians parse by means of quantification. The interpretation of quantification has not been a matter of controversy in metamathematics; ever since Frege, logicians have agreed that quantifiers should be interpreted as second-order properties. In the framework of Sections 3 and 4, then, where properties were given the semantic type $\langle s, \langle e, t \rangle \rangle$, quantifiers would have the type $\langle s, \langle \langle s, \langle e, t \rangle \rangle, t \rangle \rangle$. 'A man', for example, would be assigned the property possessed by a property N in case there is a man of whom N is true. 'No one' would be assigned the property possessed by a property N in case for all persons x, N is false of x. In many familiar logical calculi, of course, quantifiers are treated syncategorematically and there is no syntactic category of quantifier phrases. But if one wishes to have such a category this method of interpreting them in higher-order logic is well known.

Montague noticed that this interpretation can be applied to quantified noun phrases of English. Then, for instance, the sentence 'A man walks' is true if and only if the property of walking possesses the property expressed by 'a man'; 'Mary loves no one' is true if and only if the property of being loved by Mary possesses the property expressed by 'no one'. Examples such as 'John believes that Mary hopes that a man loves her', however, show the need of some more general method of talking about properties than that illustrated by 'the property of walking' or 'the property of being loved by Mary'. It is customary for logicians to use variables for this purpose. We may say, for example, that 'John believes that Mary hopes that x loves her' is true (on one reading, the one that gives the quantifier wide scope) if and only if the property expressed by the formula 'John believes that Mary hopes that x loves her' possesses the property expressed by 'a man'.

Thus, semantic considerations suggest that quantifier phrases should combine with formulas, relative to a particular variable occurring in the formula. In their artificial languages, logicians have written this semantic feature into their syntactic rule for quantifiers: '$\wedge xP(x)$', for example, comes from attaching '$\wedge x$' to the formula '$P(x)$'. But proper names, since they denote entities, will have semantic type $\langle s, e \rangle$ and so it is natural to treat them syntactically as modified by one-place verbs. 'John walks', then, is formalized by '$P(a)$', 'A man walks' by '$\vee xP(x)$'.[55] The difference in syntactic form is clear; 'a' combines with one-place verbs to form sentences, while '$\vee$' combines with a formula, relative to a variable, to make another formula.

In English syntax, however, quantifier phrases and proper nouns behave in much the same way; it is difficult to find instances in which replacement of the one kind of expression by the other affects grammaticality. And according to grammatical tradition, proper names and quantifier phrases are both classified as noun phrases, so that 'John walks' and 'A man walks' are treated as having the same form.

This approach has more to recommend it than economy. If noun phrases are divided into singular terms and quantifier phrases, the role of singular terms will be to combine, for instance, with intransitive verbs to form sentences and with transitive verbs to form intransitive verb phrases. ('John' combines with 'loves' to form the intransitive verb phrase 'loves John', which then combines with 'Mary' to form the sentence 'Mary loves John'.) Singular terms also combine with prepositions to form ad-verbs, adjectives and adformulas. Quantifier phrases, as we have said, will combine with formulas, relative to a variable, to form formulas.

But in this case our syntax will not enable us to capture certain ambiguities. Each of the following sentences, for example, has a "nonreferential" reading.

(C-11) John seeks a unicorn.
(C-12) John talks about a unicorn.
(C-13) John owes Smith a horse.

This reading of (C-11) and (C-12) is distinguished by the fact that it does not imply that there are unicorns; in the case of (C-13), this is the reading that differs in meaning from 'John owes Smith a certain horse'.

[55] For simplicity here, we have let 'x' range over men.

Since 'John frequently seeks a unicorn', for instance, is *three* ways ambiguous, the ambiguity of (C-11) cannot be explained by lexical ambiguity; if 'seek' (or both 'seek' and 'frequently') were ambiguous, this sentence would be two (or four) ways ambiguous. Data such as this must be explained by scope and so there must be a syntactic ambiguity in (C-11), (C-12), and (C-13), arising in two different ways in which the quantifier phrases have combined with other elements of the sentences. But if quantifier phrases could combine only with formulas, no reading other than the referential one would be forthcoming. For example, consider (C-11): if this is analyzed as coming from the combination of 'a unicorn' and 'John seeks x' by a rule of quantification, then under this analysis (C-11) will be true if and only if there is a unicorn that possesses the property of being sought by John.

To obtain analysis trees that will support the nonreferential readings of these sentences we must allow quantifier phrases to combine with verbs and prepositions just as singular terms do. For instance, 'a unicorn' must combine with 'seek' to form 'seek a unicorn' and with 'about' to form 'about a unicorn'. But these are just the combinations that would necessarily occur if the syntactic distinction between singular terms and quantifier phrases were abolished.

This was an argument to the effect that quantifier phrases should be treated like singular terms. Within Montague's syntactic theory of variable binding, which is adapted from logical syntax, there is also an argument suggesting that singular terms should be treated like quantifier phrases. In the grammar of Chapter 8, free variables are realized by morphological forms of 'he' to which numerical subscripts are attached. These free variables are genderless, but are marked for case; 'he', for example, is nominative, 'him' is accusative. When a formula is combined with a quantifier phrase, relative to the variable 'he$_5$', say, some occurrences of 'he$_5$' in the formula can become bound by the quantifier, and in so doing they lose their subscripts and take on a gender. For example, when 'a woman' combines with

(C-14) he$_4$ believes that Mary talks about him$_4$

relative to the variable 'he$_4$', the result is

(C-15) a woman believes that Mary talks about her.

When 'every unicorn' combines with

(C-16) he$_1$ says that he$_2$ finds a woman such that she loves him$_2$

relative to the variable 'he$_2$', the result is

(C-17) he$_1$ says that every unicorn finds a woman such that she loves it.

But as well as formulas like (C-15) and (C-17), where pronouns are bound to quantifier phrases, there are ones like

(C-18) Susan believes that Mary talks about her

and

(C-19) he$_1$ says that John finds a woman such that she loves him,

in which pronouns have been bound to proper names. To account for these constructions, singular terms must be allowed to figure in a syntactic rule just like the one for quantifier phrases, a rule that introduces them into formulas relative to a variable.

In response to considerations such as these, Montague chose in his last paper, Chapter 8, to assign singular terms and quantifier phrases to the same syntactic category. Clearly, a quantifier phrase such as 'a man', 'everyone', or 'no one' cannot be considered to denote any entity, for there will then be no way to explain the consistency of 'a man walks' with 'a man does not walk', or the ambiguity of 'Every man loves a woman', or the inconsistency of 'Some man walks' with 'No man walks'.[56] However, the reverse strategy of assigning proper names the semantic type $\langle s, \langle\langle s, \langle e, t\rangle\rangle, t\rangle\rangle$ given to quantifier phrases will lead to no such difficulties. Though it may be rather artificial to regard 'John' as expressing a property of properties, there will be no readjustment of the truth values of sentences if 'John' is made to express the property of being one of the properties

---

[56] The last of these problems is not as irreconcilable as the first two, since it might conceivably be solved by means of meaning postulates.

possessed by John. For then 'John walks' will be true if and only if the property of walking is one of those properties possessed by John, that is, if and only if John possesses the property of walking.

Though it would not affect truth values, this interpretation of singular terms weakens the logical theory to an uncomfortable degree; it treats as invalid many things, such as the sentence 'John is tall or John is not tall', which not only are valid on the standard interpretation of singular terms, but are intuited as valid. Also it finds ambiguities in many sentences, such as 'John loves Mary', which on this theory has the same syntactic form as (C-11), that are not intuited as ambiguous. As we indicated in the previous section, these difficulties can be remedied by meaning postulates; every proper name can be given a meaning postulate to the effect that for some entity, the name expresses the second-order property of being a property that is possessed by that entity. These postulates will restore the standard theory of validity for proper names.

There is another case in Chapter 8 where the natural interpretation of expressions is complicated in the interests of uniformity. To explain the apparent referential opacity of the position occupied by 'the temperature' in 'The temperature rises', Montague chose to interpret intransitive verbs as properties of individual concepts rather than as properties of entities. That is, intransitive verbs are assigned the semantic type $\langle s, \langle\langle s, e\rangle, t\rangle\rangle$ rather than the type $\langle s, \langle e, t\rangle\rangle$. Since 'the temperature' and 'ninety' would be associated with different individual concepts, this explains how 'The temperature rises' and 'Ninety rises' can differ in truth value, even though 'The temperature is ninety' may be true.

This change in the interpretation of intransitive verbs affects the interpretation of noun phrases. According to the policy we have just presented, noun phrases will denote properties of the semantic values assigned to intransitive verbs, and so will have the semantic type $\langle s, \langle \tau, t\rangle\rangle$, where τ is the type of intransitive verbs. Noun phrases, then, singular terms as well as quantifiers, will be assigned the semantic type $\langle s, \langle\langle s, \langle\langle s, e\rangle, t\rangle\rangle, t\rangle\rangle$.

Inferences such as 'John runs and John is the mayor of New York; therefore the mayor of New York runs' are rendered logically invalid by this tactic. But a meaning postulate for 'runs', together with a meaning postulate for 'John' and either a semantic rule or meaning postulate for 'the', will justify the inference.

It is interesting to note how these changes affect the interpretation of a plain sentence like 'John walks'. When both revisions are taken into account, this sentence is made to say that the property of individual concepts expressed by 'walks' possesses the second-order property of properties of individual concepts expressed by 'John'. The unnaturalness of this interpretation in such simple cases is balanced by uniformity and elegance in the overall theory. Also it should be stressed that meaning postulates for 'John' and 'run' will make the interpretation of this sentence reduce to the condition that the entity denoted by 'John' possesses a certain first-order property of entities, the property expressed by 'walks'.

D. PRAGMATICS

1. Indexicals and contexts of use

As a formal discipline, pragmatics owes much of its development to Montague and his students and associates. Chapters 3 and 4 have introductory sections that furnish historical background, and expositions and developments of further material relating to pragmatics can be found in Scott [14], Stalnaker [15], Lewis [8], and Kamp [7]. Here, therefore, our discussion of the subject will be confined to a brief general account and a single example.

Montague limits pragmatics to the study of *indexicals*, expressions whose semantic values depend on *context of use*. The personal pronoun 'I', whose denotation depends on who is giving utterance, is an indexical. This example shows that information concerning who is speaking should be included among the things specified by context of use. Other indexicals include 'now', 'tomorrow', 'here', and the demonstrative pronouns 'this' and 'that'.

The form taken by pragmatic theory differs little from that of semantics. As before, an interpretation consists of an interpretation structure and an interpretation assignment. Part of the interpretation structure is a set J of contexts of use. We no longer speak simply of the intension $\text{Int}_{\mathscr{B}}(\zeta)$ given to a phrase ζ by an interpretation $\mathscr{B}$ and of the extension $\text{Ext}_{\mathscr{B},i}(\zeta)$ given to ζ by $\mathscr{B}$ at the possible world i, but of the intension $\text{Int}_{\mathscr{B},j}(\zeta)$ relative to a context of use j and the extension $\text{Ext}_{\mathscr{B},\langle i,j \rangle}(\zeta)$ relative to an *index* $\langle i, j \rangle$.

The close similarity of pragmatic and semantic theory raises the question of whether they are separate subjects at all. It seems natural to view pragmatics as a generalization of semantics in which more—but not a great deal more—structure has been built into possible worlds. This estimate would not be entirely correct, because possible worlds and contexts of use do differ significantly; and the interaction between the two produces some effects that are not found in semantics alone.

The difference between possible worlds and contexts of use is that, though denotations are assigned to expressions relative to both, only the former enter into the construction of possible denotations.[57] The set of senses of the possible denotations belonging to a set X consists of all functions from possible worlds to X, not of all functions from contexts of use to X (or, for that matter, from indices $\langle i, j \rangle$ to X, where i is a possible world and j a context of use).

In our treatment of semantics we discussed the phenomena that suggest this construction of possible denotations, phenomena concerning intensional contexts. What analogous phenomena would force us to treat functions from contexts of use or indices as possible denotations? These would be instances in which the intensions of sentences involving indexicals depended not just on the intensions of their constituent phrases relative to a fixed context of use, but on functions taking contexts of use into intensions.

---

[57] Here the term 'possible world' is used in the general sense mentioned above in Section C.4, equivalent to 'sense-determining index'. In this sense a "possible world" may be a pair consisting of a possible world and a moment of time, or (to account for sentences like 'Somewhere the government frequently collapses') a triple consisting of a possible world, a time, and a place.

But such cases, if they occur at all, are rare and isolated.[58] Let ζ be an indexical, φ be the result of embedding the indexical in an intensional context, j be a context of use, and K be the function whose domain is the set J of all contexts of use, such that for all $j' \in J$, $K(j')$ is the intension of ζ relative to j'. Let M be $K(j)$ and N be the intension of φ relative to j. Then N depends only on the value M of ζ with respect to j, never on the whole of K. For example, 'Five minutes hence it will be the case that I am speaking' expresses, relative to a context of use j, a proposition depending only on the person who is speaking in j, not on the person who is speaking five minutes later. Similarly, 'Two days hence, it will be the case that yesterday is Tuesday' is true when uttered on Wednesday, false when uttered on Monday. Likewise, 'It might be the case that that man is guilty' would never be said to be true because the speaker might have pointed at a guilty man.

As we will see in the next section, the introduction of contexts of use also gives rise to a new species of validity that does not arise in semantics. It is natural, for instance, to treat 'I exist' as pragmatically valid, since with respect to any context of use in which it is uttered it will be true. But certainly it is not semantically valid—that is, it need not express a necessary proposition. Montague presents a pragmatic analysis of this example in Chapter 3, Section 3.

Conceived as the study of indexicals, pragmatics is not a very sweeping field of inquiry. Perhaps, however, this confinement to indexicals is only a symptom of the present state of formal pragmatics, and will be remedied by further research.[59] At present, however, this narrowness is not uncomfortable. The material at the end of Chapter 3, as well as Kamp [7] and unpublished work of David Kaplan's, suggests that the study of indexicals is by no means exhausted.

---

[58] These are cases like the sense of 'Tomorrow never comes' (if there is such a sense) in which a truth is expressed.

[59] Stalnaker's work suggests that certain kinds of presupposition can also be treated within formal pragmatics. If this is so, it will be a valuable and important extension of the subject.

2. A pragmatic language

The language $\mathfrak{A}^5$ we will discuss in this section will be an extension of the tense calculus $\mathfrak{A}^4$. To illustrate the fundamental ideas of pragmatics it will suffice to add an indexical individual constant 'y', to be thought of as standing for 'yesterday', to the vocabulary of $\mathfrak{A}^4$. Thus, $X^5_{\text{ICST}} = \{\text{'}a\text{'}, \text{'}b\text{'}, \text{'}c\text{'}, \text{'}y\text{'}\}$. Also, we will treat the one-place verb 'P' as a logical constant, standing for 'is past', as in 'The year 1972 is past'.

The interpretation of $\mathfrak{A}^5$ requires enough structural information about time to enable us to speak of days. Since our only indexical is 'yesterday' we can let the set J of contexts of use consist of days, which can be represented by sets of moments of time. An interpretation structure for $\mathfrak{A}^5$ is a quadruple $\langle E, I, <, J \rangle$, where J is a partition of I into subsets that are connected with respect to $<$. We require that $J \subseteq E$, and that for all $j \in J$ there be a unique member $Y(j)$ of J "immediately preceeding" j. More precisely, say that $j_1 < j_2$ if $j_1 \neq j_2$ and for some i_1 and i_2, $i_1 \in j_1$, $i_2 \in j_2$, and $i_1 < i_2$. Then $Y(j)$ is such that $Y(j) < j$ and there is no $j' \in J$ such that $Y(j) < j' < j$. These requirements ensure that for each context of use in J there will be a denotation for 'y' in E. $Y(j)$, of course, is the day before j.

An interpretation $\mathscr{B}$ of $\mathfrak{A}^5$ is a structure $\langle \langle E, I, <, J \rangle, f \rangle$, where the assignment f is like an interpretation assignment for $\mathfrak{A}^4$, only made relative to contexts of use. For each basic expression ζ of $\mathfrak{A}^5$ and $j \in J$, $f(\zeta, j)$ will be a possible denotation of the type specified in Table C-5.[60] Besides this, every interpretation must meet certain requirements. First there is a group of conditions relating to logical constants. If ζ is a logical constant of $\mathfrak{A}^4$, then $f(\zeta, j)$ is the same value that was stipulated in formulating the semantics of $\mathfrak{A}^4$. For instance, for all $j \in J$,

[60] This is slightly different from Montague's treatment of assignments. In Chapter 7, for instance, he treats them as associating functions from indices to possible denotations with expressions. '$F_\zeta(i, j)$' will then signify the extension of ζ relative to i and j. Our account of assignments suggests a different notation: '$F_\zeta(j)$' would signify the *intension* of ζ relative to the context of use j, according to this notation. I feel this is preferable because it separates the roles of contexts of use and possible worlds. The intension of an expression is relative to, but not constituted by, the former.

$f(`\neg', j)$ is that function $N$ from $\{0, 1\}^I$ to $\{0, 1\}^I$ such that $N_M(i) = 0$ if $M(i) = 1$ and $N_M(i) = 1$ if $M(i) = 0$. Also, $f(`P', j)$ is a function N from I to $\{0, 1\}^E$ such that for all subsets X of I, $N_i(X) = 1$ if $i' < i$ for all $i' \in X$ and $N_i(X) = 0$ if $i' \geq i$ for some $i' \in X$. Thus, 'P' is true at i of all sets of moments whose members are all prior to i, and false of all other sets of moments. This justifies our glossing of 'P' as 'is past'. The indexical 'y', a new logical constant, is interpreted so that in a context of use j it functions as a proper name of the day before j. $f(`y', j) = N$, where N is that function from I to E such that for all $i \in I$, $N(i) = Y(j)$. We will also choose to require that 'y' be the only basic expression of $\mathfrak{A}^5$ that acts as an indexical. This requirement takes the following form: for all basic expressions ζ of $\mathfrak{A}^5$ other than 'y', $f(\zeta, j) = f(\zeta, j')$ for all $j, j' \in J$.

The intension $\text{Int}_{\mathscr{B}, j}(\zeta)$ given by $\mathscr{B}$ to an arbitrary phrase ζ of $\mathfrak{A}^5$ is defined by a recursion just like the one used for $\mathfrak{A}^4$. For instance, $\text{Int}_{\mathscr{B}, j}(\zeta) = f(\zeta, j)$ if ζ is a basic expression of $\mathfrak{A}^5$, and if ξ is a one-place verb and α an individual constant, then $\text{Int}_{\mathscr{B}, j}(\ulcorner \xi(\alpha) \urcorner) = M$, where M is that function from I to $\{0, 1\}$ such that $M(i) = (\text{Int}_{\mathscr{B}, j}(\xi))(N(i))$, where $N = \text{Int}_{\mathscr{B}, j}(\alpha)$. The extension $\text{Ext}_{\mathscr{B}, \langle i, j \rangle}(\zeta)$ of ζ relative to the index $\langle i, j \rangle$ is $N(i)$, where $N = \text{Int}_{\mathscr{B}, j}(\zeta)$. According to this last definition, the extension of ζ depends on time in *two* respects: it depends on the semantic "time of evaluation" i as well as on the pragmatic "time of utterance" j. The former is the time *about which* one is talking, the latter the time *at which* one is talking.

Now in a primary sense, we always are talking about the time at which we are speaking. A past tense formula $\ulcorner \mathscr{P} + \varphi + \urcorner$ is, in this primary sense, true at the time i at which it is spoken if and only if the embedded formula φ is true at some previous i'. $\ulcorner \mathscr{P} + \varphi + \urcorner$ is "about" i' in a secondary sense, however, since in determining its truth value we must consider the truth values of its constituents at moments other than i, moments like i'.

It is this secondary kind of aboutness that creates a need for *abnormal* indices, indices $\langle i, j \rangle$ such that $i \notin j$. These are indices in which the moment spoken about is not a moment occurring in the day of utterance. Even though in determining $\text{Ext}_{\mathscr{B}, \langle i, j \rangle}(\ulcorner \mathscr{P} + \varphi + \urcorner)$ we may begin with a normal index $\langle i, j \rangle$, the process of calculating this semantic value will force us to take into account $\text{Ext}_{\mathscr{B},\langle i',j\rangle}(\varphi)$ for i' preceding i, and these indices $\langle i', j\rangle$ may be abnormal.

Nevertheless, a sentence cannot be uttered relative to an abnormal index. When 'Yesterday is past' is uttered, for instance, we use the time of utterance both to fix the referent of 'yesterday' and to gauge the truth value of the sentence uttered. It is natural, then, to define a notion of *pragmatic validity* for $\mathfrak{A}^4$. A formula φ is valid in this sense if for all interpretations $\mathscr{B} = \langle\langle E, I, <, J\rangle, f\rangle$, $\text{Ext}_{\mathscr{B},\langle i,j\rangle}(\varphi) = 1$ for all indices $\langle i, j\rangle$ such that $i \in j$. It can easily happen that pragmatically valid formulas will not be semantically valid; we have already mentioned 'I exist', the example noted by Montague in Chapter 3. In $\mathfrak{A}^5$, '$P(y)$', standing for 'Yesterday is past', is an example of such a formula. Clearly, it will be false at any index $\langle i, j\rangle$ such that i falls on a day preceding j. But for normal contexts, where $i \in j$, '$P(y)$' will be true at $\langle i, j\rangle$ because 'y' will then denote a set of moments all of which are previous to j.

Notice that for each context j, the sentence '$P(y)$' will express a different proposition at j; $\text{Int}_{\mathscr{B},j}('P(y)')$ differs from $\text{Int}_{\mathscr{B},j'}('P(y)')$ if $j \neq j'$. For if $j < j'$, for instance, $\text{Int}_{\mathscr{B},j}('P(y)')$ will be true at more moments of time than $\text{Int}_{\mathscr{B},j'}('P(y)')$. This is a typical phenomenon in pragmatics: 'I was born in California' expresses one proposition in one man's mouth, and a different proposition in another's. But though the proposition expressed by '$P(y)$' in one context j varies with j, and for each j is not a necessary proposition, nevertheless the *form of words* '$P(y)$' is true whenever it is uttered. This is the source of pragmatic validity; unlike semantic validity, which lies in a sentence, by virtue of its structure, expressing a necessary proposition, pragmatic validity originates in the general relation of the proposition expressed in a normal context by a certain sentence to features of that context.

REFERENCES

1. Church, A. The Need for Abstract Entities in Semantic Analysis. *Proceedings of the American Academy of Arts and Sciences* 80:100–12 (1951).

2. Church, A. *Introduction to Mathematical Logic*, vol. 1. Princeton, N.J., 1956.
3. Frege, G. Über Sinn und Bedeutung. *Zeitschrift für Philosophie und philosophische Kritik* 100:25–50 (1892). Translated by H. Feigl under the title "On Sense and Nominatum" in H. Feigl and W. Sellars (eds.), *Readings in Philosophical Analysis*, New York, 1949. Translated by M. Black under the title "On Sense and Reference" in P. Geach and M. Black, *Translations from the Philosophical Writings of Gottlob Frege*, Oxford, 1952.
4. Harman, G. Deep Structure as Logical Form. *Synthèse* 21:275–97 (1970).
5. Hintikka, J. Surface Information and Depth Information. In J. Hintikka and P. Suppes (eds.), *Information and Inference*, Dordrecht, 1969.
6. Kalish, D. Semantics. In P. Edwards, *The Encyclopedia of Philosophy*, New York, 1967.
7. Kamp, H. Formal Properties of 'Now'. *Theoria* 37:227–73 (1971).
8. Lewis, D. General Semantics. *Synthèse* 22:18–67 (1970).
9. Lewis, D. Anselm and Actuality. *Nous* 4:175–88 (1970).
10. Pap, A. *Semantics and Necessary Truth*. New Haven, Conn., 1958.
11. Partee, B. Comments on Richard Montague's "Quantification in Ordinary English." In J. Hintikka, J. Moravcsik, and P. Suppes (eds.), *Approaches to Natural Language*. Dordrecht, 1973.
12. Putnam, H. Is Semantics Possible? *Metaphilosophy* 1:187–201 (1970).
13. Rodman, R. *Papers in Montague Grammar*. Los Angeles, 1972. (At the present time, copies of this volume can be obtained by sending $3.00 per copy to Mr. Robert Rodman, Linguistics Department, UCLA, Los Angeles, Calif. 90024.)
14. Scott, D. Advice on Modal Logic. In K. Lambert (ed.), *Philosophical Problems in Logic*. Dordrecht, 1970.
15. Stalnaker, R. Pragmatics. *Synthèse* 22:272–89 (1970).
16. Suppes, P. *Axiomatic Set Theory*. Princeton, N.J., 1960.
17. Thomason, R. *Symbolic Logic: an Introduction*. New York, 1970.
18. Thomason, R. and R. Stalnaker. A Semantic Theory of Adverbs. *Linguistic Inquiry* 4:195–220 (1973).
19. van Fraassen, B. *Formal Semantics and Logic*. New York, 1971.
20. van Fraassen, B. A Formal Approach to the Philosophy of Science. In R. Colodny (ed.), *Paradigms and Paradoxes: the Philosophical Challenge of the Quantum Domain*. Pittsburgh, 1972.

1. Logical Necessity, Physical Necessity, Ethics, and Quantifiers

1. INTRODUCTION

This paper is intended to contribute to the problem of interpreting 'it is logically necessary that', 'it is physically necessary that', and 'it is obligatory that'. The interpretations given below were suggested by certain logical analogies between these phrases and the universal quantifier. The interpretations are to be given in an extensional metalanguage; in particular, the metalanguage is not to contain any of the phrases themselves. Further, the interpretation is to be such as to permit the use of the phrases in conjunction with quantifiers.

It is only in satisfying this last requirement that my interpretations can be called original. They are based on the following unoriginal considerations. Let Φ be a sentence. Then $\ulcorner$it is logically necessary that $\Phi\urcorner$ is true if and only if Φ is a theorem of logic; $\ulcorner$it is physically necessary that $\Phi\urcorner$ is true if and only if Φ is deducible from a certain class of physical laws which is specified in advance; $\ulcorner$it is obligatory that $\Phi\urcorner$ is true if and only if Φ is deducible from a certain class of ethical laws which is again specified in advance.[1]

Originally published in *Inquiry* 4 : 259–69 (1960). Reprinted gratis by permission. The present paper was delivered before the Annual Spring Conference in Philosophy at the University of California, Los Angeles, in May, 1955. It contains no results of any great technical interest; I therefore did not initially plan to publish it. But some closely analogous, though not identical, ideas have recently been announced by Kanger in [2, 3] and by Kripke in [4]. In view of this fact, together with the possibility of stimulating further research, it now seems not wholly inappropriate to publish my early contribution.

[1] I use corners in the sense of Quine's *Mathematical Logic*. The interpretations given at this point are highly approximate, and can be taken literally only when an infinite domain of discourse is under consideration.

In these cases, Φ was assumed to be a sentence. The interesting cases, however, are those in which the formula Φ is *not* a sentence; that is, when Φ contains free variables, as in 'for some x, it is logically necessary that x is identical with the Evening Star'. This example is advanced by Quine in [6] to support grave doubts concerning the joint use of modalities and quantification. The example seems to follow from the true sentence, 'it is logically necessary that the Evening Star is identical with the Evening Star'; yet the example itself seems to be either false or meaningless. What is that x which is necessarily identical with the Evening Star? Is it the Evening Star, that is, the Morning Star? It seems not, since it is only an empirical fact, not a matter of logical necessity, that the Morning Star is identical with the Evening Star.

For the phrase 'it is logically necessary that' Carnap in [1] has already given an interpretation which permits the introduction of quantifiers. I shall shortly indicate relations between his interpretation and mine.

In Section 3 it is observed that my interpretation of the four notions mentioned in the title fall under a certain comprehensive scheme of interpretation, and further that the valid sentences of the scheme can be axiomatically characterized by a certain system of modal logic which has hitherto not been considered in the literature.

2. AN ELEMENTARY MODAL LANGUAGE; INTERPRETATIONS

I wish to consider a language S which contains *individual variables*; an unspecified number of *individual constants*; for each $n \geqslant 0$, an unspecified number of *n-place predicates*; all the *sentential connectives*; and the additional symbol 'N'. Thus an *atomic formula* of S is the result of writing an n-place predicate followed by n *individual signs* (that is, variables or individual constants). All atomic formulas are *formulas*; any truth-functional compound of *formulas* is again a *formula*; if Φ is a *formula*, then so is $\ulcorner N\Phi \urcorner$; nothing is a *formula* except as required by the foregoing rules. In particular, the formulas of S contain no quantifiers.

Now if 'N' is read 'it is logically necessary that', our intuition convinces us of the following facts:

(1a) If Φ is tautologous (that is, passes the truth-table test), then Φ holds.

(1b) If Φ is tautologous, then $\ulcorner N\Phi \urcorner$ holds.

(2a) $\ulcorner N(\Phi \supset \Psi) \supset (N\Phi \supset N\Psi) \urcorner$ holds (for any formulas Φ and Ψ).

(2b) $\ulcorner N[N(\Phi \supset \Psi) \supset (N\Phi \supset N\Psi)] \urcorner$ holds.

(3a) $\ulcorner N\Phi \equiv NN\Phi \urcorner$ holds.

(3b) $\ulcorner N(N\Phi \equiv NN\Phi) \urcorner$ holds.

(4a) $\ulcorner \sim N\Phi \equiv N \sim N\Phi \urcorner$ holds.

(4b) $\ulcorner N(\sim N\Phi \equiv N \sim N\Phi) \urcorner$ holds.

All the formulas mentioned can be proved in the Lewis system $S5$ (one of the classical systems of modal logic proposed by C. I. Lewis, see [5]).[2] The intuition may well balk at (3a)–(4b); in fact, iterated modalities play little part in ordinary discourse, and the laws governing them are ill-determined. But the logic of modalities is considerably simplified by the principles (3a)–(4b). It is hoped, therefore, that the scrupulous reader will grant them provisionally.

But now let us read 'N' as 'it is *physically* necessary that'. We find that all the principles (1a)–(4b) continue to hold (or at least do not clearly fail). Let us read 'N' as 'it is *obligatory* that' (or 'it *ought to be the case* that'). Again (1a)–(4b) do not seem totally implausible. Also, surprisingly, we find that (1a)–(4b) hold when 'N' is read 'for all x' (the universal quantifier on the variable 'x'). Furthermore, it is possible to introduce by definition an operator dual to 'N'; in fact, $\ulcorner \Diamond \Phi \urcorner$ is put for $\ulcorner \sim N \sim \Phi \urcorner$. For each of the readings I have given for 'N', there is a corresponding natural reading for '$\Diamond$'. Thus '$\Diamond$' may be read 'it is

---

[2] In fact, if one were to add the axioms $\ulcorner N\Phi \supset \Phi \urcorner$ (where Φ is a formula of S) to 1a–4b and adopt the inference rule *modus ponens*, one would obtain exactly the theorems of $S5$. It should be mentioned that the schemata 1a–4b are not independent. Indeed, 3a and 3b can be derived from the other schemata, using *modus ponens;* a derivation sufficient to establish this fact may be found in M. Wajsberg [9].

logically possible that', 'it is physically possible that', 'it is permissible that', or 'for some x'. (Von Wright, in *An Essay in Modal Logic*, has pointed out similar analogies.)

What is the source of this strange analogy between apparently unrelated phrases? Can the analogy be exploited in order to yield interpretations for some of the phrases? In seeking interpretations let us begin in accordance with the method of Tarski [8]. Let us consider a possible formula of S:

$$(Wxa \ v \ NHx)$$

(where 'W' and 'H' are predicates, 'x' is a variable, and 'a' is an individual constant). In order to make this formula either true or false we must

(1) specify a *domain of discourse*, over which the variables are to range,

(2) assign to each descriptive constant (that is, predicate or individual constant) an *extension*, that is, assign to each individual constant an element of the domain of discourse as designatum and assign to each n-place predicate a class of n-tuples of elements of the domain of discourse, and

(3) assign *values* to the variables, that is, assign to each variable an element (to which it is supposed to refer) of the domain of discourse.

Thus we are led to *models* of our language S. These are to be ordered triples $\langle D, R, f \rangle$. D is to be a domain of discourse (that is, a non-empty set); R is to be an *extension-assignment* with respect to D, that is, a function which assigns to each descriptive constant an extension (with respect to D); and f is to be a *value-assignment* with respect to D, that is, a function which assigns to each variable an element of D.

An *interpretation* of the language S will be a definition of the phrase 'the model M satisfies the formula Φ'. Such a definition, to be interesting, must fulfill certain conditions. In the case of formulas not involving 'N' these conditions have been clearly specified by Tarski. When 'N' is involved, however, we must rely, at least for the sake of this paper, on intuition in judging the worth of a definition.

It is convenient to define first the notion of the *value* of an *individual sign* for a given model:

$$v_{\langle D,R,f\rangle}(\zeta) = \begin{cases} R(\zeta) \text{ if } \zeta \text{ is an individual constant} \\ f(\zeta) \text{ if } \zeta \text{ is a variable} \end{cases}$$

Let us now, following Tarski, attempt to construct a recursive definition of satisfaction. Certain clauses can be borrowed without alteration from Tarski:

(1) If π is an n-place predicate and $\zeta_1, \ldots, \zeta_n$ are individual signs, then $\langle D, R, f\rangle$ satisfies $\ulcorner \pi\zeta_1 \ldots \zeta_n \urcorner$ if and only if the ordered n-tuple $\langle v_{\langle D,R,f\rangle}(\zeta_1), \ldots, v_{\langle D,R,f\rangle}(\zeta_n)\rangle$ is an element of $R(\pi)$.

(2) $\langle D, R, f\rangle$ satisfies $\ulcorner \sim \Phi \urcorner$ if and only if $\langle D, R, f\rangle$ does not satisfy Φ; $\langle D, R, f\rangle$ satisfies $\ulcorner (\Phi \vee \Psi)\urcorner$ if and only if $\langle D, R, f\rangle$ satisfies Φ or $\langle D, R, f\rangle$ satisfies Ψ; and similarly for the other sentential connectives.

It is now our desire to add a clause '$\langle D, R, f\rangle$ satisfies $\ulcorner N\Phi \urcorner$ if and only if . . .' for each of the four intended readings of 'N'. We shall thus obtain four notions of satisfaction. Corresponding to the reading 'it is logically necessary that', we shall have 'satisfies$_L$'; corresponding to 'it is physically necessary that', 'satisfies$_p$'; corresponding to 'it is obligatory that', 'satisfies$_E$' ('E' for 'ethics'); and corresponding to 'for all x', 'satisfies$_Q$' ('Q' for 'quantification'). For the last reading Tarski has already supplied us with an interpretation.

Let Q be the following relation between models: $\langle D, R, f\rangle Q \langle D', R', f'\rangle$ if and only if $D = D'$, $R = R'$, and $f(\alpha) = f'(\alpha)$ for every variable α different from 'x'. Then

(3_Q) $\langle D, R, f\rangle$ satisfies$_Q \ulcorner N\Phi \urcorner$ if and only if, for every model M such that $\langle D, R, f\rangle Q M$, M satisfies$_Q \Phi$.[3]

Perhaps now, instead of the relation Q which was introduced for the sake of the universal quantifier, we can define another relation which will perform the same office for logical necessity. In fact, it seems reasonable to consider $\ulcorner$it is logically necessary

---

[3] Thus satisfaction$_Q$ is introduced by a recursive definition whose first two clauses are obtained from (1) and (2) above by replacing 'satisfies' and 'satisfy' by 'satisfies$_Q$' and 'satisfy$_Q$', and whose third and final clause is (3_Q). Similar remarks apply to satisfaction$_L$, satisfaction$_p$, and satisfaction$_E$, whose recursive definitions are composed of suitable variants of (1) and (2), together with (3_L), (3_p), or (3_E).

that $\Phi^\neg$ as asserting that Φ holds under every assignment of extensions to its descriptive constants. Accordingly, let us define the relation L as follows:

$$\langle D, R, f \rangle \; L \; \langle D', R', f' \rangle \text{ if and only if } D = D' \text{ and } f = f'.$$

Then 'satisfies$_L$' can be defined:

(3_L) $\langle D, R, f \rangle$ satisfies$_L$ $^\ulcorner N\Phi^\urcorner$ if and only if, for every model M such that $\langle D, R, f \rangle \; L \; M$, M satisfies$_L$ Φ.[3]

Using similar methods we can give an interpretation for physical necessity. We first fix a class K of sentences which may contain quantifiers but may not contain 'N'; these are thought of as *physical laws*. $^\ulcorner$It is physically necessary that $\Phi^\urcorner$ is then understood as asserting that Φ holds under every assignment of extensions under which all the physical laws hold. The relation P is defined accordingly:

$$\langle D, R, f \rangle \; P \; \langle D', R', f' \rangle \text{ if and only if } D = D', f = f', \text{ and}$$
$\langle D', R', f' \rangle$ satisfies (in Tarski's sense) all sentences of K;

and, in terms of P, 'satisfies$_p$':

(3_p) $\langle D, R, f \rangle$ satisfies$_p$ $^\ulcorner N\Phi^\urcorner$ if and only if, for every model M such that $\langle D, R, f \rangle \; P \; M$, M satisfies$_p$ Φ.[3]

In order to assure that the modal laws (1a) through (4b) be satisfied by all models, it is necessary to assume that for each domain of discourse D and each value assignment f there is an R such that $\langle D, R, f \rangle$ satisfies all the physical laws in K.

For the sake of the ethical notion 'it is obligatory that' we should first fix a class I of *ideal models*; these are the models in which the descriptive signs have just the extensions which they ought to have. The class I could, for example, be defined as the class of models which, in Tarski's sense, satisfy the ten commandments (formulated as declarative, rather than imperative, sentences; the fourth commandment, for instance, becomes '$(x)(y)(z)$ (x is a person. (y is father of x v y is mother of x) $\supset$ x honors y)'). It is important that, for any D and f, there be an R such that $\langle D, R, f \rangle$ is an element of I. The relation E is defined:

$$\langle D, R, f \rangle \; E \; \langle D', R', f' \rangle \text{ if and only if } D = D', f = f', \text{ and}$$
$\langle D', R', f' \rangle$ is an element of I;

and, in terms of E, 'satisfies$_E$':

(3_E) $\langle D, R, f \rangle$ satisfies$_E$ $\ulcorner N\Phi \urcorner$ if and only if, for every model M such that $\langle D, R, f \rangle$ E M, M satisfies$_E$ Φ.[3]

3. GENERALIZATIONS

It is seen that our four definitions of satisfaction display a common formal structure. Is this, perhaps, the reason why the four notions all obey the laws (1a)–(4b)? The answer seems affirmative, in view of the following consideration. Let X be any relation between models; let *satisfaction$_X$* be defined in precise analogy with the definitions (3_Q), (3_L), (3_P), and (3_E); and let a formula be called *valid with respect to X* if it is satisfied$_X$ by every model. Then if Φ is any formula comprehended under (1a)–(4b), Φ is valid with respect to every relation X which fulfills the following conditions:

(i)   for all M, there is an N such that M X N,

(ii) for all M, N, P, if M X N and N X P, then M X P, and

(iii) for all M, N, P, if M X N and M X P, then N X P.

Another question naturally arises. Let us consider the deductive system which has (1a)–(4b) as its axioms and *modus ponens* as its only inference rule. On the other hand, let us call a formula Φ *valid* if, for every relation X which fulfills conditions (i)–(iii), Φ is valid with respect to X. It is clear from what was just said that every theorem of the deductive system is valid. But does the converse hold? Is the deductive system complete? The answer, it turns out, is affirmative: a formula Φ is valid if and only if it is a theorem.[4] Furthermore, there is a *decision method*

---

[4] This completeness result can be stated in the following more elegant form (which permits it more easily to be compared with the principal theorem of Kripke [4]. We understand by a *complete model* an ordered couple $\langle M, K \rangle$, where M is a model and K a non-empty class of models. We define recursively the relation expressed by 'the complete model $\langle M, K \rangle$ satisfies the formula Φ', using clauses completely analogous to (1) and (2) of Section 2, together with the following:

$\langle M, K \rangle$ satisfies $\ulcorner N\Phi \urcorner$ if and only if, for every model P in K, $\langle P, K \rangle$ satisfies Φ.

It is then totally elementary to show the equivalence of the completeness result given in the text with the following result:

A formula Φ (of the language S) is a theorem of the system whose axioms are 1a–4b and whose only rule is *modus ponens* if and only if Φ is satisfied by every complete model.

for the class of valid formulas; it can be obtained by modifying suitably one of the well-known decision methods for the monadic predicate calculus.[5]

The language S may now be enlarged by the addition of infinitely many universal quantifiers, one for each variable. How is the enlarged language to be interpreted? The enlargement may be regarded as the accession to S of new modal operators. For each variable α, a relation Q_α may be defined in analogy with the relation Q (which now turns out to be $Q_{x'}$). In defining satisfaction, one retains clauses (1) and (2), as well as one of the clauses (3_L), (3_P), or (3_E), according as one understands 'N' logically, physically, or ethically. One adds the following clause:

$(3'_Q)$ $\langle D, R, f \rangle$ satisfies $\ulcorner(\alpha)\Phi\urcorner$ if and only if, for every model M such that $\langle D, R, f \rangle Q_\alpha M$, M satisfies Φ. ($(3'_Q)$ amounts to the same thing as Tarski's interpretation of quantifiers.)

Thus there is no difficulty in interpreting a system which contains both modal operators and quantifiers, and Quine's uneasiness in this regard seems to be without justification (provided, of course, that the interpretations I have given are 'good', whatever this may mean). The dubious cases which Quine mentions will shortly be examined in the light of my interpretation.

It is perhaps interesting to note that not only may quantifiers be introduced into the language S, but additional modal symbols as well. For instance, one may introduce the symbols 'PN' and 'O' for 'it is physically necessary that' and 'it is obligatory that' respectively, retaining 'N' in the sense 'it is necessary that'. To obtain an interpretation, one simply combines clauses (1), (2), (3_L), and $(3'_Q)$ with the result of replacing 'N' by 'PN' and 'O' respectively in clauses (3_P) and (3_E).

4. LOGICAL NECESSITY

It may be complained that only a very restricted sense of logical necessity has been interpreted, that the wider sense, according to which, for instance, 'No bachelor is married' is logically

---

[5] A proof of the completeness and decidability of the system 1a–4b (with *modus ponens*) can be obtained without much difficulty from the ideas in Wajsberg [9].

necessary, has been overlooked. According to the interpretations mentioned in this paper, the wider sense of logical necessity should be regarded as a kind of physical necessity. The 'physical laws' involved are what Carnap has called *meaning postulates*.

For the sake of the further discussion, let us supplement our language by the symbol of identity, ' = ', and accordingly add the following clause to our definition of satisfaction:

(4) $\langle D, R, f \rangle$ satisfies $\ulcorner \zeta = \eta \urcorner$ (where ζ, η are individual signs) if and only if $v_{\langle D,R,f \rangle}(\zeta)$ is identical with $v_{\langle D,R,f \rangle}(\eta)$.

It was mentioned that Carnap in [1] has also interpreted logical necessity in such a way as to admit quantifiers. Carnap's interpretation was given in terms of state descriptions, but to facilitate comparisons I shall express it in terms of models. In the first place, we must assume that our language contains infinitely many individual constants, and we must fix a denumerably infinite domain of discourse D and a biunique designation function Des, whose domain is the class of individual constants and whose range is D. Then a *determinate extension-assignment R* is one such that $R(\zeta)$ is Des(ζ), for each individual constant ζ. A *determinate model* $\langle D_1, R_1, f_1 \rangle$ is one such that $D_1 = D$ and R_1 is a determinate extension-assignment. Let the relation C be defined as follows:

$$\langle D_1, R_1, f_1 \rangle \ C \ \langle D_2, R_2, f_2 \rangle \text{ if and only if } D_1 = D_2 = D,$$
$$f_1 = f_2, \text{and } R_2 \text{ is a determinate extension-assignment.}$$

We have, corresponding to C, the notion of satisfaction $_C$. It can now be shown that a sentence is L-true in Carnap's Modal Functional Logic if and only if it is satisfied $_C$ by every determinate model. Carnap's interpretation is indeed suitable for certain purposes, and it can be generalized so as to apply to models which are not denumerable. But it does not permit the occurrence of two individual constants naming (under certain extension-assignments) the same thing. It is just in connection with such co-extensive constants that most of the problems involving modalities arise.

It turns out that logical necessity, according to the interpretation given in this paper, is a kind of universal quantification. In fact, $\ulcorner N\Phi \urcorner$ is logically equivalent to $\ulcorner ()\Phi \urcorner$, where '()' is to be replaced by a string of universal quantifiers, one for each of the descriptive constants in Φ. This quantification, though it can be expressed in a second-order predicate calculus, cannot appear in our language, because quantifiers on predicates would be required.

The consideration just mentioned will throw some light on the so-called modal paradoxes. First, does Leibniz' Law hold? In one form yes, in another form no. It can be shown that

$$\text{(A)} \quad (x)(y)(x = y \supset (\Phi_x \equiv \Phi_y))$$

is satisfied by every model, but that

$$\text{(B)} \quad c = d \supset (\Phi_c \equiv \Phi_d)$$

(where 'c' and 'd' are individual constants) does not in general hold. The dubious instances of Leibniz' Law, for example,

$$\text{Evening Star}_s = \text{Morning Star} \supset (N(\text{Evening Star} = \text{Evening Star}) \equiv N(\text{Evening Star} = \text{Morning Star}))$$

are indeed of form (B). But does (B) not follow from (A) simply by universal instantiation? Universal instantiation from a variable to a constant is not valid when the variable stands within the scope of 'N'. Why this should be may be seen, in a rough way, as follows: The inference in question leads, for example, from '$(x)(\exists y) N(x = y)$' to '$(\exists y)N(c = y)$'. Let us replace, in both formulas, 'N' by universal quantifiers on descriptive constants. Then the inference leads from '$(x)(\exists y)(x = y)$' to '$(\exists y)(c)(c = y)$'. This is clearly invalid because it violates the restrictions on universal instantiation; a free occurrence of 'x' in '$(\exists y)(x = y)$' has been transformed into a bound occurrence of 'c'. A similar explanation involving a clash of quantifiers accounts for the failure of (B).

Let us consider the example of Quine which was mentioned earlier. The premise, which is true, is '$N(\text{Evening Star} = \text{Evening Star})$'. The conclusion, which is false, is '$(\exists x) N(x = \text{Evening Star})$'. The invalidity of the inference is again explained by the fact that the occurrences of 'Evening Star' involved are bound by 'N'.

Thus certain paradoxes concerned with so-called non-extensional contexts can be avoided by a method no more mysterious than rigid adherence to the rules of quantification theory. One is tempted to wonder whether other non-extensional contexts, like belief contexts, may not be susceptible to a similar analysis.[6]

5. PHYSICAL NECESSITY

Let the sentences (or physical laws) of the class K relative to which we interpreted physical necessity be only finite in number. Let Ψ be their conjunction. Then it can be shown that a model satisfies $\ulcorner PN\Phi \urcorner$ if and only if it satisfies $\ulcorner N(\Psi \supset \Phi) \urcorner$. Hence in this case physical necessity may be expressed in terms of logical necessity. (Similarly, if the class I of ideal models is definable by a finite class of sentences, ethical obligation can also be expressed in terms of logical necessity.)

Physical necessity is closely related to the subjunctive conditional. I should like to distinguish two kinds of subjunctive conditionals, exemplified by the following:

(1) If a meteor were to strike a planetary atmosphere at a speed greater than 100,000 m.p.h., it would burn.

(2) If Hindemith and Stravinsky were compatriots, Hindemith would be Russian.

It is not implausible to analyze (1) in terms of physical necessity as follows:

(3) $(x) PN((x$ is a meteor . x strikes a planetary atmosphere at a speed greater than 100,000 m.p.h.) $\supset x$ burns).

It is not hard to find physical laws relative to which (3) is true.

A similar attempt in connection with (2) would yield

(4) PN(Hindemith and Stravinsky are compatriots $\supset$ Hindemith is Russian),

but this is false, if 'PN' is interpreted relative to any plausibly selected class of natural laws. What follows 'PN' in (4) seems not to be deducible from natural laws alone, but only from natural laws in conjunction with the fact that Stravinsky is Russian.

The situation is further complicated by the fact that the following sentence, as well as (2), seems to be true:

(5) If Hindemith and Stravinsky were compatriots, Stravinsky would be German.

---

[6] A treatment of belief contexts, more or less along the lines adumbrated here, has since been given in Montague and Kalish [5].

Yet there is something paradoxical in the joint assertion of (2) and (5).

I make the following proposal. Let the ordinary subjunctive conditional, ⌜If it were the case that Φ, then it would be the case that Ψ⌝, be regarded as elliptical, and let it be replaced by

(6) On the evidence that X, if it were the case that Φ, then it would be the case that Ψ.

Here explicit reference is made to the evidence on which the subjunctive conditional is based. The omission of the evidence is perhaps analogous to a similar omission, pointed out by Carnap, in connection with probability $_1$. (6) can now be expressed in terms of physical necessity, as ⌜$PN(X \cdot \Phi \supset \Psi)$⌝.

If (2) and (5) are expanded in accordance with this proposal, their apparent incompatibility disappears:

(2′) On the evidence that Stravinsky is Russian, if Hindemith and Stravinsky were compatriots, Hindemith would be Russian.

(5′) On the evidence that Hindemith is German, if Hindemith and Stravinsky were compatriots, Stravinsky would be German.

It should, perhaps, be emphasized that the interpretation given above of physical necessity (as well as of subjunctive conditionals) is relativized to a class K of natural laws. Any attempt to avoid this relativization would seem to require a characterization of the concept of a *true natural law*, but such an undertaking lies beyond the scope of the present paper.

6. A MISSING LAW

The familiar principle of modal logic,

(1) ⌜$N\Phi \supset \Phi$⌝,

is conspicuous by its absence from the system axiomatized by (1a)–(4b). This law clearly holds for logical necessity and quantification, and clearly fails for ethical obligation. It is perhaps not so clear that (1) also fails for physical necessity.

We must clarify what it means for a formula Ψ to *hold* for physical necessity; this will be said to occur just in case every model satisfies$_p$ Ψ. Then if we choose Φ to be a natural law (of the class K) and consider a model which does not satisfy Φ, it is easily seen that the corresponding instance of (1) does not hold for physical necessity.

It is of course the case that all instances of (1) are *true*, in the sense of being satisfied$_p$ by every actual model (that is, every model whose domain of discourse and extension-assignment correspond to the actual constitution of the world), on the assumption that all the natural laws in K are also true. But we are interested in the *logic* of physical necessity—hence not in those formulas which are simply true, but in those which are true in every model.

REFERENCES

1. Carnap, R. Modalities and Quantification. *Journal of Symbolic Logic* 11:33–64 (1946).
2. Kanger, S. The Morning Star Paradox. *Theoria* 23:1–11 (1957).
3. —. A Note on Quantification and Modalities. *Theoria* 23:133–34 (1957).
4. Kripke, S. A Completeness Theorem in Modal Logic. *Journal of Symbolic Logic* 24:1–14 (1959).
5. Lewis, C. and C. Langford. *Symbolic Logic*. New York and London, 1932.
6. Montague, R. and D. Kalish. 'That'. *Philosophical Studies* 10:54–61 (1959). Chap. 2 in this book.
7. Quine, W. Notes on Existence and Necessity. *Journal of Philosophy* 40:113–27 (1943).
8. Tarski, A. Der Wahrheitsbegriff in den formalisierten Sprachen. *Studia Philosophica* 1:261–405 (1936).
9. Wajsberg, M. Ein erweiterter Klassenkalkül. *Monatshefte für Mathematik und Physik* 40:113–26 (1933).

2. 'That' (with Donald Kalish)

Among the difficulties which have concerned philosophers of language, a certain type is of particular prominence. The difficulties of this type arise when systems of formal logic are applied to ordinary language, and consist in the apparent failure, in this context, of certain presumably valid rules of inference.

For example, the following two arguments seem to be valid, yet in each the premises are true and the conclusion false.[1]

(1) Tully = Cicero.
   'Tully' contains five letters.
   Therefore 'Cicero' contains five letters.
(2) The end of a thing is its perfection.
   Death is the end of life.
   Therefore death is the perfection of life.

Two kinds of remedies immediately suggest themselves. First, we might purify ordinary language in various ways—for instance, by eliminating certain contexts or by replacing a single, so-called 'ambiguous' phrase by two or more 'unambiguous' phrases. The argument (2) should clearly be treated in this fashion: We should replace the ambiguous word 'end' by at least two other words, such as 'purpose' and 'termination'.

This remedy *could* also be applied to the argument (1): we could simply abolish quotation marks. But so drastic an application of the remedy should be avoided, if possible, for it would exclude a highly convenient mode of expression.

Originally published in *Philosophical Studies* 10:54–61 (1959). Reprinted with permission. This paper was presented at the thirty-first annual meeting of the American Philosophical Association, Pacific Division, December 19, 1957. The authors wish to express their gratitude to Mr. David Kaplan and Mrs. Ruth Anna Mathers for helpful criticism.

[1] The argument (1) is taken from Quine [5] and (2) from Copi [3].

The second remedy is to revise our inference rules, and this is what seems appropriate in connection with argument (1). The rule of inference which validates (1) is a form of Leibniz' principle of the indiscernibility of indenticals and may be stated as follows: From $\ulcorner \zeta = \eta \urcorner$ and ϕ_ζ, we may infer ϕ_η, where ζ and η are names and the formula ϕ_η is obtained from the formula ϕ_ζ by replacing an occurrence of ζ by η. We should, as Quine has pointed out in [5], introduce the notion of a *proper occurrence* of a name. An adequate definition would be quite long, and would contain reference to many kinds of contexts; in particular, occurrences of names within quotation marks would be construed as improper. We should then impose on Leibniz' principle the restriction that the replaced occurrence of a name be proper. The argument (1) is no longer an instance of the revised principle.

There are some difficulties of the type mentioned in our opening paragraph for which the remedy is not obvious. Perhaps the most conspicuous among these are the cases involving the conjunction 'that'. It is to such cases that the present discussion is directed. We shall further restrict our attention to a single rule, Leibniz' principle in its revised form. Our remarks, however, will apply with slight modification to a number of other logical principles.

We begin with three examples:

(3) The number of planets = 9.

Kepler was unaware that the number of planets > 6.

Therefore Kepler was unaware that $9 > 6$.

(4) $9 = $ the number of planets.

It is necessary that $9 = 9$.

Therefore it is necessary that the number of planets = 9.

(5) $9 = $ the number of planets.

It is provable in arithmetic that 9 is not prime.

Therefore it is provable in arithmetic that the number of planets is not prime.

In each of these examples, the premises are ordinarily regarded as true and the conclusion false, and each argument seems to be an instance of Leibniz' principle. The common characteristic is the occurrence of the subordinate conjunction 'that'. (Similar paradoxes can be generated with the help of 'whether' or the interrogatives 'what', 'where', 'why', 'when', 'who', 'how', in their use as subordinate conjunctions. Our later remarks apply to these cases as well as to the case of 'that'.)

The literature already contains two treatments of 'that'-contexts (or, more accurately, of particular kinds of 'that'-contexts), neither of which we consider entirely adequate. One treatment, fundamentally due to Quine, consists in handling 'that'-contexts just as quotation contexts were handled above. That is, all occurrences of designatory expressions within a 'that'-clause are regarded as improper. Thus, none of the arguments (3)–(5) is an instance of the revised principle of Leibniz.

The other treatment which occurs in the literature is due to suggestions made by Frege, Carnap, Church, and Quine (in [4], [1], [2], and [5], respectively). It consists neither in revising inference rules nor in purifying ordinary language, but in assigning unusual meanings to its expressions. In particular, all designatory expressions are construed as referring to intensions (sometimes called *senses* or *concepts*) rather than extensions. Thus '9' no longer designates the number 9, but instead the concept corresponding to '9', which differs from the concept corresponding to 'the number of planets'. Under this interpretation, the first premise in each of the arguments (3)–(5) becomes false. (Frege's original analysis is slightly more complex: designatory expressions refer sometimes to extensions, sometimes to intensions, depending on the context.)

The second treatment suffers not only from excessive complexity, but also from the fact that no adequate account of intensions has yet been given. If we restrict our attention to contexts of the form 'it is necessary that', then we may, for example, identify the intension of a name ζ with the class of all names η such that the identity $\ulcorner \zeta = \eta \urcorner$ is necessary. But this notion of intensions is not sufficient even for contexts of the form 'it is provable (in some particular system) that', and clearly is inapplicable to contexts such as 'Kepler is unaware that'.

Let us consider now the first treatment, according to which designatory expressions cannot occur properly within 'that'-clauses. There is no indication here of how to deal with variables which are free within 'that'-clauses. Indeed, Quine, the author of the present proposal, regards the use of free variables within 'that'-clauses as meaningless. For example, consider

(6) $(\exists x)$(it is necessary that $x = 9$).

The sentence, Quine argues, seems to assert that something is necessarily identical with 9. If so, what is this thing? Is it the number 9, that is, the number of planets? If so, it would seem to follow that the number of planets is necessarily 9.

Quine's argument is obviously not conclusive. It contains a suppressed application of Leibniz' principle to occurrences of names which are improper according to Quine's own criterion. Further, there are cases in which the joint use of quantifiers and 'that'-clauses is quite natural. The sentence

(7) Herbert lost a book at Stanford, but did not discover that he had lost it until he returned to Berkeley

expresses a common state of affairs, yet it contains an implicit use of a quantifier to bind a variable which, according to Quine, occurs improperly. Using a symbolic expression for the existential quantifier, (7) becomes

$(\exists x)$ (x is a book and Herbert lost x at Stanford, but Herbert did not discover that he had lost x until he returned to Berkeley).

It is hopeless to attempt to symbolize (7) in such a way as to avoid the free occurrence of a variable within a 'that'-clause. Even more telling examples can be found in technical writing. The following, for instance, is an important mathematical fact:

(8) For each prime number x, it is provable in arithmetic that x is prime.

Further, one of the principal lemmas of Gödel's theory is frequently stated as follows:

If ϕ is any theorem of arithmetic, then it is provable that ϕ is a theorem.

We feel, then, that Quine's treatment of 'that'-clauses is at least incomplete, because it makes no provision for the joint use of 'that' and quantifiers.

We turn now to our analysis of the word 'that'. Let us begin with the second premise of argument (5):

(9) It is provable in arithmetic that 9 is not prime.

Argument (9) asserts that a certain sentence is provable in arithmetic, in fact, the sentence

9 is not prime.

The assertion is true. However, the sentence

The number of planets is not prime

is *not* provable in arithmetic. It does not follow, as some have claimed, that (9) fails to express a property of the number 9. It only follows that whatever property is expressed involves an implicit choice of names. Within arithmetic, there is one choice of names which is particularly natural. This is to choose the kth numeral as the standard name of the kth positive integer. Thus, letting N_0 be the function which assigns to each positive integer its standard name, we conclude that $N_0(1) = $ '1', $N_0(2) = $ '2', and so on. Other naming functions are possible. For example, let N_1 be that function which coincides with N_0 for all numbers other than 9, but which assigns to the number 9 the name 'the number of planets'.

The sentence (9), then, is strictly speaking ambiguous, because it is not determined exactly what sentence is asserted to be provable in arithmetic. To remove ambiguity, we should indicate somehow which naming function is to be employed. We may do this by attaching a suffix to the word 'that'. Thus the intended meaning of (9) is expressed unambiguously by

(10) It is provable in arithmetic that-N_0 9 is not prime.

This can be translated into language which avoids 'that' as follows:

(11) The result of replacing 'a' by $N_0(9)$ in 'a is not prime' is provable in arithmetic,

which asserts truly:

'9 is not prime' is provable in arithmetic.

Other renderings of (9), less natural than (10), are also possible, such as

(12) It is provable in arithmetic that-N_1 9 is not prime.

The translation of (12) is

The result of replacing 'a' by $N_1(9)$ in 'a is not prime' is provable in arithmetic,

which asserts the falsehood

'The number of planets is not prime' is provable in arithmetic.

Thus the truth-value of (9) depends on the way in which the ambiguity of 'that' is resolved.

Let us apply this suggestion to the argument (5). If we replace 'that' by 'that-N_0', the premises of (5) are true. The conclusion becomes

It is provable in arithmetic that-N_0 the number of planets is not prime,

in other words,

The result of replacing 'a' by N_0 (the number of planets) in 'a is not prime' is provable in arithmetic,

which amounts to (11). (We must observe in this connection that, since the number of planets = 9, N_0 (the number of planets) = $N_0(9)$ = '9'.) Thus, in this case, the conclusion of (5) is true, and there is no difficulty. On the other hand, if we replace 'that' by 'that-N_1', the conclusion of (5) becomes false, but so does the second premise, which then amounts to the same thing as (12).

There is a third way of viewing (5): the naming function may be construed as changing in the passage from premises to conclusion. For example, we might replace the occurrence of 'that' in the second premise by 'that-N_0', and the occurrence of 'that' in the conclusion by 'that-N_1'. Then the premises are true and the conclusion false; but the argument is no longer an instance of Leibniz' principle.

This third analysis of (5) seems particularly natural. In general there is a strong tendency to use, for each occurrence of 'that', a naming function which assigns the names that actually follow the occurrence. The tendency, however, is not irresistible; there are important cases in which another naming function is more natural, for example,

Herbert believes that the lying so-and-so is honest.[2]

Under our treatment, then, at least some occurrences of designatory expressions within 'that'-clauses may be regarded as proper and thus amenable to Leibniz' principle; in fact, under both the first and the second analysis of (5), the names '9' and 'the number of planets' may be regarded as occurring properly throughout the argument. Further, there is no longer any reason to avoid the joint use of quantifiers and 'that'. The ambiguous sentence (8) corresponds now to a number of sentences, for instance

(13) (x) (x is a prime number $\supset$ it is provable in arithmetic that-N_0 x is prime),

which is completely unobjectionable. In fact, (13) makes the assertion

(x) (x is a prime number $\supset$ the result of replacing 'a' by $N_0(x)$ in 'a is prime' is provable in arithmetic),

which is true.

Actually, the choice of a naming function is insufficient to resolve all the ambiguity connected with 'that'. Let us consider the conclusion of argument (3) and replace 'that' by 'that-N_1'. There are now *several* possible ways to eliminate 'that', for instance:

(14) Kepler was unaware of the result of replacing 'a' by $N_1(9)$ in '$a > 6$',

that is,

Kepler was unaware of 'the number of planets > 6',

<hr />

[2] This example was suggested by Mr. David Kaplan.

which is true;

(15) Kepler was unaware of the result of replacing 'a' by $N_1(6)$ in '$9 > a$',

which is false;

(16) Kepler was unaware of the result of replacing 'a' by $N_1(9)$ and 'b' by $N_1(6)$ in '$a > b$',

which is true; and

(17) Kepler was unaware of '$9 > 6$',

which is false. Thus we must not only specify a naming function, but also indicate what places in the clause following 'that' are to be controlled by the naming function. The intention in (17), for instance, is to render all places immune to the naming function; thus, in a special case, 'that' acquires the function of quotes, and, as in Quine's proposal, all subsequent occurrences of designatory expressions become improper.

The present source of ambiguity can best be eliminated by choosing certain variables—say 'a', 'b', 'c', ...—as *place-holders*, and then indicating in each case the formula in which replacements are to be made, marking with place-holders those places which are to be governed by the naming function. Thus three things must be specified in order to render 'that' univocal: (1) a naming function, (2) a formula (containing 0 or more place-holders) in which replacements are to be made, and (3) those objects whose names are to replace the place-holders. If we consider formulas containing only one place-holder, 'a', the general notion is the following:

$^x\text{that}_N(\phi)$ = the result of replacing all free occurrences of 'a' by $N(x)$ in ϕ.

If we consider two place-holders, the notion is the following:

$^{x,y}\text{that}_N(\phi)$ = the result of replacing all free occurrences of 'a' by $N(x)$ and of 'b' by $N(y)$ in ϕ.

Thus the 'that'-clauses involved in the sentences (14)–(17) are respectively

^{9}that-N_1 ('$a > 6$'),
^{6}that-N_1 ('$9 > a$'),
^{9,6}that-N_1 ('$a > b$'),

and

that-N_1 ('$9 > 6$').

Our treatment distinguishes two ways in which a designatory expression may occur within a 'that'-clause. The improper occurrences are those standing within the quoted formula which follows 'that'; the proper occurrences are those occurring as superscripts to 'that'. When, however, we are given a sentence in ordinary English, it is in general impossible to determine which occurrences are accessible to Leibniz' principle; we must first replace the sentence by one of a number of formal counterparts.

An exception to this remark is the case of variables: it seems that any free occurrence of a variable in a 'that'-clause should be construed as proper; otherwise, vacuous quantifiers will unexpectedly appear. With this point in mind, let us examine Quine's example, the sentence (6). If we were to regard the occurrences of 'x' and '9' as improper and proper respectively, we should obtain, employing N_0, the translation

($\exists x$) (it is necessary ^{9}that-N_0 ('$x = a$')),

which amounts to

($\exists x$) (the expression '$x = 9$' is necessary).

This is not only false but odd, because of the vacuous existential quantifier. If we forbid improper free occurrences of variables and restrict our attention to the two naming functions N_0 and N_1, only four formal versions of (6) are possible:

($\exists x$) (it is necessary ^{x}that-N_0 ('$a = 9$'))
($\exists x$) (it is necessary ^{x,9}that-N_0 ('$a = b$'))
($\exists x$) (it is necessary ^{x}that-N_1 ('$a = 9$'))
($\exists x$) (it is necessary ^{x,9}that-N_1 ('$a = b$')).

Of these, the third is false, and the others are true.

The purified 'that', like Russell's 'the', is theoretically dispensable but often useful. For instance, the following simple definition of ω-consistency need no longer cause discomfort:

> A system T of arithmetic is ω-consistent if and only if for no formula $\phi(a)$ is it provable in T that-N_0 ($\ulcorner(\exists a)\phi(a)\urcorner$) and, for each positive integer n, ^{n}that-N_0 ($\ulcorner \sim \phi(a)\urcorner$).

There is another difficulty which ought in justice to be mentioned. It might well be contended that

(18) Kepler was aware that the number of planets > 5

is true, but that

(19) Kepler was aware of 'the number of planets > 5'

is false, on the grounds that Kepler did not know English. Instead of identifying the meaning of (18) and (19), we could perhaps analyze (18) as

> For some sentence ϕ, ϕ is synonymous with 'the number of planets > 5' and Kepler was aware of ϕ.

But this analysis involves the exceedingly difficult notion of synonymy. Actually, we feel that the present puzzle is susceptible to a less futuristic treatment, along the lines of our treatment above.

What should be pointed out is that our treatment is quite sufficient to resolve the difficulties arising from the joint use of quantifiers and 'that', and from the application of logical rules to 'that'-contexts. It should be recognized that in some instances our analysis departs from ordinary usage, in fact whenever synonymy seems to be involved. It remains to extend our analysis in such a way as to combine the virtues of the present treatment with a closer conformity to ordinary usage.

REFERENCES

1. Carnap, R. *Meaning and Necessity*, 2d ed. with supplements. Chicago, 1956.

2. Church, A. A Formulation of the Logic of Sense and Denotation. In P. Henle, H. Kallen, and S. Langer (eds.), *Structure, Method, and Meaning: Essays in Honor of H. M. Sheffer*. New York, 1951.
3. Copi, I. *Introduction to Logic*, 1st ed. New York, 1953.
4. Frege, G. Über Sinn und Bedeutung. *Zeitschrift für Philosophie und philosophische Kritik* 100:25–50 (1892).
5. Quine, W. Reference and Modality. In *From a Logical Point of View*. Cambridge, Mass., 1953.

3. Pragmatics

The study of language (or *semiosis* or *semiotic*) was partitioned in Morris [19] into three branches—syntax, semantics, and pragmatics—that may be characterized roughly as follows. Syntax is concerned solely with relations between linguistic expressions; semantics with relations between expressions and the objects to which they refer; and pragmatics with relations among expressions, the objects to which they refer, and the users or contexts of use of the expressions.

Syntax had already been extensively developed at the time at which Morris wrote, largely by Tarski, Gödel, and members of the Hilbert school. (See Tarski [25, 26, and 28]; Gödel [6]; Hilbert and Bernays [7].) Most contemporary work in syntax falls into one of two subfields—proof theory or the as yet rather tentative field of mathematical linguistics.

The foundations of semantics had also been completely laid (in Tarski [27]) by the time of Morris' remarks; but its most extensive development has occurred since then, under the name "model theory". (See the collection Addison, Henkin, and Tarski [1] for an extensive bibliography of work in this field, as well as Robinson [24].) It has been suggested—for instance, in article VII of Quine [19]—that semantics be divided into two fields—a theory of reference, corresponding to model theory and Tarski's

Originally published in Raymond Klibansky (ed.), *Contemporary Philosophy: A Survey*. Florence, La Nuova Italia Editrice, 1968; pp. 102–22. Reprinted with permission. This paper in large part reports talks given by the author before the Philosophy Colloquium of the University of California at Los Angeles in December 1964, before the British Association for the Philosophy of Science in June 1966, and at Stockholm University in March 1966. The preparation of the paper was partly supported by U.S. National Science Foundation Grants GP-4594 and GP-7706.

work, and a theory of meaning. This suggestion turns out upon investigation probably not to represent the best division: the theory of meaning, it appears, can most naturally be accommodated within pragmatics, as in Section 2 below.

Pragmatics, however, was still futuristic at the time of Morris' monograph. It was suggested in Bar-Hillel [2] that pragmatics concern itself with what C. S. Peirce had in the last century called *indexical expressions*, that is, words and sentences of which the reference cannot be determined without knowledge of the context of use;[1] examples are the words 'I' and 'here', as well as sentences involving tenses.

Pragmatics did not, however, exhibit any precise technical structure until 1959, when the present author, later joined by others, initiated considerations that for the most part have remained unpublished until now. It seemed to me desirable that pragmatics should at least initially follow the lead of semantics, which is primarily concerned with the notion of truth (in a model, or under an interpretation), and hence concern itself also with truth—but with respect not only to an interpretation but also to a context of use.

I formulated an analysis of this notion in connection with a number of special cases; and in many of the cases an important feature was a treatment of quantifiers developed primarily by my student, Professor Nino Cocchiarella, in connection with tense logic, and persisting in the general development below. In this early work, however, truth and satisfaction were defined anew for each special case. In particular, no unified treatment of operators was seen until 1965, when full formal unity was achieved through joint work of Dr. Charles Howard and myself.

1. LANGUAGES AND INTERPRETATIONS

Let me sketch now the general treatment.

By a *pragmatic language* is understood a language having

---

[1] Other terms for these expressions include 'egocentric particulars' (Russell), 'token-reflexive expressions' (Reichenbach), 'indicator words' (Goodman), and 'non-eternal sentences' (Quine).

symbols (or atomic expressions) of the following categories:

(1) the *logical constants* $\neg$, $\wedge$, $\vee$, $\rightarrow$, $\leftrightarrow$, Λ, V, $=$ (read respectively 'it is not the case that', 'and', 'or', 'if . . . then', 'if and only if', 'for all', 'for some', 'is identical with');

(2) parentheses;

(3) the (individual) variables $v_0, \ldots, v_k, \ldots$;

(4) n-place predicates, for each natural number (that is, non-negative integer) n, including the designated one-place predicate E (read 'exists');

(5) n-place operation symbols, for each natural number n;

(6) n-place operators, for each positive integer n.

We require of every pragmatic language that it possess all symbols of categories (1), (2), and (3); we may consequently identify a pragmatic language with the set of predicates, operation symbols, and operators that it contains. Thus a pragmatic language is in general any set of such symbols.

An n-place operator is a symbol which, when placed before a string of n sentences, generates another sentence. Examples of one-place operators are the phrases 'necessarily', 'it will be the case that'; and of two-place operators the phrases 'if it were the case that . . . , it would be the case that - - -', 'on the assumption that . . . it is probable to the degree 1 that - - -'. I exclude zero-place operators because they would be indistinguishable in function from zero-place predicates.

The terms (designatory expressions) and formulas of a pragmatic language L are built up as one would expect. To be explicit, the set of *terms* of L is the smallest set Γ such that (1) all variables are in Γ and (2) Γ contains $A\zeta_0 \ldots \zeta_{n-1}$ whenever A is an n-place operation symbol in L and $\zeta_0, \ldots, \zeta_{n-1}$ are in Γ^2; and the set of *formulas* of L is the smallest set Δ such that (1) Δ contains

---

[2] The metatheory is assumed to coincide with some version of set theory with proper classes (Bernays-Morse set theory, say, with or without individuals; for a formulation of such a theory see the Appendix of Kelley [10]), supplemented by designations of various symbols and sets of symbols of the object language, a symbol of concatenation (here represented by mere juxtaposition), and certain assumptions of distinctness and disjointness concerning symbols and sets of symbols of the object language. It should perhaps be emphasized that '$\neg$', '$\wedge$', and the like are not symbols of the object language, but rather metalinguistic names of such symbols.

$P\zeta_0 \ldots \zeta_{n-1}$ whenever P is an n-place predicate of L and $\zeta_0, \ldots, \zeta_{n-1}$ are terms of L, as well as $\zeta = \eta$ whenever ζ, η are terms of L, (2) Δ contains $\neg \varphi$, $(\varphi \wedge \psi)$, $(\varphi \vee \psi)$, $(\varphi \rightarrow \psi)$, and $(\varphi \leftrightarrow \psi)$ whenever φ, ψ are in Δ, (3) Δ contains $\bigwedge u\varphi$ and $\bigvee u\varphi$ whenever u is a variable and φ is in Δ, and (4) Δ contains $N\varphi_0 \ldots \varphi_{n-1}$ whenever N is an n-place operator of L and $\varphi_0, \ldots, \varphi_{n-1}$ are in Δ.

In interpreting a pragmatic language L we shall have to take into account the possible contexts of use. It is not necessary to consider them in their full complexity; we may instead confine our attention to those among their features which are relevant to the discourse in question. Thus it will suffice to specify the set of all complexes of relevant aspects of intended possible contexts of use. We may call such complexes *indices*, or to borrow Dana Scott's term, *points of reference*. For instance, if the only indexical feature of L were the occurrence of tense operators, then the points of reference might naturally be chosen as moments of time, regarded as possible moments of utterance. On the other hand, if L contained in addition the first person pronoun 'I', as in an example below, two aspects of the context of use would become relevant, the speaker as well as the moment of utterance; and a point of reference might naturally be chosen as an ordered pair consisting of a person and a moment of time.

Another kind of information we must supply in interpreting L is the intended *intension* (or meaning) of each predicate of L. To do this for a predicate P we should determine, for each point of reference i, the *extension* (or denotation) of P with respect to i. For example, if the points of reference are moments of time and P is the one-place predicate 'is green', we should specify for each moment i the set of objects to be regarded as green at i; if P is instead the two-place predicate 'is married to', we should specify for each moment i the set of ordered pairs $\langle x, y \rangle$ such that x and y are to be regarded as married at i.

A third kind of information to be supplied is the intended intension of each operation symbol of L. This may be done, as in the case of predicates, by specifying, for each point of reference i, the intended extension of the operation symbol with respect to i.

For example, if the points of reference are again moments of time and we consider the one-place operation symbol 'the wife of', we should specify for each moment i the function which assigns to each married man the person to be regarded as his wife at i (and to every other object under consideration an arbitrarily selected 'null entity'); while if we consider the zero-place operation symbol (or *individual constant*) 'the American president', we should specify for each moment i the person to be regarded as the American president at i.

The fourth kind of information to be supplied is an interpretation of the operators of L. To provide this we associate with each n-place operator of L and each point of reference i, as the extension of the operator with respect to i, an n-place relation among sets of points of reference. It is this general way of interpreting operators, together with the corresponding clause (5) of Definition IV below, that was worked out by Howard and me in 1965; the motivation of this interpretation will perhaps best be seen later, in connection with examples.

Finally, we must specify in interpreting L the set of *possible objects* to be considered. (In the case of tense logic these would include at least all objects existing in the past, present, or future.)

The foregoing heuristic remarks lead naturally to the following definition.

Definition I. A *possible interpretation for a pragmatic language* L is an ordered triple $\langle I, U, F \rangle$ such that (1) I, U are sets; (2) F is a function with domain L; (3) for each symbol A in L, F_A is a function with domain I; (4) whenever P is an n-place predicate in L and i is in I, $F_P(i)$ is an *n-place relation on* U (that is, a set of ordered n-tuples of members of U); (5) whenever A is an n-place operation symbol in L and i is in I, $F_A(i)$ is an $(n + 1)$-place relation on U such that, for all $x_0, \ldots, x_{n-1}$ in U, there is exactly one object y in U such that $\langle x_0, \ldots, x_{n-1}, y \rangle$ is in $F_A(i)$; and (6) whenever N is an n-place operator of L and i is in I, $F_N(i)$ is an n-place relation on the set of all subsets of I.

A few remarks are in order. I use the notations 'F_P' and '$F(P)$' interchangeably for function value; this is convenient when, as above, the function value is itself a function. Finite sequences (or n-tuples) are designated with the help of angular parentheses;

for instance, $\langle x \rangle$ is the 1-tuple consisting of x. The set I in the definition above is the set of all *points of reference of* the interpretation $\langle I, U, F \rangle$. If i is a point of reference and the designated predicate E is in L, then the objects x such that $\langle x \rangle \in F_E(i)$ are understood as the objects existing with respect to i (according to $\langle I, U, F \rangle$). The set U in the definition above is regarded as the set of all *possible objects* (or *possible individuals*) *of* $\langle I, U, F \rangle$; we do not require that every possible object exist with respect to some point of reference, though this additional condition will indeed hold in many special cases. In clauses (4) and (5) we require that the extension of a predicate or operation symbol always be a relation among, or function on, *possible* objects. To see that it would be unduly restrictive to require generally that the extension with respect to a given point of reference be a relation among objects existing with respect to that point of reference or a function of which the value for such objects will again be such an object, suppose that the points of reference are moments of time, and consider the one-place predicate 'is remembered by someone' and the one-place operation symbol 'the father of'.

2. MEANING AND REFERENCE

The notions of intension and extension as applied to terms and formulas will now be introduced; and using these notions we shall characterize truth, logical validity and logical consequence.

A term will in general contain variables. Its extension, then, at a given point of reference should be that function H which assigns to each possible system of values of those variables the corresponding value of the term at the point of reference. Terms may contain varying numbers of variables, and there is no upper bound on that number; it is therefore convenient to take H as applying not to finite but to infinite sequences of possible objects.[3] Position in a sequence will indicate the intended correspondence between variables and objects; that is to say, in an infinite sequence x the nth constituent x_n will be regarded as the value of the variable v_n.

---

[3] By 'infinite sequence' I mean here an *ordinary* infinite sequence, that is, a function having as its domain the set of all natural numbers.

Definition II.   Suppose that $\mathscr{A}$ is a possible interpretation for a pragmatic language L, $\mathscr{A} = \langle I, U, F \rangle$, and i is in I. Then $\text{Ext}_{i,\mathscr{A}}(\zeta)$, or the *extension* of ζ at i (according to $\mathscr{A}$), is introduced for an arbitrary term ζ of L by the following recursive definition.

(1) $\text{Ext}_{i,\mathscr{A}}(v_n)$ is that function H having as its domain the set of all infinite sequences of possible objects of $\mathscr{A}$, and such that if x is any such sequence, $H(x) = x_n$.

(2) If A is an n-place operation symbol in L and $\zeta_0, \ldots, \zeta_{n-1}$ are terms of L, then $\text{Ext}_{i,\mathscr{A}}(A\zeta_0 \ldots \zeta_{n-1})$ is that function H having as its domain the set of all infinite sequences of possible objects of $\mathscr{A}$, and such that if x is any such sequence, $H(x)$ is the unique object y for which $\langle \text{Ext}_{i,\mathscr{A}}(\zeta_0)(x), \ldots, \text{Ext}_{i,\mathscr{A}}(\zeta_{n-1})(x), y \rangle$ is a member of $F_A(i)$.

Definition III.   Suppose that $\mathscr{A}$ is a possible interpretation for a pragmatic language L, $\mathscr{A} = \langle I, U, F \rangle$, and ζ is a term of L. Then $\text{Int}_{\mathscr{A}}(\zeta)$, or the *intension* of ζ, is that function H with domain I such that, for each i in I,

$$H(i) = \text{Ext}_{i,\mathscr{A}}(\zeta).$$

A formula will also in general contain free variables, and its extension at a given point of reference should accordingly be the set of those systems of values of its free variables by which it is satisfied. As with terms, it is convenient to regard the values of variables as given by *infinite* sequences of possible objects. We cannot, however, introduce the extensions of formulas, as we did the extensions of terms, by a simple recursion on the structure of expressions. As was observed in Frege [5], the extension of a formula containing operators will depend on the intensions rather than the extensions of certain of its parts. Accordingly, we first introduce the *intensions* of formulas, and in this connection a simple recursion is possible.

Definition IV.   Suppose that $\mathscr{A}$ is a possible interpretation for L and $\mathscr{A} = \langle I, U, F \rangle$. Then $\text{Int}_{\mathscr{A}}(\varphi)$ is introduced as follows for an arbitrary formula φ of L.

(1) If ζ, η are terms of L, then $\text{Int}_{\mathscr{A}}(\zeta = \eta)$ is that function H with domain I such that, for each i in I, $H(i)$ is the set of infinite sequences x of members of U for which $\text{Ext}_{i,\mathscr{A}}(\zeta)(x)$ is identical with $\text{Ext}_{i,\mathscr{A}}(\eta)(x)$.

(2)   If P is an n-place predicate in L and $\zeta_0, \ldots, \zeta_{n-1}$ are terms of L, then $\mathrm{Int}_{\mathscr{A}}(P\zeta_0 \ldots \zeta_{n-1})$ is that function H with domain I such that, for each i in I, $H(i)$ is the set of infinite sequences x of members of U for which $\langle \mathrm{Ext}_{i,\mathscr{A}}(\zeta_0)(x), \ldots, \mathrm{Ext}_{i,\mathscr{A}}(\zeta_{n-1})(x)\rangle$ is a member of $F_P(i)$.

(3)   If φ is a formula of L, then $\mathrm{Int}_{\mathscr{A}}(\neg\varphi)$ is that function H with domain I such that, for each i in I, $H(i)$ is the set of infinite sequences x of members of U for which x is not in $\mathrm{Int}_{\mathscr{A}}(\varphi)(i)$; and similarly for the other sentential connectives.

(4)   If φ is a formula of L, then $\mathrm{Int}_{\mathscr{A}}(\mathrm{V}\, v_n\varphi)$ is that function H with domain I such that, for each i in I, $H(i)$ is the set of infinite sequences x of members of U for which there exists y in U such that the infinite sequence $\langle x_0, \ldots, x_{n-1}, y, x_{n+1}, \ldots\rangle$ is in $\mathrm{Int}_{\mathscr{A}}(\varphi)(i)$; and similarly for $\wedge v_n\varphi$.

(5)   If N is an n-place operator in L and $\varphi_0, \ldots, \varphi_{n-1}$ are formulas of L, then $\mathrm{Int}_{\mathscr{A}}(N\varphi_0 \ldots \varphi_{n-1})$ is that function H with domain I such that, for each i in I, $H(i)$ is the set of infinite sequences x of members of U such that $\langle J_0, \ldots, J_{n-1}\rangle$ is in $F_N(i)$, where, for each $k < n$, J_k is the set of members j of I for which x is a member of $\mathrm{Int}_{\mathscr{A}}(\varphi_k)(j)$.

Definition V.   Suppose that $\mathscr{A}$ is a possible interpretation for a pragmatic language L, i is a point of reference of $\mathscr{A}$, and φ is a formula of L. Then $\mathrm{Ext}_{i,\mathscr{A}}(\varphi)$, or the *extension* of φ at i under $\mathscr{A}$, is $\mathrm{Int}_{\mathscr{A}}(\varphi)(i)$.

If φ is a *sentence* (that is, a formula without free variables), then the extension of φ will always be either the empty set or the set of all infinite sequences of possible objects; it is this consideration that underlies the following definition of truth.[4]

Definition VI.   If $\mathscr{A}$ is a possible interpretation for L, i is a point of reference of $\mathscr{A}$, and φ is a sentence of L, then φ is *true* at i under $\mathscr{A}$ if and only if $\mathrm{Ext}_{i,\mathscr{A}}(\varphi)$ is the set of all infinite sequences of possible objects of $\mathscr{A}$.

To clarify the intent of these definitions, let me state a few of their immediate consequences for the notion of truth.

Remark.   Let $\mathscr{A}$ be a possible interpretation, having the form $\langle I, U, F\rangle$, for a pragmatic language L; let i be in I; let u be a

---

[4] This consideration, as well as many of the other general ideas used in the definitions of this section, is of course due to Tarski [27].

variable; let P be a one-place predicate in L; and let c, d be zero-place operation symbols in L. Then:

(1) Pc is true at i under $\mathscr{A}$ if and only if $\langle F_c(i)(\Lambda)\rangle$ is in $F_P(i)$;[5]

(2) $c = d$ is true at i under $\mathscr{A}$ if and only if $F_c(i)(\Lambda)$ is identical with $F_d(i)(\Lambda)$;

(3)   if φ is a sentence of L, then $\neg\,\varphi$ is true at i under $\mathscr{A}$ if and only if φ is not true at i under $\mathscr{A}$;

(4)   if φ, ψ are sentences of L, then $(\varphi \wedge \psi)$ is true at i under $\mathscr{A}$ if and only if both φ and ψ are true at i under $\mathscr{A}$;

(5) $\mathsf{V}\,uPu$ is true at i under $\mathscr{A}$ if and only if there exists an object x in U such that $\langle x \rangle$ is in $F_P(i)$;

(6)   if N is a one-place operator in L and φ is a sentence of L, then $N\varphi$ is true at i under $\mathscr{A}$ if and only if $\langle J \rangle$ is in $F_N(i)$, where J is the set of members of I at which φ is true (under $\mathscr{A}$).

According to (5) above, quantification is over *possible* (and not merely *actual* or existing) objects. The desirability of this can be seen by considering, within the special case of tense logic, the sentence 'there was a man whom no one remembers'. Quantification over actual individuals can of course also be expressed, with the aid of the designated predicate E of existence; for instance, the *existential* sentence corresponding to the sentence in (5) is

$\mathsf{V}\,u(Eu \wedge Pu).$

Definition VII. We say that φ is a *logical consequence* of a set Γ (in the sense of general pragmatics) if and only if there is a pragmatic language L such that φ and all members of Γ are sentences of L, and for every possible interpretation $\mathscr{A}$ for L and every point of reference i of $\mathscr{A}$, if all members of Γ are true at i under $\mathscr{A}$, then φ is true at i under $\mathscr{A}$; and φ is *logically valid* (again in the sense of general pragmatics) if and only if φ is a logical consequence of the empty set (that is, if and only if there is a pragmatic language L of which φ is a sentence and such that φ is true at i under $\mathscr{A}$, whenever $\mathscr{A}$ is a possible interpretation for L and i a point of reference of $\mathscr{A}$).

[5] Here Λ is the empty sequence. $F_c(i)$ is a zero-place function, and its value for the zero-tuple Λ is the possible object intuitively designated by c.

It is easily seen that if φ and the members of Γ are sentences (of some pragmatic language), then φ is a logical consequence of Γ if and only if there is a conjunction ψ of members of Γ such that $(\psi \to \varphi)$ is logically valid. It is also obvious, in view of known results, that the set of logically valid sentences of a recursive language is recursively axiomatizable (under a finite set of inference rules). To *exhibit* an axiom system for this set is, however, another and more difficult matter; but this has been done by Professor David Kaplan in recent unpublished work.

3. SPECIALIZATIONS

When we come to consider special disciplines comprehended by pragmatics—disciplines such as tense logic, modal logic, the logic of personal pronouns—the notions of logical validity and consequence given in Definition VII are seen to require refinement. For instance, we shall frequently be interested not in *all* possible interpretations for a given language L, but only in a certain class K of possible interpretations. The choice of K will depend on the special discipline under consideration, and the members of K will be regarded as the *standard* interpretations for L in the sense of that discipline. The corresponding relativized notions of consequence and validity are characterized as follows.

Definition VIII. Let K be a class of possible interpretations for a pragmatic language L; and let φ and the members of the set Γ be sentences of L. Then φ is a *K-consequence* of Γ if and only if, for every $\mathscr{A}$ in K and every point of reference i of $\mathscr{A}$, if all members of Γ are true at i under $\mathscr{A}$, then so is φ; and φ is *K-valid* if and only if φ is a K-consequence of the empty set.

In some situations, one of which is illustrated below, this degree of specialization will be insufficient; we shall sometimes find it necessary to restrict the points of reference as well as the possible interpretations to be considered. Construction of the exact notions, which involve assigning to each standard interpretation a designated set of its points of reference (regarded as constituting its *standard* points of reference), is due jointly to my students Dr. J. A. W. Kamp and Mr. Perry Smith and myself.

Definition IX. Let K be a class of possible interpretations for a pragmatic language L, let J be a function assigning to each member $\mathscr{A}$ of K a set of points of reference of $\mathscr{A}$, and let φ and the members of Γ be sentences of L. Then φ is a (K, J)-*consequence* of Γ if and only if, for every $\mathscr{A}$ in K and every i in $J_{\mathscr{A}}$, if all members of Γ are true at i under $\mathscr{A}$, then so is φ; and φ is (K, J)-*valid* if and only if φ is a (K, J)-consequence of the empty set.

The necessity of these notions has been shown by Mr. Kamp: he has found interesting examples of K and J for which he has proved that there is no class K' such that the set of K'-valid sentences coincides with the set of (K, J)-valid sentences.

Let us now introduce various special classes of possible interpretations; we shall thereby indicate some of the special branches of pragmatics.

Ordinary tense logic

Let L be a a pragmatic language having as its only operators the two one-place operators $\mathscr{P}$ and $\mathscr{F}$, and let $K_1(L)$ be the class of possible interpretations $\langle I, U, G \rangle$ for L such that (1a) I is the set of real numbers; (1b) for each i in I, $G_{\mathscr{P}}(i)$ is the set of one-tuples $\langle J \rangle$ such that $J \subseteq I$ and there exists j in J such that $j < i$; and (1c) for each i in I, $G_{\mathscr{F}}(i)$ is the set of one-place sequences $\langle J \rangle$ such that $J \subseteq I$ and there exists j in J such that $i < j$. Here we regard the real numbers as the moments of time. If (1a)–(1c) hold, φ is a sentence of L, and i is in I, it is easily seen that

> $\mathscr{P}\varphi$ is true at i under $\langle I, U, G \rangle$ if and only if there exists j in I such that $j < i$ and φ is true at j under $\langle I, U, G \rangle$,

and

> $\mathscr{F}\varphi$ is true at i under $\langle I, U, G \rangle$ if and only if there exists j in I such that $j > i$ and φ is true at j under $\langle I, U, G \rangle$.

Thus it is appropriate to read '$\mathscr{P}\varphi$' as 'it has been the case that φ' and '$\mathscr{F}\varphi$' as 'it will be the case that φ'. The $K_1(L)$-valid sentences of L constitute the logical truths (of L) of ordinary tense logic. Dana Scott has pointed out in correspondence that if L contains at least one one-place predicate and two two-place operation symbols, then the set of $K_1(L)$-valid sentences of L is not recursively enumerable (and hence not recursively axiomatizable). He has also shown that under the same assumption on L (which can undoubtedly be somewhat weakened), the *compactness theorem* fails for $K_1(L)$; that is to say, it is not the case that whenever a sentence φ of L is a $K_1(L)$-consequence of a set Γ of sentences of L, φ is also a $K_1(L)$-consequence of some finite subset of Γ.

According to the interpretations in $K_1(L)$, time is continuous. If we desired to impose the condition that time is discrete, we could replace condition (1a) by 'I is the set of integers (positive and negative)'. Dana Scott has shown that the results mentioned above hold also in this connection.

Generalized tense logic

We may, however, regard the structure of time as contingent and hence be disinclined to limit attention to any particular temporal structure; it seems natural, however, to impose the minimal requirement that time be simply ordered. If L is again a pragmatic language having $\mathscr{P}$ and $\mathscr{F}$ as its only operators, we thus arrive at another class of standard interpretations for L; indeed, let $K_2(L)$ be the class of possible interpretations $\langle I, U, G \rangle$ for L such that there exists a simple ordering[6] $\leqslant$ of I for which (2a) I is nonempty; (2b) for each i in I, $G_{\mathscr{P}}(i)$ is the set of one-tuples $\langle J \rangle$ such that i is in I, $J \subseteq I$, and there exists j in J such that $j \leqslant i$ and $j \neq i$, and (2c) for each i in I, $G_{\mathscr{F}}(i)$ is the set of one-tuples $\langle J \rangle$ such that i is in I, $J \subseteq I$, and there exists j in J such that $i \leqslant j$ and $i \neq j$. We obtain in this way the tense logic of Nino Cocchiarella. It is easily seen (and was observed by Cocchiarella) that the compactness theorem holds for $K_2(L)$. Further, Cocchiarella [3, 4] has given an elegant axiomatization of the $K_2(L)$-valid sentences of L.

Personal pronouns and demonstratives

Let L be a pragmatic language having no operators at all, but having a distinguished zero-place operation symbol c. Let $K_3(L)$ be the class of possible interpretations $\langle I, U, G \rangle$ for L such that (3a) $G_A(i)$ is $G_A(j)$ for all symbols A in L other than c, and all i, j in I; and (3b) $G_c(i)$ is $\{\langle i \rangle\}$ (that is, the unit set of the one-tuple of i), for all i in I. If these conditions are satisfied, P is a one-place

---

[6] A *simple ordering* of a set I is a reflexive, antisymmetric, and transitive relation with I as its field. (R is *antisymmetric* if and only if $x = y$ whenever $x \, R \, y$ and $y \, R \, x$.)

predicate in L, and i, j are in I, it is easily seen that Pc is true at i under $\langle I, U, G \rangle$ if and only if $\langle i \rangle$ is in $G_P(j)$. Thus if the points of reference are possible speakers, c represents the first person pronoun 'I'. If the points of reference are regarded as persons to whom utterances are addressed, c will represent the second person pronoun 'thou'. Other ways of construing points of reference will endow c with the sense of the demonstrative pronouns 'this' or 'that'. It would not be unreasonable to impose on the members of $K_3(L)$ the additional condition that $\langle i \rangle$ be in $G_E(i)$ for all i in I; if this were done, but not otherwise, the sentence Ec (for example, 'I exist') would be valid. The accommodation of several demonstratives and personal pronouns at once presents no problem: we should employ several distinguished individual constants and take sequences of corresponding length (regarded, for example, as composed of the speaker, the person addressed, and the object at which the speaker is pointing) as points of reference.

To illustrate in greater detail the treatment of several indexical features in a single language, let us consider the *combination of tenses with the first person singular*. If I, J, U are sets, $\leqslant$ is a simple ordering of I, and for each i in I, $\mathscr{A}_i = \langle J, U, G_i \rangle$ and $\mathscr{A}_i$ is a possible interpretation for a pragmatic language L not containing the operators $\mathscr{P}$ and $\mathscr{F}$, then the $\leqslant$-*product* of the systems $\mathscr{A}_i$ (for i in I) is that possible interpretation $\langle K, U, H \rangle$ for $L \cup \{\mathscr{P}, \mathscr{F}\}$ such that (1) K is the set of ordered pairs $\langle i, j \rangle$ such that i is in I and j is in J, (2) for each i in I, each j in J, and each predicate or operation symbol A in L, $H_A(\langle i, j \rangle) = (G_i)_A(j)$, (3) whenever i is in I, j is in J, and N is an n-place operator in L, $H_N(\langle i, j \rangle)$ is the set of n-tuples $\langle X_0, \ldots, X_{n-1} \rangle$ such that $X_0, \ldots, X_{n-1}$ are subsets of K and $\langle Y_0, \ldots, Y_{n-1} \rangle$ is in $(G_i)_N(j)$, where, for each $k < n$, Y_k is the set of j' in J for which $\langle i, j' \rangle$ is in X_k; (4) for each i in I and j in J, $H_{\mathscr{P}}(\langle i, j \rangle)$ is the set of one-tuples $\langle X \rangle$ such that $X \subseteq K$ and there exists i' in I such that $i' \leqslant i$, $i' \neq i$, and $\langle i', j \rangle$ is in X; and (5) for each i in I and j in J, $H_{\mathscr{F}}(\langle i, j \rangle)$ is the set of one-tuples $\langle X \rangle$ such that $X \subseteq K$ and there exists i' in I such that $i \leqslant i'$, $i \neq i'$, and $\langle i', j \rangle$ is in X.

Now let L be a pragmatic language containing the operators $\mathscr{P}$ and $\mathscr{F}$, together with the particular zero-place operation symbol c mentioned above; and let $K_4(L)$ be the class of possible interpretations $\mathscr{B}$ for L such that there exist sets I, J, U, possible interpretations $\mathscr{A}_i$ in $K_3(L - \{\mathscr{P}, \mathscr{F}\})$ (for i in I), and a simple ordering $\leqslant$ of I such that J is the set of points of reference, and U the set of possible individuals, of $\mathscr{A}_i$ (for all i in I), and $\mathscr{B}$ is the $\leqslant$-product of the interpretations $\mathscr{A}_i$ (for i in I). If these conditions are satisfied, φ is a sentence of L, and $\langle i,j \rangle$ is a point of reference of $\mathscr{B}$, then it is easily seen that $\mathscr{P}\varphi$ is true at $\langle i,j \rangle$ under $\mathscr{B}$ if and only if there exists i' in I such that $i' \leqslant i$, $i' \neq i$, and φ is true at $\langle i',j \rangle$ under $\mathscr{B}$; if, in addition, P is a one-place predicate in L, then Pc is true at $\langle i,j \rangle$ under $\mathscr{B}$ if and only if $\langle j \rangle$ is in $H_P(\langle i,j \rangle)$; and if j' is any member of J, then $H_P(\langle i,j \rangle) = H_P(\langle i,j' \rangle)$.

Thus $\mathscr{P}$ behaves just as the past tense operator should, and c in just the way we expect of the pronoun 'I' (or 'thou', or a demonstrative, depending on the manner in which the second constituents of the points of reference of $\mathscr{B}$ are conceived). We cannot, however, guarantee the validity of Ec ('I exist') by any reasonable diminution of the class $K_4(L)$. We should instead have to speak of $(K_4(L), J)$-validity, where for all $\langle K, U, H \rangle$ in $K_4(L)$, $J_{\langle K,U,H \rangle}$ is the set of pairs $\langle i, j \rangle$ in K for which $\langle j \rangle$ is in $H_E(\langle i,j \rangle)$. It turns out that Ec is $(K_4(L), J)$-valid, but $\neg \mathscr{P} \neg Ec$ ('I always have existed') is not.

Standard modal logic

Let L be a pragmatic language having $\square$ as its only operator, and let $K_5(L)$ be the class of possible interpretations $\langle I, U, F \rangle$ for L such that for each i in I, $F \square (i) = \{\langle I \rangle\}$. Here we regard I as the set of all possible worlds. If $\langle I, U, F \rangle$ is in $K_5(L)$, φ is a sentence of L, and i is in I, then $\square \varphi$ is true at i under $\langle I, U, F \rangle$ if and only if, for all j in I, φ is true at j under $\langle I, U, F \rangle$. Thus necessity turns out to be truth in all possible worlds. The compactness theorem is easily seen to hold for $K_5(L)$, and the set of $K_5(L)$-valid sentences is axiomatized by a certain quantified version of S5 that may be found in Kripke [12]. Kripke has proved in that article the completeness of his axioms for interpretations differing only inessentially from the ones given here, and the present completeness result can be inferred in a trivial way from Kripke's.

Generalized modal logic

Let L be as above, let M be a class of binary relations, and let $K_6(L, M)$ be the class of possible interpretations $\langle I, U, F \rangle$ for L such that, for some R in M, (6a) R is a reflexive relation having I as its field, and (6b) for each i in I, $F \square (i)$ is the set of one-tuples $\langle J \rangle$ for which $J \subseteq I$ and, for all j such that iRj, j is in J. Here we again regard I as the set of all possible worlds; the assertion that iRj is understood as meaning that the world j is *accessible from* the world i, and the truth of $\square \varphi$ in i then amounts to the truth of φ in all worlds accessible from i. For example, we might consider one world accessible from another just in case the two were alike throughout the past, or, alternatively, alike up to some moment in the past. In both of these cases, which will be considered in greater detail below, the accessibility relation is an equivalence relation. Standard modal logic is that special case in which M is the class of all *universal* relations (that is, relations R such that iRj whenever either i or j is in the field of R).

The idea of using accessibility relations in connection with modal logic was introduced independently in the 1957 publication Kanger [9] (reporting research carried out in 1955), the 1955 talk reported in Montague [16], and the 1960 talk reported in Hintikka [8]. In these occurrences, however, accessibility relations were always relations between models; accessibility relations between points of reference, like those considered here, appear to have been first explicitly introduced in Kripke [13].

Various axiomatizability results are given in Kripke [13]. In particular, if M is either the class of reflexive relations,[7] the class of symmetric and reflexive relations, the class of transitive and reflexive relations, or the class of equivalence relations, Kripke has axiomatized the set of $K_6(L, M)$-valid sentences of L which contain neither $=$ nor any operation symbols, and in which every quantification is restricted to the predicate E of existence. For

---

[7] A *reflexive* relation is one which is sometimes called *reflexive on its field*, that is, a binary relation R such that $i R i$ for all i in the field of R.

several of these cases extensions relaxing the restrictions on the sentences considered have been obtained in the unpublished dissertation Cocchiarella [4] and in unpublished work of Kripke and Richmond Thomason.

General deontic logic emerges if we lift the requirement of reflexivity from accessibility relations, which then can better be regarded as relations of ethical relevance. In particular, we now let L be a pragmatic language having the one-place operator O as its only operator, and $K_7(L)$ be the class of possible interpretations $\langle I, U, F \rangle$ for L such that, for some binary relation S, (7a) the field of S is included in I, and (7b) for each i in I, $F_O(i)$ is the set of one-tuples $\langle J \rangle$ for which $J \subseteq I$ and, for all j, if iSj then j is in J. We read '$O\varphi$' as 'it is obligatory that φ' and regard the assertion that iSj as meaning that j is one of the better worlds among those accessible from i. The truth of $O\varphi$ in i then amounts to the truth of φ in all the better worlds among those accessible from i. The *sentential logic* of $K_7(L)$ (that is, the set of $K_7(L)$-valid sentences that contain no variables and no individual constants, and hence no predicates of more than zero places) has been axiomatized in unpublished work of E. J. Lemmon and Dana Scott; a completeness proof for the full set of $K_7(L)$-valid sentences has been found recently by Professor David Kaplan on the basis of a suggestion of E. J. Lemmon.

Special deontic logic

It appears that no limitation on the relation of ethical relevance can plausibly be imposed in all circumstances. Nevertheless, various specializations will be appropriate in certain contexts. We may, for instance, suppose that any world is accessible from (though not necessarily ethically relevant to) any other world; we should then need to consider only a single set of 'better worlds'. Accordingly, if L is as above, we let $K_8(L)$ be the class of possible interpretations $\langle I, U, F \rangle$ for L such that, for some nonempty subset J of I, $F_O(i)$ is, for all i in I, the set of one-tuples $\langle K \rangle$ for which $J \subseteq K \subseteq I$. I is again regarded as the set of all possible worlds; J is regarded as the set of better (or preferable) worlds; and the truth of $O\varphi$ in i amounts to the truth of φ in all preferable worlds.

According to a slightly more general approach we regard accessibility as an equivalence relation among worlds (like the relation of being alike throughout the past) but continue to consider only a single set of preferable worlds; $O\varphi$ is then taken as true in i if and only if φ is true in all worlds that are accessible from i and preferable. Thus we let $K_9(L)$ be the class of possible interpretations $\langle I, U, F\rangle$ for L such that there exist an equivalence relation R and a set J included in I such that (9a) for each i in I, there is j in J such that iRj, and (9b) for each i in I, $F_0(i)$ is the set of one-tuples $\langle K\rangle$ such that $K \subseteq I$ and, for each j such that iRj and j is in J, j is in K. (The optimistic assumption (9a), that from every world some preferred world is accessible, is not unreasonable if R is understood as the relation of being alike in the past, the past is considered to have finite duration, and the future is considered to have infinite duration.)

It is easily seen that the $K_8(L)$-valid sentences of L are the same as the $K_9(L)$-valid sentences of L, and that both coincide with the valid sentences (characterized model-theoretically, but in a different way) of the quantified deontic logic of the 1955 talk reported in Montague [16]. It is easily inferred from a completeness result stated in that paper that the sentential logic of $K_8(L)$ (as well as of $K_9(L)$) is axiomatized, under the rule of detachment, by the following schemata:

φ (if φ is a tautology),
$O\varphi$ (if φ is a tautology),
$O(\varphi \to \psi) \to (O\varphi \to O\psi)$,
$O(O(\varphi \to \psi) \to (O\varphi \to O\psi))$,
$\neg\, O\varphi \leftrightarrow O \neg\, O\varphi$,
$O(\neg\, O\varphi \leftrightarrow O \neg\, O\varphi)$.

As an illustration of possible combinations, let us consider the *combination of necessity with obligation.* Let L be a pragmatic language having $\Box$ and O as its only operators, let M be a class of binary relations, and let $K_{10}(L, M)$ be the class of possible interpretations $\langle I, U, F\rangle$ for L such that, for some R in M and some binary relation S, conditions (6a), (6b), and (7b) hold, and in addition $S \subseteq R$.

As another illustration, let us consider the *combination of tenses with temporally dependent necessity and temporally dependent obligation*. Let L be as above, but with the addition of the tense operators $\mathscr{P}$ and $\mathscr{F}$, let L' be a pragmatic language included in $L - \{\mathscr{P}, \mathscr{F}, \square, O\}$, and let $K_{11}(L, L')$ be the class of possible interpretations $\mathscr{C}$ for L such that, for some I, J, U, $\leqslant$, $\mathscr{A}_i$ (for i in I), F_i (for i in I), R_i (for i in I), $\mathscr{B}_i$ (for i in I), and G_i (for i in I), (11a) I, J, U are sets; (11b) $\leqslant$ is a simple ordering of I; (11c) for each i in I, $\mathscr{A}_i = \langle J, U, F_i \rangle$ and $\mathscr{A}_i$ is a possible interpretation for L'; (11d) for each i in I, R_i is that binary relation between members of J such that, for all j, j' in J, jR_ij' if and only if $(F_{i'})_A(j) = (F_{i'})_A(j')$ whenever $i' \leqslant i$, $i' \neq i$, and A is in L'; (11e) for each i in I, $\mathscr{B}_i = \langle J, U, G_i \rangle$, $F_i \subseteq G_i$, and $\mathscr{B}_i$ is in $K_{10}(L - \{\mathscr{P}, \mathscr{F}\}, \{R_i\})$; and (11f) $\mathscr{C}$ is the $\leqslant$-product of the systems $\mathscr{B}_i$, for i in I. We think of the members of I as the moments of time, $\leqslant$ as their ordering, and J as the set of possible worlds. The assertion that jR_ij' means that the worlds j and j' are alike at all times before i in the features represented by the language L'. If conditions (11a)–(11f) are satisfied, φ is a sentence of L, and $\langle i, j \rangle$ is a point of reference of $\mathscr{C}$, then it is easily seen that $\square \, \varphi$ is true at $\langle i, j \rangle$ (that is, at time i in world j) under $\mathscr{C}$ if and only if φ is true under $\mathscr{C}$ at all points of reference $\langle i, j' \rangle$ for which jR_ij' (that is, at time i in all worlds like j at all times before i). Thus '$\square \, \varphi$' can reasonably be read 'it is necessary on the basis of the past that φ', and '$O\varphi$', for similar reasons, 'it is obligatory in view of the past that φ'.

The *future subjunctive conditional* can apparently be accommodated without departing from the interpretations in $K_{11}(L, L')$. Indeed,

$$\square \, \neg \, \mathscr{F} \, \neg \, (\varphi \rightarrow \psi)$$

appears to express adequately the assertion that

> if it should be the case that φ, it would (at the same time) be the case that ψ.

Among subjunctive conditionals, it is the future that seems most relevant to ethical discourse; a treatment of other subjunctive conditionals, however, could be given along similar lines but would be more involved. The first adequate treatment of the present subjunctive conditional was given, within the framework of pragmatics, in unpublished work of Professor David Lewis; other treatments, involving what appear to be improvements and extensions, were developed by both Lewis and me. The present analysis of the future subjunctive conditional, though due to me, profits both from Professor Lewis' criticism of an earlier proposal and from discussion with J. A. W. Kamp and Dana Scott.

In all the examples above relevance or accessibility relations would have sufficed for the interpretation of operators. The following examples, for which this cannot be said, will illustrate the additional generality of the present treatment.

Kripke's semantics for nonnormal modal logics

Let L be a pragmatic language having $\square$ as its only operator; and let $K_{12}(L)$ be the class of possible interpretations $\langle I, U, F \rangle$ for L such that, for some binary relation R, (12a) the field of R is included in I; (12b) iRi whenever iRj; (12c) for all i in I, $F \square (i)$ is the set of one-tuples $\langle J \rangle$ for which $J \subseteq I$, iRi, and j is in J for all j such that iRj. Then one of the principal theorems of Kripke [13] may be stated as follows: the sentential logic of $K_{12}(L)$ is identical with the set of theorems (formulated in L) of the system E2 of Lemmon [15]. The other completeness theorems of Kripke [13] can be similarly accommodated within the conceptual framework of pragmatics.

Another general modal logic

The interpretations of Kripke mentioned above provide elegant completeness theorems for such systems as S2 and S3, but do not have strong intuitive content. Examples can be found, however, of intuitively significant interpretations of necessity which also appear not to be expressible in terms of relevance relations. For instance, let L be as above, let $\mathcal{M}$ be a class of *sets* of binary relations, and let $K_{13}(L, \mathcal{M})$ be the class of possible interpretations $\langle I, U, F \rangle$ for L such that, for some M in $\mathcal{M}$, (13a) M is a set of reflexive relations having I as their field, and (13b) for each i in I, $F_{\square}(i)$ is the set of one-tuples $\langle J \rangle$ for which

$J \subseteq I$ and there exists R in M such that J contains all objects j for which $i\,R\,j$. The members of I are again regarded as the possible worlds. The relations in M are regarded as corresponding to the various ways of accessibility; in other words, if R is in M, then to say that $i\,R\,j$ is to say that j is accessible from i *in a certain way*. The truth of $\square\,\varphi$ in a world i amounts to the truth of φ in all worlds accessible from i *in some particular way*.

We may, for instance, consider the ways of accessibility as corresponding to moments in the past, and indeed in such a manner that one world is accessible from another in the way corresponding to i if and only if the two worlds are identical in specified features up to the moment i. To go into a certain amount of detail, we might let L be as above, but with the addition of the tense operators $\mathscr{P}$ and $\mathscr{F}$, L' be a pragmatic language included in $L - \{\mathscr{P}, \mathscr{F}, \square\}$, and $K_{14}(L, L')$ be the class of possible interpretations $\mathscr{C}$ for L such that, for some $I, J, U, \leqslant, \mathscr{A}_i$ (for i in I), F_i (for i in I), M_i (for i in I), $\mathscr{B}_i$ (for i in I), and G_i (for i in I), conditions (11a)–(11c) hold, and in addition (14a) for each i in I, M_i is the set of binary relations R among members of J such that for some $i', i' \leqslant i, i' \neq i$, and for all j, j' in J, $j\,R\,j'$ if and only if $(F_{i''})_A(j) = (F_{i''})_A(j')$ whenever $i'' \leqslant i', i'' \neq i'$, and A is in L'; (14b) for each i in I, $\mathscr{B}_i = \langle J, U, G_i \rangle$, $F_i \subseteq G_i$, and $\mathscr{B}_i$ is in $K_{13}(L - \{\mathscr{P}, \mathscr{F}\}, \{M_i\})$; and (14c) $\mathscr{C}$ is the $\leqslant$-product of the systems $\mathscr{B}_i$, for i in I. If these conditions are satisfied, φ is a sentence of L, and $\langle i, j \rangle$ is a point of reference of $\mathscr{C}$, then it is easily seen that $\square\,\varphi$ is true at $\langle i, j \rangle$ (that is, at time i in world j) under $\mathscr{C}$ if and only if there exists R in M_i such that φ is true at all points of reference $\langle i, j' \rangle$ for which $j\,R\,j'$. Thus '$\square\,\varphi$' could receive the alternate reading 'it was predictable at some time in the past that it would now be the case that φ'.[8]

This example suggests several ways of specifying the class $\mathscr{M}$ in connection with $K_{13}(L, \mathscr{M})$. We might, for instance, require that as in the example each set in $\mathscr{M}$ be a set of equivalence relations which is closed under intersection; in particular, let $\mathscr{M}_1$ be the class of sets M such that, for some set I, (a) M is a nonempty set of equivalence relations having I as their field,

---

[8] This reading was suggested by Mr. Wilbur Walkoe.

and (b) $R \cap S$ is in M whenever R, S are in M. If M is in $\mathscr{M}_1$, then we may regard each member R of M as a relation between worlds of identity in certain features.

On the other hand, we may consider accessibility in terms not of identity but of *similarity* in certain features; and in that case it is reasonable to consider the class $\mathscr{M}_2$ of all sets M such that, for some set I, (a) M is a nonempty set of reflexive and symmetric relations having I as their field, (b) $R \cap S$ is in M whenever R, S are in M, and (c) for each R in M, there exists S in M such that, for all i, j, k, if $i \, S \, j$ and $j \, S \, k$, then $i \, R \, k$. If M is in $\mathscr{M}_2$, we regard each member R of M as a relation between worlds of similarity in certain features and to a certain degree. R will of course not generally be transitive. The relation S of which condition (c) asserts the existence can be understood as the relation of similarity in the features involved in R but to twice the degree involved in R.[9]

A further relaxation of assumptions leads us to the class $\mathscr{M}_3$ of all sets M such that, for some set I, (a) M is a nonempty set of reflexive relations having I as their field, (b) $R \cap S$ is in M whenever R, S are in M, and (c) whenever R is in M and i in I, there exists S in M such that, for all j, k, if $i \, S \, j$ and $j \, S \, k$, then $i \, R \, k$.

Clearly $\mathscr{M}_1 \subseteq \mathscr{M}_2 \subseteq \mathscr{M}_3$. It can also be shown that $K_{13}(L, \mathscr{M}_3)$ is exactly the class of *topological* interpretations of modal logic, that is, the class of possible interpretations $\langle I, U, F \rangle$ for L such that there exists a set T for which (a) $\langle I, T \rangle$ is a topological space,[10] and (b) for each i in I, $F \, \square \, (i)$ is the set of one-tuples $\langle J \rangle$ such that $J \subseteq J$ and, for some K in T, i is in K and $K \subseteq J$. The $K_{13}(L, \mathscr{M}_3)$-valid sentences are thus exactly the theorems of a quantified version of the Lewis system S4; this was shown for the topological interpretation in Rasiowa and Sikorski [23].

[9] The class $\mathscr{M}_2$ is closely related to the class of *uniform spaces* (in the sense of general topology; for a definition and discussion see Kelley [10, pp. 175–216]). In particular, if M is in $\mathscr{M}_2$, I is the common field of all relations in M, and N is the set of relations S between members of I such that $R \subseteq S$ for some R in M, then $\langle I, N \rangle$ is a uniform space; and conversely, if $\langle X, T \rangle$ is a uniform space and M is the set of symmetric relations in T, then M is in $\mathscr{M}_2$ and all relations in M have X as their field.

[10] For a definition of a topological space see, for instance, Kelley [10, p. 37].

Inductive logic

For each real number r such that $0 \leqslant r \leqslant 1$, let P_r be a one-place operator; and let $P_r \neq P_s$ whenever $r \neq s$. Let L be a pragmatic language having the symbols P_r (for $0 \leqslant r \leqslant 1$) as its operators; and let $K_{15}(L)$ be the class of possible interpretations $\langle I, U, F \rangle$ for L such that there exist $\mathcal{G}$, μ for which (15a) $\langle I, \mathcal{G}, \mu \rangle$ is a field of probability (in the sense of Kolmogorov [11]), and (15b) for each i in I and each real number r such that $0 \leqslant r \leqslant 1$, $F_{P_r}(i)$ is the set of one-tuples $\langle J \rangle$ for which J is a member of $\mathcal{G}$ and $\mu(J) = r$. We may thus read '$P_r \varphi$' as 'it is probable to exactly the degree r that φ'; and 'probable' may be understood in the sense of either a frequency theory or an *a priori* theory, depending on whether the points of reference are regarded as moments of time or possible worlds. '$P_1 \varphi$' may correspondingly be read as either 'it is almost always the case that φ' or 'it is almost certain that φ'.

Examples of tense operators can also be found that cannot be interpreted in terms of relevance relations. Mr. Kamp has considered two binary operators of this sort, corresponding to the locutions 'since it was the case that φ, it has (always) been the case that ψ' and 'until it is the case that φ, it will (always) be the case that ψ'. (Mr. Kamp has analyzed the general notion of a tense and has shown, in work that is still unpublished, that every tense can be expressed in terms of these two.)

I shall only mention three further developments of pragmatics. (1) Mr. Kamp has given an analysis, exhibiting several interesting features, of the indexical adverbs 'yesterday', 'today', and 'tomorrow', used in combination with tense operators. (2) A treatment of dates, as used in combination with tense operators, has been given in Prior [21] and has been further developed by Mr. Kamp.[11] (3) A kind of second-order extension of pragmatics has been developed in Montague [17] and identified with *intensional logic*; what appears to be the first fully adequate treatment of belief contexts and the like is thereby provided. A number of philosophical applications of the enlarged system are given in Montague [18].

[11] Although this is the only point at which specific attribution has been made to Arthur Prior, I should mention that the entire modern development of tense logic was initiated and stimulated by his work, particularly his books [20 and 21].

REFERENCES

1. Addison, J., L. Henkin and A. Tarski. *The Theory of Models.* Amsterdam, 1965.
2. Bar-Hillel, Y. Indexical Expressions. *Mind* 63:359–79 (1954).
3. Cocchiarella, N. A Completeness Theorem for Tense Logic. *Journal of Symbolic Logic* 31:689–90 (1966).
4. —. Tense Logic: A Study of Temporal Reference. Dissertation, University of California at Los Angeles, 1966.
5. Frege, G. Über Sinn und Bedeutung. *Zeitschrift für Philosophie und philosophische Kritik* 100:25–50 (1892).
6. Gödel, K. Über formal unentscheidbare Sätze der *Principia mathematica* und verwandter Systeme I. *Monatshefte für Mathematik und Physik* 38:173–98 (1931).
7. Hilbert, D. and P. Bernays. *Grundlagen der Mathematik.* Berlin, 1934–39.
8. Hintikka, J. Modality and Quantification. *Theoria* 27:119–28 (1961).
9. Kanger, S. *Provability in Logic.* Stockholm, 1957.
10. Kelley, J. *General Topology.* Princeton, 1955.
11. Kolmogorov, A. *Foundations of the Theory of Probability.* New York, 1956.
12. Kripke, L. A Completeness Theorem in Modal Logic. *Journal of Symbolic Logic* 24:1–14 (1959).
13. —. Semantical Considerations on Modal Logic. *Acta Philosophica Fennica* 16:83–94 (1963).
14. —. Semantical Analysis of Modal Logic, II: Non-normal Modal Propositional Calculi. In Addison, Henkin, and Tarski [1], cited above.
15. Lemmon, E. New Foundations for Lewis Modal Systems. *Journal of Symbolic Logic* 22:176–86 (1957).
16. Montague, R. Logical Necessity, Physical Necessity, Ethics, and Quantifiers. *Inquiry* 4:259–69 (1960). Chap. 1 in this book.
17. —. Pragmatics and Intensional Logic. *Synthèse* 22:68–94 (1970). Chap. 4 in this book.
18. —. On the Nature of Certain Philosophical Entities. *Monist* 53:159–94. Chap. 5 in this book.
19. Morris, C. *Foundations of the Theory of Signs.* Chicago, 1938.
20. Prior, A. *Time and Modality.* Oxford, 1957.
21. —. *Past, Present, and Future.* Oxford, 1967.
22. Quine, W. *From a Logical Point of View.* Cambridge, Mass., 1953.
23. Rasiowa, H. and R. Sikorsky. *The Mathematics of Metamathematics.* Warsaw, 1963.

24. Robinson, A. Model Theory. In R. Klibansky (ed.), *Contemporary Philosophy: A Survey*, vol. 1. Florence, 1968.

25. Tarski, A. Über einige fundamentale Begriffe der Metamathematik. In *Comptes Rendus des Séances de la Société des Sciences et des Lettres de Varsovie*, Classe III 23, Warsaw, 1930. English translation in Tarski [29], cited below.

26. —. Fundamentale Begriffe der Methodologie der deductiven Wissenschaften I. *Monatshefte für Mathematik und Physik* 37:361–404 (1930). English translation in Tarski [29].

27. —. Projecie Prawdy w Językach Nauk Dedukcyjnych (The Concept of Truth in the Languages of the Deductive Sciences). In *Travaux de la Société des Sciences et des Lettres de Varsovie*, Classe III 34, Warsaw, 1933. English translation in Tarski [29], cited below.

28. —. Grundzüge des Systemenkalküls. *Fundamenta Mathematicae* 25:503–26 (1935) and 26:283–301 (1936). English translation in Tarski [29], cited below.

29. —. *Logic, Semantics, Metamathematics*. Oxford, 1956.

4. Pragmatics and Intensional Logic

The word 'pragmatics' was used in Morris [19] for that branch of philosophy of language which involves, besides linguistic expressions and the objects to which they refer, also the users of the expressions and the possible contexts of use. The other two branches, syntax and semantics, dealing respectively with expressions alone and expressions together with their reference, had already been extensively developed by the time at which Morris wrote, the former by a number of authors and the latter in Tarski [20].

Morris' conception of pragmatics, however, was programmatic and indefinite. A step towards precision was taken by Bar-Hillel, who suggested in Bar-Hillel [2] that pragmatics concern itself with what C. S. Peirce had in the last century called *indexical expressions*.[1] An indexical word or sentence is one of which the reference cannot be determined without knowledge of the context of use; an example is the first person pronoun 'I'. Indexical sentences can be produced in various ways, for instance, by using tenses. Consider 'Caesar will die'. This sentence cannot be

Originally published in *Synthèse* 22:68–94 (1970). Reprinted with permission. This paper was delivered before the Southern California Logic Colloquium on January 6, 1967, and reports research partly supported by U.S. National Science Foundation Grant GP-4594. I should like to express gratitude to my student Dr. J. A. W. Kamp for a number of valuable suggestions beyond those explicitly acknowledged below, and to Mr. Tobin Barrozo for correcting an error. It should perhaps be mentioned that this paper was submitted to another journal on November 7, 1967, but was withdrawn after two and one-half years because of the great delay in its publication; it was thus intended to appear before either Montague [15] or Montague [16], for both of which it supplies a certain amount of background.

[1] Other terms for these expressions include 'egocentric particulars' (Russell), 'token-reflexive expressions' (Reichenbach), 'indicator words' (Goodman), and 'noneternal sentences' (Quine, for sentences that are indexical).

considered either true or false independently of the context of use; before a truth value can be determined, the time of utterance, which is one aspect of the context of use, must be specified.

Though Bar-Hillel suggested that pragmatics concern itself with indexical expressions, he was not wholly explicit as to the form this concern should take. It seemed to me desirable that pragmatics should at least initially follow the lead of semantics—or its modern version, model theory[2]—which is primarily concerned with the notions of truth and satisfaction (in a model, or under an interpretation). Pragmatics, then, should employ similar notions, though here we should speak about truth and satisfaction with respect not only to an interpretation but also to a context of use.

These notions I analyzed some years ago in connection with a number of special cases, for instance, those involving personal pronouns, demonstratives, modal operators, tenses, probability operators, contextual ambiguity, and direct self-reference.[3] An important feature of many of these analyses was a treatment of quantifiers due largely to my student Prof. Nino Cocchiarella, and persisting in the general development below.[4]

In each special case, however, truth and satisfaction had to be defined anew; in particular, no unified treatment of operators was seen. Intuitive similarities existed; but full formal unity was not achieved until 1965, and then it came about through joint work of Dr. Charles Howard and myself.

Let me sketch the general treatment. By a *pragmatic language* is understood a language of which the symbols (atomic expressions) are drawn from the following categories:

(1) the logical constants $\neg$, $\wedge$, $\vee$, $\rightarrow$, $\leftrightarrow$, $\wedge$, $\vee$, $=$, E (read respectively 'it is not the case that', 'and', 'or', 'if...then', 'if and only if', 'for all', 'for some', 'is identical with', 'exists'),

[2] For an account of the fundamental concepts of model theory see Tarski [22].

[3] This work was reported in a talk I delivered before the U.C.L.A. Philosophy Colloquium on December 18, 1964. The treatment of special cases within the general framework of the present paper will be discussed in another publication. [Editor's note: This work was apparently never completed.]

[4] Cocchiarella considered quantification only in connection with tense logic; his treatment may be found in the abstract Cocchiarella [4] and the unpublished doctoral dissertation Cocchiarella [5].

(2) parentheses, brackets, and commas,

(3) the individual variables $v_0, \ldots, v_k, \ldots,$

(4) individual constants,

(5) n-place predicate constants, for each natural number (that is, nonnegative integer) n, and

(6) operators.

(The individuals to which such a language refers will be regarded as possible objects; accordingly, the symbol E will occur in such contexts as $E[x]$, which is read 'x exists' or 'x is actual'. I consider under (6) only what might be called *one-place operators*. These are symbols which, like the negation sign, generate a sentence when placed before another sentence; examples are the modal operators 'necessarily' and 'possibly', as well as the expressions 'it will be the case that', 'usually', and 'it is probable to at least the degree one-half that'. Purely for simplicity I have disallowed operation symbols, descriptive phrases, and many-place operators; but an extension of the present treatment to accommodate such expressions would be completely routine. Indeed, many-place operators can be expressed in both extended pragmatics and intensional logic, which are considered below; and a partial theory of descriptive phrases occurs within intensional logic.)

The *formulas* of a pragmatic language L are built up exactly as one would expect. To be explicit, the set of formulas of L is the smallest set Γ such that (1) Γ contains all expressions

$E[\zeta],$

$\zeta = \eta,$

$P[\zeta_0, \ldots, \zeta_{n-1}],$

where each of $\zeta, \eta, \zeta_0, \ldots, \zeta_{n-1}$ is an individual constant of L or an individual variable and P is an n-place predicate constant of L; (2) Γ is closed under the application of sentential connectives; (3) $\bigwedge u\phi$ and $\bigvee u\phi$ are in Γ whenever u is an individual variable and ϕ is in Γ; and (4) $N\phi$ is in Γ whenever N is an operator of L and ϕ is in Γ.

To interpret a pragmatic language L we must specify several things. In the first place, we must determine the set of all possible contexts of use—or rather, of all complexes of relevant aspects of possible contexts of use; we may call such complexes *indices*, or to borrow Dana Scott's term, *points of reference*. For example, if the only indexical features of L were the presence of tense operators and the first person pronoun 'I', then a point of reference might be an ordered pair consisting of a person and a real number, understood respectively as the utterer and the moment of utterance.

In the second place, we should have to specify, for each point of reference i, the set A_i of objects present or existing with respect to i. For example, if the points of reference were moments of time, A_i would be understood as the set of objects existing at i.

In the third place, we should have to specify the meaning or *intension* of each predicate and individual constant of L. To do this for a constant c, we should have to determine, for each point of reference i, the denotation or *extension* of c with respect to i. For example, if the points of reference were moments of time and c were the predicate constant 'is green', we should have to specify for each moment i the set of objects to be regarded as green at i. If, on the other hand, c were an individual constant, say 'the Pope', we should have to specify, for each moment i, the person regarded as Pope at i.

The fourth thing we must provide is an interpretation of the operators of L. To do this we associate with each operator of L a relation between points of reference and sets of points of reference. The role played by such relations, as well as the intuitive reasons for regarding them as interpreting operators, can best be discussed later.

In order to be a bit more precise about interpretations, let us introduce a few auxiliary notions. Understand by a $\langle U_0, \ldots, U_{n-1} \rangle$-*relation* a subset of $U_0 \times \ldots \times U_{n-1}$ (by which we intend the Cartesian product $\prod_{i<n} U_i$ of the sets $U_0, \ldots, U_{n-1}$), and by an $\langle I, U_0, \ldots, U_{n-1} \rangle$-*predicate* a function from the set I into the set of all $\langle U_0, \ldots, U_{n-1} \rangle$-relations. (I use the word 'relation' for a possible candidate for the extension of a predicate constant, while 'predicate' is reserved for the intension of such a constant. Consider the special case in which $n = 1$. Then the $\langle U_0 \rangle$-relations will coincide with the sets of elements of U_0, the $\langle I, U_0 \rangle$-predicates are what we might

regard as *properties* (indexed by I) of elements of U_0, and both will correspond to one-place predicate constants. In case $n = 0$, we should speak of Λ-relations (where Λ is the empty sequence, that is, the empty set); and these are the subsets of the empty Cartesian product, which is of course $\{\Lambda\}$. Thus the only Λ-relations will be the empty set Λ and its unit set $\{\Lambda\}$; let us think of these two objects as the truth-values F and T respectively. The corresponding predicates are $\langle I \rangle$-predicates; and they will be functions from the set I to truth-values, that is, what we might regard as *propositions*[5] indexed by I.)

By a *k-place relation among members* of a set U and by a *k-place I-predicate of members of U* are understood a $\langle U_0, \ldots, U_{k-1} \rangle$-relation and an $\langle I, U_0, \ldots, U_{k-1} \rangle$-predicate respectively, where each U_p (for $p < k$) is U.

Definition I. A *possible interpretation for a pragmatic language* L is a triple $\langle A, F, R \rangle$ such that (1) A is a function; (2) for each i in the domain of A, A_i is a set (I use the notations 'A_i' and '$A(i)$' indiscriminately for function value); (3) F is a function whose domain is the set of predicate and individual constants of L; (4) whenever c is an individual constant of L, F_c is a function whose domain is the domain of A and such that, for all j in the domain of A, $F_c(j)$ is a member of the union of the sets A_i for i in the domain of A; (5) whenever P is an n-place predicate constant of L, F_P is an n-place $\mathbf{D}A$-predicate of members of the union of the sets A_i (for $i \in \mathbf{D}A$), where $\mathbf{D}A$ is the domain of A; (6) R is a function whose domain is the set of operators of L, and (7) whenever N is in the domain of R, R_N is a $\langle \mathbf{D}A, \mathbf{S}\mathbf{D}A \rangle$-relation, where $\mathbf{S}\mathbf{D}A$ is the power set (set of all subsets) of $\mathbf{D}A$.

A few remarks are perhaps in order in connection with this definition. Let $\mathfrak{A}$ be a possible interpretation for a pragmatic language L, and let $\mathfrak{A}$ have the form $\langle A, F, R \rangle$. We understand the domain of the function A to be the set of all points of reference according to $\mathfrak{A}$. If i is a point of reference, A_i is understood as the set of objects existing with respect to i (according to $\mathfrak{A}$). The union of the sets A_i for i in $\mathbf{D}A$ is thus what we might regard as the set of all possible individuals (according to $\mathfrak{A}$). By the definition

---

[5] The idea of construing propositions, properties, and relations-in-intension as functions of the sorts above occurs first, I believe, in Kripke [12].

above, an individual constant denotes a *possible* individual, and a one-place predicate constant a set of *possible* individuals, with respect to a given point of reference. To see that it would be overly restrictive to demand that the respective denotations be an individual that exists with respect to the given point of reference or a set of such individuals, suppose that the points of reference are instants of time, and consider the individual constant 'the previous Pope' and the predicate constant 'is remembered by someone'. A similar point can be made in connection with predicate constants of more than one place. Consider, for instance, the two-place predicate constant 'thinks of' (as in 'Jones thinks of Jove'). Under a standard interpretation of which the points of reference are possible worlds, the extension of this constant with respect to a given world would be a relation between individuals existing in that world and possible individuals (that is, objects existing in some world).[6]

The notions central to pragmatics, those of *truth* and *satisfaction*, are expressed by the phrases 'the sentence (that is, formula without free variables) ϕ is true with respect to the point of reference i under the interpretation $\mathfrak{A}$' and 'the possible individual x satisfies the formula ϕ with respect to the point of reference i under the interpretation $\mathfrak{A}$', which we may abbreviate by 'ϕ is true$_{i,\mathfrak{A}}$' and 'x sat$_{i,\mathfrak{A}}$ ϕ' respectively. The following clauses do not constitute definitions of truth and satisfaction, but are rather to be regarded as true assertions exhibiting the salient features of those notions; the full definitions will be given later.

Criteria of pragmatic truth and satisfaction. Let $\mathfrak{A}$ be a possible interpretation, having the form $\langle A, F, R \rangle$, for a pragmatic language L; let $i \in \mathbf{D}A$; let x be a member of the union of the sets A_j (for $j \in \mathbf{D}A$); let P be a two-place predicate constant of L; and let u be an individual variable. Then:

(1) $P[c, d]$ is true$_{i,\mathfrak{A}}$ if and only if $\langle F_c(i), F_d(i) \rangle \in F_P(i)$;

(2) x sat$_{i,\mathfrak{A}}$ $P[c, u]$ if and only if $\langle F_c(i), x \rangle \in F_P(i)$;

---

[6] This simple and obvious approach is not the only possible treatment of 'thinks of', a phrase that has been discussed in the philosophical literature, for instance, in Anscombe [1], with incomplete success; but it is, I think, *one* possible treatment of *one* sense—the referential—of that phrase. For a treatment of the non-referential sense see Montague [15].

(3) x sat$_{i,\mathfrak{A}}$ $c = u$ if and only if $F_c(i)$ is identical with x;

(4) x sat$_{i,\mathfrak{A}}$ $\mathsf{E}[u]$ if and only if $x \in A_i$;

(5) if ϕ is a sentence of L, then $\neg\phi$ is true$_{i,\mathfrak{A}}$ if and only if ϕ is not true$_{i,\mathfrak{A}}$;

(6) if ϕ, ψ are sentences of L, then $(\phi \wedge \psi)$ is true$_{i,\mathfrak{A}}$ if and only if both ϕ and ψ are true$_{i,\mathfrak{A}}$;

(7) if ϕ is a formula of L of which the only free variable is u, then $\mathsf{V}u\phi$ is true$_{i,\mathfrak{A}}$ if and only if there is an object y in the union of the sets A_j (for $j \in \mathbf{D}A$) such that y sat$_{i,\mathfrak{A}}$ ϕ;

(8) if ϕ is a sentence of L and N an operator of L, then $N\phi$ is true$_{i,\mathfrak{A}}$ if and only if $\langle i, \{j : j \in \mathbf{D}A$ and ϕ is true$_{j,\mathfrak{A}}\}\rangle \in R_N$.

According to (8), $N\phi$ is true at i (under $\mathfrak{A}$) if and only if i bears the relation R_N to the set of points of reference at which ϕ is true (under $\mathfrak{A}$). To see that (8) comprehends the proper treatment of, for example, the past tense operator, consider an interpretation $\mathfrak{A}$ in which $\mathbf{D}A$ is the set of real numbers (that is, instants of time) and R_N is the set of pairs $\langle i, J\rangle$ such that $i \in \mathbf{D}A, J \subseteq \mathbf{D}A$, and there exists $j \in J$ such that $j < i$. Then, by (8), $N\phi$ will be true at i (under $\mathfrak{A}$) if and only if there exists $j < i$ such that ϕ is true at j (under $\mathfrak{A}$); and therefore N will correctly express 'it has been the case that'. It is clear that the future tense, as well as the modal operators (interpreted by relevance relations) of Kripke [12], can be similarly accommodated. These examples, however, could all be treated within a simpler framework, in which R_N is always a relation between two points of reference (rather than having as its second relatum a *set* of points of reference). To see the necessity of the more general approach, we could consider probability operators, conditional necessity, or, to invoke an especially perspicuous example of Dana Scott, the present progressive tense. To elaborate on the last, let the interpretation $\mathfrak{A}$ again have the real numbers as its points of reference; and let R_N be the set of pairs $\langle i, J\rangle$ such that $i \in \mathbf{D}A, J \subseteq \mathbf{D}A$, and J is a neighborhood of i (that is, J includes an open interval of which i is a member). Then, by (8), $N\phi$ will be true at i (under $\mathfrak{A}$) if and only if there is an open interval containing i throughout which ϕ is true (under $\mathfrak{A}$). Thus N might receive the awkward reading 'it is being the case that', in the sense in which 'it is being the case that Jones leaves' is synonymous with 'Jones is leaving'.

According to (7), quantification is over *possible* (and not merely *actual*) individuals. The desirability of this can be seen by considering, within the special case of tense logic, the sentence 'there was a man whom no one remembers'. One can of course express quantification over actual individuals by combining quantifiers with the symbol E of existence.

To be quite precise, the desiderata (1)–(8) can be achieved by the following sequence of definitions; that is to say, (1)–(8) are simple consequences of Definitions II–V below. We assume for these that $\mathfrak{A}$ is a possible interpretation for a pragmatic language L, $\mathfrak{A} = \langle A, F, R \rangle$, U is the union of the sets A_j for $j \in \mathbf{D}A$, U^ω is the set of all infinite sequences (of type ω) of members of U, $i \in \mathbf{D}A$, and n is a natural number.

Definition II. If ζ is an individual variable or individual constant of L, then by $\mathrm{Ext}_{i,\mathfrak{A}}(\zeta)$, or the *extension* of ζ at i (with respect to $\mathfrak{A}$) is understood that function H with domain U^ω which is determined as follows:

(1) if ζ is the variable v_n and $x \in U^\omega$, then $H(x) = x_n$;

(2) If ζ is an individual constant and $x \in U^\omega$, then $H(x) = F_\zeta(i)$.

The *extension* of a *formula* of L at a point of reference (and with respect to $\mathfrak{A}$) is introduced by the following recursive definition.

Definition III. (1) If ζ is an individual constant of L or an individual variable, then $\mathrm{Ext}_{i,\mathfrak{A}}(E[\zeta])$ is $\{x : x \in U^\omega \text{ and } (\mathrm{Ext}_{i,\mathfrak{A}}(\zeta))(x) \in A_i\}$.

(2) If each of ζ, η is either an individual constant of L or an individual variable, then $\mathrm{Ext}_{i,\mathfrak{A}}(\zeta = \eta)$ is $\{x : x \in U^\omega \text{ and } (\mathrm{Ext}_{i,\mathfrak{A}}(\zeta))(x)$ is identical with $(\mathrm{Ext}_{i,\mathfrak{A}}(\eta))(x)\}$.

(3) If P is an n-place predicate constant of L and each of $\zeta_0, \ldots, \zeta_{n-1}$ is an individual constant of L or an individual variable, then $\mathrm{Ext}_{i,\mathfrak{A}}(P[\zeta_0, \ldots, \zeta_{n-1}])$ is $\{x : x \in U^\omega \text{ and } \langle (\mathrm{Ext}_{i,\mathfrak{A}} \times (\zeta_0))(x), \ldots, (\mathrm{Ext}_{i,\mathfrak{A}}(\zeta_{n-1}))(x) \rangle \in F_P(i)\}$.

(4) If ϕ, ψ are formulas of L, then $\mathrm{Ext}_{i,\mathfrak{A}}(\neg \phi)$ is $U^\omega - \mathrm{Ext}_{i,\mathfrak{A}}(\phi)$, $\mathrm{Ext}_{i,\mathfrak{A}}((\phi \wedge \psi))$ is $\mathrm{Ext}_{i,\mathfrak{A}}(\phi) \cap \mathrm{Ext}_{i,\mathfrak{A}}(\psi)$, and similarly for the other sentential connectives.

(5) If ϕ is a formula of L, then $\mathrm{Ext}_{i,\mathfrak{A}}(\vee v_n \phi)$ is $\{x : x \in U^\omega$ and, for some $y \in U$, the sequence $\langle x_0, \ldots, x_{n-1}, y, x_{n+1}, \ldots \rangle \in \mathrm{Ext}_{i,\mathfrak{A}}(\phi)\}$, and similarly for $\wedge v_n \phi$.

(6) If ϕ is a formula of L and N an operator of L, then $\text{Ext}_{i,\mathfrak{A}}(N\phi)$ is $\{x : x \in U^\omega$ and $\langle i, \{j : j \in \mathbf{D}A$ and $x \in \text{Ext}_{j,\mathfrak{A}}(\phi)\}\rangle \in R_N\}$.

Definition IV. If ϕ is a sentence of L, then ϕ is true$_{i,\mathfrak{A}}$ if and only if $\text{Ext}_{i,\mathfrak{A}}(\phi) = U^\omega$.

Definition V. If ϕ is a formula of L of which the only free variable is v_n, then y sat$_{i,\mathfrak{A}}\phi$ if and only if there exists $x \in \text{Ext}_{i,\mathfrak{A}}(\phi)$ such that $x_n = y$.

It is seen from the definitions above that the extension of a formula (at a point of reference) is a set of sequences (indeed, the set of sequences 'satisfying' that formula at that point of reference, in the sense in which sequences, rather than individuals satisfy) and that the extension of an individual constant or variable (again, at a given point of reference) is a function assigning a possible individual to each sequence in U^ω. How does this construction accord with the fundamental discussion in Frege [9]? It should be remembered that Frege considered explicitly the extensions only of expressions without free variables—thus, as far as our present language is concerned, only of sentences and individual constants. For Frege the extension (or *ordinary extension*) of a sentence was a truth value; but it is easily seen that according to Definition III the extension of a sentence of L will always be either U^ω or the empty set, which in this context can be appropriately identified with truth and falsehood respectively. For Frege the extension (or *ordinary extension*) of an individual constant was the object it denotes, while for us the extension is the constant function with that object as value (and with U^ω as domain). Apart from set-theoretic manipulations, then, Frege's extensions agree with ours in all common cases.

I introduce for the sake of later discussion the *intensions* of certain expressions with respect to $\mathfrak{A}$, as well as the notions of *logical consequence*, *logical truth*, and *logical equivalence* appropriate to pragmatics.

Definition VI. If ϕ is an individual constant of L, a formula of L, or an individual variable, then $\text{Int}_\mathfrak{A}(\phi)$ is that function H with domain $\mathbf{D}A$ such that, for each $i \in \mathbf{D}A$, $H(i) = \text{Ext}_{i,\mathfrak{A}}(\phi)$.

Definition VII. A sentence ϕ is a *logical consequence* (in the sense of pragmatics) of a set Γ of sentences if and only if for every pragmatic language L and all $\mathfrak{A}$, A, F, R, i, if $\mathfrak{A} = \langle A, F, R \rangle$,

$\mathfrak{A}$ is a possible interpretation for L, $i \in \mathbf{D}A$, $\Gamma \cup \{\phi\}$ is a set of sentences of L, and for every $\psi \in \Gamma$, ψ is true$_{i,\mathfrak{A}}$, then ϕ is true$_{i,\mathfrak{A}}$. A sentence is *logically true* if and only if it is a logical consequence of the empty set. A sentence ϕ is *logically equivalent* to a sentence ψ if and only if the sentence $(\phi \leftrightarrow \psi)$ is logically true.[7]

If we understand the extension of a predicate constant P (at i and with respect to $\mathfrak{A}$) to be $F_P(i)$, then inspection of Definition III will show that Frege's functionality principle applies fully to our notion of extension: the extension of a formula is a function of the extensions (ordinary extensions) of those of its parts not standing within indirect contexts (that is, for the present language, not standing within the scope of an operator), together with the intensions (what Frege also called *indirect extensions*) of those parts that do stand within indirect contexts. It is clause (6) of Definition III which creates the dependence of certain extensions on intensions, and which consequently makes it impossible to regard Definition III as a simple recursion on the length of formulas. Instead, the recursion is on a well-founded relation S between ordered pairs, characterized as follows: $\langle\langle j, \psi\rangle,$ $\langle i, \phi\rangle\rangle \in S$ if and only if $i, j \in \mathbf{D}A$, ϕ, ψ are formulas of L, and ψ is a proper part of ϕ.[8]

On the other hand, we could have adopted another order, introducing intensions first and defining extensions explicitly in terms of them. In that case, as is easily seen, we could have introduced intensions by a simple recursion on the length of formulas; in other words, the intension of a complex expression is a function purely of the intensions of its components. (We thus answer negatively, for pragmatic languages at least, a question

---

[7] Let us call an interpretation $\langle A, F, R \rangle$ *empty* if the union of the sets A_i for $i \in \mathbf{D}A$ is the empty set. We have not excluded empty interpretations from consideration, and it might be feared that minor difficulties might consequently arise in connection with the notions introduced in Definition VII. Such fears would be unjustified; it can easily be shown that the definition given above of logical consequence is equivalent to the result of adding to it the restriction that $\mathfrak{A}$ be a nonempty interpretation. On the other hand, some of the criteria given above of truth and satisfaction would fail for empty interpretations; but the case of empty interpretations is excluded by the assumption 'x is a member of the union of the sets A_j'.

[8] Recursion on well-founded relations was first explicitly introduced in Montague [13].

raised by Frege, whether we need to consider *indirect intensions* as well as ordinary extensions and ordinary intensions. The answer remains negative even for the richer languages considered below.)

The general treatment of operators, embodied in clause (6) of Definition III and due to Charles Howard and me, has the advantage of comprehending all known special cases but the drawback of a seemingly *ad hoc* and unintuitive character. This semblance can be removed, and at the same time a theoretical reduction accomplished, by the consideration of *intensional logic*. Attempts to construct intensional languages suitable for handling belief contexts and the like have been made previously, but without complete success; I report now my own efforts in this direction.

By an *intensional language* is understood a language of which the symbols are drawn from the following categories:

(1) the logical constants of pragmatic languages;

(2) parentheses, brackets, and commas;

(3) the individual variables $v_0, \ldots, v_n, \ldots$;

(4) individual constants;

(5) the *n*-place predicate variables $G_{0,n}, \ldots, G_{k,n}, \ldots$, for each natural number n;

(6) predicate constants of type s, for each finite sequence s of integers ≥ -1;

(7) the operator $\square$ (read 'necessarily');

(8) the descriptive symbol T (read 'the unique ... such that' and regarded, along with the symbols under (1) and (7), as a logical constant).

Under (6) we admit predicate constants taking predicate variables, as well as individual symbols, as arguments. The type of such a constant indicates the grammatical categories of a suitable sequence of arguments, -1 indicating an individual symbol and a nonnegative integer n indicating an n-place predicate variable. Thus our previous n-place predicate constants are comprehended, and can be identified with predicate constants of type $\langle s_0, \ldots, s_{n-1} \rangle$, where each s_i (for $i < n$) is -1. The descriptive symbol will be applied only to predicate variables; this is because it will be needed only in such contexts and because its use in connection with individual variables would require some small but extraneous attention to the choice of a 'null entity'.[9] The descriptive phrases we admit will be completely eliminable, and are introduced solely to facilitate certain later examples.

The set of *formulas* of an *intensional* language L is the smallest set Γ such that (1) Γ contains the expressions

$$E[\zeta],$$
$$\zeta = \eta,$$
$$G[\zeta_0, \ldots, \zeta_{n-1}],$$

where each of $\zeta, \eta, \zeta_0, \ldots, \zeta_{n-1}$ is an individual constant of L or an individual variable and G is an n-place predicate variable of L, as well as all expressions

$$P[\zeta_0, \ldots, \zeta_{n-1}],$$

where P is a predicate constant of L having type $\langle s_0, \ldots, s_{n-1} \rangle$ and, for each $i < n$, either $s_i \geqslant 0$ and ζ_i is an s_i-place predicate variable, or $s_i = -1$ and ζ_i is an individual constant of L or an individual variable; (2) Γ is closed under the application of sentential connectives; (3) $\wedge u\phi$ and $\vee u\phi$ are in Γ whenever ϕ is in Γ and u is either an individual variable or a predicate variable; (4) $\square\phi$ is in Γ whenever ϕ is in Γ; and (5) whenever ϕ, ψ are in Γ, and G is a predicate variable, then Γ also contains the result of replacing in ϕ all occurrences of G which do not immediately follow $\wedge$, $\vee$, or T by $TG\psi$.

By a *term* of L is understood either an individual constant of L, a variable, or an expression $TG\phi$, where G is a predicate variable and ϕ a formula of L.

Definition VIII. A *possible interpretation for an intensional language* L is a pair $\langle A, F \rangle$ such that clauses (1)–(4) of Definition I hold, and in addition (5') whenever P is a predicate constant of L having type $\langle s_0, \ldots, s_{n-1} \rangle$, F_P is a $\langle \mathbf{D}A, U_0, \ldots, U_{n-1} \rangle$-predicate, where, for each $i < n$, either $s_i = -1$ and U_i is the

---

[9] The present system could, however, be extended so as to contain a full theory of definite descriptions in any of the well-known ways, for instance, that of Montague and Kalish [17]. It is partly in order to avoid irrelevant controversy over the best treatment of descriptions that I introduce them so sparingly here.

union of the sets A_i for $i \in \mathbf{D}A$, or $s_i \geq 0$ and U_i is the set of all s_i-place $\mathbf{D}A$-predicates of members of the union of the sets A_i for $i \in \mathbf{D}A$.

Clause (5) of Definition I is a special case of the present (5'), taking $s_0 = \ldots = s_{n-1} = -1$.

Again we shall be primarily interested in notions of truth and satisfaction, expressed by the phrases 'the sentence ϕ is true with respect to the point of reference i under the interpretation $\mathfrak{A}$', and 'x satisfies the formula ϕ with respect to the point of reference i under the interpretation $\mathfrak{A}$'. Since, however, our formulas may now contain free predicate variables as well as free individual variables, we must understand 'x' to refer either to a possible individual or to a predicate of individuals. The intuitions underlying the present development will become clear upon consideration of the following criteria.

Criteria of intensional truth and satisfaction. Let $\mathfrak{A}$ be a possible interpretation, having the form $\langle A, F \rangle$, for an intensional language L; let $i \in \mathbf{D}A$; let U be the union of the sets A_j (for $j \in \mathbf{D}A$); let $x \in U$; let P be a predicate constant of L of type $\langle -1, -1 \rangle$; let c, d be individual constants of L; and let u be an individual variable. Then:

(1)–(7) of the criteria of pragmatic truth and satisfaction.

(8') If ϕ is a formula of L of which the only free variable is the n-place predicate variable G, then $\vee G\phi$ is true$_{i,\mathfrak{A}}$ if and only if there is an n-place $\mathbf{D}A$-predicate X of members of U such that X sat$_{i,\mathfrak{A}}\phi$.

(9') If G is an n-place predicate variable, $\mathscr{P}$ a predicate constant of L of type $\langle n \rangle$, and X an n-place $\mathbf{D}A$-predicate of members of U, then X sat$_{i,\mathfrak{A}}\mathscr{P}[G]$ if and only if $\langle X \rangle \in F_P(i)$.

(10') If ϕ is a sentence of L, then $\square\phi$ is true$_{i,\mathfrak{A}}$ if and only if ϕ is true$_{j,\mathfrak{A}}$ for all $j \in \mathbf{D}A$.

(11') If G is an n-place predicate variable, $\mathscr{P}$ a predicate constant of L of type $\langle n \rangle$, and ϕ a formula of L of which the only free variable is G, then $\mathscr{P}[TG\phi]$ is true$_{i,\mathfrak{A}}$ if and only if either there is exactly one n-place $\mathbf{D}A$-predicate X of members of U such that X sat$_{i,\mathfrak{A}}\phi$, and that predicate is in $F_{\mathscr{P}}(i)$; or it is not the case that there is exactly one such predicate, and the empty predicate (that is, $\mathbf{D}A \times \{\Lambda\}$) is in $F_{\mathscr{P}}(i)$.

(12′) If G is a zero-place predicate variable and X a $\langle DA \rangle$-predicate, then X sat$_{i,\mathfrak{A}}G[$ $]$ if and only if the empty sequence is a member of $X(i)$ (hence, if and only if $X(i) = \{\Lambda\}$).

In view of (8′), predicate variables range over predicates of possible individuals. In view of (10′), $\square$ should be regarded as the *standard* necessity operator. In view of (8′) and earlier remarks, zero-place predicate variables range over propositions; accordingly, we may, by (12′), read $G[$ $]$ as 'the proposition G is true'.

Quantification over individual concepts and over relations (in the extensional sense) is lacking, but its effect can nevertheless be achieved. Let $\langle A, F \rangle$ be a possible interpretation for an intensional language, and let U be the union of the sets A_i for $i \in DA$. By an *individual concept* of $\langle A, F \rangle$ is understood a function from DA into U. But individual concepts of $\langle A, F \rangle$ can be identified with $\langle DA, U \rangle$-predicates satisfying the formula

$$\square \mathrm{V} u \, \Lambda v (G[v] \leftrightarrow v = u).$$

Further, as J. A. W. Kamp has observed, $\langle U, U \rangle$-relations can be identified with $\langle DA, U, U \rangle$-predicates satisfying the formula

$$\Lambda u \wedge v \, (\square G[u, v] \vee \square \neg \, G[u, \, v]);$$

and a similar identification can be performed for relations of more or fewer places.

Let us now introduce precise definitions having Criteria (1)–(12′) as consequences. We assume that $\mathfrak{A}$ is a possible interpretation for an intensional language L, $\mathfrak{A} = \langle A, F, \rangle$, U is the union of the sets A_j for $j \in DA$, and $i \in DA$. We can no longer regard simple infinite sequences as assigning values to variables; the presence of variables of various sorts requires the consideration of *double* sequences in which one of the indices determines the sort of variable in question. In particular, let us understand by a *system* associated with $\mathfrak{A}$ a function x having as its domain the sets of pairs $\langle n, k \rangle$ for which n is a natural number and k an integer ≥ -1, and such that whenever $\langle n, k \rangle$ is such a pair, either $k = -1$ and $x(\langle n, k \rangle) \in U$, or $k \geq 0$ and $x(\langle n, k \rangle)$ is a k-place DA-predicate of members of U. We assume that S is the set of all systems associated with $\mathfrak{A}$; as is customary, we shall understand by $x_{n,k}$ the function value $x(\langle n, k\rangle)$. In addition, we assume that n, k are natural numbers; and if x is a function, we understand by x_b^a the function obtained from x by substituting b for the original value of x for the argument a, that is, the function $(x - \{\langle a, x(a)\rangle\}) \cup \{\langle a, b\rangle\}$.

The *extension* of a *term* or *formula* is introduced by a single recursion.

Definition IX. (1) If c is an individual constant of L, then $\text{Ext}_{i,\mathfrak{A}}(c)$ is that function H with domain S such that, for all $x \in S$, $H(x) = F_c(i)$.

(2) $\text{Ext}_{i,\mathfrak{A}}(v_n)$ is that function H with domain S such that, for all $x \in S$, $H(x) = x_{n,-1}$.

(3) $\text{Ext}_{i,\mathfrak{A}}(G_{n,k})$ is that function H with domain S such that, for all $x \in S$, $H(x) = x_{n,k}$.

(4) If ϕ is a formula of L, then $\text{Ext}_{i,\mathfrak{A}}(\mathsf{T}G_{n,k}\phi)$ is that function H with domain S such that, for all $x \in S$, either $\{H(x)\} = \{Y : x_Y^{\langle n,k\rangle} \in \text{Ext}_{i,\mathfrak{A}}(\phi)\}$, or there is no Z for which $\{Z\} = \{Y : x_Y^{\langle n,k\rangle} \in \text{Ext}_{i,\mathfrak{A}}(\phi)\}$, and $H(x)$ is $\mathbf{D}A \times \{\Lambda\}$.

(5) If ζ is an individual constant of L or an individual variable, then $\text{Ext}_{i,\mathfrak{A}}(\mathsf{E}[\zeta])$ is $\{x : x \in S \text{ and } (\text{Ext}_{i,\mathfrak{A}}(\zeta))(x) \in A_i\}$.

(6) If each of ζ, η is either an individual constant of L or an individual variable, then $\text{Ext}_{i,\mathfrak{A}}(\zeta = \eta)$ is $\{x : x \in S \text{ and } (\text{Ext}_{i,\mathfrak{A}}(\zeta))(x)$ is identical with $(\text{Ext}_{i,\mathfrak{A}}(\eta))(x)\}$.

(7) If η is an n-place predicate variable or a term $\mathsf{T}G\phi$ (with G an n-place predicate variable), and each of $\zeta_0, \ldots, \zeta_{n-1}$ is an individual constant of L or an individual variable, then $\text{Ext}_{i,\mathfrak{A}}(\eta[\zeta_0, \ldots, \zeta_{n-1}])$ is $\{x : x \in S \text{ and } \langle(\text{Ext}_{i,\mathfrak{A}}(\zeta_0))(x), \ldots, (\text{Ext}_{i,\mathfrak{A}}(\zeta_{n-1}))(x)\rangle \in (\text{Ext}_{i,\mathfrak{A}}(\eta))(x)(i)\}$.

(8) If P is a predicate constant of L of type $\langle s_0, \ldots, s_{n-1}\rangle$ and, for each $i < n$, either $s_i \geqslant 0$ and ζ_i is either an s_i-place predicate variable or a term $\mathsf{T}G\phi$ in which G is an s_i-place predicate variable and ϕ a formula of L, or $s_i = -1$ and ζ_i is an individual constant of L or an individual variable, then $\text{Ext}_{i,\mathfrak{A}}(P[\zeta_0, \ldots, \zeta_{n-1}])$ is $\{x : x \in S \text{ and } \langle(\text{Ext}_{i,\mathfrak{A}}(\zeta_0))(x), \ldots, (\text{Ext}_{i,\mathfrak{A}}(\zeta_{n-1}))(x)\rangle \in F_P(i)\}$.

(9) If ϕ, ψ are formulas of L, then $\text{Ext}_{i,\mathfrak{A}}(\neg \phi)$ is $S - \text{Ext}_{i,\mathfrak{A}}(\phi)$, and similarly for the other sentential connectives.

(10) If ϕ is a formula of L, then $\text{Ext}_{i,\mathfrak{A}}(\mathsf{V} v_n\phi)$ is $\{x : x \in S \text{ and, for}$

some $y \in U$, the system $x^{\langle n,\, \overline{y}^{1} \rangle} \in \mathrm{Ext}_{i,\mathfrak{A}}(\phi)\}$, and similarly for $\bigwedge v_n \phi$.

(11) If ϕ is a formula of L, then $\mathrm{Ext}_{i,\mathfrak{A}}(\bigvee G_{n,k}\phi)$ is $\{x : x \in S$ and, for some k-place $\mathbf{D}A$-predicate Y of members of U, the system $x^{\langle n,k \rangle}_Y \in \mathrm{Ext}_{i,\mathfrak{A}}(\phi)\}$, and similarly for $\bigwedge G_{n,k}\phi$.

(12) If ϕ is a formula of L, then $\mathrm{Ext}_{i,\mathfrak{A}}(\square \phi)$ is $\{x : x \in S$ and, for all $j \in \mathbf{D}A, x \in \mathrm{Ext}_{j,\mathfrak{A}}(\phi)\}$.

Definition X. If ϕ is a sentence of L, then ϕ is true$_{i,\mathfrak{A}}$ if and only if $\mathrm{Ext}_{i,\mathfrak{A}}(\phi) = S$.

Definition XI. If ϕ is a formula of L with exactly one free variable, then y sat$_{i,\mathfrak{A}}\phi$ if and only if either there is a natural number n such that the free variable of ϕ is v_n and there exists $x \in \mathrm{Ext}_{i,\mathfrak{A}}(\phi)$ such that $x_{n,-1} = y$, or there are natural numbers n, k such that the free variable of ϕ is $G_{n,k}$ and there exists $x \in \mathrm{Ext}_{i,\mathfrak{A}}(\phi)$ such that $x_{n,k} = y$.

Definition XII. If ϕ is a term or formula of L, then $\mathrm{Int}_{\mathfrak{A}}(\phi)$, or the *intension* of ϕ with respect to $\mathfrak{A}$, is that function H with domain $\mathbf{D}A$ such that, for each $i \in \mathbf{D}A$, $H(i) = \mathrm{Ext}_{i,\mathfrak{A}}(\phi)$.

Definition XIII. A sentence ϕ is a *logical consequence* (in the sense of intensional logic) of a set Γ of sentences if and only if for every intensional language L and all $\mathfrak{A}, A, F, i$, if $\mathfrak{A} = \langle A, F \rangle$, $\mathfrak{A}$ is a possible interpretation for L, $i \in \mathbf{D}A$, $\Gamma \cup \{\phi\}$ is a set of sentences of L, and for every $\psi \in \Gamma$, ψ is true$_{i,\mathfrak{A}}$, then ϕ is true$_{i,\mathfrak{A}}$. A sentence is *logically true* if and only if it is a logical consequence of the empty set. A sentence ϕ is *logically equivalent* to a sentence ψ if and only if the sentence $(\phi \leftrightarrow \psi)$ is logically true.

The remarks about extensions and intensions made in connection with pragmatic languages continue to apply here, with infinite sequences everywhere replaced by systems. Further, Criteria (1)–(12′) are immediate consequences of Definitions IX–XI.

It was said earlier that descriptive phrases of the sort we admit, that is, descriptive phrases involving predicate variables, are eliminable. We can now make a more precise statement: if ϕ is any sentence of an intensional language L, then there is a sentence of L without descriptive phrases that is logically equivalent to ϕ. For instance, if ϕ is

$$\mathscr{P}[\mathbf{T}G\mathscr{2}[G]],$$

where G is a one-place predicate variable and $\mathscr{P}$, $\mathscr{Q}$ are predicate constants of type $\langle 1 \rangle$, then ϕ is logically equivalent to

$$\bigvee G(\mathscr{Q}[G] \wedge \bigwedge H(\mathscr{Q}[H] \to \Box \wedge x(H[x] \leftrightarrow G[x]))$$
$$\wedge \mathscr{P}[G]) \vee (\neg \bigvee G(\mathscr{Q}[G] \wedge \bigwedge H(\mathscr{Q}[H] \to$$
$$\Box \wedge x(H[x] \leftrightarrow G[x]))) \wedge \bigvee G(\Box \wedge x \neg G[x] \wedge \mathscr{P}[G])).$$

The convenience of descriptive phrases is found in the construction of names of specific predicates. For instance, we can distinguish as follows expressions designating properties or two-place predicates expressed by particular formulas (with respect to places marked by particular individual variables): if ϕ is a formula and u, v are distinct individual variables, understand by $\hat{u}\phi$ (which may be read 'the property of u such that ϕ') the term $\mathsf{T}G \wedge u \Box(G[u] \leftrightarrow \phi)$, and by $\hat{u}\hat{v}\phi$ (read 'the predicate of u and v such that ϕ') the term $\mathsf{T}H \wedge u \wedge v \Box(H[u, v] \leftrightarrow \phi)$, where G, H are respectively the first one-place and the first two-place predicate variables not occurring in ϕ. We can of course proceed upward to three variables or more; but—and this is more interesting—we can proceed downward to the empty sequence of variables. In particular, if ϕ is any formula, understand by $^\wedge\phi$ the term $\mathsf{T}G\Box(G[\ ] \leftrightarrow \phi)$; this term designates the proposition expressed by the formula ϕ, may be read 'the proposition that ϕ' or simply 'that ϕ', and serves the purposes for which the term '$\bar{\phi}$' of Kaplan [11] was constructed.

It is clear from Definition IX that sentences of intensional languages, unlike those of pragmatic languages, may contain indirect components—that is, components of which the *intension* must be taken into account in determining the *extension* of the compound—of only one sort; and these are components standing within the scope of the particular operator $\Box$. An equivalent construction would have taken the indirect context $^\wedge\phi$ rather than $\Box\phi$ as basic, together with the notion of identity of propositions; we could then have defined $\Box\phi$ as $^\wedge\phi = {}^\wedge\wedge v_0 v_0 = v_0$.

Now let us see how to accommodate operators within intensional languages. (The observation that this can be done, as well as the present way of doing it, is due jointly to J. A. W. Kamp and me.) Suppose that L is any pragmatic language and $\langle A, F, R \rangle$ any possible interpretation for it. Let the operators N of L be mapped biuniquely onto predicate constants N' of type $\langle 0 \rangle$. Let L' be an intensional language of which the individual constants are those of L, and the predicate constants are those of L together with the symbols N', for N an operator of L. Let F' be such that $\langle A, F' \rangle$ is a possible interpretation for the intensional language L', $F \subseteq F'$, and for each operator N of L and each $i \in \mathbf{D}A$, $F'_{N'}(i)$ is $\{\langle U \rangle : U$ is a $\langle \mathbf{D}A \rangle$-predicate and $\langle i, \{j : j \in \mathbf{D}A$ and $U(j) = \{\Lambda\}\}\rangle \in R_N\}$. Then we can easily prove the following: if ϕ is a sentence of L, ϕ' is obtained from ϕ by replacing each subformula of the form $N\psi$, where N is an operator of L and ψ a formula of L, by

$$\bigvee G(\Box(G[\ ] \leftrightarrow \psi) \wedge N'[G]),$$

and $i \in \mathbf{D}A$, then ϕ is true with respect to i and the *pragmatic* interpretation $\langle A, F, R \rangle$ if and only if ϕ' is true with respect to i and the *intensional* interpretation $\langle A, F' \rangle$.

We thus have a reduction of pragmatics to intensional logic which amounts, roughly speaking, to treating *one-place modalities* (that is, relations between points of reference and sets of points of reference) as properties of propositions. Conversely, every property of propositions corresponds to a one-place modality. Indeed, if $\langle A, F \rangle$ is an interpretation for an intensional language and $\mathscr{X}$ is a property of propositions with respect to $\langle A, F \rangle$ (that is, a $\langle \mathbf{D}A, U \rangle$-predicate, where U is the set of all $\langle \mathbf{D}A \rangle$-predicates), then the corresponding one-place modality will be the set of pairs $\langle i, J \rangle$ such that $i \in \mathbf{D}A$ and there exists $Y \in \mathscr{X}(i)$ such that $J = \{j : j \in \mathbf{D}A$ and $Y(j) = \{\Lambda\}\}$.

Let us be a little more precise about the sense in which intensional logic can be *partially* reduced to pragmatics. Let L be an intensional language of which the predicate constants are all of type $\langle 0 \rangle$ or $\langle s_0, \ldots, s_{n-1} \rangle$, where $s_p = -1$ for all $p < n$, and let $\langle A, F \rangle$ be any interpretation for L. Let the predicate constants $\mathscr{P}$ of L having type $\langle 0 \rangle$ be mapped biuniquely onto operators $\mathscr{P}'$, and let N be an operator not among these. Let L' be a pragmatic language of which the individual constants are those of L, the predicate constants are those of L not having type $\langle 0 \rangle$, and the operators consist of N together with the symbols $\mathscr{P}'$ for $\mathscr{P}$ a predicate constant of L of type $\langle 0 \rangle$. Let F', R

be such that $\langle A, F', R \rangle$ is a possible interpretation for the pragmatic language L', $F' \subseteq F$, R_N is the set of pairs $\langle i, J \rangle$ such that $i \in \mathbf{D}A$ and $J = \mathbf{D}A$, and for each predicate $\mathscr{P}$ of L of type $\langle 0 \rangle$, $R_{\mathscr{P}'}$ is the set of pairs $\langle i, J \rangle$ such that $i \in \mathbf{D}A$ and there exists $Y \in F_{\mathscr{P}}(i)$ such that $J = \{j : j \in \mathbf{D}A$ and $Y(j) = \{\Lambda\}\}$. Then we can easily show that if $i \in \mathbf{D}A$, ϕ is a sentence of L, ϕ' is obtained from ϕ by replacing each subformula $\mathscr{P}[^{\frown}\psi]$, where $\mathscr{P}$ is a predicate constant of type $\langle 0 \rangle$ and ψ is a formula of L, by $\mathscr{P}'\psi$, and ϕ' is a sentence of the pragmatic language L' (this imposes certain limitations on the form of ϕ), then ϕ is true with respect to i and the *intensional* interpretation $\langle A, F \rangle$ if and only if ϕ' is true with respect to i and the *pragmatic* interpretation $\langle A, F', R \rangle$.

The fact that one-place modalities coincide in a sense with properties of propositions is what lends interest to those modalities and provides intuitive sanction for using them to interpret operators. (A completely analogous remark would apply to many-place modalities and many-place operators if these had been included in our system of pragmatics.) The relations among various systems can be roughly expressed as follows. If we understand by *modal logic* that part of intensional logic which concerns formulas containing no predicate variables, then intensional logic can be regarded as *second-order modal logic*, and pragmatics is in a sense contained in it; indeed, pragmatics can be regarded as a first-order reduction of part of intensional logic.

Nothing of course compels us to stop at *second-order* modal logic. We could extend the present construction in a fairly obvious way to obtain various higher-order systems, even of transfinite levels. Only the second-order system, however, is required for the rather direct philosophical applications for which the present paper is intended to provide the groundwork.

For example, belief can be handled in a natural way within intensional logic. Let L be an intensional language containing a predicate constant $\mathscr{B}$ of type $\langle -1, 0 \rangle$. If $\langle A, F \rangle$ is a possible interpretation for L, we now regard the domain of A as the set of all possible worlds, A_i as the set of objects existing within the possible world i, and $F_c(i)$ as the extension of the nonlogical constant c within the world i. Then a $\langle DA \rangle$-predicate can reasonably be regarded as a proposition in the full philosophical sense, not merely the extended sense considered earlier, and the intension of a sentence with respect to $\langle A, F \rangle$ as the proposition expressed by that sentence (under the interpretation $\langle A, F \rangle$). We regard $\mathscr{B}$ as abbreviating 'believes', and accordingly regard $F_{\mathscr{B}}(i)$ as the set of pairs $\langle x, U \rangle$ such that x believes the proposition U in the possible world i. The proposal to regard belief as an empirical relation between individuals and propositions is not new. A number of difficulties connected with that proposal are, however, dispelled by considering it within the present framework; in particular, there remains no problem either of quantifying into belief contexts or of iteration of belief.[10] Consider the assertion 'there exists an object of which Jones believes that Robinson believes that it is perfectly spherical'. This involves both iteration and quantification into indirect contexts, but is represented in L (with respect to $\langle A, F \rangle$) by the simple sentence

$$\bigvee x(\mathsf{E}[x] \wedge \mathscr{B}[J, \,^\frown\mathscr{B}[R, \,^\frown S[x]]]),$$

where J and R are individual constants regarded as designating Jones and Robinson respectively and S is a predicate constant regarded as expressing the property of being perfectly spherical; or, if we prefer to avoid descriptive phrases, by the logically equivalent sentence

$$\bigvee x \bigvee G(\mathsf{E}[x] \wedge \mathscr{B}[J, G] \wedge \Box(G[\;] \leftrightarrow \bigvee H(\mathscr{B}[R, H] \wedge$$
$$\Box(H[\;] \leftrightarrow S[x])))).$$

Two objections might be raised. In the first place, what empirical sense can be assigned to belief as a relation between persons and propositions? As much, I feel, as is customary with empirical predicates. One can give confirmatory criteria for belief, though probably not a definition, in behavioristic terms. I present two unrefined and incompletely analyzed examples:

   (1) If ϕ is any sentence expressing the proposition G, then the

---

[10] Problems of the first sort have been pointed out many times by Quine, for instance, in Quine [20]; and problems of the second sort arose in connection with Kaplan [11], the system of which appeared incapable of being extended in such a way as adequately to accommodate iteration of belief.

assertion that x assents to ϕ confirms (though certainly not conclusively) the assertion that x believes G.

(2) If ϕ is any formula with exactly one free variable that expresses the property H (in the sense that, for all $i \in \mathbf{D}A$, $H(i)$ is the set of possible individuals satisfying ϕ with respect to i and a given interpretation), then the assertion that x assents to ϕ when y is pointed out to x confirms (though again not conclusively) the assertion that x believes the proposition that $H[y]$.

A second objection might concern the fact that if ϕ and ψ are any logically equivalent sentences, then the sentence

$$\mathcal{B}[J, {}^\frown\phi] \to \mathcal{B}[J, {}^\frown\psi]$$

is logically true, though it might under certain circumstances appear unreasonable. One might reply that the consequence in question seems unavoidable if propositions are indeed to be taken as the objects of belief, that it sheds the appearance of unreasonableness if (1) above is seriously maintained, and that its counterintuitive character can perhaps be traced to the existence of another notion of belief, of which the objects are sentences or, in some cases, complexes consisting in part of open formulas.[11]

As another example, let us consider the verb 'seems', as in

u seems to be perfectly spherical to v.

We let L be as above, except that it is now to contain a predicate constant $\mathcal{S}$ of type $\langle -1, 1, -1 \rangle$; if $\langle A, F \rangle$ is a possible interpretation for L and $i \in \mathbf{D}A$, $F_{\mathcal{S}}(i)$ is to be regarded as the set of triples $\langle x, U, y \rangle$ such that, in the possible world i, x seems to y to have the property U. The formula displayed above would then be represented in L by the formula

$$\mathcal{S}[u, \hat{w}S[w], v].$$

We have made no attempt to *define* 'believes' or 'seems'. But that need not prevent us from clarifying the logical status

---

[11] A partial treatment of such a notion may be found in Montague and Kalish [18]. The discussion there is, however, incomplete in that it fails to provide for such cases as those for which the confirmatory criterion (2) was designed—cases in which beliefs may concern objects for which the believer has no name.

of these verbs and the notions of logical truth and logical consequence for discourse involving them; and this would appear to be the main requirement for the evaluation of a number of philosophical arguments. The philosophical utility of intensional logic, however, is not in my opinion thereby exhausted; more important applications can be found in other areas, notably metaphysics and epistemology, and are to some extent discussed in Montague [15].

It is perhaps not inappropriate to sketch here an intermediate system, due to Dana Scott and me, which may be called *extended pragmatics*.[12] The symbols of an *extended pragmatic language* are drawn from the following categories:

(1) the logical constants of pragmatics,

(2) parentheses, brackets, commas,

(3) individual variables,

(4) individual constants,

(5) operators of degree $\langle m, n, p \rangle$, for all natural numbers m, n, p.

The set of *formulas* of such a language L is the smallest set Γ satisfying certain expected conditions, together with the condition that

$$N u_0 \ldots u_{m-1} [\zeta_0, \ldots, \zeta_{n-1}, \phi_0, \ldots, \phi_{p-1}]$$

is in Γ whenever N is an operator of L having degree $\langle m, n, p \rangle$, $u_0, \ldots, u_{m-1}$ are distinct individual variables, each of $\zeta_0, \ldots, \zeta_{n-1}$ is either an individual constant of L or an individual variable, and $\phi_0, \ldots, \phi_{p-1}$ are in Γ. A *possible interpretation for an extended pragmatic language* L is a pair $\langle A, F \rangle$ satisfying conditions (1), (2), (4) of Definition I, and in addition such that (3′) F is a function whose domain is the set of individual constants and operators of L, and (5′) whenever N is an operator of L of degree $\langle m, n, p \rangle$, F_N is a $\langle \mathbf{D}A, U_0, \ldots, U_{n-1}, V_0, \ldots, V_{p-1} \rangle$-predicate, where each U_i (for $i < n$) is the union of the sets A_j

---

[12] The outline of extended pragmatics did not occur in the original version of this paper, but was added after I had seen a treatment of modal logic developed by Scott in June, 1967, and had discussed it with him and David Kaplan. The principal difference between Scott's system and extended pragmatics is that in the former no allowance is made for quantification over individuals, but only over individual concepts.

for $j \in \mathbf{D}A$, and each V_i (for $i < p$) is the set of m-place $\mathbf{D}A$-predicates of members of the union of the sets A_j (for $j \in \mathbf{D}A$). The *extension* of an individual variable, an individual constant, or a formula with respect to a possible interpretation $\mathfrak{A}$ having the form $\langle A, F \rangle$ and at a point of reference $i \in \mathbf{D}A$ is characterized as in Definition II, together with a recursion consisting of clauses (1), (2), (4), (5) of Definition III, together with the following clause: if N is an operator of L of degree $\langle m, n, p \rangle$, $k_0, \ldots, k_{m-1}$ are distinct natural numbers, each of $\zeta_0, \ldots, \zeta_{n-1}$ is either an individual constant of L or an individual variable, and $\phi_0, \ldots, \phi_{p-1}$ are formulas of L, then $\mathrm{Ext}_{i,\mathfrak{A}}(Nv_{k_0} \ldots v_{k_{m-1}}[\zeta_0, \ldots, \zeta_{n-1}, \phi_0, \ldots, \phi_{p-1}])$ is $\{x : x \in U^{\omega}$ and $\langle \mathrm{Ext}_{i,\mathfrak{A}}(\zeta_0)(x), \ldots, \mathrm{Ext}_{i,\mathfrak{A}}(\zeta_{n-1})(x), Y_{0,x}, \ldots, Y_{p-1,x} \rangle \in F_N(i)\}$, where, for each $q < p$ and $x \in U^{\omega}$, $Y_{q,x}$ is $\{\langle j, \{\langle y_0, \ldots, y_{m-1} \rangle : x_{y_0}^{k_0} \ldots {}_{y_{m-1}}^{k_{m-1}} \in \mathrm{Ext}_{j,\mathfrak{A}}(\phi_q)\} \rangle : j \in \mathbf{D}A\}$.

Thus, in particular, if N is an operator of degree $\langle 0, n, 0 \rangle$, then $\mathrm{Ext}_{i,\mathfrak{A}}(N[\zeta_0, \ldots, \zeta_{n-1}])$ is $\{x : x \in U^{\omega}$ and $\langle \mathrm{Ext}_{i,\mathfrak{A}}(\zeta_0)(x), \ldots, \mathrm{Ext}_{i,\mathfrak{A}}(\zeta_{n-1})(x) \rangle \in F_N(i)\}$, and N will play the role of an n-place predicate constant; and if N has degree $\langle 0, 0, 1 \rangle$, then $\mathrm{Ext}_{i,\mathfrak{A}}(N[\phi])$ is $\{x : x \in U^{\omega}$ and $\langle \{\langle j, \{\Lambda\} \rangle : j \in \mathbf{D}A$ and $x \in \mathrm{Ext}_{j,\mathfrak{A}}(\phi)\} \cup \{\langle j, \Lambda \rangle : j \in \mathbf{D}A$ and $x \notin \mathrm{Ext}_{j,\mathfrak{A}}(\phi)\} \rangle \in F_N(i)\}$, and N will accordingly serve as a substitute for a (one-place) operator of pragmatics. Further, an operator of extended pragmatics of arbitrary degree $\langle m, n, p \rangle$ can be replaced within intensional logic by a predicate constant of type $\langle s_0, \ldots, s_{n-1}, t_0, \ldots, t_{p-1} \rangle$, where each s_i (for $i < n$) is -1 and each t_i (for $i < p$) is m.

Thus, in a sense, pragmatics is contained in extended pragmatics, which is in turn contained in intensional logic. We can regard extended pragmatics as providing another first-order reduction, more comprehensive than that supplied by ordinary pragmatics, of part of intensional logic. For instance, if $\mathscr{B}$ is, like 'believes', a predicate constant of type $\langle -1, 0 \rangle$ of intensional logic, we could replace $\mathscr{B}$ by an operator $\mathscr{B}'$ of degree $\langle 0, 1, 1 \rangle$ (of extended pragmatics) and express the assertion

$$\mathscr{B}[x, {}^{\smallfrown}\phi]$$

equivalently (under a suitable interpretation) by

$$\mathscr{B}'[x, \phi].$$

Similarly, if $\mathscr{S}$ is, like 'seems', a predicate constant of type $\langle 1, 1, -1 \rangle$, we could replace $\mathscr{S}$ by an operator $\mathscr{S}'$ of degree $\langle 1, 2, 1 \rangle$ and express the assertion

$$\mathscr{S}[u, \hat{w}\phi, v]$$

by

$$\mathscr{S}'w[u, v, \phi].$$

(It should be clear from this example, as well as from the general definition of extension, that the m variables immediately following an operator of degree $\langle m, n, p \rangle$ are to be regarded as *bound*.) There is of course no contention that all formulas of intensional logic involving $\mathscr{B}$ or $\mathscr{S}$ can be paraphrased within extended pragmatics; for instance, the assertion 'Jones believes something which Robinson does not believe' does not correspond to any formula of extended pragmatics.

We may now consider various technical properties of the three systems introduced in this paper. Notice first that the compactness theorem does not hold for intensional logic. In other words, let us call a set of sentences *satisfiable* if there is a nonempty interpretation $\mathfrak{A}$ and a point of reference i of $\mathfrak{A}$ such that all sentences in the set are true with respect to i and $\mathfrak{A}$; then it is not the case that for every set Γ of sentences of intensional logic,

(3)   if every finite subset of Γ is satisfiable, then Γ is satisfiable.

This is obvious in view of the reduction, at which we hinted earlier, of ordinary second-order logic to intensional logic, together with the well-known failure of the compactness theorem for second-order logic. On the other hand, let us call ϕ a *predicative* sentence if ϕ is a sentence of intensional logic not containing the descriptive symbol and such that (1) whenever G is a predicate variable, ψ is a formula, and $\wedge G\psi$ is a subformula of ϕ, there are $\mathscr{P}, \zeta_0, \ldots, \zeta_n, \chi$ such that $\mathscr{P}$ is a predicate constant, each ζ_i (for $i \leqslant n$) is either an individual constant, an individual variable, or a predicate variable, χ is a formula, ψ is the formula $(\mathscr{P}[\zeta_0, \ldots, \zeta_n] \rightarrow \chi)$, and G is ζ_i for some $i \leqslant n$; and (2) whenever G is a predicate variable, ψ is a formula, and $\vee\, G\psi$ is a subformula of ϕ, there are $\mathscr{P}, \zeta_0, \ldots, \zeta_n, \chi$ satisfying the same conditions as in (1) except that ψ is now to be $(\mathscr{P}[\zeta_0, \ldots, \zeta_n] \wedge \chi)$. For the *predicative* sentences of intensional logic we do have a compactness theorem; in other words, (3) holds for every set Γ of predicative sentences.[13] From this assertion we can infer full compactness theorems for pragmatics and extended pragmatics, in other words, the assertion that (3) holds for *every* set Γ of sentences of pragmatics and for *every* set Γ of sentences of extended pragmatics; we use reductions of the sort sketched above of those disciplines to intensional logic and notice that the reductions can be performed in such a way as to result exclusively in predicative sentences.

Similar remarks apply to the recursive enumerability of the logical truths of the three systems we have considered. We must, however, say a word about the meaning of recursive enumerability in this context. We have not required that the symbols from which our languages are constructed form a countable set; it would thus be inappropriate to speak of a Gödel numbering of all expressions. We may, however, suppose that a Gödel numbering satisfying the usual conditions has been given for a certain denumerable *subset S* of the set of all expressions; we may further suppose that all logical constants, the parentheses and brackets, the comma, all individual variables, all predicate variables, infinitely many n-place predicate constants (for each n), infinitely many predicate constants of each type, infinitely many one-place operators, and infinitely many operators of each degree are in S, and that S is closed under the concatenation of two expressions. When we say that a set of expressions is recursive or recursively enumerable we shall understand that it is a subset of S which is recursive or recursively enumerable under our fixed Gödel numbering.

Let us identify a language with the set of symbols it contains; we may accordingly speak of recursive languages. It is then easily shown, by the same methods as those sketched in connection

---

[13] This assertion, the formulation of which is partly due to J. A. W. Kamp, can be shown rather easily on the basis of the completeness theorem for ω-order logic of Henkin [10], and is not peculiar to *second*-order modal logic: indeed, the compactness theorem would hold for the predicative sentences of a higher-order modal logic containing variables of all finite levels.

with compactness, that (1) there are recursive intensional languages of which the sets of logical truths are not recursively enumerable; (2) if L is any recursive intensional language, then the set of predicative sentences of L which are logically true is recursively enumerable; (3) if L is any recursive pragmatic language, then the set of all logical truths of L is recursively enumerable; (4) if L is any recursive extended pragmatic language, then the set of all logical truths of L is recursively enumerable.

On the basis of (2)–(4), together with a theorem of Craig [6], we can of course show for each of the three sets mentioned in (2)–(4) the existence of a recursive subset which axiomatizes the set in question under the rule of detachment. It would be desirable, however, to find natural and simple recursive axiomatizations of these sets. Of the three problems that thus arise one has been definitely solved: David Kaplan has recently axiomatized the set of logical truths of (ordinary) pragmatics. He has also axiomatized the set of logical truths of a system closely resembling extended pragmatics; and it is likely that when his axiomatization becomes available, it will be capable of adaptation to extended pragmatics. The problem, however, of axiomatizing predicative intensional logic remains open.

In connection with problems of axiomatizability it is perhaps not inappropriate to mention that all three of our systems are purely referential in one sense, specifically, in the sense that

$$(4) \quad \wedge u \wedge v \, (u = v \to (\phi \leftrightarrow \phi'))$$

is logically true whenever u, v are individual variables, ϕ is a formula of the language in question, and ϕ' is obtained from ϕ by replacing a free occurrence of u by a free occurrence of v, but *not* purely referential in another sense: it is not generally true that whenever c, d are individual constants, ϕ is a formula of one of the languages under consideration, and ϕ' is obtained from ϕ by replacing an occurrence of c by d, the formula

$$(5) \quad c = d \to (\phi \leftrightarrow \phi')$$

is logically true. It follows, of course, that the principle of universal instantiation does not always hold; it holds when one instantiates to variables but not in general when one instantiates to individual constants.

There is rather general (though not universal) agreement that (5) ought not to be regarded as logically true when modal and belief contexts are present; for consider the following familiar example of (5):

> If the Morning Star = the Evening Star, then Jones believes that the Morning Star appears in the morning if and only if Jones believes that the Evening Star appears in the morning.

This viewpoint has led some philosophers, however, to reject also the logical truth of (4). The desirability of maintaining (4) as a logical truth but not (5) was, to my knowledge, first explicitly argued in the 1955 talk reported in Montague [14], but has more recently been advanced in Føllesdal [8] and Cocchiarella [4], and in addresses of Professors Richmond Thomason and Dagfinn Føllesdal.

Let me conclude with a few historial remarks concerning intensional logic. The first serious and detailed attempt to construct such a logic appears to be that of Church [3]. Carnap had independently proposed in conversation that intensional objects be identified with functions from possible worlds to extensions of appropriate sorts, but that, in distinction from the later proposal of Kripke adopted in the present paper, possible worlds be identified with models. David Kaplan, in his dissertation Kaplan [11], pointed out certain deficiencies of Church's system, presented a modified version designed to correct these, and supplied a model theory for the revised system based on Carnap's proposal. Kaplan's system, however, suffered from the drawback indicated above involving the iteration of empirical properties of propositions; the difficulty stemmed largely from Carnap's suggestion that possible worlds be identified with models. More recent attempts by Charles Howard, David Kaplan, and Dana Scott (some preceding and some following the talk reported by the main body of the present paper) have avoided this difficulty but have shared with Kaplan [11] the drawback of not allowing unrestricted quantification over ordinary individuals. Without such quantification, however, I do not believe that one can treat ordinary language in a natural way or meet adequately Quine's objections to quantification into indirect contexts.

REFERENCES

1. Anscombe, E. The Intentionality of Sensation: A Grammatical Feature. In R. Butler (ed.), *Analytical Philosophy, Second Series.* Oxford, 1965.
2. Bar-Hillel, Y. Indexical Expressions. *Mind* 63:359–79 (1954).
3. Church, A. A Formulation of the Logic of Sense and Denotation. In P. Henle, H. Kallen, and S. Langer (eds.), *Structure, Method, and Meaning.* New York, 1951.
4. Cocchiarella, N. A Completeness Theorem for Tense Logic. *Journal of Symbolic Logic* 31:689–90 (1966).
5. —. Tense Logic: A Study of Temporal Reference. Dissertation, University of California at Los Angeles, 1966.
6. Craig, W. On Axiomatizability within a System. *Journal of Symbolic Logic* 18:30–32 (1953).
7. Feigl, H. and W. Sellars. *Readings in Philosophical Analysis.* New York, 1949.
8. Føllesdal, D. Referential Opacity and Modal Logic. Dissertation, Harvard University, 1961.
9. Frege, G. Über Sinn und Bedeutung. *Zeitschrift für Philosophie und philosophische Kritik* 100:25–50 (1892). English translation in Feigl and Sellars [7], cited above.
10. Henkin, L. Completeness in the Theory of Types. *Journal of Symbolic Logic* 15:81–91 (1950).
11. Kaplan, D. Foundations of Intensional Logic. Dissertation, University of California at Los Angeles, 1964.
12. Kripke, S. Semantical Considerations on Modal Logic. *Acta Philosophica Fennica* 16:83–94 (1963).
13. Montague, R. Well-founded Relations: Generalizations of Principles of Induction and Recursion. *Bulletin of the American Mathematical Society* 61:442 (1955).
14. —. Logical Necessity, Physical Necessity, Ethics, and Quantifiers. *Inquiry* 4:259–69 (1960).
15. —. On the Nature of Certain Philosophical Entities. *Monist* 53:159–94 (1969). Chap. 5 in this book.
16. —. Pragmatics. In R. Klibansky (ed.), *Contemporary Philosophy: A Survey*, vol. 1. Florence, 1968. Chap. 3 in this book.

17. Montague, R. and D. Kalish. Remarks on Descriptions and Natural Deduction, I. *Archiv für mathematische Logik und Grundlagenforschung* 3:50–64 (1957).
18. —. 'That'. *Philosophical Studies* 10: 54–61 (1959). Chap. 2 in this book.
19. Morris, C. Foundations of the Theory of Signs. In *International Encyclopedia of Unified Science* 1 (1938).
20. Quine, W. *Word and Object*. Cambridge, Mass., 1960.
21. Tarski, A. Pojęcie prawdy w językach nauk dedukcyjnych (The Concept of Truth in the Languages of the Deductive Sciences). Translation in *Logic, Semantics, Metamathematics*, cited below.
22. —. Contributions to the Theory of Models, Part I. *Indagationes Mathematicae* 16:572–88 (1954) and 17:56–64 (1955).
23. —. *Logic, Semantics, Metamathematics*. Oxford, 1956.

5. On the Nature of Certain Philosophical Entities

It has been maintained that we need not tolerate such entities as pains, events, tasks, and obligations. They are indeed not required in connection with sentences like 'Jones has a pain', 'the event of the sun's rising occurred at eight', 'Jones performed at eight the task of lifting a stone', or 'Jones has the obligation to give Smith a horse', which can be paraphrased without reference to the entities in question—for instance, in the case of the second example, as 'the sun rose at eight'.

There are, however, other sentences that most of us on occasion accept and that entail the existence of such dubious epistemological, metaphysical, and ethical entities as pains, tasks, events, and obligations. I have in mind sentences like 'Jones just had a pain similar to one he had yesterday', 'not all psychological events have physiological correlates', 'God cannot perform every possible task', and 'Jones has not discharged all his obligations'. We cannot lightly dismiss sentences like these; they play a conspicuous role in philosophy, perceptual psychology, and everyday discourse. It therefore appears desirable to investigate the nature of the entities in question, construct an

Originally published in *The Monist* 53:159–94 (1960). Reprinted with permission. This paper corresponds to a talk given before the UCLA Philosophy Colloquium on February 24, 1967. I should like to express gratitude to my student, Dr. J. A. W. Kamp, who participated in discussions leading to that talk and to whom I am indebted for many valuable criticisms and suggestions, too pervasive to be mentioned specifically below; and to Professor Benson Mates, whose talk "Sense Data," given before the UCLA Philosophy Colloquium on November 18, 1966, largely provoked the present considerations. In connection with certain points mentioned below, I profited also from conversations with Professors Charles Chastain and David Lewis. Much of the work reported here was supported by National Science Foundation Grants GP-4594 and GP-7706.

exact and convenient language in which to speak of them, and analyze the pertinent notion of logical consequence. The last task would seem a necessary preliminary to the rational treatment of certain philosophical paradoxes.

To see what an *event* is, consider the sentence 'the sun rose at eight'. This can be regarded as, in a sense, made up of two linguistic components—the individual constant (or definite singular term) 'eight' and a formula (or open sentence) containing one free variable—'the sun rises at t'.[1] Now 'the sun rose at eight' expresses the assertion that a certain event occurred at eight (that is, at the moment designated by the first linguistic component of the sentence). Thus it is not unreasonable to regard the event as corresponding to the second linguistic component, the formula with one free variable. But in what sense are we to understand this correspondence? One possibility is to regard it as identity; that is to say, we might identify the event of the sun's rising with the formula 'the sun rises at t'. But this is not good; if extended to a general practice, it would not allow for the existence of inexpressible events.

Let us examine a second possibility. Another object naturally corresponding to the formula 'the sun rises at t' is a set—in particular, the set of all objects satisfying the formula. Thus we might identify the event of the sun's rising with the set of all moments at which the sun rises. Because there are sets of moments which do not correspond in this way with any formulas, we do not, as in our first attempt, exclude the possible existence of inexpressible events. But the present attempt is for another reason inadmissible; it does not allow for the existence of two different events which occur always at the same time—two different but coextensive events, we might say.

A third possibility, and one that seems to be the only reasonable suggestion, is to take as the event corresponding to a formula the property expressed by that formula. Thus the event of the sun's rising will be the property of being a moment at which the sun

---

[1] For simplicity it is best at this point to disregard the tenses of verbs, that is, to speak tenselessly, and fictitiously regard 'the sun rises at eight' and 'the sun rose at eight' as synonymous. Also, for simplicity, we may suppose time to extend over a single twelve-hour period, so that 'eight' will designate a unique moment.

rises, and events in general will form a certain class of properties of moments of time. I shall say more about the nature of properties, but this much is clear at the outset. There are inexpressible properties; and two properties are identical just in case they are coextensive in every *possible* world, not simply if they are coextensive in the actual world. Thus the two objections raised in connection with the earlier proposals do not apply here.

One advantage of identifying events with properties of moments is that it is easy to analyze the notion of occurrence. To say that an event *P occurs* at a moment *t* is simply to say that *t* possesses (or partakes of, or participates in) the property *P*.

What I have had in mind so far are events of only one kind, what we might call *instantaneous generic events*. There are other kinds, for instance, *protracted generic events* like the American presidential campaign. Such events should be identified with properties of intervals, rather than moments, of time (or more generally with properties of unions of intervals of time) and present no special problems; nevertheless, we shall avoid considering them here. Events of another kind, what we might call *instantaneous individual events*, like *a* rising of the sun, should not, however, be dismissed, and will be considered later, after the development of a certain amount of technical equipment.

Before proceeding to pains, tasks, and the like, we must consider the nature of relations, which have traditionally been construed in two ways. According to the modern mathematical use, an *n*-place relation is a set of sequences of length *n*; relations are then understood as *extensional* objects. According to an older and perhaps more philosophical use, relations are instead *intensional*, in the sense that two different relations can correspond to a single set of sequences. Relations of the latter sort are sometimes called *relations-in-intension*, and I shall use that designation for them, as well as the term 'predicate'. (I believe that the *propositional functions* of *Principia Mathematica* should be understood as predicates; but this contention, like several other exegetical hypotheses concerning that work, is not beyond controversy.) Thus predicates will not be linguistic entities; for the latter we shall reserve such terms as 'predicate constant', 'predicate variable', and 'predicate symbol'. One-place predicates will coincide with what I have called properties, and zero-place predicates with propositions.

I mention relations-in-intension in order to proceed to *tasks*, which I believe should be regarded as certain two-place relations-in-intension between persons and moments. For example, the task of lifting a stone is the predicate of lifting a stone at a given moment, that is, the relation-in-intension born by x to t just in case x lifts a stone at t. To say that x *performs* the task R at t is to say that x bears the relation-in-intension R to t. The importance of allowing for inexpressible tasks (as well as for inexpressible events) becomes evident if we consider not the task of lifting a stone but the quite different task of lifting a particular stone. (There are stones that have no names; the task of lifting any one of them will be inexpressible.)

What should we say about *pains*? They, and more generally *experiences*, are of the same ontological sort as tasks: they form a certain class of relations-in-intension between persons and moments. For example, the experience of seeing a tree is the relation-in-intension born by x to t just in case x sees a tree at t. For x to *have* the experience R at t is for x again to bear the relation-in-intension R to t. It should be observed that the basic notion of partaking of a property or predicate is expressed in ordinary English by several different verbs, depending on context; by 'perform' in the case of a task, 'have' in the case of an experience, and 'occur' in the case of an event.

Obligations can probably best be regarded as the same sort of thing as tasks and experiences, that is, as relations-in-intension between persons and moments; for instance, the obligation to give Smith a horse can be identified with the predicate expressed by 'x gives Smith a horse at t'. We should scrutinize, in this context also, the notion of partaking of a predicate. Notice that if R is an obligation, to say that x bears the relation-in-intension R to t is not to say that x *has the obligation* R at t, but rather that x *discharges* or *fulfills* the obligation R at t. But how could we say that x *has* at t *the obligation* R? This would amount to the assertion that it is *obligatory* at t that x *bear the relation-in-intension* R to some moment equal or subsequent to t.

We have thus reduced four types of entities—experiences,

events, tasks, obligations—to predicates. I leave to the reader's imagination a number of completely analogous reductions—of acts, actions, rights, responsibilities, and the like; and I shall contend below, that sense data too can be so construed. I do not pretend to have *defined* the notion of an experience, event, or the like, even in terms of the notion of a predicate. For instance, I have said that experiences form a *certain class* of two-place predicates. In other words, the property of being an experience is to be regarded as a property of two-place predicates. It is not my object to define that property; I do not imagine that all two-place predicates of persons and moments are experiences, and I have proposed no criterion for singling out those that are.

Thus I have done no more than to reduce several dubious ontological categories to one, that of predicates; and one might well question the point of applying Occam's razor here.

There are two reasons for the reductions. In the first place, predicates should not be regarded as wholly dubious. They are not much more mysterious than sets; and if we are willing to speak of possible worlds and possible individuals, we can easily say exactly what predicates are. To be more specific, let I be the set of all *possible worlds;* for each member i of I, let A_i be the set of *individuals existing in the possible world* i; and let U be the set of all *possible individuals.* Then U will include the union of all sets A_i for i in I, and may indeed coincide with it, though we need not explicitly impose such a limitation. A *property of individuals* is a function having I as its domain and subsets of U as its values. (If P is such a property and i a possible world, $P(i)$ is regarded as the set of possible individuals that partake of P in i. For example, the property of being red is the function that assigns to each possible world the set of possible individuals which in that world are red.) More generally, an *n-place predicate of individuals* is a function having I as its domain and of which the values are sets of n-place sequences of members of U. If P is a predicate of individuals and i a possible world, we regard $P(i)$ as the *extension* of P in i; the extension of an n-place predicate will always be an n-place relation (in the extensional sense).

We should consider zero-place predicates for a moment. These will be functions with domain I of which the values are sets of zero-place sequences. But there is only one zero-place sequence, the empty sequence Λ; hence there are only two sets of zero-place sequences, the empty set and the unit set of Λ. These two sets are according to some developments of set theory identified with the numbers 0 and 1; in any case, we can regard them as representing falsehood and truth respectively. Thus a zero-place predicate will be a function from possible worlds to truth-values, and hence a *proposition*, as was claimed earlier.

It might appear natural to impose an additional condition on predicates, that their extension with respect to a given possible world always be a relation among possible individuals *existing in that world*. This condition is satisfied by the property of being red, but its general imposition would be unwarranted, as consideration of, for example, the property of being an object thought of by Jones will reveal. This property, of which more will be said later, is quite likely possessed by some objects, perhaps Zeus, which exist in some possible worlds but not in the actual world.

It might also at first be supposed that a possible world could be identified with the set of possible individuals existing in it. But this is unreasonable: there are other ways of differentiating possible worlds than by the individuals they contain, for instance, by the relative positions of those individuals.

A construction of predicates similar to the one given here was introduced by Carnap in unpublished work and adopted by Kaplan in his dissertation [7]. The only essential divergence is that in the earlier construction possible worlds were always identified with *models* for a given language (in the technical sense of Tarski [16]). From the intuitive viewpoint, such a proposal suffers from a defect similar to that of the proposal considered in the last paragraph: two possible worlds may differ even though they are indistinguishable in all respects expressible in a given language (even by open formulas). For instance, if the language refers only to physical predicates, then we may consider two possible worlds, consisting of exactly the same persons and physical objects, all of which have exactly the same physical properties and stand in exactly the same physical relations; then the two corresponding models for our physical language will be identical. But the two possible worlds may still differ, for example, in that in one everyone believes the proposition that snow is white, while in the other someone does not believe it. (To say that there are correlations between physical properties and beliefs would be irrelevant; though there may be such correlations in the actual world, they need not exist in all possible worlds.) This point might seem unimportant, but it looms large in any attempt to treat belief as a relation between persons and propositions. And indeed, the identification of possible worlds with models was the main obstacle to a successful treatment of iterated belief contexts within the intensional logic of Kaplan [7].[2]

The present analysis of predicates is essentially, and I believe for the first time, to be found in Kripke [8], where Kripke employs, however, a different terminology and has in mind somewhat different objectives.

The second reason for reducing a number of dubious philosophical entities to predicates is that it enables us now to realize the second and third goals mentioned in the second paragraph of this paper, that is, to construct an exact language capable of naturally accommodating discourse about the dubious entities, and to introduce an intuitively satisfactory notion of logical consequence for sentences of that language. These goals can now be reached in connection with discourse about predicates.

It has for fifteen years been possible for at least one philosopher (myself) to maintain that philosophy, at this stage in history, has as its proper theoretical framework set theory with individuals and the possible addition of empirical predicates. It might initially appear a trivial matter to extend such a framework so as to encompass talk of predicates: we might regard (as perhaps we always have) set theory as referring to possible, and not only actual, objects; and we might add to the language of set theory two definite singular terms, one to designate the set of possible worlds, and the other the set of possible individuals. Within such a framework the general definition given above of a predicate can obviously be repeated, and general assertions about predicates can be formulated. The trouble is that we cannot yet form names of specific predicates, except in very special cases. Consider the

[2] For a treatment of belief contexts, including arbitrary iterations of belief, see Montague [11].

property of being red, and suppose that we have at our disposal the empirical one-place predicate constant 'is red'. This constant applies truly only to existing objects (or such is the convention to which I shall adhere) and therefore will not assist us in defining the property of being red; to use the characterization given above of that property we should need instead the two-place predicate constant 'is red in, or with respect to' (a given possible world). (The assertion that x is red in i would clearly not be equivalent to the assertion that x exists in i and is a *red possible individual*, even if we were willing to admit the meaningfulness of the last phrase.) By the time such two-place predicate constants had been added, and provision made for the apparent referential opacity of predicate names (for instance, Scott is the author of *Waverley*, but the property of being Scott is not the property of being the author of *Waverley*), we should have altered our philosophical framework to a point at which we could perhaps no longer feel entirely within it.

Thus we have arrived at a moment anticipated in my fifteen years' dogmatism. Philosophy is always capable of enlarging itself; that is, by metamathematical or model-theoretic means—means available within set theory—one can 'justify' a language or theory that transcends set theory, and then proceed to transact a new branch of philosophy within the new language. It is now time to take such a step and to lay the foundations of intensional languages.

Although this step might at first sight appear completely trivial, one might suppose on reflection, in view of serious questions raised by Quine[3] concerning the meaningfulness of quantification into intensional contexts, as well as the inconclusive character of attempts in Carnap [1], Church [2], and Kaplan [7] to construct systems of intensional logic, that the possibility of an adequate intensional logic would be at least controversial. Let me say quite dogmatically that I consider this no longer to be the case. One system of intensional logic now exists which fully meets the objections of Quine and others, which possesses a simple structure as well as a close conformity to ordinary

[3] For example, in Quine [13], [14], and [15].

language, and concerning the adequacy of which I believe no serious doubts can be entertained.[4] I shall confine myself here to a bare description of the system; for additional technical details, for arguments as to the system's intuitive adequacy, and for applications to belief contexts, the reader is referred to Montague [11] and the talk cited under footnote 4.

We consider a formal language having *basic expressions* of the following five categories: (1) logical constants, in particular, the sentential connectives $\neg$, $\wedge$, $\vee$, $\rightarrow$, $\leftrightarrow$ (respectively 'it is not the case that', 'and', 'or', 'if ... then', 'if and only if'), [,], (,), the quantifiers $\wedge$ and $\vee$ (respectively 'for all' and 'for some'), the identity symbol $=$, the descriptive operator T ('the unique object ... such that'), and the modal operator $\square$ ('necessarily'); (2) individual variables; (3) individual constants; (4) n-place predicate variables, for each nonnegative integer n; and (5) predicate constants of type s, for each finite sequence s of integers ≥ -1.

The *atomic formulas* of this language are of the following sorts: (1) $\zeta = \eta$, where each of ζ, η is either an individual constant or an individual variable; (2) $P = Q$, where, for some n, both P and Q are n-place predicate variables; (3) $P[\zeta_0, \ldots, \zeta_{n-1}]$, where P is a predicate constant of some type $\langle s_0, \ldots, s_{n-1} \rangle$ and, for each $k < n$, either s_k is -1 and ζ_k is an individual variable or individual constant, or $s_k \geq 0$ and ζ_k is an s_k-place predicate variable; and (4) $P[\zeta_0, \ldots, \zeta_{n-1}]$, where P is an n-place predicate variable and each of $\zeta_0, \ldots, \zeta_{n-1}$ is an individual constant or an individual variable. (Taking $n = 0$, we have as a special case of (4) the atomic formula $P[\,]$, where P is a zero-place predicate variable; this is understood as asserting that the proposition represented by P holds, or is true.)

Formulas in general are built up from atomic formulas in the expected way using logical symbols. To be explicit, the set of formulas is the intersection of all sets Γ such that (1) all atomic

---

[4] This system was constructed by me on the partial basis of ideas of Kripke and Cocchiarella, reflects in my judgment the intentions of Frege [5], was presented, along with other material, in a talk before the Southern California Logic Colloquium on January 6, 1967, and appears in Montague [11]. The system outlined below differs from the one in Montague [11] in one inessential respect only: in Montague [11] the set of possible individuals is required always to coincide with the set of individuals that exist in some possible world.

formulas are in Γ; (2) $\neg \varphi$, $(\varphi \wedge \psi)$, $(\varphi \vee \psi)$, $(\varphi \rightarrow \psi)$, $(\varphi \leftrightarrows \psi)$, and $\square \; \varphi$ are in Γ whenever φ and ψ are in Γ; (3) $\wedge u\varphi$ and $\vee u\varphi$ are in Γ whenever φ is in Γ and u is either an individual variable or a predicate variable; and (4) whenever φ, ψ are in Γ, P, Q are, for some n, both n-place predicate variables, and neither $\wedge P$, $\vee P$, nor TP occurs in φ, then the result of replacing P by $TQ\psi$ in φ is in Γ. A *sentence* is as usual a formula without free variables; the notion of a free variable is understood as usual.

This language looks suspiciously like an ordinary second-order predicate calculus (with the perhaps not too significant addition of the symbol $\square$, and the perhaps not too remarkable improvement of replacing atomic formulas consisting simply of a zero-place predicate constant or predicate variable P by the more intelligible combination $P[\,]$). The novelty comes in the interpretation.

If I, U_0, ..., U_{n-1} are any sets, then by a *predicate of type* $\langle I, U_0, \ldots, U_{n-1} \rangle$ is understood a function from I into the set of all subsets of the Cartesian product $U_0 \times \ldots \times U_{n-1}$. (In accordance with the remarks above, such a predicate will be regarded as an n-place predicate corresponding to the choice of I as the set of all possible worlds and having as its extension, in each possible world, an n-place relation of which the relata are drawn from the respective sets $U_0, \ldots, U_{n-1}$.)

An *interpretation* differs from a model in that the latter assigns extensions, while the former assigns intensions. To be explicit, an interpretation (or a possible interpretation) for our language is an ordered triple $\langle I, U, F \rangle$ satisfying the following conditions: (1) I, U are sets; (2) F is a function of which the domain is the set of predicate constants and individual constants (of our language); (3) whenever c is an individual constant, F_c is a function with domain I and taking values in U; and (4) whenever P is a predicate constant of type $\langle s_0, \ldots, s_{n-1} \rangle$ F_P is a predicate of type $\langle I, U_0, \ldots, U_{n-1} \rangle$, where, for each $k < n$, either s_k is -1 and U_k is U, or $s_k \geqslant 0$ and U_k is the set of all predicates of type $\langle I, V_0, \ldots, V_{s_k - 1} \rangle$, where V_p is U for all $p < s_k$. (I is the set of possible worlds according to the interpretation $\langle I, U, F \rangle$; U the set of possible individuals; and, for each predicate constant or individual constant c, F_c the *intension* of c, which is itself a function assigning to each possible world i the *extension* $F_c(i)$ of c in i (according to $\langle I, U, F \rangle$).)[5]

We now consider the notions of *truth* and *satisfaction*, or more specifically, the notions expressed by the two phrases 'the sentence φ is true of the possible world i under the interpretation $\mathfrak{A}$', and 'the object x (or the sequence $\langle x_0, \ldots, x_{n-1} \rangle$ of objects) satisfies the formula φ in the possible world i with respect to the interpretation $\mathfrak{A}$'. (By an object we may understand here either a possible individual or a predicate of individuals.) I shall not define these notions here, but rather confine myself to presenting a number of examples of their use, from which I believe the general intent will be apparent.[6]

Let $\mathfrak{A} = \langle I, U, F \rangle$, let $\mathfrak{A}$ be a possible interpretation, and let i be a member of I. (1) If u is an individual variable and c an individual constant, then the possible individual x satisfies the formula $u = c$ (in i, with respect to $\mathfrak{A}$) if and only if x is identical with $F_c(i)$. (2) If in addition P is a predicate constant of type $\langle -1, -1 \rangle$, then x satisfies the formula $P[u, c]$ (in i, with respect to $\mathfrak{A}$) if and only if the pair $\langle x, F_c(i) \rangle$ is a member of $F_P(i)$. (3) If u is an individual variable, Q a one-place predicate variable, $\mathscr{P}$ a predicate constant of type $\langle -1, 1 \rangle$, x a member of U, and A a predicate of type $\langle I, U \rangle$, then the pair $\langle x, A \rangle$ satisfies the formula $\mathscr{P}[u, Q]$ (in i, with respect to $\mathfrak{A}$) if and only if $\langle x, A \rangle$ is a member of $F_{\mathscr{P}}(i)$. (4) If P is a zero-place predicate variable and A a predicate of type $\langle I \rangle$ (that is, a proposition), then A satisfies the formula $P[\,]$ (in i, with respect to $\mathfrak{A}$) if and only if the empty sequence is a member of $A(i)$ (that is, if and only if $A(i)$ is truth). (5) If φ is a sentence, then $\neg \varphi$ is true (in i, with respect to $\mathfrak{A}$) if and only if φ is not true (in i, with respect to $\mathfrak{A}$); similarly for other sentential connectives. (6) If u is an individual variable and φ a formula of which u is the only free variable, then $\vee u\varphi$ is true (in i, with respect to $\mathfrak{A}$) if and only if there is an object x in U such that x satisfies φ (in i, with respect to $\mathfrak{A}$). (7) If Q is an n-place predicate variable and φ a formula of which Q is the

---

[5] I use the notations 'F_x' and '$F(x)$' interchangeably for the value of the function to which 'F' refers for the argument to which 'x' refers.

[6] For precise general definitions see Montague [11].

only free variable, then $\vee Q\varphi$ is true (in i, with respect to $\mathfrak{A}$) if and only if there is a predicate of type $\langle I, U_0, \ldots, U_{n-1}\rangle$ which satisfies φ (in i, with respect to $\mathfrak{A}$), where each U_k (for $k < n$) is U. (8) If φ is a sentence then $\Box\, \varphi$ is true in i (with respect to $\mathfrak{A}$) if and only if φ is true in j (with respect to $\mathfrak{A}$), for every j in I. (9) If u is an individual variable, Q a one-place predicate variable, $\mathscr{P}$ a predicate constant of type $\langle -1, 1\rangle$, φ a formula of which the only free variable is Q, and x a member of U, then x satisfies $\mathscr{P}[uTQ\varphi]$ (in i, with respect to $\mathfrak{A}$) if and only if $\langle x, A\rangle$ is in $F_{\mathscr{P}}(i)$, where either (i) there is exactly one predicate of type $\langle I, U\rangle$ which satisfies φ (in i, with respect to $\mathfrak{A}$), and A is that predicate, or (ii) it is not the case that there is exactly one such predicate, and A is the empty predicate (that is, $I \times \{\Lambda\}$).

In view of (6), quantification on an individual variable is quantification over all *possible* individuals. It would be natural to include among our predicate constants a symbol E of *existence*, having type $\langle -1\rangle$; $F_E(i)$ would then be regarded as the set of individuals existing in the possible world i, according to the interpretation $\langle I, U, F\rangle$. Using such a predicate constant, we can express quantification over *actual* individuals by combinations of the form $\vee u(E[u] \wedge \varphi)$ and $\wedge u(E[u] \to \varphi)$. In view of (7), quantification on a predicate variable is quantification over all predicates of individuals of an appropriate number of places. If we understand the extension of a formula to be the set of objects or sequences that satisfy it (so that in the special case of a sentence the extension is a truth value), then (1)–(3), (5)–(9), illustrate Frege's principle that the extension of a formula is a function of the extensions of its direct components and the *intensions* (or *indirect extensions*) of its indirect components.

Having the notion of truth in a world *under any possible interpretation*, we can immediately characterize *logical truth* and *logical consequence*. Thus a sentence is *logically true* if, for every interpretation $\langle I, U, F\rangle$ and every i in I, the sentence is true of i with respect to $\langle I, U, F\rangle$; and a sentence φ is a *logical consequence* of a set Γ of sentences just in case, for every interpretation $\langle I, U, F\rangle$ and every i in I, if all members of Γ are true of i with respect to $\langle I, U, F\rangle$, then φ is true of i with respect to $\langle I, U, F\rangle$.

We have thus constructed what might be called a *second-order calculus of predicates*. The construction of a calculus of predicates containing variables of all finite levels would constitute a routine extension of what we have done, but is not required here; neither is the somewhat more involved but still rather obvious extension to all finite and transfinite levels.

The modal operator provides a means of constructing names of specific predicates. (There are other ways of accomplishing this, but each would require some supplementation of the pure second-order calculus.) For instance, if u, v are distinct individual variables and φ is a formula, then we understand by $\hat{u}\varphi$ the expression

$$\ulcorner P \wedge u \,\square\, (P[u] \leftrightarrows \varphi),$$

which designates the property expressed by φ (with respect to the place marked by u), and by $\hat{u}\hat{v}\varphi$ the expression

$$\ulcorner Q \wedge u \wedge v \,\square\, (Q[u, v] \leftrightarrows \varphi),$$

which designates the two-place predicate expressed by φ (with respect to the places marked by u and v, in that order); here P is to be a particular one-place, and Q a particular two-place, predicate variable not occurring in φ. We can of course proceed upward to three variables and more, but we can also proceed downward to the empty sequence of variable. In particular, we let $\hat{\ }\varphi$ be the expression

$$\ulcorner R \,\square\, (R[\,] \leftrightarrows \varphi),$$

where R is a particular zero-place predicate variable not in the formula φ; this expression designates the proposition expressed by φ.

In ordinary English, $\hat{\ }\varphi$ amounts to $\ulcorner$that $\varphi\urcorner$ or (to use apposition) $\ulcorner$the proposition that $\varphi\urcorner$; for instance, $\hat{\ }$(Bald [Socrates]) may be regarded as synonymous with 'the proposition that Socrates is bald'. English provides no such natural and generally applicable synonym for $\hat{u}\varphi$ or $\hat{u}\hat{v}\varphi$; we may, however, use for this purpose the rather awkward phrases $\ulcorner$the property of u such that $\varphi\urcorner$ and $\ulcorner$the predicate of u and v such that $\varphi\urcorner$

respectively.[7] In special cases, when the formula in question is not too complex, English employs a gerund or infinitive phrase in place of $\hat{u}\varphi$ or $\hat{u}\hat{v}\varphi$; this appears to be the canonical use of infinitives. For instance 'to be bald', 'being bald', 'the property of being bald', and $\hat{u}$ (Bald [u]) may all be regarded as synonymous, as may all of $\ulcorner$to raise $x\urcorner$, $\ulcorner$raising $x\urcorner$, $\ulcorner$the property of raising $x\urcorner$, and $\hat{u}$ (Raises [u, x]), and all of 'to raise', 'raising', 'the (intensional) relation of raising', and $\hat{u}\hat{v}$ (Raises [u, v]).[8] But when confronted

[7] Let me say a word about my syntactic conventions, in case they are not already clear. Single quotes are employed as usual to form names of specific expressions of English. Corners (or quasi-quotes) are also used in connection with expressions of English, but in situations in which not all constituents of the expressions are definitely specified. The general use should be clear from the following example: if u is any individual variable and φ any expression of English, then $\ulcorner$ the property of u such that $\varphi \urcorner$ is that expression of English obtained by writing 'the property of' followed by u followed by 'such that' followed by φ.

On the other hand, neither quotes nor corners are needed when we refer to expressions of our formal language. We have names of the various logical constants of that language; for instance, $\neg$ is a logical constant, but '$\neg$' is a name of a logical constant. Further, we use juxtaposition to indicate concatenation. Thus, for example, if φ is any expression of our formal language, then $\neg \varphi$ is the expression obtained by writing the negation symbol of the object language (however it may look; we need not inquire into its appearance) followed by φ.

I shall of course take occasional liberties in the interests of conciseness.

[8] A problem might seem to arise if we were to replace 'raises' by 'loves'. We may say not only 'to love is to exalt', in which both infinitives rather clearly designate two-place predicates, but also 'to love is to exult', in which it seems we must take 'to love' as designating a one-place predicate, because there is no other alternative for 'to exult'. We are not, however, compelled by these examples to regard the infinitive construction as ambiguous; it is better to regard the ambiguity as residing in 'loves', which, unlike 'raises', 'exalts', and 'exults', can be either transitive (and hence require two arguments) or intransitive (requiring one argument, and in one sense synonymous with 'loves some individual'). The rule is that infinitives and gerunds formed from one-place verbs designate properties, and those formed from two-place verbs two-place predicates. If a verb may be either transitive or intransitive, its infinitive and gerund will be correspondingly ambiguous. Notice, though, that the *sentences* 'to love is to exalt' and 'to love is to exult' are not ambiguous; the number of places of 'loves' may be regarded as determined in the two cases (and as a matter of fact differently) by appropriate rules of grammar, taken in conjunction with the syntactically unambiguous character of 'exalts' and 'exults'. (The same rules would exclude 'to raise is to exult' as ungrammatical.) On the other hand, 'to love is to hate' is genuinely ambiguous, and could be represented by either

$\qquad \hat{u}\hat{v}$ (u loves v) $= \hat{u}\hat{v}$ (u hates v)

or $\qquad \hat{u}$ (u loves) $= \hat{u}$ (u hates)

—that is, synonymously,

$\qquad \hat{u} \vee v$ (u loves v) $= \hat{u} \vee v$ (u hates v).

with a more complex binary abstract,

$\hat{u}\hat{v}$ (u loves the sister of v),

English style shuns the straightforward 'the relation of loving the sister of' and requires some such clumsy combination as 'the relation of loving the sister of a given person'. Notice that in such phrases as 'the property of being bald', 'the property of loving x' and 'the relation of loving' the 'of' is otiose; the construction is apposition, as in 'the city of Amsterdam'.

For simplicity let us for the time being ignore the passage of time. More specifically, let us confine attention to a single moment, the present, so that tasks, experiences, and obligations may be treated as *properties* of persons rather than as *two-place* relations-in-intension between persons and moments. (When, however, we come to a reconsideration of events, we shall have to restore the temporal element.) Accordingly, the phrases 'is a task', 'is an experience', 'is an obligation' become predicate constants of type $\langle 1 \rangle$.

Before proceeding further, we should consider an objection to our treatment that is implicit in the literature. It is easily seen that the sentence

(1) $\wedge P (P = \hat{u}P[u])$

is a logical truth, if u is an individual variable and P a one-place predicate variable; and hence also the sentence

(2) $\wedge P (\text{Experience} [P] \rightarrow P = \hat{u}P[u])$,

which we might paraphrase as

(3)   'Every experience is identical with the attribute of having that experience'.

Yet David Lewis has written in [9] that 'we must not identify an experience itself with the attribute that is predicated of somebody by saying that he is having that experience,' and this would seem to conflict with (3).

As Lewis has pointed out in conversation, there are other interpretations of his assertion than those that construe it as denying (3); nevertheless, it is that denial, together with a supporting argument that parallels the argument in Lewis' paper, which will interest us here.

The argument is this. Suppose that a certain person, Jones, is having just one experience, say seeing a tree, but in another possible world he is having another experience instead, say hearing a bell, and no other experience. Then it would be plausible to maintain the following three assertions.

(4) Experience $[\hat{u}\,(u \text{ sees a tree})]$,

(5) $TQ\,(\text{Experience } [Q] \wedge Q \,[\text{Jones}]) = \hat{u}\,(u \text{ sees a tree})$,

(6) $\hat{u}TQ\,(\text{Experience } [Q] \wedge Q \,[\text{Jones}])\,[u] \neq \hat{u}\,(u \text{ sees a tree})$.

Sentences (4) and (5) assert that seeing a tree is an experience, and that it is the experience Jones has. Sentence (6) says that the property of having the experience Jones has is not the property of seeing a tree. This is true because if the two properties were identical, they would be coextensive in all possible worlds; yet in the world in which Jones is hearing a bell they have different extensions.

It is a logical consequence of (5) and (6) that

(7) $TQ\,(\text{Experience } [Q] \wedge Q \,[\text{Jones}]) \neq \hat{u}TQ\,(\text{Experience } [Q] \wedge Q \,[\text{Jones}])\,[u]$.

But (2) (the symbolic version of (3)) would appear to imply, simply by universal instantiation, that

(8) $\text{Experience } [TQ\,(\text{Experience } [Q] \wedge Q \,[\text{Jones}])] \to TQ\,(\text{Experience } [Q] \wedge Q \,[\text{Jones}]) = \hat{u}TQ\,(\text{Experience } [Q] \wedge Q \,[\text{Jones}])\,[u]$.

It would follow by (4) and (5) that

$TQ\,(\text{Experience } [Q] \wedge Q \,[\text{Jones}]) = \hat{u}TQ\,(\text{Experience } [Q] \wedge Q \,[\text{Jones}])\,[u]$,

which contradicts (7).

The fallacy is the inference of (8) from (2). In intensional logic universal instantiation is not in all circumstances valid; indeed, it is easily verified that though (2) is logically true, its instance (8) is not.

This much of universal instantiation can be maintained: (i) if φ is a formula, P is an n-place predicate variable, ψ is like

φ except for having free occurrences of some n-place *predicate variable* wherever φ has free occurrences of P, and $u_0, \ldots, u_{k-1}$ comprehend all the free variables of ψ, then the sentence $\Lambda u_0 \ldots \Lambda u_{k-1} (\Lambda P\varphi \to \psi)$ is logically true; (ii) if φ, ψ are formulas having no variables in common, P, Q are n-place predicate variables, χ is like φ except for having $TQ\psi$ wherever φ has free occurrences of P, $u_0, \ldots, u_{k-1}$ comprehend all the free variables of χ, *and P does not occur in φ within the scope of $\square$*, then $\Lambda u_0 \ldots \Lambda u_{k-1} (\Lambda P\varphi \to \chi)$ is logically true; (iii) if φ, ψ are formulas having no variables in common, P, Q, R are n-place predicate variables such that R does not occur in ψ, χ is like φ except for having $TQ\psi$ wherever φ has free occurrences of P, and $u_0, \ldots, u_{k-1}$ comprehend all the free variables of ψ and χ, then $\Lambda u_0 \ldots \Lambda u_{k-1} (\vee R \square (R = TQ\psi) \to (\Lambda P\varphi \to \chi))$ is logically true.

The last hypothesis of (ii) excludes the fallacious application above; there φ is the formula $P = \hat{u}P[u]$, which, when we recall the characterization of $\hat{u}\varphi$, is seen to contain P within the scope of the modal operator. If the principle (iii) were to be used to sanction the inference of (8) from (2), we should need the additional hypothesis

$$\vee R \square (R = TQ\psi),$$

where ψ is the formula (Experience $[Q] \wedge Q$ [Jones]). But a little consideration will reveal that hypothesis to be false under the circumstances described above.[9]

Wholly analogous restrictions apply when an individual variable is to be instantiated, and prevent the inference from Leibniz' Law—that is, the correct principle that $\Lambda u \Lambda v (u = v \to (\varphi \leftrightarrows \psi))$ is logically true whenever u, v are individual variables, φ is a formula of which u is the only free variable, and ψ is like φ except for having a free occurrence of v where φ has a free occurrence of u—to a corresponding incorrect principle in which u

---

[9] The principle (iii) is nevertheless useful in other situations. For instance, if $TQ\psi$ is one of the expressions $\hat{}\psi'$, $\hat{u}\psi'$, or $\hat{u}\hat{v}\psi'$ (for some formula ψ' and some distinct individual variables u, v), then

$$\Lambda u_0 \ldots \Lambda u_{k-1} \vee R \square (R = TQ\psi)$$

is logically true.

and v are replaced by individual constants (and the pertinent quantifiers dropped).

We are now in a position to apply intensional logic to several matters of traditional philosophical concern. For a first example, notice that the argument

'Jones finds a unicorn; therefore there is a unicorn'

is valid, as attested by the following symbolization:

V x (Unicorn [x] ∧ Finds [Jones, x]); therefore V x Unicorn [x].

Yet, as Quine has pointed out in [15], the seemingly analogous argument

(9)   'Jones seeks a unicorn; therefore there is a unicorn'

is not valid. How can we account for the difference without adopting Quine's radical course of regarding 'seeks a unicorn' and all its analogues as unanalyzable predicate constants—a course that would raise the psychological problem of explaining how a natural language containing infinitely many primitive predicate constants can be learned? What we should observe is that 'seeks' can be regarded as abbreviating 'tries to find'. Keeping this in mind, we may represent (9) as

(10)   Tries [Jones, $û$ V x (Unicorn [x] ∧ Finds [u, x])]; therefore V x Unicorn [x].

(Here 'tries', as its use with an infinitive would suggest, is represented by a predicate constant of type $\langle -1, 1 \rangle$.) The premise of (10) explicitly exhibits the existential quantification indicated by the indefinite article, but not in such a way as to render the argument valid (that is, such that its conclusion is a logical consequence of its premise). Indeed, in order to make a valid argument out of (10) we should have to replace its premise by

(11)   V x (Unicorn [x] ∧ Tries [Jones, $û$ Finds [u, x]]).

When saying 'Jones tries to find a unicorn' or 'Jones seeks a unicorn', we ordinarily, I believe, intend to assert the premise of

(10); if we have (11) in mind, we should generally say instead
'Jones tries to find a certain (or a particular) unicorn' or 'Jones
seeks a certain (or a particular) unicorn'.[10] It is possible, however,
to construe the premise of (9) as ambiguous, with (11) and the
premise of (10) as expressing its two possible meanings. I shall
not discuss whether this would be a desirable course; but if it
were adopted, we should have to say of (9), as of many syntactically
ambiguous arguments in English, that under one analysis it is
valid while under others not.

It was not Quine who first called attention to the kind of
difficulty we have just examined. Indeed, Buridan pointed out
that the argument

(12)   'Jones owes Smith a horse; therefore there is a horse
        which Jones owes Smith',

though intuitively invalid, would appear to be validated by
formal criteria. The solution is just as before. We notice that
'owes' amounts roughly to 'is obliged to give'; more precisely,
we may regard '... owes———to - - -' as abbreviating '- - - is
such that ... is obliged to give———to him'. For example, if
c, d, e are individual constants, then

(13) $\ulcorner c$ owes d to $e \urcorner$

is taken as

$$V u [u = e \wedge \text{Obliged } [c, \hat{v} \text{ Gives } [v, d, u]]],$$

where Obliged and Gives are predicate constants of types
$\langle -1, 1 \rangle$ and $\langle -1, -1, -1 \rangle$; Gives $[x, y, z]$ is read $\ulcorner x$ gives
y to $z \urcorner$, and Obliged $[x, P]$ is read $\ulcorner x$ is obliged $P \urcorner$ or $\ulcorner x$ has the
obligation $P \urcorner$. It would not be quite correct to take (13) as

$\ulcorner c$ is obliged to give d to $e \urcorner$,

that is,

Obliged $[c, \hat{v} \text{ Gives } [v, d, e]]$,

because examination of examples would reveal that in (13) e (though

---

[10] 'A certain' and 'a particular' ordinarily serve in English as existential quantifiers of wide scope, just as 'any' is a universal quantifier of wide scope.

not of course d) is 'purely referential.'[11] The argument (12) may then be represented as

$V u$ (u = Smith $\wedge$ Obliged [Jones, $\hat{v} V x$ (Horse [x] $\wedge$ Gives [v, x, u])]); therefore $V x$ (Horse [x] $\wedge V u$ (u = Smith $\wedge$ Obliged [Jones, $\hat{v}$ Gives [v, x, u]])),

which is easily shown invalid.

The solution proposed in these two cases is substantially to reject 'seeks' and 'owes' as predicate constants, and to insist on circumlocution when we might be tempted to use those verbs. We may wonder whether it is possible to approximate English more closely within our intensional language. What we can do in the case of 'seeks'—and that of 'owes' would be completely analogous—is to introduce *several* predicate constants; and it would be possible to define them by means of the following equivalences:

(14) $\square \wedge x \wedge y$ (x Seeks y $\leftrightarrows$ Tries [x, $\hat{u}$ Finds [u, y]]),

(15) $\square \wedge x \wedge P$ (x Seeks-a P $\leftrightarrows$ Tries [x, $\hat{u} V y$ ($P[y] \wedge$ Finds [u, y])]).

(16) $\square' \wedge x \wedge P$ (x Seeks-the P $\leftrightarrows$ Tries [x, $\hat{u} V y$ ($\wedge z$ ($P[z] \rightleftarrows z = y) \wedge$ Finds [u, y])]),

(17) $\square \wedge x \wedge P$ (x Seeks-two-objects-having P $\leftrightarrows$ Tries [x,$\hat{u} V y V z$ ($P[y] \wedge P[z] \wedge y \neq z \wedge$ Finds [u, y] $\wedge$ Finds [u, z])]).

Notice that if c, d are individual constants, the equivalence

(18) c Seeks d $\leftrightarrows$ Tries [c, $\hat{u}$ Finds [u, d]]

is *not* a logical consequence of (14), but rather the equivalence

c Seeks d $\leftrightarrows V y$ ($y = d \wedge$ Tries [c, $\hat{u}$ Finds [u, y]]).

[11] For similar reasons

Obliged [c, P]

is not synonymous with

Is-obligatory [$^\frown P[c]$],

but rather with

$V u$ [$u = c \wedge$ Is-obligatory [$^\frown P[u]$]].

Thus the predicate constant introduced by (14) expresses the
'referential' sense of 'seeks'. The 'nonreferential' sense given by the
right side of (18) can be expressed in terms of 'seeks-a' (that is,
'seeks-an-object-having'), in view of the following logical consequence of (15):

$$c \text{ Seeks-a } \hat{u} \ [u = d] \leftrightarrows \text{Tries } [c, \hat{u} \text{ Finds } [u, d]].$$

The list of equivalences (14)–(17) can of course be expanded
indefinitely on the pattern of (17). If this were done, we should
again find ourselves with infinitely many primitive predicate constants. Though certain reductions are possible (for instance, of the
constants introduced by (14) and (16) to that introduced by (15)),
it does not appear possible to introduce, within the framework of
our present formal language, a finite number of notions of seeking
that will accommodate all the contemplated contexts of 'seeks'.
If, however, we were to pass to a *third-order*, rather than a
second-order, language, the situation would change: we should
then be able to introduce a single predicate constant in terms of
which all notions analogous to those introduced by (14)–(17)
could be expressed; I shall give a more detailed account of the
situation in a later paper.[12]

As far as 'seeks' and 'owes' are concerned, circumlocution
involving infinitives is possible. It is not, however, in the case of all
English verbs sharing the logical peculiarities of 'seeks' and 'owes',
despite the apparent contention to the contrary in Quine [15];
four counter-examples are 'worships', 'conceives', 'is about'
and 'thinks of'.[13] It does not follow that discourse involving such
verbs is beyond the compass of our formal framework. In connection with each such verb we can introduce (though not define)
primitive predicate constants—either infinitely many or, if we

[12] [Editor's note: This paper, which was to have been titled "Indefinite Terms,
Intensional Verbs, and Unconceived Trees," was never written.]

[13] The example of 'worships' is due to Dr. Kamp. The fact that 'thinks of'
cannot be adequately represented by an ordinary predicate constant in no way
contradicts the earlier intimation that 'is an object thought of by' can be so
represented. The construction leading to the latter phrase, as well as the one
leading to 'is such that ... thinks of it', is among the devices to which Quine
called attention in [15] as producing transparent contexts from contexts that are
at least under some interpretations referentially opaque.

were to shift to a third-order language, just one—exactly like those considered in connection with 'seeks'. To spell out the consequences of this suggestion, and in particular to evaluate Berkeley's famous argument about the tree in the park, would be a routine matter, but will be deferred to the aforementioned paper.

The verb 'sees' would appear to be in the same boat as 'seeks' or 'worships', for one is not prevented from seeing a unicorn by the fact that there are no unicorns; or rather, there would appear to be two senses of 'sees', the veridical and the nonveridical, and according to the latter 'there is a unicorn' is not a logical consequence of 'Jones sees a unicorn'. I can see no serious objection to distinguishing two senses of 'sees' (and other perceptual verbs) along these lines. Nevertheless, another course seems simpler, and is the one I shall adopt. It is to reject entirely the nonveridical sense of 'sees' (and thus to treat 'sees' always as a predicate constant of type $\langle -1, -1 \rangle$) and to use instead of the nonveridical sense the circumlocution 'seems to see'. Accordingly, 'Jones sees a unicorn' is unambiguously false, no matter what Jones seems to see.

Actually, it would not be quite accurate to express the nonveridical (or rather, not necessarily veridical) situation we have in mind by 'Jones seems to see a unicorn'. This sentence is probably best regarded as elliptical; while it would generally be taken in the desired sense of 'Jones seems to Jones to see a unicorn', it could also mean that Jones seems to a certain observer to see a unicorn. Thus our purposes appear to require a predicate constant Seems having type $\langle -1, -1, 1 \rangle$, and read, in the context Seems $[x, y, P]$,

$\ulcorner x$ seems to y $P \urcorner$[14]

We may then express the assertion that Jones sees, in the nonveridical sense, a unicorn by

Seems [Jones, Jones, $\hat{u} \vee v$ (Unicorn $[v] \wedge$ Sees $[u, v]$)].

Now Benson Mates (in the talk to which the introductory footnote refers) raised the interesting problem of describing in

[14] See page 170 for footnote.

an exact way such situations as that about which we might ordinarily say

> (19) 'Jones sees a unicorn having the same height as a table actually before him';

it was this problem that gave rise to the present paper, as well as to the construction of the intensional logic which it contains. In the light of that logic, the treatment of (19) is fairly obvious. Since we have decided to use 'sees' only in the veridical sense, we must first reformulate (19) as

> 'Jones seems to Jones to see a unicorn having the same height as a table actually before him'.

And this can be represented as follows:

> (20) $\vee x$ (Table $[x] \wedge$ Before $[x,$ Jones$] \wedge$ Seems [Jones, Jones, $\hat{u} \vee y$ (Unicorn $[y] \wedge$ Sees $[u, y] \wedge y$ Has-the-same-height-as x)]).

----

[14] Another familiar locution involving 'seems' is exemplified by 'it seems to Jones that Smith is tall', or, synonymously, 'that Smith is tall seems true to Jones', and could be represented by a predicate constant of type $\langle 0, -1 \rangle$. If x, y are individual variables and P a one-place predicate variable, then the connection between the two uses is given by the following equivalence:

$\square \wedge x \wedge y \wedge P$ (Seems $[x, y, P] \leftrightarrow \hat{}P[y]$ Seems-true-to x).

The usual *caveat* against direct instantiation to individual constants should be reiterated here; thus

Seems [Jones, Jones, $\hat{u} \vee v$ (Unicorn $[v] \wedge$ Sees $[u, v]$)] $\leftrightarrow$
$\hat{}\vee v$ (Unicorn $[v] \wedge$ Sees [Jones, v]) Seems-true-to Jones

is not a logical consequence of the equivalence above, but rather

Seems [Jones, Jones, $\hat{u} \vee v$ (Unicorn $[v] \wedge$ Sees $[u, v]$)] $\leftrightarrow$
$\vee y$ [y = Jones $\wedge \hat{}\vee v$ (Unicorn $[v] \wedge$ Sees $[y, v]$) Seems-true-to Jones].

It would be a temptation but inaccurate simplification to say that seeming and believing amount to the same thing. Indeed, we do not have an implication in either direction; for one can seem to see water without believing that one sees water, and believe that one sees an unbroken desert without seeming to see an unbroken desert. 'It seems to x P' appears to refer to only one component of belief and perhaps means something like 'x has sensory evidence for P'. Such a reading would give a narrower sense than the ordinary, for we sometimes say 'it seems to me that Plato wrote the *Republic*'; but this narrowing would perhaps be desirable in the light of our epistemological purposes.

Mates also considered the possibility of using a 'seems' locution, but rejected it because of the consequent necessity, not obtaining in the simpler case of 'Jones seems to see a unicorn', of quantifying into indirect contexts; and before Montague [11] it was not clear that this could be done intelligibly. Thus Mates was led to regard (19) as implying the existence of certain sense data. The possibility of giving the symbolization (20), however, appears to show that an argument for sense data based on (19) would not be conclusive.

This is not to say that sense data do not exist. We can provide for them if we wish. Indeed, we have already considered the nature of pains, and pains form a special class of sense data. It is reasonable to regard sense data as, like pains, experiences of a particular sort, and hence as two-place relations between persons and moments—or rather, since we are for the moment ignoring the temporal coordinate—as properties of persons. To say that *x has* the sense datum *P* is to assert that *x* has the property *P*. (If *P* is, say, a visual experience, some epistemologists might wish to say that *x sees* the sense datum *P* when we say that *x* has *P*. To introduce additional senses of perceptual verbs along this line would certainly be possible, but to all appearances useless.)

Can we be more specific in our account of sense data? In the first place, not all experiences qualify. For instance, the experience of seeing (in, as always, the veridical sense) a particular tree is not a sense datum, because it violates the principle that no being can seem (to itself) to have a sense datum without actually having it. We may symbolize this principle as follows:

(21) $\wedge P$ (Sense-datum $[P] \rightarrow \wedge x \,\square$ (Seems $[x, x, P] \rightarrow P[x]$)).

Dr. Kamp has suggested imposing an additional, analogous condition, to which I see no clear objection but to which I should also not like to commit myself:

$\wedge P$ (Sense-datum $[P] \rightarrow \wedge x \,\square$ ($P[x] \rightarrow$ Seems $[x, x, P]$)).

From this, together with (21), it would follow that every sense datum is seeming to have an experience:

$\wedge P$ (Sense-datum $[P] \to \vee Q$ (Experience $[Q] \wedge P = \hat{u}$ Seems $[u, u, Q]$)).

It is not unnatural to call experiences P satisfying the consequent of (21) (that is, such that no being can seem to have them without actually having them) *direct* or *infallible* experiences. We may, however, wonder whether any such experiencés exist. It is, I think, not unreasonable to assume that if Q is any experience, then seeming to have Q both is a direct experience and satisfies Kamp's condition:

(22) $\wedge Q$ (Experience $[Q] \to \wedge x \ \square$ (Seems $[x, x, \hat{u}$ Seems $[u, u, Q]] \leftrightarrows$ Seems $[x, x, Q]$)).

Now let us consider the experience of seeming to see a tree. In view of (22), this is a direct experience. But is it a sense datum? I think not, because of insufficient particularity; loosely speaking, there are many widely divergent 'mental images' (for instance, of different sorts of trees), and hence many different sense data, corresponding to the experience of seeming to see a tree. But is the experience of seeming to see a *particular* tree always a sense datum? In other words, is the following assertion true:

(23) $\wedge x$ (Tree $[x] \to$ Sense-datum $[\hat{u}$ Seems $[u, u, \hat{v}$ Sees $[v, x]]])$?

I think not, again on grounds of insufficient particularity. We can see, and seem to see, a single tree in different ways, for instance, from different angles and distances, and under different lighting conditions; and these differences would ordinarily be taken to correspond to different sense data. Further, even if (23) were true, it would fail to comprehend a good many tree-like sense data—in particular, those not corresponding to existing trees. Thus I should regard, as better candidates for sense data, such experiences as seeming to see, in a very particular way, a tree of a very particular sort.

Not all sense data will be of this kind, that is, seeming to have a veridical sense experience of a certain sort; counterexamples are provided by certain pains, for instance, toothaches. But all sense data have at least this much in common: they are direct and very particular experiences.

It is possible that we shall in no case be able to express the required particularity; that is to say, it may be that for no sense datum P is there a formula φ of our language such that the expression $\hat{u}\varphi$ designates P. This would not be an objection; the same can be said for many tasks, events, and the like. We may also find ourselves unable to characterize in general the degree of particularity required of sense data. This again would produce a situation which is neither unusual nor seriously objectionable; as with tasks and events we could introduce an undefined predicate constant to express the property of being a sense datum.

Thus there is little doubt as to the theoretical feasibility of talking about sense data, but one may well question its practicality and desirability. The difference is only one of degree, but we do appear to be worse off with sense data than with experiences, tasks, events, and obligations. We are confronted with an apparent paucity of noncontroversial general principles concerning sense data, and a complete absence of principles providing specific examples of them. It is thus a serious question whether their introduction would be worthwhile. Perhaps the purposes of epistemology, perceptual psychology, and ordinary speech could be better served by talk of experiences, direct experiences, and experiences that consist of seeming to have other experiences.

Be this as it may, there is at least one traditional question about sense data for which our reduction provides an answer—in particular, whether two different persons can have the same sense datum. The answer is affirmative; sense data are very narrow properties to be sure, so that perhaps no two persons ever *have* had the same sense datum, but nevertheless not so narrow as to make it *impossible* for such a situation to occur.

It is now time to resume the discussion of events. Let us first observe that according to our present policy of ignoring the temporal coordinate, events of the sort considered earlier, that is, *instantaneous generic events*, would become propositions; for instance, ⌜the rising of x⌝ would be expressed by

$\hat{\ }(x \text{ rises})$

and $\ulcorner$the raising of $x\urcorner$ by

$\qquad \hat{\ }(x$ is raised$).^{15}$

But to confine ourselves in this way is undesirable if we are to consider events of other sorts. Let us therefore restore the temporal element;[16] then if x is an individual variable, the English locution $\ulcorner$the rising of $x\urcorner$ will be expressed by

$\qquad$ (24) $\hat{\imath}$ Rises $[x, t]$,

and $\ulcorner$the raising of $x\urcorner$ by either

$\qquad \hat{\imath}$ Is-raised $[x, t]$

or

$\qquad \hat{\imath} \vee y$ Raises $[y, x, t]$;

here we use predicate constants for 'rises at', 'is raised at', and 'raises . . . at'.

The occurrence of the definite article in 'the rising of x' suggests the introduction of the property of being a rising, in the generic sense, of a given object. Accordingly, let us extend English by using the phrase $\ulcorner P$ is a (generic) rising of $x\urcorner$, whenever P is a one-place predicate variable and x an individual variable,

---

[15] The rule for English appears to be roughly that if P is a one-place (or intransitive) verb, then the P'ing of x is the proposition that x has P, while if P is a two-place (or transitive) verb, then the P'ing of x is the proposition that x is P'd, that is, the proposition that something P's x. The ambiguity in Chomsky's example, 'the shooting of x', is then accounted for by the ambiguity of 'shoots', which may be either transitive or intransitive; cf. footnote 8.

[16] Neither of the forms of expression we consider in this paper, that is, a language applying to a single instant and a tenseless language referring explicitly to many instants, is a close approximation of ordinary English. A much closer approximation would be a formal language that combines tenses with modalities and perhaps in addition allows, but does not require, explicit reference to instants; event names in such a language could be made to look more like their English counterparts. It is perfectly clear how to construct and interpret a language of this sort, on the basis of Montague [10] and the discussion in Prior [12, pages 103–105] (later elaborated in unpublished work of Kamp) of how to fit the phrase 'at t' into the framework of tense logic; one feature would be the replacement of possible worlds by ordered pairs consisting of an instant and a possible world. I do not introduce this more elaborate development, because the points I wish to make can also be brought out, albeit at the expense of some awkwardness, in connection with the simpler tenseless language.

as synonymous with

$P = \hat{t} \text{Rises} [x, t].$

In *ordinary* English we shall never encounter instances of the new usage, that is, occurrences of '*a* rising of *x*' when the reference is to a generic event; we shall always find instead '*the* rising of *x*'. Because it is logically true that there is exactly one generic rising of any given object, what can be expressed in the one way can be equally well expressed in the other. Nevertheless, it appears desirable to supplement English in the indicated manner in order to maintain the standard use of 'the'; for then the (generic) rising of *x* will be identical with the unique object *P* such that *P* is a (generic) rising of *x*.

Some names of instantaneous generic events contain an explicit reference to the time of occurrence; we may say, for instance, 'the rising of Jones at 5:00 a.m., February 22, 1966, is an unprecedented event'. In this connection it would be feasible to introduce events of another kind, again to be identified with propositions rather than properties; the rising of *x* at *t* would then be the proposition that *x* rises at *t*. One would not say that such an event *occurs at a given moment*, but only *occurs*; this is to say that the proposition in question *holds* or *is true*.

Despite the feasibility of such a treatment, it involves an unnecessary proliferation. Rather than construing the rising of *x* at *t* as a proposition, I prefer to identify it with the property of being a moment at which *x* rises and which is identical with *t*; that is to say, if *x*, *t* are individual variables, I regard ⌜the rising of *x* at *t*⌝ as synonymous with

(25) $\hat{s} (\text{Rises} [x, s] \wedge s = t).$

An event such as the rising of *x* at *t* can meaningfully be said to occur at any given moment; but there is at most one moment (indeed, *t*) at which it *can occur*. If we say of such an event simply that it *occurs*, we mean as usual that it occurs at some moment.

Thus the rising of *x* at *t* is, like the rising of *x*, a property of moments of time. But what are we to say of *instantaneous individual events*, like the individual risings of an object *x*? I should like to make a proposal, but it should be regarded as more tentative than those I have so far advanced.

I propose that the· individual risings of x be identified, like other instantaneous events, with properties of moments of time, but in this case with properties of a great degree of particularity, what we might regard as the various particular occurrences that constitute risings of x. As usual, we should introduce, without at this stage any attempt at definition, a primitive predicate constant of type $\langle 1 \rangle$ meaning 'is an individual event'. I propose, moreover, that we introduce a predicate constant Rising of type $\langle 1, -1 \rangle$; the formula Rising $[P, x]$ is understood as expressing $\ulcorner P$ is an (individual) rising of $x \urcorner$.

I make no attempt to *define* the notion of being an individual rising of x. It may also be that, because of its particularity, no individual rising of x is definable in our language. We may nevertheless consider a few postulates. First, every rising of an object is an individual event:

$$\wedge P \wedge x \text{ (Rising } [P, x] \rightarrow \text{Individual-event } [P]).$$

Secondly, it appears harmless and possibly convenient to assume that every individual event is an event in our earlier sense (that is, a generic event):

$$\wedge P \text{ (Individual-event } [P] \rightarrow \text{Event } [P]).$$

Thirdly, every individual event occurs:

$$\wedge P \text{ (Individual-event } [P] \rightarrow \vee tP[t]).$$

This is because if we were to maintain that Zeus sees every rising of the sun, we should not regard ourselves as adequately controverted by the observation that Zeus does not see those risings of the sun that do not occur.[17] Fourthly, it seems plausible to

---

[17] As the example indicates, 'sees' (as well as other perceptual verbs, except perhaps 'tastes') may take events as well as individuals as objects. In this case too we could distinguish between a veridical sense, which requires the occurrence of the perceived event, and a nonveridical or neutral sense, which could again be replaced by 'seems to see'. The pertinence of the example in the text would not be affected by the choice between these two senses; for definiteness, however, let us settle upon the veridical sense.

assume that no individual event can occur at more than one time:

(26) $\wedge P$ (Individual-event $[P] \rightarrow \square \neg \vee s \vee t$ $(s \neq t \wedge$
$P[s] \wedge P[t]))$.

This assumption, however, is probably not forced on us. Considerations of convenience might lead us to reject (26) and adopt the viewpoint that though the particularity of individual events is such that they are extremely unlikely to recur, it is still possible that they should. According to such a view, if x rises twice in exactly the same way (in all the features now considered relevant to individuating individual events), we should say not that two risings of x have occurred, but that a single rising of x has occurred twice.

Even if we assume (26), however, it would be unreasonable to make the stronger assumption $\wedge P$ (Individual-event $[P] \rightarrow$
$\vee t \square \wedge s (P[s] \rightarrow s = t))$, for there would seem to be risings of certain objects which have occurred at certain times but could have occurred at others. The same consideration shows that the risings of x should not be identified with those events which are, for some t, the (generic) rising of x at t.

The fifth principle we may assume is that whenever a rising of an object occurs, that object rises:

$\wedge P \wedge x \wedge t$ (Rising $[P, x] \wedge P[t] \rightarrow$ Rises $[x, t]$).

It would be tempting, but probably incorrect, to make the stronger assumption that whenever a rising of an object occurs, that object necessarily rises, or more precisely

(27) $\wedge P \wedge x$ (Rising $[P, x] \rightarrow \wedge t \square (P[t] \rightarrow$ Rises $[x, t]))$.

The implausibility of this assertion can best be argued if we vary the example. It would not be unreasonable to maintain that a certain falling of a certain object x happened to accomplish the destruction of x, but only contingently. (Other fallings of x did not accomplish the destruction of x, and this one might not have.) We should then be inclined to say that some falling of x was a destroying of x, but could have occurred at a time at which x was not destroyed:

$\vee P$ (Falling $[P, x] \wedge$ Destroying $[P, x] \wedge \vee t \neg \square \neg (P[t] \wedge$
$\neg$ Is-destroyed $[x, t]))$.

This, however, would contradict an analogue of (27). Roughly speaking, the connection between destroyings of x and the (generic) destroying of x appears to be a matter not of necessity but (in some cases) of causation.[18]

Once we are prepared to speak of risings of particular objects, there is no problem in saying what a rising is; specifically, we may regard ⌜P is a rising⌝ as synonymous with

$$\lor x \text{ Rising } [P, x].$$

There is also no problem in extending the remarks above to examples in which more than one argument of individual type are involved, for instance, raisings of x by y and givings of x by y to z.

If the analyses we have given are correct, we may expect to encounter unusually numerous ambiguities in the English locutions referring to specific events. One source of ambiguity would be the failure of English to distinguish between the generic and the individual sense of 'rising'. As was already observed, no ambiguity arises when we use '*a* rising of x'; English always takes this as meaning 'an *individual* rising of x'. But when we use '*the* rising', ambiguities are indeed possible. For instance, the rising of x at t may be taken either as in (25) above, or as that one among the individual risings of x which occurs at t; that is to say, if x, t are individual variables, then ⌜the rising of x at t⌝ may be understood as either

$$\hat{s} \text{ (Rises } [x, s] \land s = t)$$

or

$$TP \text{ (Rising } [P, x] \land P[t]).$$

These two expressions, besides designating different events in general, will have quite different logical properties. For instance,

---

[18] I believe that what I have said about individual events is compatible with the remarks about them in Davidson [3] and [4]. In particular, Davidson introduces undefined predicate constants like our Rising. (He does not, however, raise in those papers the question of the ontological status or logical type of the event-argument of such predicate constants.) Also, Davidson [3] contains (on p. 84, third paragraph) an example, more complicated but perhaps more convincing than ours, serving the same purpose as the one just given in the text.

the first expression but not the second will yield logical truths when substituted for Q in the formulas

$$\Lambda x \Lambda t \lor P \, (P = Q \land \Box \land s \, (P[s] \rightarrow \text{Rises } [x, s])),$$
$$\Lambda x \Lambda t \lor P \, (P = Q \land \Box \land s \, (P[s] \rightarrow s = t)).$$

A similar ambiguity arises in connection with the phrase 'the rising of x', but is more conspicuous if we replace 'rising' by 'dying'. To be specific, ⌜the dying of x⌝ may be understood either as

$$\hat{t} \, \text{Dies } [x, t],$$

along the lines of (24), or as

$$\mathrm{T}P \, \text{Dying } [P, x].$$

The ambiguities are multiplied if in the locutions considered above we replace variables by individual constants or indefinite singular terms. In most cases the place occupied by the variable x may be regarded as either purely referential or not. The choice is immaterial as long as only variables are involved, but, as we have seen in earlier connections, is of considerable moment when other sorts of singular terms are brought into consideration.

Observe, however, that our decision to use a predicate constant for 'is an individual rising of' removes one *conceivable* source of ambiguity. In our formal language the arguments of a predicate constant can occur only referentially. Thus, for example, if c is any individual constant, the following equivalence is logically true:

$$\Lambda P \, (\text{Rising } [P, c] \rightleftarrows \lor x (x = c \land \text{Rising} [P, x])).$$

It would have been possible to arrange things otherwise, so that c would not be represented as referential in ⌜P is an individual rising of c⌝; we should then have treated 'is an individual rising of' not as a predicate constant, but in the manner of 'seeks', 'worships', 'is about', and 'thinks of'. There seems, however, no good reason to take the latter course, or to dispute the claim in Davidson [3] that individual constants always occur referentially in such contexts as the one under consideration.

I once entertained a specious argument to the contrary. If we are willing to treat 'is an (individual) rising of' as a predicate constant, the intuitively invalid argument

(28) 'the morning star is the evening star; Jones reports a rising of the morning star; therefore Jones reports a rising of the evening star'

would appear to become valid, in view of the symbolization

$c = d$; V P (Rising [P, c] ∧ Reports [Jones, P]); therefore V P (Rising [P, d] ∧ Reports [Jones, P]).

David Kaplan questioned, however, whether the situation was so simple, and suggested that peculiar obliquities of the verb 'reports' might be involved. He was correct: the difficulty here is not with Rising, but in representing 'reports' by a predicate constant. For if such a representation were invariably correct, the argument

(29) 'Jones reports a rising of a unicorn; therefore there is a rising of a unicorn'

would be invariably valid. But 'reports' should instead be treated like 'seeks'. (The only important difference is that 'reports' is of higher type; that is to say, the ostensible object of 'reports' is not an individual but a property.) To see the resemblance, we might observe that to report an event is more or less to assert that it occurs, just as to seek an object is to try to find it. In other words, ⌜x reports P⌝ may be taken as standing for

Asserts [x, ˆ V $tP[t]$]].

But how are we to represent 'Jones reports a rising of a unicorn'? We could take it either as

V P (V x (Unicorn [x] ∧ Rising [P, x]) ∧ Asserts [Jones, ˆ V $tP[t]$]]),

which could also be read 'Jones reports a particular rising of a unicorn', is certainly false, and would make the argument (29) valid; or as

Asserts [Jones, ˆ V P (V x (Unicorn [x] ∧ Rising [P, x]) ∧ V $tP[t]$)],

which is a more likely rendering and would make (29) invalid.

Now if we treat (28) in the latter style, it becomes

$c = d$; Asserts [Jones, ˆ $\vee$ P (Rising [P, c] $\wedge$ $\vee$ $tP[t]$)]; therefore Asserts [Jones, ˆ $\vee$ P (Rising [P, d] $\wedge$ $\vee$ $tP[t]$)],

which is invalid despite the decision to represent 'is an (individual) rising of' by a predicate constant.[19]

A general remark of clarification is perhaps needed. The so-called 'locutions' we have considered, like 'x finds y', 'x seeks y', and the like, are not to be regarded as part of our formal language, but as expressions of English. We have correlated with these English locutions expressions of our formal language that we regard as synonymous with them (in a sense that we do not attempt to analyze in general). In some cases the correlation is very simple: a predicate constant is used as the exact counterpart of an English verb or verb phrase. For instance, with ⌜x finds y⌝, ⌜x sees y⌝, ⌜x tries P⌝ are correlated the respective formal expressions

Finds [x, y],
Sees [x, y],
Tries [x, P].

(In the case of 'sees' the possibility of such a simple correlation depends on our understanding that verb in the veridical sense.) In other cases, however, the correlation is less simple. For instance, ⌜x seeks y⌝ is represented by

Tries [$x, \hat{u}$ Finds [u, y]];

⌜x conceives y⌝ by

Conceives* [$x, \hat{u} (u = y)$], ·

where Conceives* is a predicate constant of type $\langle -1, 1 \rangle$ and Conceives* [x, P] is regarded as synonymous with ⌜x conceives-an-object-having P⌝; and ⌜P is a generic rising of x⌝ by

$P = \hat{t}$ (Rises [x, t]).

---

[19] It is, I hope, clear that the point of the last paragraph does not depend on the particular analysis given there of 'reports', against which objections could perhaps be raised.

This is, as we have seen, how things must be as long as our formal language contains no atomic formulas other than identities and those generated by predicate constants and predicate variables. Another approach, which will not be adopted here but perhaps deserves some attention, is possible. We could add to our symbolism a stock of *locution symbols* of the various types admitted in connection with predicate constants, and allow each of these new symbols to appear in formulas in precisely the ways in which a predicate constant of the same type may appear. We could then, in a regular manner, correlate with each atomic English locution, at least of the sorts we have considered, an *atomic* formula of the enlarged formal language. For instance, if a, b are any individual variables *or individual constants*, and P any one-place predicate variable or well-formed proper description of a one-place predicate, we might represent $\ulcorner a$ seeks $b \urcorner$ by

$S[a, b]$,

$\ulcorner a$ conceives $b \urcorner$ by

$C[a, b]$,

and $\ulcorner P$ is a generic rising of $a \urcorner$ by

$R[P, a]$,

where S, C, R are locution symbols of the respective types $\langle -1, -1 \rangle, \langle -1, -1 \rangle, \langle 1, -1 \rangle$. We might continue to represent by predicate constants those English locutions (if any) of which we feel confident that they behave in a 'normal' manner.

I can see no good way of extending our semantics (or theory of interpretations) to formulas containing locution symbols, and such formulas would have to remain uninterpreted; more precisely, interpretations would as at present assign intensions only to predicate constants and individual constants, and the assertion that φ is true under an interpretation $\mathfrak{A}$ with respect to a possible world i would entail that φ is a sentence containing no locution symbols. We could nevertheless extend our notions of logical truth and logical consequence to the new sentences in what appears to be an appropriate way. For example, if φ is a sentence of the enlarged formal language, then φ could be considered *logically true* if every sentence obtained from φ by substituting (in a proper way, with due precautions against the clash of bound variables; for a precise characterization of the notion of substitution involved, see, for instance, Kalish and Montague [6, chap. 4]) formulas not containing locution symbols for the locution symbols of φ is logically true in our earlier sense. Then if x is an individual variable and c an individual constant, the sentence

$$(\wedge xF[x] \rightarrow F[c])$$

will be logically true if F is a predicate constant, but not if F is a locution symbol. It might be of some interest to investigate the new logical truths in some generality, and perhaps to axiomatize them.

This extension, it is true, would not bring our formal language *very* much closer to ordinary English. In particular, we should still not have a simple way of treating locutions that contain indefinite singular (or plural) terms. For instance, 'x seeks a unicorn' and 'x seeks all unicorns' either would be treated in the earlier way, in terms of 'tries to find', or else would be represented by means of predicate constants or locution symbols bearing no special relation to the one used for 'x seeks y'. This is a situation which I believe could be relieved, but only after one has provided a general and adequate treatment of indefinite terms in English. Such a treatment can indeed be devised without much difficulty,[20] and would suggest a further extension of our formal language; but it would lead us too far afield to supply the details here.

Let us return from our digression to the consideration of events. Despite our decision to express 'is an individual rising of' by means of a predicate constant, there remain areas of ambiguity as yet unexplored. For instance, in $\hat{t}$ Rises $[x, t]$ the place occupied by x may be taken as either referential or not; and accordingly, if c is an individual constant and $\mathscr{R}$ a predicate constant of type $\langle 1 \rangle$,

(30) $\ulcorner \mathscr{R}$ [the (generic) rising of c]$\urcorner$

---

[20] I am aware that some mathematical linguists have attempted treatments of indefinite terms; but I do not refer to their attempts, which can only be regarded as inadequate for precise scientific purposes.

could be taken as either

(31) $\mathsf{V}\,x\,(x = c \wedge \mathscr{Q}\,[\hat{t}\,\text{Rises}\,[x, t]])$

or

(32) $\mathscr{Q}\,[\hat{t}\,\text{Rises}\,[c, t]],$

and

(33) $\ulcorner \mathscr{Q}\,[\text{the (generic) rising of a unicorn}]\urcorner$

as either

(34) $\mathsf{V}\,x\,(\text{Unicorn}\,[x] \wedge \mathscr{Q}\,[\hat{t}\,\text{Rises}\,[x, t]])$

or

(35) $\mathscr{Q}\,[\hat{t}\,\mathsf{V}\,x\,(\text{Unicorn}\,[x] \wedge \text{Rises}\,[x, t])].$

Evidence that the referential situation (that is, the one exemplified in (31) and (34)) may actually occur is provided by 'the rising of a star failed to occur', which in most cases would be understood as meaning 'the rising of a *particular* star failed to occur'.

My evidence for the occurrence of the nonreferential situation (the one exemplified in (32) and (35)) is less conclusive. Perhaps better evidence can be found; one must take care, however, to avoid examples like the one involving 'reports'. The sentence

'the rising of a unicorn fails to occur'

would in most cases not be understood in the manner of (34), and in those cases would apparently be correctly represented by (35). The fact that in third-order intensional logic (which has not been explicitly introduced in the present paper) $\ulcorner P$ fails to occur$\urcorner$ can be represented more explicitly by Fails $[P, \hat{Q}\,\mathsf{V}\,tQ\,[t]]$ would not affect the example.

Notice, however, that if we were to replace the example by 'the rising of a unicorn does not occur',

we should not be driven to a nonreferential reading; for the last sentence (in its most likely meaning) can be expressed equivalently either by

$\neg\,\mathsf{V}\,x\,(\text{Unicorn}\,[x] \wedge \mathsf{V}\,s\,(\hat{t}\,\text{Rises}\,[x, t])\,[s])$

or (in the nonreferential manner) by

$\neg \: V \: s\hat{\imath} \: V \: x$ (Unicorn $[x] \wedge$ Rises $[x, t]$) $[s]$.

Thus the cogency of the example above depends on a literal treatment of 'fails to occur', in which we refrain from introducing a negation sign. This is, I believe, the correct approach. I should, however, point out a consequence that some might find dubious: the sentence 'a rising of a unicorn fails to occur', unlike 'a rising of a unicorn does not occur' and 'no rising of a unicorn occurs', will according to this approach be unambiguously false; for apart from logically equivalent variants, it can be expressed only as follows:

$V \: x \: V \: P$ (Unicorn $[x] \wedge$ Rising $[P, x] \wedge$ Fails-to-occur $[P]$).

I do not find this consequence unacceptable. When we tend to assert 'a rising of a unicorn fails to occur', we should perhaps regard that sentence (though well-formed and expressing something) as incorrectly expressing the intended assertion, which could correctly (though somewhat ambiguously) be expressed by '*the* rising of a unicorn fails to occur'.[21]

Other ambiguities arise, purely as a matter of quantificational scope, if we replace the atomic contexts (30) and (33), which involve only a predicate constant, by more complex formulas. For instance, if we employ a predicate constant Sees* of type $\langle -1, 1 \rangle$ to express the seeing of *events*, the sentence

⌜Jones seems (to Jones) to see the (generic) rising of c⌝

may be taken as either the fully nonreferential

Seems [Jones, Jones, $\hat{u}$ Sees* $[u, \hat{\imath}$ Rises $[c, t]]]$,

the half-referential

Seems [Jones, Jones, $\hat{u} \: V \: x \: (x = c \wedge$ Sees* $[u, \hat{\imath}$ Rises $[x, t]])]$,

or the fully referential

$V \: x \: (x = c \wedge$ Seems [Jones, Jones, $\hat{u}$ Sees* $[u, \hat{\imath}$ Rises $[x, t]]])$.

[21] Another example corresponding to (35), though one that for reasons I shall not elaborate is no stronger than the one in the text, is 'the killing of a policeman occurred repeatedly'.

Indeed, the ambiguities associated with (30) and (33) can also be regarded as matters of quantificational scope. This is obvious in the case of (33); in connection with (30) we should observe that (32) is logically equivalent to

$$\mathcal{2} \; [\hat{t} \lor x \, (x = c \land \text{Rises} \, [x, t])].$$

Thus all the ambiguities we have considered in connection with the generic rising of an object can be regarded as having to do with the placing of a bounded existential quantifier; in some cases the bound is Unicorn $[x]$, and in others $x = c$.

If we now take into account not only these ambiguities but also those proceeding from the failure of English to distinguish between the generic and the (possibly unique) individual rising of an object, then such a simple sentence as

'the rising of a unicorn is not seen'

will have the following six readings, all of which are to some extent and under some circumstances plausible, and no two of which are logically equivalent:

$\neg$ Is-seen $[TP \lor x \, (\text{Unicorn} \, [x] \land \text{Rising} \, [P, x])]$,
$\neg \lor x \, (\text{Unicorn} \, [x] \land \text{Is-seen} \, [TP \, \text{Rising} \, [P, x]])$,
$\lor x \, (\text{Unicorn} \, [x] \land \neg \, \text{Is-seen} \, [TP \, \text{Rising} \, [P, x]])$,
$\neg$ Is-seen $[\hat{t} \lor x \, (\text{Unicorn} \, [x] \land \text{Rises} \, [x, t])]$,
$\neg \lor x \, (\text{Unicorn} \, [x] \land \text{Is-seen} \, [\hat{t} \, \text{Rises} \, [x, t]])$,
$\lor x \, (\text{Unicorn} \, [x] \land \neg \, \text{Is-seen} \, [\hat{t} \, \text{Rises} \, [x, t]])$.

What I have said about events is certainly incomplete and not completely certain; but I have reason to hope that the ambiguities I have pointed out will confirm two points sometimes mistakenly supposed incompatible: there is philosophic interest in attempting to analyze ordinary English; and ordinary English is an inadequate vehicle for philosophy.

REFERENCES

1. Carnap, R. *Meaning and Necessity.* 2nd ed. with supplements, Chicago, 1956.

2. Church, A. A Formulation of the Logic of Sense and Denotation. In P. Henle, H. Kallen, and S. Langer (eds.), *Structure, Method, and Meaning: Essays in Honor of H. M. Sheffer*. New York, 1951.

3. Davidson, D. The Logical Form of Action Sentences. In N. Rescher (ed.), *The Logic of Decision and Action*. Pittsburgh, 1967.

4. —. Causal Relations. *Journal of Philosophy* 64:691–703 (1967).

5. Frege, G. Über Sinn und Bedeutung. *Zeitschrift für Philosophie und philosophische Kritik* 100:25–50 (1892).

6. Kalish, D. and R. Montague. *Logic: Techniques of Formal Reasoning*. New York, 1964.

7. Kaplan, D. Foundations of Intensional Logic. Dissertation, University of California at Los Angeles, 1964.

8. Kripke, S. Semantical Considerations on Modal Logic. *Acta Philosophica Fennica* 16:83–94 (1963).

9. Lewis, D. An Argument for the Identity Theory. *Journal of Philosophy* 63:17–25 (1966).

10. Montague, R. Pragmatics. In R. Klibansky (ed.), *Contemporary Philosophy: A Survey*, vol. 1. Florence, 1968. Chap. 3 in this book.

11. —. Pragmatics and Intensional Logic. *Synthèse* 22:68–94 (1970). Chap. 4 in this book.

12. Prior, A. *Past, Present, and Future*. Oxford, 1967.

13. Quine, W. Notes on Existence and Necessity. *Journal of Philosophy* 40:113–27 (1943).

14. —. The Problem of Interpreting Modal Logic. *Journal of Symbolic Logic* 12:43–48 (1947).

15. —. *Word and Object*. Cambridge, Mass., 1960.

16. Tarski, A. Contributions to the Theory of Models, Part I. *Indagationes Mathematicae* 16:572–88 (1954) and 17:56–64 (1955).

6. English as a Formal Language

1. INTRODUCTION

I reject the contention that an important theoretical difference exists between formal and natural languages. On the other hand, I do not regard as successful the formal treatments of natural languages attempted by certain contemporary linguists. Like Donald Davidson[1] I regard the construction of a theory of truth—or rather, of the more general notion of truth under an arbitrary interpretation—as the basic goal of serious syntax and semantics; and the developments emanating from the Massachusetts Institute of Technology offer little promise towards that end.

In the present paper I shall accordingly present a precise treatment, culminating in a theory of truth, of a formal language that I believe may be reasonably regarded as a fragment of ordinary English. I have restricted myself to a very limited fragment, partly because there are portions of English I do not yet know how to treat, but also for the sake of simplicity and the clear exposition

Originally published in Bruno Visentini et al., *Linguaggi nella Società e nella Tecnica*. Milan, Edizioni di Comunità, 1970; pp. 189–224. Reprinted with permission. Some of the ideas in the present paper were adumbrated in seminar lectures in Amsterdam in January and February of 1966 and in Los Angeles in March of 1968. An earlier version of the present paper was delivered at the University of British Columbia in July of 1968. Much of the work reported here was supported by U.S. National Science Foundation Grant GP-7706. I should like to express my appreciation, for valuable criticism and suggestions, to Professors Yehoshua Bar-Hillel, David Lewis, Terence Parsons, Barbara Hall Partee, Dana Scott, and J. F. Staal, Messrs. Donald Berkey, John Cooley, and Perry Smith, and especially my student Dr. J. A. W. Kamp, without whose suggestions the present paper would not have been possible.

[1] In his paper Davidson [5].

of certain basic features. It is already known how to extend the treatment rather widely in various directions, and some of the extensions will be sketched in Part II of this paper;[2] the present fragment is, however, sufficiently comprehensive to illuminate the following features of English: its apparatus of quantification, the function of the definite article, the nature of ambiguity, and the role of adjectives and adverbs. The fragment may also hold some interest for those not concerned with natural languages; it provides an example of a fairly rich formal language—capable of accommodating modal operators, indirect contexts, and the definite article—not requiring for its interpretation a distinction between sense and denotation.

The treatment given here will be found to resemble the usual syntax and model theory (or semantics) of the predicate calculus,[3] but leans rather heavily on the intuitive aspects of certain recent developments in intensional logic.[4] In my semantic categories will be found echoes of the *syntactic* categories of Ajdukiewicz [1], and in my syntactic rules traces of the observations in Chapters 3 and 4 of Quine [12]. My treatment of quantification bears some resemblance to the rather differently motivated treatment in Bohnert and Backer [2]—a work that certainly antedates mine, but with which I did not become acquainted until after completing the present development. An important aspect of the present treatment—the semantics of adjectives and adverbs[5]—is due independently to J. A. W. Kamp and Terence Parsons, neither of whom has yet published his work in this domain.[6]

2. BASIC SYNTACTIC CATEGORIES

The basic, or unanalyzed, expressions of our formal language fall into the following nine categories, $B_0, \ldots, B_8$.

---

[2] [Editor's note: Part II of this paper was never written.]

[3] The model theory of the predicate calculus is of course due to Alfred Tarski; see for instance Tarski [15, 16, and 17].

[4] In particular, those of Montague [9].

[5] It is Donald Davidson who, in [3] and [4], has emphasized that adverbs appear to present special problems.

[6] [Editor's note: See Parsons [10], which appeared in 1971. Kamp's work on adjectives and adverbs remains unpublished.]

B_0 (or the set of *basic name phrases*) consists of all proper nouns of English, together with the symbols $v_0, \ldots,$ $v_n, \ldots$, which are known as (individual) *variables*.[7]

B_1 (or the set of *basic formulas*) = $\{\ulcorner \text{it rains} \urcorner\}$.[8]

B_2 (or the set of *basic one-place verb phrases*) = $\{\ulcorner \text{walks} \urcorner\}$.

B_3 (or the set of *basic two-place verb phrases*) = $\{\ulcorner \text{walks} \urcorner,$ $\ulcorner \text{loves} \urcorner, \ulcorner \text{cuts} \urcorner, \ulcorner \text{is} \urcorner\}$.

B_4 (or the set of *basic common noun phrases*) consists of all common nouns of English (as listed, say, in some standard dictionary), together with the phrase $\ulcorner$brother of $v_0 \urcorner$.

B_5 (or the set of *basic adformula phrases*) = $\{\ulcorner \text{not} \urcorner, \ulcorner \text{neces-}$ sarily$\urcorner, \ulcorner v_0$ believes that$\urcorner\}$.

B_6 (or the set of *basic ad-one-verb phrases*) = $\{\ulcorner \text{rapidly} \urcorner,$ $\ulcorner$in $v_0 \urcorner$, $\ulcorner$with $v_0 \urcorner$, $\ulcorner$through $v_0 \urcorner$, $\ulcorner$between v_0 and $v_1 \urcorner\}$.

B_7 (or the set of *basic ad-two-verb phrases*) = B_6.

B_8 (or the set of *basic adjective phrases*) consists of all «ordinary» descriptive adjectives of English (that is to say, with the exception of such «indexical» adjectives as $\ulcorner$former$\urcorner$, such «quantificational» adjectives as $\ulcorner$every$\urcorner$, $\ulcorner$most$\urcorner$, and $\ulcorner$three$\urcorner$, and adjectives of certain

---

[7] Thus v_n is to be the nth *variable* (of the object language). Strictly speaking, then, the expressions 'v_0', 'v_1', and the like are not variables but metalinguistic names of object language variables. (We need not specify the exact form of the latter, but it would certainly be possible to do so; for instance, v_n might be identified with the result of appending n primes to the letter 'x'.)

[8] By $\{\alpha\}$ I understand the unit set of α, by $\{\alpha, \beta\}$ the set having the objects α and β as its only members, and so on. Corners (or quasi-quotes) are used in the manner of Quine [11]. Roughly speaking, the convention is this. If $\Gamma_0, \ldots, \Gamma_n$ are designatory expressions of the metalanguage (in particular, names of English expressions or variables referring to English expressions; we shall employ lower-case Greek letters as variables of this sort), then the expression

$$\ulcorner \Gamma_0, \ldots, \Gamma_n \urcorner$$

is to designate the concatenation of the expression to which $\Gamma_0, \ldots, \Gamma_n$ refer. If, however, any of $\Gamma_0, \ldots, \Gamma_n$ are not designatory expressions of the metalanguage but rather individual words of the object language, we first replace such words by their quotation names. For instance, if λ is an expression of English, then $\ulcorner \text{walks } \lambda \urcorner = \ulcorner \text{'walks' } \lambda \urcorner$ = the result of writing 'walks' followed by λ; $\ulcorner \text{walks} \urcorner = \ulcorner \text{'walks'} \urcorner$ = 'walks'; and $\ulcorner \text{it rains} \urcorner = \ulcorner \text{'it' 'rains'} \urcorner$ = the result of writing 'it' followed by 'rains' = 'it rains'.

other exceptional varieties), together with the phrases $\ulcorner$bigger than $v_0\urcorner$, $\ulcorner$in $v_0\urcorner$, and $\ulcorner$between v_0 and $v_1\urcorner$.

A few remarks are in order. We speak here of *basic* name phrases, *basic* formulas, and the like. This is because we shall later extend the categories $B_0, B_1, \ldots$ to sets $C_0, C_1, \ldots$, which will be regarded as the full categories of name phrases, of formulas, and so on.

Roughly speaking, basic one-place and two-place verb phrases (apart from $\ulcorner$is$\urcorner$), are what one usually calls *intransitive* and *transitive verbs* respectively. There are examples in English of three-place verb phrases, like $\ulcorner$gives$\urcorner$, and possibly of verb phrases having a still greater number of places; but for simplicity we ignore these in our fragment. (In connection with a more highly inflected language such as Latin, the maximum number of places of verbs could perhaps be fixed more easily and naturally, as the number of *cases* in the language that have uses associated with verbs; we thus exclude the vocative.) Notice that $\ulcorner$walks$\urcorner$ is both intransitive (as in $\ulcorner$John walks rapidly$\urcorner$) and transitive (as in $\ulcorner$John walks a dog$\urcorner$). $\ulcorner$Cuts$\urcorner$ and $\ulcorner$loves$\urcorner$ also have intransitive uses, but for simplicity we ignore them.

Traditional grammar groups together modifiers of formulas, of verbs of various numbers of places, of adjectives, and of adverbs, and calls them all adverbs. It will be important, however, to distinguish these various sorts of modifiers. Accordingly, we shall speak of *adformulas* and *adverbs*, the latter in the narrow sense of modifiers of verbs, and subdivided into *ad-one-verbs* and *ad-two-verbs* according as the verbs modified are of one or two places; and we could, in an extension of the present fragment, speak of adadjectives, adad-one-verbs, adad-two-verbs, adadadjectives, adadad-one-verbs, and adadad-two-verbs as well. (The word $\ulcorner$very$\urcorner$ would for instance belong to all of these categories.) It may seem artificial, in view of the coincidence of the categories B_6 and B_7, to introduce them both; and it is perhaps not really necessary to do so in the present context. (It has, however, been suggested that $\ulcorner$and conversely$\urcorner$ appears to qualify as an ad-two-verb that is not an ad-one-verb.) Still, it is certainly possible to imagine languages in which it would be highly desirable on semantic grounds to countenance two co-extensive syntactic categories.

3. SEMANTIC CATEGORIES

In the following we think of A as the set of possible individuals to which our object language refers and I as the set of possible worlds. We consider now the possible denotations of English expressions relative to A and I; these will fall into nine categories, $U_{0,A,I}, \ldots, U_{8,A,I}$, corresponding to the syntactic categories $B_0, \ldots, B_8$. (I shall, however, generally suppress the subscripts 'A' and 'I', and write simply 'U_0', $\ldots$, 'U_8'.)

Fundamental categories

U_0 (or the universe of possible denotations of name phrases, relative to A and I) $= A$.

U_1 (or the universe of possible denotations of formulas) $= 2^I$.

(Here we use two common set-theoretical notations. The number 2 is identified with the set $\{0, 1\}$; and if X, Y are any sets, X^Y is to be the set of functions with domain Y and range included in X. Further, we identify 0 and 1 with the respective truth values falsehood and truth; thus U_1 becomes the set of all functions from possible worlds to truth values, that is, the set of all *propositions* (relative to I).)

Derived categories

All other semantic categories to be considered will have the form $V_0^{V_1 \times \cdots \times V_n}$, where $n \geqslant 1$ and $V_0, \ldots, V_n$ are themselves semantic categories. (By $V_1 \times \ldots \times V_n$ is understood the Cartesian product of the sets $V_1, \ldots, V_n$, that is, the set of ordered n-tuples of which the respective constituents are members of $V_1, \ldots, V_n$; thus $V_0^{V_1 \times \cdots \times V_n}$ is the set of n-place functions with arguments drawn from $V_1, \ldots, V_n$ respectively and with values in V_0.) Not every such combination generated by the fundamental categories is exemplified in English, and still fewer are exemplified in the fragment we treat here. In particular, we consider the following seven additional categories.

U_2 (or the universe of possible denotations of one-place verb phrases) $= U_1{}^{U_0}$.

(The members of U_2 are thus what we might regard as *properties* of individuals, or, as we shall sometimes say, one-place *predicates* of individuals.[9])

U_3 (or the universe of possible denotations of two-place verb phrases) $= U_1{}^{U_0 \times U_0}$.

(The members of U_3 are thus two-place *relations-in-intension*, or *predicates*, of individuals.)

U_4 (or the universe of possible denotations of common noun phrases) $= U_1{}^{U_0} (= U_2)$.

U_5 (or the universe of possible denotations of adformula phrases) $= U_1{}^{U_1}$.

U_6 (or the universe of possible denotations of ad-one-verb phrases) $= U_2{}^{U_2}$.

U_7 (or the universe of possible denotations of ad-two-verb phrases) $= U_3{}^{U_3}$.

U_8 (or the universe of possible denotations of adjective phrases) $= U_4{}^{U_4}$.

4. MODELS

A *model* is an ordered 11-tuple $\langle A, I, G_0, \ldots, G_8 \rangle$ such that (1) A is a set containing at least two elements,[10] (2) I is a nonempty set, and (3) $G_0, \ldots, G_8$ are functions assigning appropriate denotation functions to the members of $B_0, \ldots, B_8$ respectively.

I shall of course spell out clause (3) in exact terms. The idea is this. We have supplemented the «usual» basic expressions of English by expressions containing free variables. Such an expression will not in general denote anything in an absolute sense, but only *with respect to* a given infinite sequence of individuals. This

---

[9] The present notion of a property, as well as those of a relation-in-intension and a proposition, are essentially those of Kripke [8].

[10] This assumption is for convenience only. We could manage with assuming simply that A is nonempty, but the stronger assumption somewhat simplifies a few definitions given below and explicitly noted.

sequence will provide the values of all variables, and in such a way that the nth constituent of the sequence will be regarded as the value of v_n. Thus a model should assign to a basic expression not a denotation but a *denotation function*, that is, a function that maps each infinite sequence of individuals onto a possible denotation of the expression. The exact clauses corresponding to (3) are accordingly the following. (As above, A and I are regarded as the sets of possible individuals and possible worlds respectively. Recall also that in set-theoretical usage ω is the set of natural numbers; hence A^ω is the set of infinite sequences of members of A.)

(3a) $G_0, \ldots, G_8$ are functions with the respective domains $B_0, \ldots, B_8$.

(3b) $G_0(\alpha) \in U_0^{A^\omega}$ whenever $\alpha \in B_0$; ...; $G_8(\alpha) \in U_8^{A^\omega}$ whenever $\alpha \in B_8$.

(3c) If H is any one of $G_0, \ldots, G_8$, α is in the domain of H, x and y are in A^ω, and $x_n = y_n$ for all n such that v_n occurs in α, then $H(\alpha)(x) = H(\alpha)(y)$. (Thus although each denotation function, regarded as a function on individuals, is infinitary, its value will always be determined by the arguments occupying a certain finite set of argument places—and indeed, just those places that correspond to variables of the corresponding expression.)

The remaining clauses require that certain definite denotation functions be assigned to certain basic expressions, in particular, variables, $\ulcorner$is$\urcorner$, $\ulcorner$not$\urcorner$, $\ulcorner$entity$\urcorner$, and $\ulcorner$necessarily$\urcorner$, which are thus treated as logically determinate.

(3d) $G_0(v_n)$ is that function f in A^{A^ω} such that, for all $x \in A^\omega$, $f(x) = x_n$.

(3e) G_3 ($\ulcorner$is$\urcorner$) is that function f in $((2^I)^{A \times A})^{A^\omega}$ such that, for all $x \in A^\omega$, all $t, u \in A$, and all $i \in I$, $f(x)(t, u)(i) = 1$ if and only if $t = u$.

(3f) G_4 ($\ulcorner$entity$\urcorner$) is that function f in $((2^I)^A)^{A^\omega}$ such that, for all $x \in A^\omega$, all $t \in A$, and all $i \in I$, $f(x)(t)(i) = 1$. (Thus with respect to every infinite sequence $\ulcorner$entity$\urcorner$ denotes the universal property of individuals.)

(3g) G_5 ($\ulcorner$not$\urcorner$) is that function f in $((2^I)^{2^I})^{A^\omega}$ such that for all $x \in A^\omega$, all $p \in 2^I$, and all $i \in I$, $f(x)(p)(i) = 1$ if and only if $p(i) = 0$.

(3h) G_5 ($\ulcorner$necessarily$\urcorner$) is that function f in $((2^I)^{2^I})^{A^\omega}$ such that for all $x \in A^\omega$, all $p \in 2^I$, and all $i \in I$, $f(x)(p)(i) = 1$ if and only if $p(j) = 1$ for all $j \in I$. (We thus employ *standard*, or *universal*, or *Leibnizian* necessity, amounting to truth in all possible worlds.)

It is because the categories of basic expressions overlap that we must have separate functions $G_0, \ldots, G_8$, rather than a single function assigning denotation functions to all basic expressions.

5. SYNTACTIC CATEGORIES

In this section we shall extend the basic syntactic categories $B_0, B_1, \ldots, B_8$ to the full syntactic categories C_0 (or the set of name phrases), C_1 (or the set of formulas), ..., C_8 (or the set of adjective phrases). These sets will be «introduced», in a sense that will be made precise below, by the following *syntactical* (or *grammatical*) *rules*, S1–S17; let it only be said that $C_0, \ldots, C_8$ will be defined in such a way as to make S1–S17 true. (I use '&' as an abbreviation of 'and' and '→' as an abbreviation 'if... then').

Rule of basic expressions:

S1. $B_0 \subseteq C_0, \ldots, B_8 \subseteq C_8$.

Rules corresponding to functional application:

S2. $\delta \in C_2$ & $\alpha \in C_0$ & $\langle \delta, \alpha, \varphi \rangle \in R_2 \rightarrow \varphi \in C_1$,

where R_2 is that three-place relation among expressions such that if δ, α, φ are any expressions, then δ, α, φ stand in the relation R_2—that is, $\langle \delta, \alpha, \varphi \rangle \in R_2$—if and only if $\varphi = \ulcorner \alpha \delta \urcorner$. (According to S2, if δ is a one-place verb phrase and α a name phrase, and $\varphi = \ulcorner \alpha\, \delta \urcorner$, then φ is a formula. For example, if $\delta = \ulcorner$walks$\urcorner$ and $\alpha = \ulcorner$John$\urcorner$, then $\ulcorner$John walks$\urcorner$ is a formula in view of S2.)

S3. $\delta \in C_3$ & $\alpha, \beta, \in C_0$ & $\langle \delta, \alpha, \beta, \varphi \rangle \in R_3 \rightarrow \varphi \in C_1$,

where $\langle \delta, \alpha, \beta, \varphi \rangle \in R_3$ if and only if there exist a (possibly empty) expression μ and an expression $\gamma \in B_3$ such that $\delta = \ulcorner \gamma \, \mu \urcorner$ and $\varphi = \ulcorner \alpha \, \gamma \, \beta \, \mu \urcorner$. (For example, if $\delta = \ulcorner \text{cuts} \urcorner$ and α, β are the respective variables v_0, v_1, then δ, α, β, «bear the relation R_3 to $\ulcorner v_0$ cuts $v_1 \urcorner$»—that is to say, $\langle \delta, \alpha, \beta, \ulcorner v_0$ cuts $v_1 \urcorner \rangle \in R_3$—and hence $\ulcorner v_0$ cuts $v_1 \urcorner$ is a formula. Also, if $\delta = \ulcorner \text{cuts rapidly} \urcorner$, then δ, v_0, v_1 bear the relation R_3 to $\ulcorner v_0$ cuts v_1 rapidly $\urcorner$. As far as the present fragment is concerned, we could replace the «syntactical relations» R_2–R_{17} by *total functions*, that is relations for which the last argument (the *value*) is uniquely determined by the preceding arguments, and which are *total* in the sense that a value will exist for any choice of expressions[11] as occupants of the preceding argument places. The former condition, of functionality, is indeed satisfied by the syntactical relations we consider, but would naturally and conveniently be violated in connection with languages having a more flexible word order than English, or indeed in connection with richer fragments of English that admit synonymous sets of expressions of various sorts. Most of our syntactical relations—for instance, R_3—fail, on the other hand, to be total; but this feature is a pure convenience and could be eliminated at the expense of complicating their definitions.)

S4. $\delta \in C_5 \ \& \ \varphi \in C_1 \ \& \ \langle \delta, \varphi, \psi \rangle \in R_4 \rightarrow \psi \in C_1$,

where $\langle \delta, \varphi, \psi \rangle \in R_4$ if and only if either (i) $\delta \neq \ulcorner \text{not} \urcorner$ and $\ulcorner \delta \varphi \urcorner = \psi$, or (ii) $\delta = \ulcorner \text{not} \urcorner$, φ does not end with $\ulcorner \text{not} \urcorner$, and $\ulcorner \varphi \, \delta \urcorner = \psi$. (For instance, if $\varphi = \ulcorner \text{John loves Jane} \urcorner$, then $\ulcorner \text{necessarily John loves Jane} \urcorner$ and $\ulcorner \text{John loves Jane not} \urcorner$ are formulas according to S4. As the second example indicates, our fragment involves an archaic style of negation. The more modern form (for example, $\ulcorner \text{John does not love Jane} \urcorner$) involves certain complications that will be discussed later. The clause 'φ does not end with $\ulcorner \text{not} \urcorner$' in the characterization of R_4 is included in order to avoid double negations, but for simplicity is stronger than necessary for this

---

[11] I have used the word 'expression' without indicating its precise meaning. For our present purposes an expression (of the object language) could be understood as a finite and possibly empty concatenation of various words—in particular, the words (including variables) that make up basic expressions, together with the words $\ulcorner \text{every} \urcorner$, $\ulcorner \text{that} \urcorner$, $\ulcorner \text{a} \urcorner$, $\ulcorner \text{an} \urcorner$, and $\ulcorner \text{the} \urcorner$. A fairly obvious enlargement of the basic constituents of expressions would be necessary for the extensions of our present fragment that are proposed later.

purpose; it also prevents the formation of such combinations as $\ulcorner$John loves a woman such that that woman loves John not not$\urcorner$.)

S5. $\delta \in C_6 \ \& \ \mu \in C_2 \ \& \ \langle \delta, \mu, v \rangle \in R_5 \rightarrow v \in C_2$,

where $\langle \delta, \mu, v \rangle \in R_5$ if and only if $v = \ulcorner \mu \ \delta \urcorner$. (Thus the result of appending an ad-one-verb to a one-place verb phrase is a one-place verb phrase. For instance, the one-place verb phrase $\ulcorner$walks rapidly$\urcorner$ is «obtained» by S5 from the one-place verb phrase $\ulcorner$walks$\urcorner$.)

S6. $\delta \in C_7 \ \& \ \mu \in C_3 \ \& \ \langle \delta, \mu, v \rangle \in R_6 \rightarrow v \in C_3$,

where $\langle \delta, \mu, v \rangle \in R_6$ if and only if $\ulcorner \mu \ \delta \urcorner = v$. (For instance, $\ulcorner$cuts with $v_0\urcorner$ is obtained by S6 from $\ulcorner$cuts$\urcorner$.)

S7. $\delta \in C_8 \ \& \ \zeta \in C_4 \ \& \ \langle \delta, \zeta, \eta \rangle \in R_7 \rightarrow \eta \in C_4$,

where $\langle \delta, \zeta, \eta \rangle \in R_7$ if and only if either δ is one word long and $\eta = \ulcorner \delta \ \zeta \urcorner$, or δ is not one word long and $\eta = \ulcorner \zeta \ \delta \urcorner$. (For instance, the common noun phrases $\ulcorner$big house$\urcorner$ and $\ulcorner$house between v_0 and $v_1\urcorner$ are obtained by S7 from the common noun phrase $\ulcorner$house$\urcorner$.)

Rules of substitution and quantification for formulas:

S8. $\varphi \in C_1 \ \& \ \alpha, \beta \in C_0 \ \& \ \langle \varphi, \alpha, \beta, \psi \rangle \in R_8 \rightarrow \psi \in C_1$,

where $\langle \varphi, \alpha, \beta, \psi \rangle \in R_8$ if and only if α is a variable and ψ is obtained from φ by replacing all occurrences of α by β. (For instance, the formulas $\ulcorner$John walks through $v_1\urcorner$ and $\ulcorner$John walks through Amsterdam$\urcorner$ are obtained by S8 from the formula $\ulcorner$John walks through $v_0\urcorner$.)

S9. $\varphi \in C_1 \ \& \ \alpha \in C_0 \ \& \ \zeta \in C_4 \ \& \ \langle \varphi, \alpha, \zeta, \psi \rangle \in R_9 \rightarrow \psi \in C_1$,

where $\langle \varphi, \alpha, \zeta, \psi \rangle \in R_9$ if and only if α is a variable and ψ is obtained from φ by replacing the first occurrence of α by $\ulcorner$every $\zeta\urcorner$ and all other occurrences of α by $\ulcorner$that $\eta\urcorner$, where η is the member of B_4 that occurs first in ζ. (For instance, the formulas $\ulcorner$every tall man in Amsterdam loves a woman such that that woman loves that man$\urcorner$ is obtained by S9 from the formula $\ulcorner v_0$ loves a woman such that that woman loves $v_0\urcorner$. It would be a little more natural to say $\ulcorner$every tall man in Amsterdam loves a woman such that that woman loves *him*$\urcorner$. Thus the phrase $\ulcorner$that $\eta\urcorner$, where η is a basic common noun phrase, plays the role of a pronoun, but is a little more flexible and avoids the complications associated with gender and case. As another example of S9, notice that ⌜every man loves that man⌝ can be obtained from ⌜v_0 loves v_0⌝; here it would be much more natural to say ⌜every man loves *himself*⌝. It would be quite possible to give rules providing for such locutions, but I decline to do so because of the rather uninteresting complications that would be involved.[12])

---

[12] There may, however, be some interest in the following tentative observation, which would be relevant to the formulation of such rules. If the first occurrence of a variable α in a formula φ is as the "subject" of a basic verb phrase, and ζ is a common noun phrase, then it appears that we may construct a "universal generalization" of φ (restricted to ζ) by replacing the first occurrence of α by ⌜ every ζ⌝ and each other occurrence of α by a reflexive pronoun (⌜himself⌝, ⌜herself⌝, or ⌜itself⌝, depending on ζ) or an ordinary pronoun (⌜he⌝, ⌜him⌝, ⌜she⌝, ⌜her⌝, ⌜it⌝, depending on considerations of gender and case), according as the occurrence of α in question does or does not stand as an argument of the same occurrence of a basic verb phrase as the first occurrence of α. Thus from ⌜v_0 loves v_0⌝, ⌜v_0 loves a woman such that that woman loves v_0⌝, and ⌜v_0 loves a woman such that v_0 knows that woman⌝ we may obtain ⌜every man loves himself⌝, ⌜every man loves a woman such that that woman loves him⌝, and ⌜every man loves a woman such that he knows that woman⌝ respectively; but from the second we may not obtain ⌜every man loves a woman such that that woman loves himself⌝. Also, the present rule will not allow us to obtain ⌜every man loves him⌝ from ⌜v_0 loves v_0⌝. This is as it should be; for although ⌜every man loves him⌝ is grammatically correct, it is not a universal generalization of ⌜v_0 loves v_0⌝.

The present rule, if, as appears somewhat doubtful, it is indeed accurate, would give us a way of distinguishing between those verb phrases that ought to be taken as basic and those that ought to be regarded as generated by simpler components. For instance, ⌜gives ... to⌝ could only be basic, because ⌜every man gives v_1 to himself⌝, and not ⌜every man gives v_1 to him⌝, is a universal generalization of ⌜v_0 gives v_1 to v_0⌝; the same comment would apply to ⌜sends ... to⌝. On the other hand, ⌜takes ... with⌝ would not be basic, because ⌜v_0 takes v_1 with v_0⌝ has ⌜every man takes v_1 with him⌝ and not ⌜every man takes v_1 with himself⌝ as a universal generalization. In some cases, as with ⌜v_0 keeps v_1 near v_0⌝, one feels that a correct universal generalization can be obtained in either way—that is, with the use of either a reflexive or an ordinary pronoun; this may be taken either as reflecting indecision as to whether ⌜keeps ... near⌝ is to be basic or as indicating that ⌜v_0 keeps v_1 near v_0⌝ may be generated in two ways—either from a basic verb phrase ⌜keeps ... near⌝, or from ⌜keeps⌝ together with an adverbial phrase ⌜near v_0⌝.

By way of clarification I should mention that in the tentative rule considered above we should understand 'argument' in such a way that v_0 qualifies as an argument of ⌜gives ... to⌝ in ⌜v_0 gives a book to v_0⌝, ⌜v_0 gives the book to v_0⌝, and ⌜v_0 gives every book to v_0⌝ as well as in ⌜v_0 gives v_1 to v_0⌝.

We have spoken about universal generalizations, which are introduced by S9; but completely parallel remarks could be made about the operations involved in S10, S11, S13–S16 below.

S10. $\varphi \in C_1 \,\&\, \alpha \in C_0 \,\&\, \zeta \in C_4 \,\&\, \langle \varphi, \alpha, \zeta, \psi \rangle \in R_{10} \rightarrow \psi \in C_1$,

where $\langle \varphi, \alpha, \zeta, \psi \rangle \in R_{10}$ if and only if α is a variable and ψ is obtained from φ by replacing the first occurrence of α by $\ulcorner$a $\zeta \urcorner$ (or $\ulcorner$an $\zeta \urcorner$, according as ζ begins with a consonant or not) and all other occurrences of α by $\ulcorner$that $\eta \urcorner$, where η is the member of B_4 that occurs first in ζ. (For instance, the formulas $\ulcorner$a woman in Amsterdam loves a man such that that man loves that woman$\urcorner$ and $\ulcorner$John is a man$\urcorner$ are obtained by S10 from the formulas $\ulcorner v_0$ loves a man such that that man loves $v_0 \urcorner$ and $\ulcorner$John is $v_1 \urcorner$ respectively.)

S11. $\varphi \in C_1 \,\&\, \alpha \in C_0 \,\&\, \zeta \in C_4 \,\&\, \langle \varphi, \alpha, \zeta, \psi \rangle \in R_{11} \rightarrow \psi \in C_1$,

where $\langle \varphi, \alpha, \zeta, \psi \rangle \in R_{11}$ if and only if α is a variable and ψ is obtained from φ by replacing the first occurrence of α by $\ulcorner$the $\zeta \urcorner$ and all other occurrences of α by $\ulcorner$ that $\eta \urcorner$, where η is the member of B_4 that occurs first in ζ. (For instance, $\ulcorner$the woman in Amsterdam loves a man such that that man loves that woman$\urcorner$ is obtained by S11 from $\ulcorner v_0$ loves a man such that that man loves $v_0 \urcorner$.)

Rules of substitution and quantification for common noun phrases:

S12. $\zeta \in C_4 \,\&\, \alpha, \beta \in C_0 \,\&\, \langle \zeta, \alpha, \beta, \eta \rangle \in R_{12} \rightarrow \eta \in C_4$,

where $R_{12} = R_8$. (For instance, the common noun phrase $\ulcorner$brother of John$\urcorner$ is obtained by S12 from the common noun phrase $\ulcorner$brother of $v_0 \urcorner$.)

S13. $\zeta, \eta \in C_4 \,\&\, \alpha \in C_0 \,\&\, \langle \eta, \alpha, \zeta, \theta \rangle \in R_{13} \rightarrow \theta \in C_4$,

where $R_{13} = R_9$. (For instance, $\ulcorner$man such that that man loves every woman$\urcorner$ is obtained by S13 from $\ulcorner$man such that that man loves $v_1 \urcorner$.)

S14. $\zeta, \eta \in C_4 \,\&\, \alpha \in C_0 \,\&\, \langle \eta, \alpha, \zeta, \theta \rangle \in R_{14} \rightarrow \theta \in C_4$,

where $R_{14} = R_{10}$. (For instance, $\ulcorner$man such that that man loves a woman$\urcorner$ is obtained by S14 from $\ulcorner$man such that that man loves $v_1 \urcorner$.)

S15. $\zeta, \eta \in C_4 \,\&\, \alpha \in C_0 \,\&\, \langle \eta, \alpha, \zeta, \theta \rangle \in R_{15} \rightarrow \theta \in C_4$,

where $R_{15} = R_{11}$. (For instance, $\ulcorner$man such that that man loves the woman in Amsterdam$\urcorner$ is obtained by S15 from $\ulcorner$man such that that man loves $v_1 \urcorner$.)

Rule of relative clauses:

S16. $\zeta \in C_4 \ \& \ \varphi \in C_1 \ \& \ \alpha \in C_0 \ \& \ \langle \zeta, \varphi, \alpha, \eta \rangle \in R_{16} \rightarrow \eta \in C_4$,

where $\langle \zeta, \varphi, \alpha, \eta \rangle \in R_{16}$ if and only if α is a variable and $\eta = \ulcorner \zeta$ such that $\psi \urcorner$, where ψ comes from φ by replacing all occurrences of α by $\ulcorner$ that $\theta \urcorner$ where θ is the member of B_4 that occurs first in ζ. (For instance, if $\zeta = \ulcorner$ tall woman in Amsterdam $\urcorner$, $\varphi = \ulcorner v_0$ loves every man such that that man loves $v_0 \urcorner$, and $\alpha = v_0$, we obtain by S16 the common noun phrase $\ulcorner$ tall woman in Amsterdam such that that woman loves every man such that that man loves that woman $\urcorner$. The latter could be more idiomatically formulated as $\ulcorner$ tall woman in Amsterdam such that that woman loves every man such that that man loves *her* $\urcorner$—which, as intimated earlier, will be avoided because of the minor complications of gender and case it would introduce—or as $\ulcorner$ tall woman in Amsterdam that loves every man such that that man loves that woman $\urcorner$, or, applying the same principle of formulation to the inner relative clause, as $\ulcorner$ tall woman in Amsterdam that loves every man that loves that woman $\urcorner$. This usage too would involve complications that I should prefer here to avoid.[13])

[13] Let me indicate, briefly and rather vaguely, how to account for the last style of relative clause. It would perhaps be best to retain S16, because it is applicable to any formula φ whatever, and to add a rule of less generality having roughly the following content: if ζ is a common noun phrase, φ is a formula, α is a variable occurring in φ, and the first occurrence of α in φ is as an argument of the main occurrence of a verb phrase in φ, then $\ulcorner \zeta$ that $\delta \urcorner$ is a common noun phrase, where δ comes from φ by deleting the first occurrence of α and replacing all other occurrences of α by $\ulcorner$ that $\theta \urcorner$, where θ is the basic common noun phrase that occurs first in ζ. By this rule we could obtain the last example in the text, as well as the common noun phrase $\ulcorner$ woman that John loves $\urcorner$. The fourth hypothesis of the rule is required to avoid such ungrammatical combinations as $\ulcorner$ room that John walks through $\urcorner$ (traditionally a borderline case of grammaticality), $\ulcorner$ man that a brother of is tall $\urcorner$, $\ulcorner$ city that Amsterdam is between and Paris $\urcorner$, and $\ulcorner$ man that a woman that loves is tall $\urcorner$. The complications connected with the present rule all derive from its fourth hypothesis, and have to do with precisely characterizing the notions of an *argument* and a *main occurrence of a verb phrase*; for an analogous situation see the discussion below of modern negation and the *main occurrence of a verb*.

I should perhaps mention that S16 leads to such "vacuous" common noun phrases as $\ulcorner$ woman such that John loves Mary $\urcorner$. It would be easy enough to exclude them, simply by adding 'α occurs in φ' to the characterization of R_{16}; but there seems to be no particular point in doing so.

Rule of predicate adjectives:

S17. $\alpha \in C_0 \ \& \ \delta \in C_8 \ \& \ \langle \alpha, \delta, \varphi \rangle \in R_{17} \ \rightarrow \ \varphi \in C_1$,

where $\langle \alpha, \delta, \varphi \rangle \in R_{17}$ if and only if $\varphi = \ulcorner \alpha$ is $\delta \urcorner$. (For example, we obtain by S17 the formulas $\ulcorner$John is big$\urcorner$ and $\ulcorner$John is in $v_0 \urcorner$.)

Having stated the syntactical rules, we now address ourselves to their precise role. The following theorem, due in large part to Mr. Perry Smith, has a simple proof that will not be given here.

Theorem. There is exactly one «minimal sequence» of sets satisfying S1–S17—that is, exactly one sequence $\langle C_0, \ldots, C_8 \rangle$ such that S1–S17 hold for $C_0, \ldots, C_8$ and such that, for every sequence $\langle D_0, \ldots, D_8 \rangle$, if S1–S17 hold for $D_0, \ldots, D_8$ (taken in place of $C_0, \ldots, C_8$ respectively), then $C_0 \subseteq D_0, \ldots, C_8 \subseteq D_8$.

We are now in a position to define in an exact way the full syntactic categories $C_0, \ldots, C_8$: C_0 (or the set of *name phrases*), $\ldots, C_8$ (or the set of *adjective phrases*) are respectively the $0^{\text{th}}, \ldots, 8^{\text{th}}$ constituents of the minimal sequence satisfying S1–S17. (Thus the precise formal role of S1–S17 is simply to occur as a part of the present definition, as well as of the Theorem above.)

We can also characterize exactly the set of sentences of our fragment: φ is a *sentence* if and only if $\varphi \in C_1$ and no variable occurs in φ.

6. SEMANTIC OPERATIONS

Corresponding to the syntactic rules S2, $\ldots$, S17 (and to given sets A and I) we introduce semantic operations $F_{2,A,I}, \ldots, F_{17,A,I}$ with the following intuitive significance: if the expression μ is «obtained» by the nth syntactic rule from the expressions $\delta_0, \ldots, \delta_k$—that is to say, if $\langle \delta_0, \ldots, \delta_k, \mu \rangle \in R_n$—and if $g_0, \ldots, g_k$ are possible denotation functions of $\delta_0, \ldots, \delta_k$ respectively, then $F_{n,A,I}(g_0, \ldots, g_k)$ is to be the corresponding denotation function of μ. (The possibility of introducing such an operation $F_{n,A,I}$ imposes a *semantic restriction* on the relation R_n: though, as observed above, R_n is not required to be a function (or «uni-valued»), its values for a given sequence of initial arguments must all have the same intended denotation.)

The operations $F_{n,A,I}$ will of course have various numbers of arguments, depending on the numbers of arguments of the corresponding relations R_n. We may as well assume, however, that the domain of definition for each argument place of each $F_{n,A,I}$ is always the same, and indeed is the set of all possible denotation functions corresponding to A and I, that is, the union of the sets $U_{0,A,I}^{A^\omega}, \ldots, U_{8,A,I}^{A^\omega}$. We may therefore completely characterize $F_{2,A,I}, \ldots, F_{17,A,I}$ by specifying their values for arbitrary sequences of arguments; as usual we shall suppress the subscripts 'A' and 'I', and write simply 'F_2', ..., 'F_{17}'.

> $F_2(d, a) =$ that function p with domain A^ω such that, for all $x \in A^\omega$, $p(x) = d(x)(a(x))$.

(The right side makes *some* (conventionally determined) sense no matter what d, a are. We shall of course be interested only in the case in which d, a are denotation functions «of the right sort» —that is, in this instance, are in $U_2^{A^\omega}$, $U_0^{A^\omega}$ respectively; and in this case the right side makes *intuitive* sense. Similar remarks will apply to the characterizations of $F_3, \ldots, F_{17}$.)

> $F_3(d, a, b) =$ that function p with domain A^ω such that, for all $x \in A^\omega$, $p(x) = d(x)(a(x), b(x))$.
> $F_4(d, p) = F_2(d, p)$.
> $F_5(d, m) = F_2(d, m)$.
> $F_6(d, m) = F_2(d, m)$.
> $F_7(d, z) = F_2(d, z)$.

(Thus we see why syntactical rules S2–S7 were grouped together as corresponding to «functional application».)

> $F_8(p, a, b) =$ that function $q \in U_1^{A^\omega}$ such that, for all $x \in A^\omega$, $q(x) = p(x_{b(x)}^n)$, where n is the index of the variable represented by a (that is, the unique natural number n such that, for all $y \in A^\omega$, $a(y) = y_n$), and x_t^n is in general the sequence exactly like x except that the nth constituent is t.

(It is for the sake of this rather intuitive characterization of F_8 (as well as of F_9–F_{16} below) that A was required to contain at least two elements. With the weaker assumption that A simply be nonempty, the following somewhat less transparent characterization of F_8 gives the correct result: $F_8(p, a, b) =$ the unique function $q \in U_1{}^{A^\omega}$ such that, for all $x \in A^\omega$ and all $n \in \omega$, if $a(y) = y_n$ for all $y \in A^\omega$, then $q(x) = p(x_{b(x)}^n)$. Similar alternative characterizations would be possible in the cases of F_9–F_{16} as well.)

$F_9(p, a, z) =$ that function $q \in U_1{}^{A^\omega}$ such that, for all $x \in A^\omega$ and all $i \in I$, $q(x)(i) = 1$ if and only if $p(x_t^n)(i) = 1$ whenever t is a member of A for which $z(x)(t)(i) = 1$, where n is as above (in the characterization of F_8).

$F_{10}(p, a, z) =$ that function $q \in U_1{}^{A^\omega}$ such that, for all $x \in A^\omega$ and all $i \in I$, $q(x)(i) = 1$ if and only if $p(x_t^n)(i) = 1$ for some $t \in A$ such that $z(x)(t)(i) = 1$, where n is as above.

$F_{11}(p, a, z) =$ that function $q \in U_1{}^{A^\omega}$ such that, for all $x \in A^\omega$ and all $i \in I$, $q(x)(i) = 1$ if and only if there exists $t \in A$ such that $\{t\}$ is the set of objects $u \in A$ for which $z(x)(u)(i) = 1$, and $f(x_t^n)(i) = 1$, where n is is as above.

$F_{12}(z, a, b) =$ that function $e \in U_4{}^{A^\omega}$ such that, for all $x \in A^\omega$, $e(x) = z(x_{b(x)}^n)$, where n is as above.

$F_{13}(e, a, x) =$ that function $h \in U_4{}^{A^\omega}$ such that, for all $x \in A^\omega$, all $u \in A$, and all $i \in I$, $h(x)(u)(i) = 1$ if and only if $e(x_t^n)(u)(i) = 1$ whenever t is a member of A for which $z(x)(t)(i) = 1$, where n is as above.

$F_{14}(e, a, z) =$ that function $h \in U_4{}^{A^\omega}$ such that, for all $x \in A^\omega$, all $u \in A$, and all $i \in I$, $h(x)(u)(i) = 1$ if and only if $e(x_t^n)(u)(i) = 1$ for some $t \in A$ such that $z(x)(t)(i) = 1$, where n is as above.

$F_{15}(e, a, z) =$ that function $h \in U_4{}^{A^\omega}$ such that, for all $x \in A^\omega$, all $u \in A$, and all $i \in I$, $h(x)(u)(i) = 1$ if and only if there exists $t \in A$ such that $\{t\}$ is the set of objects $v \in A$ for which $z(x)(v)(i) = 1$, and $e(x_t^n)(u)(i) = 1$, where n is as above.

$F_{16}(z, p, a) =$ that function $e \in U_4{}^{A^\omega}$ such that, for all $x \in A^\omega$, all $t \in A$, and all $i \in I$, $e(x)(t)(i) = 1$ if and only if $z(x)(t)(i) = 1$ and $p(x_t^n)(i) = 1$, where n is as above.

$F_{17}(a, d) =$ that function $p \in U_1{}^{A^\omega}$ such that, for all $x \in A^\omega$ and all $i \in I$, $p(x)(i) = 1$ if and only if $d(x)(z(x))(a(x))(i) = 1$, where z is that function in $U_4{}^{A^\omega}$ such that, for all $x \in A^\omega$, all $t \in A$, and all $i \in I$, $z(x)(t)(i) = 1$.

7. ANALYSES AND DENOTATIONS

Models, as we have seen, assign denotations (or, strictly speaking, denotation functions) to basic expressions only. Using the semantic operations, we shall wish to assign denotations to arbitrary *denoting expressions* (that is, arbitrary members of the union of $C_0, \ldots, C_8$). This task is complicated by the fact that we have no unique readability theorem for English, or even the present fragment. Many denoting expressions are syntactically ambiguous, in the sense that they can be built up in several essentially different ways on the basis of the syntactic rules. We may, however, construct *trees* to represent the various possible analyses of a denoting expression, in a manner indicated by the following example.

Let φ be the formula $\ulcorner$a woman loves every man$\urcorner$. Then φ has two essentially different analyses, and we may represent them by the following two trees. (There are other analyses, but each of them will differ only trivially—indeed, only in a choice of variables—from one of the following two.) In these trees each nonbasic expression is accompanied by the number of the syntactic rule among S2–S17 *by* which it is obtained, and we place beneath it the expressions *from* which it is obtained, in the order in which they appear as arguments of the syntactical relation in question (among R2–R17). Each *basic* expression is accompanied by the index of its intended syntactic category.

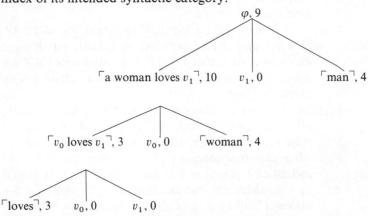

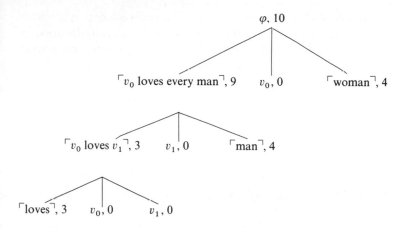

We may indeed call these trees *analyses* of φ, and corresponding to each of them (as well as to a given model) we may assign a denotation function to φ. In particular, let $\mathscr{A}$ be a model, let $\mathscr{A} = \langle A, I, G_0, \ldots, G_8 \rangle$, and let f, g be the two analyses given above, in the order in which they are displayed. Then, «reading» the tree f and using the semantic operation $F_2, \ldots, F_{17}$, we may «compute» the denotation function of φ that corresponds to f and $\mathscr{A}$ as $F_9(F_{10}(F_3(G_3\ (\ulcorner \text{loves} \urcorner),\ G_0(v_0),\ G_0(v_1)),\ G_0(v_0),\ G_4\ (\ulcorner \text{woman} \urcorner)),\ G_0(v_1),\ G_4\ (\ulcorner \text{man} \urcorner))$. Similarly, the denotation function of φ corresponding to the analysis g and the model $\mathscr{A}$ is $F_{10}(F_9(F_3(G_3\ (\ulcorner \text{loves} \urcorner),\ G_0(v_0),\ G_0(v_1)),\ G_0(v_1),\ G_4\ (\ulcorner \text{man} \urcorner)),\ G_0(v_0),\ G_4\ (\ulcorner \text{woman} \urcorner))$.

Although the notions of an analysis and of the denotation function corresponding to an analysis are probably already clear, I shall put down for reference the exact definitions. (The impatient reader may skip these safely.) We understand *sequences* in such a way that they may have any ordinal, finite or transfinite, as their length. By Λ is understood the empty sequence, by $\langle x \rangle$ the one-place sequence of which the only constituent is the object x, and by $s\,\widehat{\ }\,t$ the concatenation of the sequences s and t. A *tree-indexing* is a set T of sequences satisfying the following conditions: (1) T is a set of sequences of ordinals; (2) T is closed under the taking of initial segments (including the empty segment); and (3) whenever s is a sequence and k, n ordinals such that $s\,\widehat{\ }\,\langle n \rangle \in T$ and $k < n$, the sequence $s^\frown\langle k\rangle$ is also a member of T. A *tree* is a function of which the domain is a tree-indexing.[14] (Here a *function* is understood in the usual way, as a set of ordered pairs satisfying the «many-one condition»; and if f is a function, then $\langle x, y\rangle \in f$ if and only if x is a member of the domain of f and $f(x) = y$.)

For instance, the two trees f and g displayed above have as their domain the same tree-indexing—indeed, the set of which the members are $\Lambda, \langle0\rangle, \langle1\rangle, \langle2\rangle, \langle0,0\rangle, \langle0,1\rangle, \langle0,2\rangle, \langle0,0,0\rangle$, $\langle0, 0, 1\rangle$, and $\langle0, 0, 2\rangle$; these correspond to the nodes in the displays above, reading from top to bottom, and within a line from left to right. In most cases, however, the values of f and g differ. For example, $f(\Lambda) = \langle\varphi, 9\rangle$, but $g(\Lambda) = \langle\varphi, 10\rangle$; and $f(\langle1\rangle) = \langle v_1, 0\rangle$, but $g(\langle1\rangle) = \langle v_0, 0\rangle$.

By an *analysis* is understood a finite, nonempty tree h such that every value of h is an ordered pair, and, further, whenever $\langle s, \langle\delta, k\rangle\rangle \in h$, one of the following conditions holds: (1) k is a natural number less than 9, $\delta \in B_k$, and $s^\frown\langle0\rangle$ is not in the domain of h; or (2) k is a natural number, $2 \leqslant k \leqslant 17$, and there exist natural numbers $n, p_0, \ldots, p_{n-1}$ and expressions $\alpha_0, \ldots, \alpha_{n-1}$ such that $\langle\alpha_0, \ldots, \alpha_{n-1}, \delta\rangle \in R_k$, the pairs $\langle s^\frown\langle0\rangle, \langle\alpha_0, p_0\rangle\rangle, \ldots,$ $\langle s^\frown\langle n - 1\rangle, \langle\alpha_{n-1}, p_{n-1}\rangle\rangle$ are all members of h, and the sequence $s^\frown\langle n\rangle$ is not in the domain of h. (The condition that h be finite is actually superfluous here, and, in view of the particular character of the syntactical rules S1–S17, follows from the other conditions. It is possible, however, to imagine systems of syntactical rules in connection with which this could not be said. It is obvious that every finite tree, and hence every analysis, is such that its domain is a finite set of finite sequences of finite ordinals (that is, natural numbers).)

An *analysis of* an expression δ is an analysis h such that, for some k, $\langle\Lambda, \langle\delta, k\rangle\rangle \in h$. It is easily seen that an expression is a

---

[14] What we have called *tree-indexings* are customarily called *trees;* and no term is generally reserved for what we have called trees, despite the fact that the latter form an important class of mathematical objects. For a lucid exposition of the customary mathematical notions see Gaifman and Specker [7]. Our tree-indexings form a special case of what Gaifman and Specker call *sequential trees*. The specialization consists in imposing conditions (1) and (3), but is not seriously restrictive: every sequential tree is isomorphic to a tree-indexing.

denoting expression if and only if there is an analysis of it. Also, each analysis of a denoting expression assigns to that expression an intended syntactic category, as follows: if h is an analysis of δ, then the *category index of δ according to h* is the unique natural number k such that either (1) $\langle \Lambda, \langle \delta, k \rangle \rangle \in h$ and $\langle 0 \rangle$ is not in the domain of h; or (2) $\langle 0 \rangle$ is in the domain of h, either $\langle \Lambda, \langle \delta, 2 \rangle \rangle$, $\langle \Lambda, \langle \delta, 3 \rangle \rangle$, $\langle \Lambda, \langle \delta, 4 \rangle \rangle$, $\langle \Lambda, \langle \delta, 8 \rangle \rangle$, $\langle \Lambda, \langle \delta, 9 \rangle \rangle$, $\langle \Lambda, \langle \delta, 10 \rangle \rangle$, $\langle \Lambda, \langle \delta, 11 \rangle \rangle$, or $\langle \Lambda, \langle \delta, 17 \rangle \rangle$ is in h, and $k = 1$; or (3) $\langle 0 \rangle$ is in the domain of h, $\langle \Lambda, \langle \delta, 5 \rangle \rangle \in h$, and $k = 2$; or (4) $\langle 0 \rangle$ is in the domain of h, $\langle \Lambda, \langle \delta, 6 \rangle \rangle \in h$, and $k = 3$; or (5) $\langle 0 \rangle$ is in the domain of h, $\langle \Lambda, \langle \delta, 7 \rangle \rangle$, $\langle \Lambda, \langle \delta, 12 \rangle \rangle$, $\langle \Lambda, \langle \delta, 13 \rangle \rangle$, $\langle \Lambda, \langle \delta, 14 \rangle \rangle$, $\langle \Lambda, \langle \delta, 15 \rangle \rangle$, or $\langle \Lambda, \langle \delta, 16 \rangle \rangle$ is in h, and $k = 4$.

Because a denoting expression may, like φ above, have two or more essentially different analyses, we cannot assign to each denoting expression a unique denotation function corresponding to a given model, but rather a denotation function corresponding to a given model and a given analysis. It is obvious, however, that for each analysis there is exactly one expression of which it is an analysis. We may therefore speak of *the denotation function, corresponding to a model $\mathscr{A}$ and an analysis h, of the expression of which h is an analysis*, or, more briefly, $D(\mathscr{A}, h)$.

Before defining '$D(\mathscr{A}, h)$', it is necessary to introduce a little more auxiliary terminology. If a is an ordered pair, then by $1 [a]$ and $2 [a]$ are understood the first and second constituents, respectively, of a. If h is a tree and the one-place sequence $\langle k \rangle$ is in the domain of h, then by $h_{(k)}$, or *the kth immediate subtree of h*, is understood the set of pairs $\langle s, a \rangle$ for which s is a sequence of ordinals and $\langle \langle k \rangle^{\frown} s, a \rangle \in h$. By the *rank* of a tree h is understood the least upper bound of the lengths of sequences in the domain of h. Every analysis, being finite, will have a finite rank. In such a case—that is, when the tree h has a finite rank—it is clear that the rank of each immediate subtree of h will be one less than the rank of h.

Assume henceforth that $\mathscr{A}$ is a model, that $\mathscr{A} = \langle A, I, G_0, \ldots, G_8 \rangle$, and that h is an analysis. We can now define $D(\mathscr{A}, h)$ recursively as follows. (The recursion is on the rank of the analysis h).

(1) If the rank of h is 0, then $D(\mathscr{A}, h) = G_{2[h(\wedge)]}(1[h(\Delta)])$.

(2) If the rank of h is not 0, then $D(\mathscr{A}, h) = F_{2[h(\wedge)]}(D(\mathscr{A}, h_{(0)})$, $\ldots, D(\mathscr{A}, h_{(n)}))$, where $\{0, \ldots, n\}$ is the set of natural members k for which $\langle k \rangle$ is in the domain of h.

The following theorem is completely straightforward.

Theorem. Suppose that h is an analysis of δ, and that k is the category index of δ according to h. (1) $D(\mathscr{A}, h) \in U_k{}^{A^\omega}$. (2) If x, $y \in A^\omega$ and $x_n = y_n$ for all n such that v_n occurs in δ, then $D(\mathscr{A}, h)(x) = D(\mathscr{A}, h)(y)$. Hence: (3) If δ is a sentence and $k = 1$, then $D(\mathscr{A}, h) \in (2^I)^{A^\omega}$ and for all $x, y \in A^\omega$, $D(\mathscr{A}, h)(x) = D(\mathscr{A}, h)(y)$.

8. TRUTH AND LOGICAL TRUTH

The third part of the last theorem indicates that we may define a true sentence of our fragment in the manner suggested in Tarski [15] for mathematical languages, as one «satisfied» by every infinite sequence (or, equivalently, by *some* infinite sequence). For convenience, however, we define truth not only for sentences but for arbitrary formulas; variables will behave as though universally quantified: if $\mathscr{A} = \langle A, I, G_0, \ldots, G_8 \rangle$, then φ is *true* with respect to $\mathscr{A}$, the analysis h, and the possible world i if and only if h is an analysis of φ, the category index of φ according to h is 1, $i \in I$, and, for every $x \in A^\omega$, $D(\mathscr{A}, h)(x)(i) = 1$.

A formula φ is *logically true with respect to* an analysis h if and only if h is an analysis of φ, the category index of φ according to h is 1, and for every model $\langle A, I, G_0, \ldots, G_8 \rangle$ and every $i \in I$, φ is true with respect to $\langle A, I, G_0, \ldots, G_8 \rangle$, h, and i. If φ, ψ are sentences having f, g respectively as analyses, then φ *logically implies* ψ *with respect to* f and g if and only if the category index of φ with respect to f, as well as that of ψ with respect to g, is 1, and for every model $\langle A, I, G_0, \ldots, G_8 \rangle$ and every $i \in I$, if φ is true with respect to $\langle A, I, G_0, \ldots, G_8 \rangle$, f, and i, then ψ is true with respect to $\langle A, I, G_0, \ldots, G_8 \rangle$, g, and i. (This notion can be extended in an obvious way to the case in which φ is replaced by several, even infinitely many, sentences.) If α, β are denoting expressions having f, g respectively as analyses, then α is *logically equivalent to β with respect to* f and g if and only if the category index of α according to f is the same as the category index of β according to g, and, for every model $\mathscr{A}$, $D(\mathscr{A},f) = D(\mathscr{A}, g)$.

Professor Partee and Mr. Cooley have pointed out a reasonable way of removing the relativization to f and g. We might call two denoting expressions α and β simply *logically equivalent* if for every analysis f of α there is an analysis g of β such that α is logically equivalent to β with respect to f and g, and, conversely, for every analysis g of β there is an analysis f of α such that α is equivalent to β with respect to f and g.

A denoting expression α is *ambiguous with respect to* a model $\mathscr{A}$ if and only if there are analyses f and g of α such that $D(\mathscr{A},f) \neq D(\mathscr{A}, g)$. A denoting expression is called *structurally ambiguous* if there is a model with respect to which it is ambiguous. (I use the qualification 'structurally' rather unhappily, and wish I could think of a better term. In particular, I do not use 'syntactically', because an expression may have several «essentially different» *analyses* but still not be ambiguous in the sense given here. Yet some qualification is needed, for there is a type of ambiguity (rather uninteresting, to be sure) that is not covered by the present notion. I refer to *lexical* ambiguity, or, roughly, that ambiguity of complex expressions that stems from the ambiguity of basic expressions occurring within them. Such ambiguity could be formally construed as follows. The use of a language would ideally involve not only the determination of the collection of *all* models of the language (a determination sufficient for the *logical* notions, that is, logical truth, logical implication, logical equivalence), but also the specification of a particular, *actual* model; this would be involved in characterizing *absolute* truth (as opposed to truth *with respect to* a model).[15] But in connection with ordinary English there are *several* equally natural choices of the actual model, arising from the fact that certain basic expressions (most prominently, certain common

---

[15] To be specific, a sentence would be considered *true with respect to an analysis* h *and a possible world* i if it were true (in the sense given earlier) with respect to the actual model, h, and i. The relativization to i would be eliminable in the same way once we were able to single out the actual world among all possible worlds.

nouns and verbs) have several alternative denotations. We are
thus led to consider a *set* of actual models, and not a single actual
model. If the denotation of a denoting expression varies from one
actual model to another (with respect to a fixed analysis), then the
expression may be considered *lexically ambiguous* (with respect
to the analysis in question). It should, perhaps, be pointed out
that throughout our development models play the role of *possible
dictionaries*, with the one oddity that alternative definitions are
never allowed within a single dictionary, but instead involve the
consideration of several dictionaries.[16]

9. REMARKS ON THE PRESENT FRAGMENT

(i) Some linguists roughly sharing the main goal of the present
paper, that is, to define the notion of a *true sentence of English*
(or *English sentence true with respect to a given interpretation*),
have proposed that syntax—that is, the analysis of the notion
of a (correctly formed) sentence—be attacked first, and that only
after the completion of a syntactical theory consideration be given
to semantics, which would then be developed on the basis of that
theory. Such a program has almost no prospect of success. There
will often be many ways of syntactically generating a given set of
sentences, but only a few of them will have semantic relevance;
and these will sometimes be less simple, and hence less superficially
appealing, than certain of the semantically uninteresting modes of
generation. Thus the construction of syntax and semantics must
proceed hand in hand.

As a very simple example, observe that the set of formulas,
and hence of sentences, of our fragment would remain unchanged
if we deleted S12–S15 from the syntactical rules. The corresponding semantics, however, would be inadequate; it would provide,
for instance, no account of the intuitive ambiguity of the sentence
⌜every brother of a man in Amsterdam loves Jane⌝.

---

[16] Notice that the use of an expression, like our ⌜walks⌝, that belongs to more
than one basic category will not in itself produce either lexically or structurally
ambiguous formulas, even though several denotations may be associated with
the expression, depending on the category under which it is considered. In such
cases we would informally speak of "ambiguity that is resolved by context."

(ii) The denotation of an adjective phrase is always a function from properties to properties. (This was one of the proposals advanced by Kamp and Parsons.) The standard denotations of many adjectives—for instance, ⌜green⌝ and ⌜married⌝—may be taken as *intersection functions*, that is, functions H such that, for some property P, $H(Q)$ is, for every property Q, the property possessed by a given individual with respect to a given possible world if and only if the individual possesses both P and Q with respect to that possible world. It would be a mistake, however, to suppose that all adjectives could be so interpreted. Compare the common noun phrases ⌜big flea⌝ and ⌜big entity⌝. If the denotation of ⌜big⌝ were an intersection function, then there would be a single set B of individuals such that the extension of ⌜big flea⌝ with respect to the actual world (that is, the set of big fleas) would be the intersection of B with the set of fleas, and the extension of ⌜big entity⌝, again with respect to the actual world (that is, the set of big entities), would be the intersection of B with the set of entities (that is, the set B itself). But this is impossible, because not all big fleas (indeed, probably no big fleas) are big entities. (A big flea is, roughly, a flea bigger than most *fleas*, and a big entity an entity bigger than most *entities*.)

It would also be a mistake to impose in general the weaker assumption, satisfied by ⌜green⌝, ⌜married⌝, and ⌜big⌝, that the denotation of an adjective is a function that always assigns to a property one of its *subproperties*; for consider ⌜false friend⌝, ⌜reputed millionaire⌝, ⌜ostensible ally⌝, ⌜possible president⌝, ⌜alleged intruder⌝.

(iii) Accordingly, the sentence ⌜every big flea is big⌝ is not logically true (under any analysis). Indeed, it is logically equivalent to ⌜every big flea is a big entity⌝ (with respect to the most natural analysis of the latter), and the latter is probably not even true.

It appears that everyday usage is not quite decided as to the truth-conditions of sentences having adjectives like ⌜big⌝ in predicative position. Other conventions than ours (which is due to Kamp) are possible, but would be more complicated. The fact that our convention is in accordance with at least some varieties of ordinary usage is indicated by the plausibility of simultaneously maintaining the two sentences ⌜no flea is big⌝ and ⌜Jones finds a big flea⌝. On the other hand, ⌜every married man is married⌝ is certainly true; but it is not logically true, because its truth depends on the special circumstance that ⌜married⌝ denotes an intersection function. (Still less can we ascribe logical truth to the celebrated example ⌜every husband is married⌝.)

It would of course be possible to single out two special classes of basic adjective phrases, one a subclass of the other, and require the members of the larger class always to denote functions satisfying the subproperty condition and those of the smaller always to denote intersection functions. Then if δ is a one-word basic adjective phrase and ζ a common noun phrase, ⌜every δ ζ is a ζ⌝ would be logically true if δ is in the larger class, and so would ⌜every δ ζ is δ⌝ if δ is in the smaller. Such a course would, however, somewhat detract from the conceptual simplicity of our treatment. We should have to countenance as universes not only $U_{0,A,I}, \ldots,$ $U_{8,A,I}$ but also the set of members of $U_{8,A,I}$ that satisfy the subproperty assumption and the set of intersection functions in $U_{8,A,I}$; and the last two universes cannot be constructed in the same simple manner as the others.

Rather than altering the notion of logical truth, as under this proposal, we could perhaps more conveniently consider the logical consequences of certain *postulates*, in particular, the formulas

⌜every δ ζ is a ζ⌝,

where ζ is a common noun phrase and δ a one-word adjective phrase in the larger class mentioned above, as well as

⌜every δ ζ is a ζ such that that ζ is δ⌝

and

⌜every ζ such that that ζ is δ is a δ ζ⌝,

where ζ is again a common noun phrase and δ is a one-word adjective phrase in the smaller class mentioned above, as well as certain obvious analogues appropriate to the case in which δ is an adjective phrase of more than one word. To be a little more explicit, we might call a sentence φ *analytic* with respect to one of its analyses h if φ is a logical consequence of the set of postulates given above, with respect to h and the most natural analyses of those postulates (that is, analyses according to which the postulates are understood as universal rather than existential generalizations); and for some purposes we might be more concerned with analyticity than with logical truth.

(iv) Adverbial phrases are interpreted in very much the same way as adjective phrases, and remarks analogous to those in (ii) and (iii) are applicable to them. Notice, for instance, that ⌜Jones kills Smith in a dream⌝ does not logically imply ⌜Jones kills Smith⌝; hence neither does ⌜Jones kills Smith with a knife⌝, even though ⌜necessarily if Jones kills Smith with a knife, then Jones kills Smith⌝ might well turn out to be *true* (though not logically true) once we provide a proper analysis of ⌜if . . . then⌝.

(v) Examples above reveal that the ⌜is⌝ of such formulas as ⌜v_0 is a horse⌝ may be identified with the ⌜is⌝ of identity, and the indefinite singular term ⌜a horse⌝ treated, as usual, existentially. The same point was tentatively suggested in Quine [12] and emphasized in Bohnert and Backer [2]. Our examples also show that the ⌜is⌝ of ⌜John is big⌝, though not *identifiable* with the ⌜is⌝ of identity, is very simply *reducible* to it; for instance, ⌜John is big⌝ is logically equivalent to ⌜John is a big entity⌝.

(vi) For simplicity I have treated only the restrictive use of adjectives, relative clauses, adformulas, and adverbs, though ordinary English recognizes also a nonrestrictive use. For instance, the sentence ⌜Mary loves the esteemed doctor⌝ is within our treatment unambiguous, whereas intuitively it could be regarded as having roughly the same meaning as either the restrictive ⌜Mary loves the doctor such that that doctor is esteemed⌝ or the nonrestrictive ⌜Mary loves the doctor, and that doctor is esteemed⌝. It would not be too difficult to introduce such ambiguities in a formal way.

As far as relative clauses are concerned, we have confined ourselves to a ⌜such that⌝ locution, as in ⌜Mary loves the doctor such that that doctor is esteemed⌝, which is unambiguously synonymous with ⌜Mary loves the doctor who is esteemed⌝. The nonrestrictive $\ulcorner$Mary loves the doctor, who is esteemed$\urcorner$ has no direct counterpart in our fragment.

Adformulas also may sometimes be intuitively construed as nonrestrictive, though again we must go beyond our fragment for examples. For instance, $\ulcorner$the man such that that man fortunately loves Mary is tall$\urcorner$ may be understood either restrictively as $\ulcorner$the man such that it is fortunate that that man loves Mary is tall$\urcorner$ or unrestrictively as $\ulcorner$the man such that that man loves Mary is tall, and it is fortunate that that man loves Mary$\urcorner$. It is probable that nonrestrictive uses of adverbial phrases also exist, but I have been unable to find any clear-cut examples.

(vii) It appears to be purely a matter of taste whether certain additional syntactic (and corresponding semantic) categories should be recognized. I have in mind such categories as those of *one-place adjectival prepositions* (for instance, $\ulcorner$in$\urcorner$), which would denote functions in $U_8{}^{U_0}$, and of *two-place adjectival prepositions* (for instance, $\ulcorner$between$\urcorner$), which would designate functions in $U_8{}^{U_0 \times U_0}$. To introduce these categories would not enlarge the compass of the present fragment, though there are other categories (such as those of *adadjective phrases, adad-one-verb phrases, adad-two-verb phrases,* and *binary conjunction phrases,* interpreted by functions in $U_8{}^{U_8}$, $U_6{}^{U_6}$, $U_7{}^{U_7}$, and $U_1{}^{U_1 \times U_1}$ respectively) of which this could not be said.

(viii) Our fragment is rich in structural ambiguities, all roughly describable as arising from the various possible orders in which the «syntactic operations» R_2–R_{17} may be applied; but in this respect I believe our fragment captures the character of ordinary English in a rather revealing way. For instance, the *de re* and *de dicto* interpretations of $\ulcorner$necessarily the father of Cain is Adam$\urcorner$ (of which the former is true and the latter false) correspond to two ways of generating the sentence in question; the *de re* interpretation is obtained when the syntactical rule S4 is applied (in connection with $\ulcorner$necessarily$\urcorner$) before S11 and the *de dicto* interpretation when the opposite order is adopted. (A related suggestion, concerned with modal and belief contexts, was made in Russell [13] and amplified in Smullyan [14], but seems not to have received adequate attention. I should point out one drawback, of both my treatment and that of Russell: one must either prohibit the existence of two genuine proper names of the same individual (so that, say, ⌜Samuel Clemens⌝ would be allowed in the language, but the purported name phrase ⌜Mark Twain⌝ would be replaced by the common noun phrase ⌜person called 'Mark Twain'⌝) or else reconcile oneself to the unambiguous truth of such sentences as ⌜necessarily Samuel Clemens is Mark Twain⌝. Since descriptive phrases are not affected and the intuition is a little vague on the issues raised, this appears to me to be a price it is possible to pay for the simple semantics outlined above. It is nevertheless possible to circumvent these paradoxes, and to do so with only minor departures from the present treatment; the procedure, because of its intimate connection with the treatment of indexical features of language, will be described in Part II of this paper.)

English has, however, certain (by no means complete) devices for reducing ambiguity. These include the use of several different styles of quantification having various scopes—for instance, the use of ⌜any⌝ and ⌜a certain⌝ as universal and existential «quantifiers» of wide scope. The scope of quantifiers can also sometimes be resolved by word order (though not always according to the naive rule that the «quantificational phrase» occurring first be given the widest scope) and sometimes by the relative length of the «quantified» common noun phrases. Such features of English could be accounted for in precisely the style of our present treatment, but would require more complicated syntactical relations that R_2–R_{17}. For instance, if we were to include ⌜any⌝, we should have to make the following changes, among others: we should add rules precisely analogous to S9 and S13, but with ⌜every⌝ replaced by ⌜any⌝; corresponding semantical operations, identical with F_9 and F_{13}, would be added; R_9, R_{10}, R_{13}, and R_{14}, by which ⌜every⌝ and ⌜a⌝ are introduced, would be modified in such a way as not to apply to formulas or common noun phrases in which ⌜any⌝ already occurs; similarly, R_4 would be modified so as not to allow the appending of ⌜not⌝ to a formula containing ⌜any⌝. Such rules would restrict the variety of possible analyses of sentences containing ⌜any⌝; exact details must be postponed to another occasion.

(ix) I have deliberately, and for the sake of simplicity, ignored another source of ambiguity. We have taken the indefinite article ⌜a⌝ as always indicating existential quantification, but in some situations it may also be used universally, and indeed, in precisely the same way as ⌜any⌝; such is the case with one reading of the ambiguous sentence ⌜a woman loves every man such that that man loves that woman⌝.

(x) Considerable discussion has taken place as to what theory of descriptions best mirrors ordinary usage. It is therefore perhaps of some interest to see how ⌜the⌝ really and literally functions in English, and I believe that the treatment above provides a correct description. ⌜The⌝ turns out to play the role of a quantifier, in complete analogy with ⌜every⌝ and ⌜a⌝, and does *not* generate (in combination with common noun phrases) denoting expressions. (This does not mean that it would not be *possible* to assign complex and artificial denotations to such phrases as ⌜the ζ⌝, ⌜every ζ⌝, and ⌜a ζ⌝, but in no case would the denotation be an individual.[17])

Two special points should be noted. Within our treatment ⌜the⌝ introduces ambiguities of scope (or of order of construction) of exactly the same sort as those associated with ⌜every⌝ and ⌜a⌝. Further, English sentences contain no variables, and hence no such locutions as ⌜the v_0 such that v_0 walks⌝; ⌜the⌝ is always accompanied by a common noun phrase. In these two features virtually all artificial theories of descriptions differ from English, as well they might: it is sometimes desirable to avoid ambiguity, and the introduction of bound variables in place of property names permits a first-order treatment of a good deal of what would otherwise require nonelementary second-order methods.

The moral for artificial languages ought I think to be this. If such a language is to avoid ambiguity completely, or is to fit within a first-order framework, then it should not attempt in its theory of descriptions to mirror English too closely; it should rather be influenced by other considerations, for instance, simplic-

---

[17] It is in fact sometimes important to assign such denotations, in particular, in connection with intensional verbs. [Editor's note: Montague projected a paper on this topic, which was to have been titled 'Indefinite Terms, Intensional Verbs, and Unconceived Trees.' But it was never written.]

ity. Such an attitude is already customary in connection with artificial theories of quantification, but for reasons not at all clear to me is still resisted in some quarters in connection with descriptive phrases.

(xi) It is wrong to maintain—as Frege possibly did in [6]—that an analysis of ordinary English (or German) requires a notion of *sense* as well as one of *denotation*. The fact that we have been able to do with denotation alone depends on two novelties of our treatment—our theory of descriptions, according to which descriptive phrases do not denote individuals (or anything else, for that matter; recall that Frege's famous example involves ⌜*the morning star*⌝); and our decision to regard sentences as denoting propositions rather than truth values (and hence to regard verbs as denoting relations-in-intension rather than relations-in-extension). Frege's «argument» that sentences cannot denote propositions depends of course on the assumption that descriptive phrases denote individuals.

I should not be understood as suggesting that it is *impossible* to apply a sense-denotation distinction to English according to which formulas will denote truth values. Further, I believe that a treatment like Frege's, involving both sense and denotation, is the best way of dealing with certain interesting *artificial* languages; see Montague [9].

It would be pointless to dispute whether what I have called denotation should instead be called sense. Perhaps the only real point that can be made in this connection is the following. Our basic objective, like Frege's, is to assign truth values to sentences. Like Frege, we seek to do this by assigning extra-linguistic entities to all expressions involved in the generation of sentences (including, among these, sentences themselves) in such a way that (a) the assignment to a compound will be a function of the entities assigned to its components, and (b) the truth-value of a sentence can be determined from the entity assigned to it. But whereas Frege's approach involves assigning at least two (and perhaps infinitely many) entities to each expression, we have done with one—what I prefer to call the denotation.

I should point out that the situation need not change even when (as in Part II of this paper) we admit context-dependent names of individuals; but the reader cannot be expected to accept this claim until he has seen the details in Part II.[18]

(xii) It may not be quite clear why, within our treatment, formulas could not be taken as denoting truth values, verbs as denoting relations-in-extension, and common nouns as denoting sets. The reason should, however, become clear if one considers the effect of modifiers on such expressions, as in ⌜necessarily the father of Cain is Adam⌝, ⌜walks rapidly⌝, and ⌜possible president⌝. The denotations of the compounds—whether taken as we have taken them or taken as such extensional entities as truth values or sets—could not be obtained from the truth values or sets corresponding to the components.[19]

(xiii) It is a little ugly to include ⌜v_0 believes that⌝ among our adformulas without giving a more comprehensive account of the various uses of ⌜believes⌝ and grammatically analogous verbs and some of the presentation would be smoother without that adformula. The reason for its inclusion is to indicate that such locutions, though sometimes regarded as serious obstacles to an adequate treatment of natural language, can be accommodated within our framework. I should point out, however, that if φ and ψ are logically equivalent sentences (with respect to given analyses f and g), then ⌜John believes that φ⌝ and ⌜John believes that ψ⌝ will turn out also to be logically equivalent (with respect to analyses that contain f and g as parts). This may at first appear strange, but is a conclusion that I believe we should accept; for a brief discussion of the issues involved, in connection with an artificial rather than a natural language, see Montague [9].

(xiv) The method of presentation adopted here has been influenced by a general algebraic theory of languages and their interpretations recently constructed by the author, and exhibits the present fragment and those in Part II as special cases. The general theory contains, for instance, theorems according to

---

[18] [Editor's note: Part II of this chapter was never written. But the details to which Montague refers here are incorporated in Chapter 7 of this book.]

[19] Let me spell out what is meant, in, say, the case of ⌜possible⌝. One can find two common nouns ζ and η corresponding to the same set of individuals—or having, as we should ordinarily say, the same extension (with respect to the actual world and the standard model)—but such that ⌜possible ζ⌝ and ⌜possible η⌝ have different extensions.

which the syntactic categories of a very wide class of languages will be recursive (that is, decidable); the recursiveness of the categories $C_0, \ldots, C_8$ of our fragment, though independently rather obvious, is a consequence.

10. EXTENDING THE PRESENT FRAGMENT

Certain extensions, comprehending larger portions of English (for instance, indexical or context-dependent portions), will be given in Part II; and still wider extensions are known. In no case need one abandon the essential features of the treatment above, and in most cases the semantics remains simple.

Often, however, the syntax becomes more complicated and requires the introduction of additional devices beyond those contemplated above. For instance, if we wish to include modern negation (rather than, or in addition to, the archaic negation employed above), we must be able to single out the *main verb occurrence* within a formula; this would also be required for the formation of tenses other than the present. The word ⌜all⌝ would behave very much like ⌜every⌝, but its syntax would require the ability to single out (for purposes of pluralization) both the main verb occurrence of a formula and the *main common noun occurrence* of a common noun phrase. (Once we can do this, the treatment of *cardinals*, as in ⌜three men walk⌝, presents no problem. Because there are infinitely many cardinals, we might wish to introduce a syntactic category of *quantifiers*, to which ⌜every⌝ and ⌜a⌝ would also belong, and each member of which would designate a function in $U_1{}^{U_4 \times U_2}$.[20]) The introduction of *adadjectives* (that

[20] For instance, a model would assign to ⌜every⌝ (as its denotation function) that function d in $(U_1{}^{U_4 \times U_2})^{A^\omega}$ such that, for all $x \in A^\omega$, all $z \in U_4$, all $w \in U_2$, and all $i \in I$, $d(x)(z, w)(i) = 1$ if and only if $w(u)(i) = 1$ for all $u \in A$ for which $z(u)(i) = 1$. Quantifiers would enter formulas by way of the following syntactical rule: if φ is a formula, α a name phrase (and in particular a variable), δ a quantifier, and ζ a common noun phrase, and $\langle \varphi, \alpha, \delta, \zeta, \psi \rangle \in R$, then ψ is a formula, where R is a syntactical relation containing such quintuples as $\langle ⌜v_0$ walks⌝, v_0, ⌜every⌝, ⌜man⌝, ⌜every man walks⌝$\rangle$ and $\langle ⌜v_0$ walks⌝, v_0, ⌜two⌝, ⌜man⌝, ⌜two men walk⌝$\rangle$. The corresponding semantical operation F would be characterized as follows: $F(p, a, d, z)$ is that function $q \in U_1{}^{A^\omega}$ such that, for all $x \in A^\omega$, $q(x) = d(x)(z(x), w)$, where w is the set of all pairs $\langle u, p(x_u^n) \rangle$ such that $u \in A$, where n is the index of the variable represented by a. One would of course require also a syntactical rule (with a corresponding semantical operation) whereby quantifiers could enter common noun phrases.

is, modifiers of adjective phrases) would require the ability to single out the *main adjective occurrence* of an adjective phrase. For then the simple syntactical rule S7 could no longer be maintained; the general rule seems to be that an adjective phrase δ should be placed before or after the common noun phrase it modifies according as the main occurrence of an adjective in δ stands at the end of δ or not. If binary connectives are included, we must be able to tell whether a given formula is (according to every possible analysis) compounded by means of a connective, and what that connective is; for there are some compounds (as with 'and' and 'or') that are not susceptible of negation. But I shall reserve for another occasion the detailed discussion of these and other extensions.

REFERENCES

1. Ajdukiewicz, K. *Język i Poznanie* (*Language and Knowledge*). Warsaw, 1960.
2. Bohnert, H. and P. Backer. Automatic English-to-Logic Translation in a Simplified Model. IBM Research Paper RC-1744, 1967.
3. Davidson, D. The Logical Form of Action Sentences. In N. Rescher (ed.), *The Logic of Decision and Action*. Pittsburgh, 1967.
4. —. Causal Relations. *Journal of Philosophy* 64:691–703 (1967).
5. —. Semantics for Natural Languages. In B. Visentini et al., *Linguaggi nella Società e nella Tecnica*. Milan, 1970.
6. Frege, G. Über Sinn und Bedeutung. *Zeitschrift für Philosophie und philosophische Kritik* 100:25–50 (1892).
7. Gaifman, H. and E. Specker. Isomorphism Types of Trees. *Proceedings of the American Mathematical Society* 15:1–7 (1964).
8. Kripke, S. Semantical Considerations on Modal Logic. *Acta Philosophica Fennica* 16:83–94 (1963).
9. Montague, R. Pragmatics and Intensional Logic. *Synthèse* 22:68–94 (1970). Chap. 4 in this book.
10. Parsons, T. Some Problems Concerning the Logic of Grammatical Modifiers. *Synthèse* 21:320–34 (1970).
11. Quine, W. *Mathematical Logic*, rev. ed. Cambridge, Mass., 1951.
12. —. *Word and Object*. Cambridge, Mass., 1960.
13. Russell, B. On Denoting. *Mind* 14:479–93 (1905).
14. Smullyan, A. Modality and Description. *Journal of Symbolic Logic* 13:31–37 (1948).

15. Tarski, A. Der Wahrheitsbegriff in den formalisierten Sprachen. *Studia Philosophica* 1:261–405 (1936).

16. —. Some Notions and Methods on the Borderline of Algebra and Metamathematics. *Proceedings of the 1950 International Congress of Mathematicians* 1:705–20 (1952).

17. —. Contributions to the Theory of Models, Part I. *Indagationes Mathematicae* 16:572–88 (1954) and 17:56–64 (1955).

7. Universal Grammar

There is in my opinion no important theoretical difference between natural languages and the artificial languages of logicians; indeed, I consider it possible to comprehend the syntax and semantics of both kinds of languages within a single natural and mathematically precise theory. On this point I differ from a number of philosophers, but agree, I believe, with Chomsky and his associates. It is clear, however, that no adequate and comprehensive semantical theory has yet been constructed,[1] and

Originally published in *Theoria* 36:373–98 (1970). Reprinted with permission. The present paper was delivered at a joint symposium of the Association for Symbolic Logic and the American Philosophical Association in December, 1969, and before the U.C.L.A. Philosophy Colloquium in February, 1970; its preparation was supported in part by U.S. National Science Foundation Grant GS-2785. The ideas presented here were developed in lectures at U.C.L.A., beginning in the Spring of 1967. I am indebted to Mr. Dan Gallin, Prof. David Lewis, and Dr. Perry Smith for valuable criticisms and suggestions. In particular, Mr. Gallin and Prof. Lewis are responsible for important improvements in certain notions.

[1] Or even a reasonable semantics for a reasonably comprehensive fragment of any natural language, with the single exception of the treatment in Montague [5] of a fragment of English. There is, however, a significant difference between that treatment and the treatment below of an overlapping fragment. The novelty lies in the interpretation of singular terms and verbs, and is introduced in order to provide (for the first time, I believe, in the literature; the proposals in question were first made in my talks before the Southern California Logic Colloquium and the Association for Symbolic Logic in April and May of 1969) a reasonable semantics for discourse involving intensional verbs. (Another approach is also possible, more along the lines of Montague [5]; it remains to be seen which of the two is preferable.)

It should be pointed out that the treatment of English in Montague [5] is fully compatible with the present *general* theory, and indeed, like the conflicting treatment below, can be represented as a special case of it. I should like, however, to withdraw my emphasis in Montague [5] on the possibility of doing without a distinction between sense and denotation. While such a distinction can be avoided in special cases, it remains necessary for the general theory, and probably provides the clearest approach even to the special cases in question.

arguable that no comprehensive and semantically significant syntactical theory yet exists.[2]

The aim of the present work is to fill this gap, that is, to develop a universal syntax and semantics. I shall also consider the resulting notions in connection with two examples—the first a rather important artificial language and the second a fragment of ordinary English. This merely illustrative fragment is intentionally circumscribed in the interests of simplicity but is perhaps sufficiently rich to indicate the manner in which various more extensive portions of natural language may be subsumed within the general framework. The intensional logic which constitutes the first example below has some derivative importance apart from whatever intrinsic interest it may possess. Very extensive portions of natural languages can, like the illustrative fragment considered in this paper, be adequately interpreted by way of translation (in the precise general sense analyzed here) into that system of intensional logic.

For the sake of brevity I shall content myself with the mere statement of definitions, omitting all theorems apart from a few (called Remarks) directly related to comprehension, and avoiding almost all discussion and intuitive amplification. The resulting exposition will, I realize, be cryptic and unsatisfactory, but a more extended development must be deferred to a book.[3]

[2] The basic aim of semantics is to characterize the notions of a true sentence (under a given interpretation) and of entailment, while that of syntax is to characterize the various syntactical categories, especially the set of declarative sentences. It is to be expected, then, that the aim of syntax could be realized in many different ways, only some of which would provide a suitable basis for semantics. It appears to me that the syntactical analyses of particular fragmentary languages that have been suggested by transformational grammarians, even if successful in correctly characterizing the declarative sentences of those languages, will prove to lack semantic relevance; and I fail to see any great interest in syntax except as a preliminary to semantics. (One could also object to existing syntactical efforts by Chomsky and his associates on grounds of adequacy, mathematical precision, and elegance; but such criticism should perhaps await more definitive and intelligible expositions than are yet available. In particular, I believe the transformational grammarians should be expected to produce a rigorous definition, complete in all details, of the set of declarative sentences of some reasonably rich fragment of English—at least as rich as the fragments treated below or in Montague [5]—before their work can be seriously evaluated.)

[3] [Editor's note: This book, which was to have been titled *The Analysis of Language*, was never completed. Apparently, much of it was to have been devoted to making the set theoretic foundations of this chapter fully explicit and rigorous.]

1. BACKGROUND NOTIONS

In Sections 1–5, I use 'α', 'β', 'ξ', 'η' to refer to ordinal numbers. A β-*place relation* (among members of a set A) is a set of β-place sequences (of members of A). A β-*place operation* (on A) is a $(\beta + 1)$-place relation F (among members of A) such that whenever $\langle a_\xi \rangle_{\xi < \beta}$ is a β-place sequence (of members of A) there is exactly one object x (in A) such that the concatenation of $\langle a_\xi \rangle_{\xi < \beta}$ with the one-place sequence $\langle x \rangle$ is in F; we let $F(\langle a_\xi \rangle_{\xi < \beta}) = x$. F is an *operation* (on A) if and only if F is a β-place operation (on A), for some ordinal number β. A *function* is a one-place operation; if f is a function, we let $f(x) = f(\langle x \rangle)$.

An *algebra* is a system $\langle A, F_\gamma \rangle_{\gamma \in \Gamma}$, where A is a nonempty set, Γ is a set of any sort, and each F_γ (for $\gamma \in \Gamma$) is an operation on A. If A is any set, x is any object, and $\alpha < \beta$, then $I_{\alpha,\beta,A}$ (or the αth β-*place identity operation on A*) and $C_{x,\beta,A}$ (or the β-*place constant operation on A with value x*) are those β-place operations on A such that $I_{\alpha,\beta,A}(a) = a_\alpha$ and $C_{x,\beta,A}(a) = x$ for every β-place sequence a of members of A. If G is an a-place operation on a nonempty set A and $\langle H_\xi \rangle_{\xi < \alpha}$ is an α-place sequence of β-place operations on A, then $G^A \langle H_\xi \rangle_{\xi < \alpha}$ (or the *composition*, relative to A, of the operation G with the sequence $\langle H_\xi \rangle_{\xi < \alpha}$ of operations) is that β-place operation on A such that $G^A \langle H_\xi \rangle_{\xi < \alpha}(a) = G(\langle H_\xi (a) \rangle_{\xi < \alpha})$ for every β-place sequence a of members of A. If $\langle A, F_\gamma \rangle_{\gamma \in \Gamma}$ is an algebra, then the class of *polynomial operations* over $\langle A, F_\gamma \rangle_{\gamma \in \Gamma}$ is the smallest class K such that (1) $F_\gamma \in K$ for all $\gamma \in \Gamma$; (2) $I_{\alpha,\beta,A} \in K$ for all ordinals α, β such that $\alpha < \beta$; (3) $C_{\lambda,\beta,A} \in K$ whenever $x \in A$ and β is an ordinal; and (4) for all ordinals α and β, all α-place operations G on A, and all α-place sequences $\langle H_\xi \rangle_{\xi < \alpha}$ of β-place operations on A, if $G \in K$ and, for all $\xi < \alpha$, $H_\xi \in K$, then $G^A \langle H_\xi \rangle_{\xi < \alpha} \in K$.[4]

---

[4] For those interested in set-theoretic technicalities I might point out that in this characterization the word 'class' is used deliberately rather than 'set'. In any of the usual axiomatic formulations of set theory one can prove that there is no *set* K satisfying (1)–(4), but in those formulations that recognize proper classes in addition to sets one can prove that there *is* a proper class satisfying those conditions.

If $\langle A, F_\gamma \rangle_{\gamma \in \Gamma}$ and $\langle B, G_\gamma \rangle_{\gamma \in \Delta}$ are algebras, then h is a *homomorphism from* $\langle A, F_\gamma \rangle_{\gamma \in \Gamma}$ *into* $\langle B, G_\gamma \rangle_{\gamma \in \Delta}$ if and only if (1) $\langle A, F_\gamma \rangle_{\gamma \in \Gamma}$ and $\langle B, G_\gamma \rangle_{\gamma \in \Delta}$ are *similar* (in the sense that $\Gamma = \Delta$ and, for each $\gamma \in \Gamma$, F_γ and G_γ are operations of the same number of places); (2) h is a function with domain A and range included in B; and (3) whenever $\gamma \in \Gamma$ and $\langle a_\xi \rangle_{\xi < \beta}$ is a sequence in the domain of F_γ, $h(F_\gamma(\langle a_\xi \rangle_{\xi < \beta})) = G_\gamma(\langle h(a_\xi) \rangle_{\xi < \beta})$. We say that h is a *homomorphism from* $\langle A, F_\gamma \rangle_{\gamma \in \Gamma}$ *to* $\langle B, G_\gamma \rangle_{\gamma \in \Delta}$ if, in addition, B coincides with the range of h.

Remark. If $\langle A, F_\gamma \rangle_{\gamma \in \Gamma}$ is an algebra, h is a homomorphism from $\langle A, F_\gamma \rangle_{\gamma \in \Gamma}$ to some algebra, and, for each $\gamma \in \Delta$, G_γ is a polynomial operation over $\langle A, F_\gamma \rangle_{\gamma \in \Gamma}$, then there is éxactly one algebra $\langle B, H_\gamma \rangle_{\gamma \in \Delta}$ such that h is a homomorphism from $\langle A, G_\gamma \rangle_{\gamma \in \Delta}$ to $\langle B, H_\gamma \rangle_{\gamma \in \Delta}$.

2. SYNTAX

A *disambiguated language* is a system $\langle A, F_\gamma, X_\delta, S, \delta_0 \rangle_{\gamma \in \Gamma, \delta \in \Delta}$ such that (1) $\langle A, F_\gamma \rangle_{\gamma \in \Gamma}$ is an algebra; (2) for all $\delta \in \Delta$, X_δ is a subset of A; (3) A is the smallest set including as subsets all the sets X_δ (for $\delta \in \Delta$) and closed under all the operations F_γ (for $\gamma \in \Gamma$); (4) X_δ and the range of F_γ are disjoint whenever $\delta \in \Delta$ and $\gamma \in \Gamma$; (5) for all $\gamma, \gamma' \in \Gamma$, all sequences a in the domain of F_γ, and all sequences a' in the domain of $F_{\gamma'}$, if $F_\gamma(a) = F_{\gamma'}(a')$, then $\gamma = \gamma'$ and $a = a'$; (6) S is a set of sequences of the form $\langle F_\gamma, \langle \delta_\xi \rangle_{\xi < \beta}, \varepsilon \rangle$, where $\gamma \in \Gamma$, β is the number of places of the operation F_γ, $\delta_\xi \in \Delta$ for all $\xi < \beta$, and $\varepsilon \in \Delta$; and (7) $\delta_0 \in \Delta$. (Here the sets X_δ are regarded as the categories of basic expressions of the disambiguated language, the operations F_γ as its structural operations, the set A as the set of all its proper expressions (that is, expressions obtainable from basic expressions by repeated application of structural operations), δ_0 as the index of its category of declarative sentences, and S as the set of its syntactic rules; these play a role that will be clarified by the next definition. It is clear that if conditions (1)–(5) are satisfied, then $\langle A, F_\gamma \rangle_{\gamma \in \Gamma}$ is what is known as a *free algebra* generated by $\bigcup_{\delta \in \Delta} X_\delta$ (that is, the union of the sets X_δ for $\delta \in \Delta$).)

If $\mathfrak{A} = \langle A, F_\gamma, X_\delta, S, \delta_0 \rangle_{\gamma \in \Gamma, \delta \in \Delta}$, then $\mathfrak{A}$ *generates* the family C of syntactic categories if and only if (1) C is a family, indexed by Δ, of subsets of A; (2) $X_\delta \subseteq C_\delta$ for all $\delta \in \Delta$; (3) whenever $\langle F, \langle \delta_\xi \rangle_{\xi < \beta}, \varepsilon \rangle \in S$ and $a_\xi \in C_{\delta_\xi}$ for all $\xi < \beta$, $F(\langle a_\xi \rangle_{\xi < \beta}) \in C_\varepsilon$; and (4) whenever C' satisfies (1)–(3), $C_\delta \subseteq C'_\delta$ for all $\delta \in \Delta$.

Remark. If $\mathfrak{A}$ is any disambiguated language, then $\mathfrak{A}$ generates exactly one family of syntactic categories.

A *language* is a pair $\langle \langle A, F_\gamma, X_\delta, S, \delta_0 \rangle_{\gamma \in \Gamma, \delta \in \Delta}, R \rangle$ such that $\langle A, F_\gamma, X_\delta, S, \delta_0 \rangle_{\gamma \in \Gamma, \delta \in \Delta}$ is a disambiguated language and R is a binary relation with domain included in A. Suppose that $\mathfrak{A} = \langle A, F_\gamma, X_\delta, S, \delta_0 \rangle_{\gamma \in \Gamma, \delta \in \Delta}$ and $L = \langle \mathfrak{A}, R \rangle$. Then PE_L (or the set of *proper expressions* of L) is the range of R; OI_L (or the set of *operation indices* of L) is Γ; CI_L (or the set of *category indices* of L) is Δ; SR_L (or the set of *syntactical rules* of L) is S; $BS_{\delta, L}$ (or the δth *basic set* of L) is the set of objects ζ such that $\zeta' R \zeta$ for some $\zeta' \in X_\delta$; $\text{Cat}_{\delta, L}$ (or the δth *syntactic category* of L) is the set of objects ζ such that $\zeta' R \zeta$ for some $\zeta' \in C_\delta$, where C is the family of syntactic categories generated by $\mathfrak{A}$; ME_L (or the set of *meaningful expressions* of L) is $\bigcup_{\delta \in \Delta} \text{Cat}_{\delta, L}$; DS_L (or the set of *declarative sentences* of L) is $\text{Cat}_{\delta_0, L}$; and the class of *derived syntactical rules* of L is the smallest class K such that (1) $S \subseteq K$; (2) whenever α, β are ordinals, $\alpha < \beta$, and $\langle \delta_\xi \rangle_{\xi < \beta}$ is a β-place sequence of members of Δ, the triple $\langle I_{\alpha, \beta, A}, \langle \delta_\xi \rangle_{\xi < \beta}, \delta_\alpha \rangle \in K$; (3) whenever β is an ordinal, $\langle \delta_\xi \rangle_{\xi < \beta}$ is a β-place sequence of members of Δ, $\varepsilon \in \Delta$, and $x \in X_\varepsilon$, the triple $\langle C_{x, \beta, A}, \langle \delta_\xi \rangle_{\xi < \beta}, \varepsilon \rangle \in K$; and (4) whenever α, β are ordinals, $\langle G, \langle \delta_\xi \rangle_{\xi < \alpha}, \varepsilon \rangle \in K$, and $\langle H_\xi \rangle_{\xi < \alpha}$ is a sequence such that $\langle H_\xi, \langle \gamma_\eta \rangle_{\eta < \beta}, \delta_\xi \rangle \in K$ for all $\xi < \alpha$, then $\langle G^A \langle H_\xi \rangle_{\xi < \alpha}, \langle \gamma_\eta \rangle_{\eta < \beta}, \varepsilon \rangle \in K$. If $\zeta \in ME_L$, then ζ is *syntactically ambiguous in* L if and only if there are at least two objects $\zeta' \in \bigcup_{\delta \in \Delta} C_\delta$ such that $\zeta' R \zeta$, where C is the family of syntactic categories generated by $\mathfrak{A}$. The *language L is syntactically ambiguous* if and only if there is a meaningful expression of L that is syntactically ambiguous in L.

Remark. If L is a language, $L = \langle \mathfrak{A}, R \rangle$, $\langle H, \langle \delta_\xi \rangle_{\xi < \beta}, \varepsilon \rangle$ is a derived syntactical rule of L, C is the family of syntactic categories generated by L, and $a_\xi \in C_{\delta_\xi}$ for all $\xi < \beta$, then $H(\langle a_\xi \rangle_{\xi < \beta}) \in C_\varepsilon$.

3. SEMANTICS: THEORY OF MEANING

Suppose that $\mathfrak{A} = \langle A, F_\gamma, X_\delta, S, \delta_0 \rangle_{\gamma \in \Gamma, \delta \in \Delta}$, $L = \langle \mathfrak{A}, R \rangle$, and L is a language. An *interpretation* for L is a system $\langle B, G_\gamma, f \rangle_{\gamma \in \Gamma}$ such that $\langle B, G_\gamma \rangle_{\gamma \in \Gamma}$ is an algebra similar to $\langle A, F_\gamma \rangle_{\gamma \in \Gamma}$ and f is a function from $\bigcup_{\delta \in \Delta} X_\delta$ into B. (Here B is regarded as the set of meanings prescribed by the interpretation, G_γ is the semantic operation corresponding to the structural operation F_γ, and f assigns meanings to the basic expressions of the language.) Suppose in addition that $\mathscr{B} = \langle B, G_\gamma, f \rangle_{\gamma \in \Gamma}$. Then the *meaning assignment* for L determined by $\mathscr{B}$ is the unique homomorphism g from $\langle A, F_\gamma \rangle_{\gamma \in \Gamma}$ into $\langle B, G_\gamma \rangle_{\gamma \in \Gamma}$ such that $f \subseteq g$. Further, if $\zeta \in ME_L$, then ζ *means* b in L according to $\mathscr{B}$ if and only if there exists $\zeta' \in \bigcup_{\delta \in \Delta} C_\delta$ such that $\zeta' R \zeta$ and $g(\zeta') = b$, where C is the family of syntactic categories generated by $\mathfrak{A}$ and g is the meaning assignment for L determined by $\mathscr{B}$. Also, ζ is *semantically ambiguous* in L according to $\mathscr{B}$ if and only if ζ means at least two different things in L according to $\mathscr{B}$; ζ is *strongly synonymous* with θ in L according to $\mathscr{B}$ if and only if $\zeta, \theta \in ME_L$ and, for every $\delta \in \Delta$, $\{g(\zeta') : \zeta' \in C_\delta \text{ and } \zeta' R \zeta\} = \{g(\theta') : \theta' \in C_\delta \text{ and } \theta' R \theta\}$, where C and g are as above; and ζ is *weakly synonymous* with θ in L according to $\mathscr{B}$ if and only if $\zeta, \theta \in ME_L$ and $\{b : \zeta \text{ means } b \text{ in } L \text{ according to } \mathscr{B}\} = \{b : \theta \text{ means } b \text{ in } L \text{ according to } \mathscr{B}\}$. Suppose, in addition to the assumptions above, that L' is also a language and $\mathscr{B}'$ is an interpretation for L'. Then ζ is *interlinguistically synonymous* with ζ' (with respect to $L, \mathscr{B}, L', \mathscr{B}'$) if and only if $\zeta \in ME_L, \zeta' \in ME_{L'}$, and $\{b : \zeta \text{ means } b \text{ in } L \text{ according to } \mathscr{B}\} = \{b : \zeta' \text{ means } b \text{ in } L' \text{ according to } \mathscr{B}'\}$.

4. SEMANTICS: THEORY OF REFERENCE

Let e, t, s be the respective numbers $0, 1, 2$. (The precise choice of these objects is unimportant; the only requirements are that they be distinct and that none of them be an ordered pair.) By T, or the set of *types*, is understood the smallest set such that (1) e and t (which are regarded as the type of entities and the type of truth values respectively) are in T; (2) whenever $\sigma, \tau \in T$, the ordered pair $\langle \sigma, \tau \rangle$ (which is regarded as the type of functions from objects of type σ to objects of type τ) is in T; and (3) whenever $\tau \in T$, the pair $\langle s, \tau \rangle$ (which is regarded as the type of senses corresponding to objects of type τ) is in T. In connection with any sets E and I and any $\tau \in T$, we characterize $D_{\tau,E,I}$, or the set of *possible denotations of type* τ based on the set E of entities (or possible individuals) and the set I of possible worlds, as follows: $D_{e,E,I} = E$; $D_{t,E,I} = \{\Lambda, \{\Lambda\}\}$ (where Λ is as usual the empty set, and Λ, $\{\Lambda\}$ are identified with falsehood and truth respectively); if σ, $\tau \in T$, then $D_{\langle \sigma,\tau \rangle,E,I} = (D_{\tau,E,I})^{D\sigma,E,I}$ (where in general A^B is the set of functions with domain B and range included in A); if $\tau \in T$, then $D_{\langle s,\tau \rangle,E,I} = (D_{\tau,E,I})^I$. If J is also a set, then $M_{\tau,E,I,J}$, or the set of possible *meanings* of type τ based on the set E of entities, the set I of possible worlds, and the set J of contexts of use, is $(D_{\tau,E,I})^{I \times J}$. (By $I \times J$ is understood as usual the set of ordered pairs $\langle i, j \rangle$ such that $i \in I$ and $j \in J$. Thus *meanings* are functions of two arguments—a possible world and a context of use. The second argument is introduced in order to permit a treatment, in the manner of Montague [3], of such indexical locutions as demonstratives, first- and second-person singular pronouns, and free variables (which are treated in Section 6 below as a kind of demonstrative). *Senses* on the other hand—that is, members of $D_{\langle s,\tau \rangle,E,I}$ for some τ—are functions of only one argument, regarded as a possible world. The intuitive distinction is this: meanings are those entities that serve as interpretations of expressions (and hence, if the interpretation of a compound is always to be a function of the interpretations of its components, cannot be identified with functions of possible worlds alone), while senses are those intensional entities that are sometimes *denoted* by expressions. No such distinction was necessary in Frege [1], because there consideration of indexical locutions was deliberately avoided. It is a slight oversimplification to call the members of I possible worlds. In connection with tensed languages, for instance, it is convenient to take I as the set of all ordered *pairs* consisting of a possible world and a moment of time, and J as the set of all complexes of remaining relevant features of possible contexts of use.

Suppose that L is a language and

$$L = \langle\langle A, F_\gamma, X_\delta, S, \delta_0 \rangle_{\gamma \in \Gamma, \delta \in \Delta}, R \rangle.$$

A *type assignment* for L is a function σ from Δ into T such that $\sigma(\delta_0) = t$. A *Fregean interpretation* for L is an interpretation $\langle B, G_\gamma, f \rangle_{\gamma \in \Gamma}$ for L such that, for some nonempty sets E, I, J, and some type assignment σ for L, (1) $B \subseteq \bigcup_{\tau \in T} M_{\tau, E, I, J}$; (2) whenever $\delta \in \Delta$ and $\zeta \in X_\delta, f(\zeta) \in M_{\sigma(\delta), E, I, J}$; and (3) whenever $\langle F_\gamma, \langle \delta_\xi \rangle_{\xi < \beta}, \varepsilon \rangle \in S$ and $b_\xi \in M_{\sigma(\delta_\xi), E, I, J}$ for all $\xi < \beta$, then $G_\gamma(\langle b_\xi \rangle_{\xi < \beta}) \in M_{\sigma(\varepsilon), E, I, J}$. Here $I \times J$ is uniquely determined and is called the set of *points of reference* of the Fregean interpretation. By a *Fregean interpretation* for L *connected with* E, I, J and σ is understood an interpretation $\langle B, G_\gamma, f \rangle_{\gamma \in \Gamma}$ for L such that conditions (1)–(3) above are satisfied. A *model* for L is a pair $\langle \mathscr{B}, \langle i, j \rangle \rangle$ such that $\mathscr{B}$ is a Fregean interpretation for L and $\langle i, j \rangle$ is a point of reference of $\mathscr{B}$. (Here i and j are respectively regarded as the actual world and the actual context of use specified by the model.) Suppose that $\langle \mathscr{B}, \langle i, j \rangle \rangle$ is a model for L. Then the *denotation assignment* for L determined by $\langle \mathscr{B}, \langle i, j \rangle \rangle$ is that function h with domain A such that, for all $\zeta \in A$, $h(\zeta) = g(\zeta)(i, j)$, where g is the meaning assignment for L determined by $\mathscr{B}$. Further, η *has x as a denotation* according to L and $\langle \mathscr{B}, \langle i, j \rangle \rangle$ if and only if there exists b such that η means b in L according to $\mathscr{B}$, and $b(i, j) = x$. Also, φ is a *true sentence of L with respect to* $\langle \mathscr{B}, \langle i, j \rangle \rangle$ *and the analysis* φ' if and only if $\varphi' \in C_{\delta_0}$, $\varphi' R \varphi$, and $h(\varphi') = \{\Lambda\}$, where C is the family of syntactic categories generated by $\langle A, F_\gamma, X_\delta, S, \delta_0 \rangle_{\gamma \in \Gamma, \delta \in \Delta}$ and h is the denotation assignment for L determined by $\langle \mathscr{B}, \langle i, j \rangle \rangle$.

For simplicity, let us now suppose, in addition to the assumptions made in the last paragraph, that L is a syntactically unambiguous language. Then the relativization to an analysis may of course be removed from the characterization of truth: φ is a *true sentence of L with respect to the model* $\langle \mathscr{B}, \langle i, j \rangle \rangle$ if and only if $\varphi \in DS_L$ and φ is a true sentence of L with respect to $\langle \mathscr{B}, \langle i, j \rangle \rangle$ and the analysis φ', where φ' is the unique member of C_{δ_0} such that $\varphi' R \varphi$, and C is as in the last paragraph. Let us add the assumption that K is a class of models for L. (The most important cases are those in which K is regarded as the class of logically possible models for L; among the conditions characterizing K might then appear the requirement that the "logical operations" and "logical words" of L receive their usual interpretations.) Then φ is *K-valid* in L if and only if φ is a true sentence of L with respect to every member of K. (In case K is understood in the way just indicated, the present notion amounts to logical validity.) If ζ, $\eta \in ME_L$, then ζ is K-*equivalent* to η in L if and only if (1) ζ, $\eta \in Cat_{\delta,L}$ for some $\delta \in CI_L$, and (2) whenever $\langle \mathscr{B}, \langle i, j \rangle \rangle \in K$, the denotation of ζ according to L and $\langle \mathscr{B}, \langle i, j \rangle \rangle$ is the same as the denotation of η according to L and $\langle \mathscr{B}, \langle i, j \rangle \rangle$. By a *token* in L is understood a pair $\langle \zeta, p \rangle$ such that $\zeta \in PE_L$ and p is any ordered pair. (Here we regard p as a possible point of reference. The useful idea of construing a token as a pair consisting of a type and a point of reference originates with Bar-Hillel.) It is usual to regard entailment (or logical consequence) as a relation between sentence types; but when indexical locutions may come into consideration, it is desirable to consider two relations, one between sentence types and one between sentence tokens.[5] (It is the latter notion that is involved when we say that 'I am hungry', when said by Jones to Smith, entails 'thou art hungry', when said on the same occasion by Smith to Jones. More precisely, let us suppose that the language in question contains, as its only indexical features, the pronouns 'I' and 'thou'. Then a context of use could reasonably be construed as an ordered pair of persons, regarded as the speaker and the person addressed respectively; and the situation under consideration can be described by saying that, for every i, the token $\langle$ 'I am hungry', $\langle i, \langle$ Jones, Smith $\rangle \rangle \rangle$ entails the token $\langle$ 'thou art hungry', $\langle i$, $\langle$ Smith, Jones $\rangle \rangle \rangle$.) The precise characterizations are the following. If $\langle \varphi, p \rangle$ and $\langle \psi, q \rangle$ are tokens in L, then $\langle \varphi, p \rangle$ K-*entails* $\langle \psi, q \rangle$ in L if and only if φ, $\psi \in DS_L$ and, for every Fregean interpretation $\mathscr{B}$ for L, if $\langle \mathscr{B}, p \rangle$ is in K and φ is a true sentence of L with respect to $\langle \mathscr{B}, p \rangle$, then $\langle \mathscr{B}, q \rangle$ is in K and ψ is a true sentence of L with respect to $\langle \mathscr{B}, q \rangle$. If φ, $\psi \in DS_L$, then the sentence *type* φ K-*entails* the sentence *type* ψ in L if and only if $\langle \varphi, p \rangle$ K-*entails* $\langle \psi, p \rangle$ for every ordered pair p. (It is clear then φ is K-equivalent to ψ in L if and only if each of φ and ψ K-entails the other in L.)

---

[5] For simplicity, I explicitly define entailment only between two sentences or sentence tokens. The more general and useful notion of entailment between a *set* of sentences or sentence tokens and a sentence or sentence token can be characterized in a completely analogous fashion.

Now synonymy with respect to all logically possible inter-pretations implies logical equivalence, but not conversely. To be a little more exact, if (i) the assumptions of the last two para-graphs are satisfied; (ii) ζ, η are meaningful expressions of L belonging to a common syntactic category of L; and (iii) ζ is weakly synonymous with η in L according to every inter-pretation $\mathscr{B}$ such that, for some i and j, $\langle \mathscr{B}, \langle i, j \rangle \rangle \in K$, then (iv) ζ is K-equivalent to η in L; but there are instances in which (i), (ii), and (iv) hold, but (iii) fails. The reason is roughly that the logical equivalence of two expressions depends on their extensions only at *designated* points of reference of logically possible models, while synonymy of those expressions depends on their extensions at *all* points of reference. (And it might for instance happen that "logical words" and "logical operations" receive their usual extensions at all designated points of reference but not at certain other, "unactualizable" points of reference.) Similarly, there will be cases in which two logically equivalent expressions will not be interchangeable in a sentence without changing its truth value, although synonymous expressions always may be so interchanged. This is because the extension of a compound expression may depend on the full meanings of certain components, that is, their extensions at all points of reference, and not simply their extensions at designated points of reference. In particular, it is possible to provide within the present frame-work a natural treatment of belief contexts that lacks the contro-versial property of always permitting interchange on the basis of logical equivalence. Previous model-theoretic treatments of belief contexts (for instance, the one in Montague [2]) had always possessed that property, and so does the treatment proposed in Section 7 below. But even to those who, like myself, believe that the best and most elegant approach is to permit unrestricted interchange on the basis of logical equivalence it may be of some interest to learn that this approach has genuine alternatives and is not forced upon us.

5. THEORY OF TRANSLATION

There appears to be no natural theory of definitions which will apply to arbitrary languages. But instead of generalizing the notion of a definition, we may rather consider the translation functions from one language into another that are induced by systems of definitions, and attempt to develop suitable general notions on this basis.

Assume throughout this section that L, L' are languages, $L = \langle \mathfrak{A}, R \rangle$, $L' = \langle \mathfrak{A}', R' \rangle$, $\mathfrak{A} = \langle A, F_\gamma, X_\delta, S, \delta_0 \rangle_{\gamma \in \Gamma, \delta \in \Delta}$, and $\mathfrak{A}' = \langle A', F'_\gamma, X'_\delta, S', \delta'_0 \rangle_{\gamma \in \Gamma', \delta \in \Delta'}$. By a *translation base* from L into L' is understood a system $\langle g, H_\gamma, j \rangle_{\gamma \in \Gamma}$ such that (1) g is a function from Δ into Δ'; (2) j is a function with domain $\bigcup_{\delta \in \Delta} X_\delta$; (3) whenever $\delta \in \Delta$ and $\zeta \in X_\delta$, $j(\zeta) \in C'_{g(\delta)}$, where C' is the family of syntactic categories generated by $\mathfrak{A}'$; (4) for all $\gamma \in \Gamma$, H_γ is a polynomial operation, of the same number of places as F_γ, over the algebra $\langle A', F'_\gamma \rangle_{\gamma \in \Gamma'}$; (5) whenever $\langle F_\gamma, \langle \delta_\xi \rangle_{\xi < \beta}, \varepsilon \rangle \in S$, $\langle H_\gamma, \langle g(\delta_\xi) \rangle_{\xi < \beta}, g(\varepsilon) \rangle$ is a derived syntactical rule of L'; and (6) $g(\delta_0) = \delta'_0$. If $\mathscr{T}$ $(= \langle g, H_\gamma, j \rangle_{\gamma \in \Gamma})$ is such a translation base, then the *translation function* from L into L' determined by $\mathscr{T}$ is the unique homomorphism k from $\langle A, F_\gamma \rangle_{\gamma \in \Gamma}$ into $\langle A', H_\gamma \rangle_{\gamma \in \Gamma}$ such that $j \subseteq k$; and ζ' *is a translation* of ζ from L into L' on the basis of $\mathscr{T}$ if and only if there are η, η' such that $\eta R \zeta$, $\eta' R' \zeta'$, $\eta \in \bigcup_{\delta \in \Delta} C_\delta$, $\eta' \in \bigcup_{\delta \in \Delta'} C'_\delta$, and $k(\eta) = \eta'$, where C, C' are the families of syntactic categories generated by $\mathfrak{A}$ and $\mathfrak{A}'$ respectively, and k is the translation function from L into L' determined by $\mathscr{T}$.

The principal use of translations is the semantical one of inducing interpretations. Indeed, if we are given a translation base from L into L', together with an interpretation for the 'already known' language L', then an interpretation for L is determined in the natural manner prescribed below.

Assume for the remainder of this section that $\mathscr{T}$ $(= \langle g, H_\gamma, j \rangle_{\gamma \in \Gamma})$ is a translation base from L into L', and that $\mathscr{B}'$ $(= \langle B', G'_\gamma, f' \rangle_{\gamma \in \Gamma'})$ is an interpretation for L'. Then the *interpretation for L induced by* L', $\mathscr{B}'$, *and* $\mathscr{T}$ is the interpretation $\langle B, G_\gamma, f \rangle_{\gamma \in \Gamma}$ for L such that (1) $\langle B, G_\gamma \rangle_{\gamma \in \Gamma}$ is the unique algebra such that h' is a homomorphism from $\langle A', H_\gamma \rangle_{\gamma \in \Gamma}$ to $\langle B, G_\gamma \rangle_{\gamma \in \Gamma}$, where h' is the meaning assignment for L' determined by $\mathscr{B}'$; and (2) for all $\zeta \in \bigcup_{\delta \in \Delta} X_\delta$, $f(\zeta) = h'(j(\zeta))$, where h' is as in (1).

It is in order to insure the existence of an algebra satisfying condition (1) that we require in the definition of a translation base that the operations H_γ be polynomial operations over $\langle A', F'_\gamma \rangle_{\gamma \in \Gamma'}$; compare the Remark at the end of Section 1.

Remark.   Suppose that $\mathscr{B}$ is the interpretation for L induced by L', $\mathscr{B}'$, and $\mathscr{T}$. Then (1) if $\mathscr{B}'$ is a Fregean interpretation for L', then $\mathscr{B}$ is a Fregean interpretation for L; (2) if h is the meaning assignment for L determined by $\mathscr{B}$, h' is the meaning assignment for L' determined by $\mathscr{B}'$, and k is the translation function from L into L' determined by $\mathscr{T}$, then h is the relative product of k and h'.

6. INTENSIONAL LOGIC

I wish now to illustrate the application of the general notions of this paper to artificial, "symbolic" languages. To this end I shall construct within the present framework the syntax and semantics of a rather rich system of intensional logic.[6]

The *letters of intensional logic* are to be [,], $\equiv$, ˇ, ^, together with symbols λ_τ, $v_{n,\tau}$, and $c_{n,\tau}$ for each natural number n and each $\tau \in T$. (We regard $v_{n,\tau}$ as the nth *variable of type* τ and $c_{n,\tau}$ as the nth *constant of type* τ. Thus, for definiteness, we employ only denumerably many constants; but a relaxation of this restriction, according to which the constants of any given type could be indexed by an arbitrary initial segment of the ordinals, would involve no important change in our considerations.) We assume that all letters are one-place sequences; but apart from this requirement and normal distinctness conditions, the precise nature of the letters need not concern us. An *expression of intensional logic* is a finite concatenation of letters of intensional logic.

Let $J_0, \ldots, J_3, J_{\langle 4, \tau \rangle}$ (for $\tau \in T$) be those operations, of 2, 2, 1, 1, 2 places respectively, on the set of expressions of intensional logic such that whenever ζ, η are such expressions and $\tau \in T$,

$$J_0(\zeta, \eta) = [\zeta\eta],$$
$$J_1(\zeta, \eta) = [\zeta \equiv \lambda],$$
$$J_2(\zeta) = \check{}\,\zeta,$$
$$J_3(\zeta) = \hat{}\,\zeta,$$
$$J_{\langle 4, \tau \rangle}(\zeta, \eta) = [\lambda_\tau \zeta \eta].$$

(We indicate concatenation by juxtaposition.) Let us understand

---

[6] This system has not appeared previously in the literature, but has been presented in talks before the Southern California Logic Colloquium in April 1969 and the Association for Symbolic Logic in May 1969. It comprehends as a part the intensional logic of Montague [2] and [4].

by Var_τ the set of all expressions $v_{n,\tau}$ for n a natural number, and by Con_τ the set of all expressions $c_{n,\tau}$ for n a natural number.

By L_0, or the *language of intensional logic*, is understood the system $\langle\langle A, F_\gamma, X_\delta, S, t\rangle_{\gamma\in\Gamma,\delta\in\Delta}, R\rangle$ where (1) A is the smallest set including all sets Con_τ and Var_τ (for $\tau \in T$) and closed under $J_0, \ldots, J_3, J_{\langle 4,\tau\rangle}$ (for all $\tau \in T$); (2) Γ is the set consisting of the numbers 0, 1, 2, 3, together with all pairs $\langle 4, \tau\rangle$ for $\tau \in T$; (3) for each $\gamma \in \Gamma$, F_γ is J_γ restricted to A; (4) $\Delta = T \cup (\{T\} \times T)$; (5) for each $\tau \in T$, $X_\tau = \mathrm{Con}_\tau \cup \mathrm{Var}_\tau$ and $X_{\langle T,\tau\rangle} = \mathrm{Var}_\tau$; (6) S is the set consisting of all sequences

$$\langle F_0, \langle\sigma,\tau\rangle, \sigma, \tau\rangle,$$
$$\langle F_1, \tau, \tau, t\rangle,$$
$$\langle F_2, \tau, \langle s, \tau\rangle\rangle,$$
$$\langle F_3, \langle s, \tau\rangle, \tau\rangle,$$
$$\langle F_{\langle 4,\sigma\rangle}, \langle T, \sigma\rangle, \tau, \langle\sigma,\tau\rangle\rangle,$$

where $\sigma, \tau \in T$; and (7) R is the identity relation on A.

Remark. Assume that $\sigma, \tau \in T$.

    (1) $\mathrm{Con}_\tau \cup \mathrm{Var}_\tau \subseteq \mathrm{Cat}_{\tau,L_0}$.

    (2) If $\zeta \in \mathrm{Cat}_{\langle\sigma,\tau\rangle,L_0}$ and $\eta \in \mathrm{Cat}_{\sigma,L_0}$ then $[\zeta\eta] \in \mathrm{Cat}_{\tau,L_0}$.

    (3) If $\zeta, \eta \in \mathrm{Cat}_{\tau,L_0}$, then $[\zeta \equiv \eta] \in \mathrm{Cat}_{t,L_0}$.

    (4) If $\zeta \in \mathrm{Cat}_{\tau,L_0}$, then $\hat{\ }\zeta \in \mathrm{Cat}_{\langle s,\tau\rangle,L_0}$.

    (5) If $\zeta \in \mathrm{Cat}_{\langle s,\tau\rangle,L_0}$, then $\check{\ }\zeta \in \mathrm{Cat}_{\tau,L_0}$.

    (6) If $\zeta \in \mathrm{Var}_\sigma$ and $\eta \in \mathrm{Cat}_{\tau,L_0}$, then $[\lambda_\sigma \zeta\eta] \in \mathrm{Cat}_{\langle\sigma,\tau\rangle,L_0}$.

    (7) L_0 is a syntactically unambiguous language.

If E, I are any sets, then a *value assignment* relative to E and I is a function j having as its domain the set of ordered pairs $\langle n, \tau\rangle$ for which n is a natural number and $\tau \in T$, and such that whenever $\langle n, \tau\rangle$ is such a pair, $j(n, \tau) \in D_{\tau,E,I}$. If j is such a value assignment, then $j_x^{n,\tau}$ is to be that function j' with the same domain as j such that (1) $j'(n, \tau) = x$ and (2) $j'(m, \sigma) = j(m, \sigma)$ for every pair $\langle m, \sigma\rangle$ in the domain of j other than $\langle n, \tau\rangle$.

Let σ_0 be that type assignment for L_0 such that, for all $\tau \in T$, $\sigma_0(\tau) = \sigma_0(\langle T, \tau\rangle) = \tau$. By K_0, or the class of *logically possible models for* L_0, is understood the class of models $\langle\langle B, G_\gamma, f\rangle_{\gamma\in\Gamma}, \langle i_0, j_0\rangle\rangle$ for L_0 such that, for some nonempty sets E, I, J, (1)

$\langle B, G_\gamma, f\rangle_{\gamma \in \Gamma}$ is a Fregean interpretation for L_0 connected with E, I, J, and σ_0; (2) J is the set of value assignments relative to E and I; (3) whenever $\alpha \in U_{\tau \in T}$ Con_τ, $i \in I$, and $j, j' \in J$, $f(\alpha)(i, j) = f(\alpha)(i, j')$; (4) whenever n is a natural number, $\tau \in T$, $i \in I$, and $j \in J$, $f(v_{n,\tau})(i, j) = j(n, \tau)$; and (5) for all $a, b \in B$, $i \in I$, $j \in J$, σ, $\tau \in T$, and natural numbers n,

$G_0(a, b)(i, j) = a(i, j)(b(i, j))$ if $a \in M_{\langle \sigma, \tau \rangle, E, I, J}$ and $b \in M_{\sigma, E, I, J}$,

$G_1(a, b)(i, j) = \{\Lambda\}$ if and only if $a(i, j) = b(i, j)$,

$G_2(a)(i, j)$ is that function p on I such that, for all $k \in I$,
$\quad p(k) = a(k, j)$,

$G_3(a)(i, j) = a(i, j)(i)$ if $a \in M_{\langle \sigma, \tau \rangle, E, I, J}$, and if $a = f(v_{n,\tau})$, then $G_{\langle 4, \tau \rangle}(a, b)(i, j)$ is that function p on $D_{\tau, E, I}$ such that, for all $x \in D_{\tau, E, I}$, $p(x) = b(i, j_x^{n,\tau})$.

Remark. Assume that $\langle \mathscr{B}, \langle i_0, j_0 \rangle \rangle \in K_0$; E, I, J are nonempty sets; $\mathscr{B}$ is a Fregean interpretation connected with E, I, J, and σ_0; g is the meaning assignment for L_0 determined by $\mathscr{B}$; h is the denotation assignment for L_0 determined by $\langle \mathscr{B}, \langle i_0, j_0 \rangle \rangle$; σ, τ T; and n is a natural number. Then:

(1) If $\zeta \in Con_\tau$, then $h(\zeta) \in D_{\tau, E, I}$, and $g(\zeta)(i, j) = g(\zeta)(i, j')$ for all $i \in I$ and $j, j' \in J$.

(2) If $\zeta \in Var_\tau$, then $h(\zeta) \in D_{\tau, E, I}$ and $g(\zeta)(i, j) = g(\zeta)(i', j)$ for all $i, i' \in I$ and $j \in J$.

(3) If $\zeta \in Cat_{\langle \sigma, \tau \rangle, L_0}$ and $\eta \in Cat_{\sigma, L_0}$, then $h([\zeta \eta]) = h(\zeta)(h(\eta))$.

(4) If $\zeta, \eta \in Cat_{\tau, L_0}$, then $h([\zeta = \eta]) = \{\Lambda\}$ if and only if $h(\zeta) = h(n)$.

(5) If $\zeta \in Cat_{\tau, L_0}$, then $h(\check{}\zeta)$ is that function p on I such that, for all $i \in I$, $p(i) = g(\zeta)(i, j_0)$.

(6) If $\zeta \in Cat_{\langle s, \tau \rangle, L_0}$, then $h(\check{}\zeta) = h(\zeta)(i_0)$.

(7) If $\zeta \in Cat_{\tau, L_0}$, then $h(\lambda_\sigma v_{n,\sigma} \zeta)$ is that function p on $D_{\sigma, E, I}$ such that, for all $x \in D_{\sigma, E, I}$, $p(x) = g(\zeta)(i_0, j_{0x}^{n,\sigma})$.

It is convenient to introduce a few metamathematical abbreviations designating expressions of L_0. Among them will be found combinations corresponding to all the usual notions of propositional, quantificational, and modal logic; in these cases the expected truth conditions will be satisfied in connection with all models in K_0.[7] In particular, suppose that $\alpha \in \bigcup_{\tau \in T} \text{Var}_\tau$, φ, $\psi \in \text{Cat}_{t,L_0}$, and ρ, σ, $\tau \in T$. Then we set

$\lambda \alpha \zeta = [\lambda_\pi \alpha \zeta]$, where π is the unique member of T such that $\alpha \in \text{Var}_\pi$;

$\bigwedge \alpha \varphi = [\lambda \alpha \varphi \equiv \lambda \alpha[\alpha \equiv \alpha]]$;

$\neg \varphi = [\varphi \equiv \bigwedge \beta \beta]$, where $\beta = v_{0,t}$;

$\varphi \wedge \psi = \bigwedge \beta[\psi \equiv [[\beta \varphi] \equiv [\beta \psi]]]$, where $\beta = v_{0,\langle t,t \rangle}$;

$\varphi \rightarrow \psi = \neg(\varphi \wedge \neg \psi)$;

$\varphi \vee \psi = \neg \varphi \rightarrow \psi$;

$\bigvee \alpha \varphi = \neg \bigwedge \alpha \neg \varphi$;

$\delta\{\zeta\} = [\ulcorner \delta \zeta]$, if $\zeta \in \text{Cat}_{\sigma,L_0}$ and $\delta \in \text{Cat}_{\langle s,\langle \sigma,\tau \rangle \rangle,L_0}$;

$\delta\{\zeta,\eta\} = \delta\{\eta\}\{\zeta\}$, if $\zeta \in \text{Cat}_{\rho,L_0}$, $\eta \in \text{Cat}_{\sigma,L_0}$, and $\delta \in \text{Cat}_{\langle s,\langle \sigma,\langle s,\langle \rho,\tau \rangle \rangle \rangle \rangle,L_0}$;

$\square \varphi = [\ulcorner \varphi \equiv \hat{\ } \bigwedge \beta[\beta \equiv \beta]]$, where $\beta = v_{0,e}$;

$\zeta \equiv \eta = \square[\zeta \equiv \eta]$, if ζ, $\eta \in \text{Cat}_{\tau,L_0}$;

$\hat{\alpha} \varphi = \hat{\ }(\lambda \alpha \varphi)$.

If ζ, $\eta \in ME_{L_0}$ and $\alpha \in \bigcup_{\tau \in T} \text{Var}_\tau$, then let us understand by ζ_η^α the result of replacing all "free occurrences" of α by η in ζ; we do not bother to construct an exact definition here. The following remark indicates the extent to which principles of substitutivity of identity and of universal instantiation—always questionable in the context of modal or intensional logic—hold within the present system.

Remark. If σ, $\tau \in T$ and $\varphi \in \text{Cat}_{t,L_0}$, then the following expressions are K_0-valid in L_0:

$\bigwedge \alpha \varphi \rightarrow \varphi_\beta^\alpha$, if α, $\beta \in \text{Var}_\tau$ and β is not bound in φ;

$\bigwedge \alpha \varphi \rightarrow \varphi_\zeta^\alpha$, if $\alpha \in \text{Var}_\tau$, $\zeta \in \text{Cat}_{\tau,L_0}$, α does not stand within the scope of $\hat{\ }$ in φ, and no variable free in ζ is bound in φ;

$(\bigwedge \alpha \varphi \wedge \bigvee \alpha(\alpha \equiv \zeta)) \rightarrow \varphi_\zeta^\alpha$, if $\alpha \in \text{Var}_\tau$, $\zeta \in \text{Cat}_{\tau,L_0}$, no variable free in ζ is bound in φ, and α is not free in ζ;

$\bigvee \alpha(\alpha \equiv \hat{\ } \zeta)$, if $\zeta \in \text{Cat}_{\tau,L_0}$, $\alpha \in \text{Var}_{\langle s,\tau \rangle}$, and α is not free in ζ;

$[\beta \equiv \gamma] \rightarrow [\zeta_\beta^\alpha \equiv \zeta_\gamma^\alpha]$, if α, β, $\gamma \in \text{Var}_\tau$, $\zeta \in ME_{L_0}$, and neither β nor γ is bound in ζ;

---

[7] The methods of expressing negation and conjunction are due to Tarski [6]. I am grateful to Dr. Mohammed Amer for suggesting their use in this connection.

$(\eta \equiv \theta) \rightarrow [\zeta_{\eta}^{\alpha} \equiv \zeta_{\theta}^{\alpha}]$, if $\zeta \in ME_{L_0}$, η, $\theta \in \text{Cat}_{\tau, L_0}$, $\alpha \in \text{Var}_{\tau}$, and no variable free in η or θ is bound in ζ;

$[\eta \equiv \theta] \rightarrow [\zeta_{\eta}^{\alpha} \equiv \zeta_{\theta}^{\alpha}]$, if $\zeta \in ME_{L_0}$, η, $\theta \in \text{Cat}_{\tau, L_0}$, $\alpha \in \text{Var}_{\tau}$, α does not stand within the scope of $\hat{\ }$ in ζ, and no variable free in η or θ is bound in ζ;

$([\eta \equiv \theta] \wedge \vee \alpha (\alpha \equiv \eta) \wedge \vee \alpha (\alpha \equiv \theta)) \rightarrow [\zeta_{\eta}^{\alpha} \equiv \zeta_{\theta}^{\alpha}]$, if $\zeta \in ME_{L_0}$, η, $\theta \in \text{Cat}_{\tau, L_0}$, $\alpha \in \text{Var}_{\tau}$, no variable free in η or θ is bound in ζ, and α is not free in η or θ.

7. A FRAGMENT OF ENGLISH

As our second example we may take a natural language—indeed, a deliberately restricted fragment of English. The letters of this fragment are **a**, . . . , **z**, the blank, *, $\dashv$, $\vdash$, $\nvdash$, $\nvDash$, $\nvdash$, $\nVdash$, $\nVDash$, $\nVdash$, together with symbols v_n for each natural number n. Again we assume normal distinctness conditions, and that all letters are one-place sequences; and an *expression* is again to be a finite concatenation of letters. We let

BDS (or the set of basic declarative sentences) $= \Lambda$,

BPDE (or the set of basic proposition-denoting expressions) $= \Lambda$,

BIE (or the set of basic individual expressions) $=$ the set consisting of the symbols v_{2n+1} for n a natural number,

BCNP (or the set of basic common noun phrases) $=$ the set of common count nouns of English,

BST (or the set of basic singular terms) $=$ the set of proper nouns of English that are not in BCNP,

BAP (or the set of basic adjective phrases) $=$ the set of 'ordinary' English adjectives that are not in BCNP or BST,

BVPPO (or the set of basic verb phrases taking a propositional object) $= \{$**believe**, **assert**, **deny**, **know**, **prove**$\}$,

BTVP (or the set of basic transitive verb phrases) $=$ the set of transitive verbs of English, including **be**, that are not in BCNP, BST, BAP, or BVPPO,

BIVP (or the set of basic intransitive verb phrases) $=$ the set of intransitive verbs of English that are not in BCNP, BST, BAP, BVPPO, or BTVP.

Let Y be the unique 11-place sequence such that (i) $Y_0, \ldots, Y_8$ are sets of expressions; (ii) Y_9, Y_{10} are binary relations between expressions; (iii) for all $\zeta, \alpha, \varphi, \delta, \beta, \delta'$;

(1) $\mathrm{BDS} \subseteq Y_0$, $\mathrm{BPDE} \subseteq Y_1$, $\mathrm{BIE} \subseteq Y_2$, $\mathrm{BCNP} \subseteq Y_3$, $\mathrm{BST} \subseteq Y_4$, $\mathrm{BAP} \subseteq Y_5$, $\mathrm{BVPPO} \subseteq Y_6$, $\mathrm{BTVP} \subseteq Y_7$, $\mathrm{BIVP} \subseteq Y_8$;

(2) if $\zeta \in Y_3$, then **every** ζ, **no** ζ, **the** ζ, **a** $\zeta \in Y_4$;

(3) if $\alpha \in Y_2$, then **he** $\alpha \in Y_4$;

(4) if $\varphi \in Y_0$, then **that** $\varphi \in Y_1$;

(5) if $\delta \in Y_7$, and $\beta \in Y_4$, then $+\delta\beta'+\, \in Y_8$, where either (a) for some $\alpha \in \mathrm{BIE}$, $\beta = $ **he** α and $\beta' = $ **him** α, or (b) there is no $\alpha \in \mathrm{BIE}$ such that $\beta = $ **he** α, and $\beta' = \beta$;

(6) if $\delta \in Y_6$ and $\beta \in Y_1$, then $+\delta\beta+\, \in Y_8$;

(7) if $\alpha \in Y_2$ and $\varphi \in Y_0$, then **such** α **that** $\varphi \in Y_5$;

(8) if $\delta \in Y_5$ and $\zeta \in Y_3$, then $\theta \in Y_3$, where (a) either δ does not have the form **such** α **that** φ for $\alpha \in \mathrm{BIE}$ and φ an expression, or no member of BCNP properly occurs (that is, as a full word) in ζ, and $\theta = \, \mp\delta\zeta\mp\,$, or (b) $\delta = $ **such** α **that** φ, the member of BCNP that properly occurs first in ζ is of

$$\left\{\begin{array}{l}\text{masculine}\\ \text{feminine}\\ \text{neuter}\end{array}\right\}\text{gender, and } \theta = \, \mp\zeta \text{ \textbf{such} } \alpha \text{ \textbf{that} } \varphi'\mp,$$

where φ' is obtained from φ by replacing each free occurrence of **he** α or **him** α (that is, occurrence that does not stand in a part of φ of the form **such** α **that** χ, where χ is an expression in which all parentheses are matched), by

$$\left\{\begin{array}{l}\textbf{he } \alpha\\ \textbf{she } \alpha\\ \textbf{it } \alpha\end{array}\right\} \text{ or } \left\{\begin{array}{l}\textbf{him } \alpha\\ \textbf{her } \alpha\\ \textbf{it } \alpha\end{array}\right\} \text{ respectively;}$$

(9) if $\delta \in \mathrm{BVPPO} \cup \mathrm{BTVP} \cup \mathrm{BIVP}$, then $\delta Y_9 \delta$ and $*Y_{10}\delta$;

(10) if $\delta \in Y_7$, $\beta \in Y_4$, and $\alpha Y_9 \delta$, then $\alpha Y_9 + \delta\beta'+\,$, where β' is as in (5);

(11) if $\delta \in Y_7$, $\beta \in Y_4$, and $\delta' Y_{10} \delta$, then $+\delta'\beta'+\, Y_{10} +\delta\beta'+\,$, where β' is as in (5);

(12) if $\delta \in Y_6$, $\beta \in Y_1$, and $\alpha Y_9 \delta$, then $\alpha Y_9 + \delta \beta +$;

(13) if $\delta \in Y_6$, $\beta \in Y_1$, and $\delta' Y_{10} \delta$, then $+ \delta' \beta + Y_{10} + \delta \beta +$;

(14) if $\alpha \in Y_4$ and $\delta \in Y_8$, then $\not\equiv \alpha \delta'' \not\equiv \in Y_0$, where either (a) there exist δ', β, β' such that $\delta' Y_{10} \delta$, $\beta Y_9 \delta$, β' is the third person singular of β, and δ'' is the result of substituting β' for * in δ', or (b) there do not exist δ', β, β' such that $\delta' Y_{10} \delta$, $\beta Y_9 \delta$, and β' is the third person singular of β, and $\delta'' = \delta$;

(15) if $\alpha \in Y_4$ and $\delta \in Y_8$, then $\not\equiv \alpha \delta'' \not\equiv \in Y_0$, where either (a) there exist δ', β such that $\delta' Y_{10} \delta$, $\beta Y_9 \delta$, $\beta \neq$ **be**, and δ'' is the result of substituting **does not** β for * in δ', or (b) there exists δ' such that $\delta' Y_{10} \delta$, **be**, $Y_9 \delta$, and δ'' is the result of substituting **is not** for * in δ', or (c) there do not exist δ', β such that $\delta' Y_{10} \delta$ and $\beta Y_9 \delta$, and $\delta'' = \delta$;

and (iv) for every 11-place sequence Z, if (i)–(iii) hold for Z, then $Y_0 \subseteq Z_0, \ldots, Y_{10} \subseteq Z_{10}$. (It is a consequence of a simple theorem on simultaneous recursion, due to Dr. Perry Smith and me, that there is exactly one sequence satisfying these conditions. We regard '$\alpha Y_9 \delta$' and '$\delta' Y_{10} \delta$' as meaning 'α is the main verb of the verb phrase δ' and 'δ' is the main verb location in the verb phrase δ' respectively.)

Let $K_0, \ldots, K_{10}$ be those operations on the set of expressions, of 1, 1, 1, 1, 1, 1, 2, 2, 2, 2, 2 places respectively, such that, for all expressions α, β, δ, ζ, φ,

$K_0(\zeta) =$ **every** ζ,

$K_1(\zeta) =$ **no** ζ,

$K_2(\zeta) =$ **the** ζ,

$K_3(\zeta) =$ **a** ζ,

$K_4(\zeta) =$ **he** ζ,

$K_5(\varphi) =$ **that** φ,

$K_6(\delta, \beta) = + \delta \beta' +$, where β' is as in (5),

$K_7(\alpha, \varphi) =$ **such** α **that** φ,

$K_8(\delta, \zeta) = \theta$, where θ is as in (8),

$K_9(\alpha, \delta) = \not\equiv \alpha \delta'' \not\equiv$, where δ'' is as in (14),

$K_{10}(\alpha, \delta) = \not\equiv \alpha \delta'' \not\equiv$, where δ'' is as in (15).

(In the definitions above some terms from traditional grammar—for instance, 'common count noun' and 'the third person singular of the verb _____'—have been employed without explicit analysis. These terms are admittedly vague but can cause no problem. Unlike certain other traditional grammatical terms, for example, 'declarative sentence', they all have a finite range of application and could therefore be replaced by precise terms exactly characterized by simple enumeration (in case no shorter and more elegant procedure should come to hand).)

By L_1 let us understand the system $\langle\langle A, F_\gamma, X_\delta, S, 0\rangle_{\gamma\in\Gamma,\delta\in\Delta}, R\rangle$, where (1) $\Delta = \{0, \ldots, 8\}$; (2) $X_0 = \text{BDS}$, $X_1 = \text{BPDE}$, $X_2 = \text{BIE}, X_3 = \text{BCNP}, X_4 = \text{BST}, X_5 = \text{BAP}, X_6 = \text{BVPPO}$, $X_7 = \text{BTVP}, X_8 = \text{BIVP}$; (3) A is the smallest set including all the sets X_δ (for $\delta \in \Delta$) and closed under the operations $K_0, \ldots, K_{10}$; (4) $\Gamma = \{0, \ldots, 10\}$; (5) for each $\gamma \in \Gamma, F_\gamma$ is K_γ restricted to A; (6) S is the set consisting of the sequences

$$\langle F_0, 3, 4\rangle,$$
$$\langle F_1, 3, 4\rangle,$$
$$\langle F_2, 3, 4\rangle,$$
$$\langle F_3, 3, 4\rangle,$$
$$\langle F_4, 2, 4\rangle,$$
$$\langle F_5, 0, 1\rangle,$$
$$\langle F_6, 7, 4, 8\rangle,$$
$$\langle F_6, 6, 1, 8\rangle,$$
$$\langle F_7, 2, 0, 5\rangle,$$
$$\langle F_8, 5, 3, 3\rangle,$$
$$\langle F_9, 4, 8, 0\rangle,$$
$$\langle F_{10}, 4, 8, 0\rangle;$$

and (7) R is that function with domain A such that, for all $\zeta \in A$, $R(\zeta)$ is the result of deleting all parentheses and members of BIE from ζ.

Remark. (1) L_1 is a syntactically ambiguous language. (2) If $L_1 = \langle \mathfrak{A}, R\rangle$ and C is the family of syntactic categories generated by $\mathfrak{A}$, then $C_i = Y_i$ for $i = 0, \ldots, 8$.

Suppose that L_1 has, as above, the form $\langle\langle A, F_\gamma, X_\delta, S, 0\rangle_{\gamma\in\Gamma,\delta\in\Delta}, R\rangle$. By $\mathcal{T}_0$, or the *standard translation base* from L_1

into L_0, is understood the system $\langle g, H_\gamma, j \rangle_{\gamma \in \Gamma}$ such that (1) g is that function with domain $\{0, \ldots, 8\}$ such that

$$g(0) = t,$$
$$g(1) = \langle s, t \rangle,$$
$$g(2) = \langle T, e \rangle,$$
$$g(3) = \langle e, t \rangle,$$
$$g(4) = \langle s, \langle \langle s, g(3) \rangle, t \rangle \rangle,$$
$$g(5) = \langle \langle s, g(3) \rangle, g(3) \rangle,$$
$$g(6) = \langle g(1), \langle g(4), t \rangle \rangle,$$
$$g(7) = \langle g(4), \langle g(4), t \rangle \rangle,$$
$$g(8) = \langle g(4), t \rangle;$$

(2) $H_0, \ldots, H_{10}$ are those operations over PE_{L_0}, of 1, 1, 1, 1, 1, 1, 2, 2, 2, 2, 2 places respectively, such that, for all ζ, α, φ, δ, $\beta \in PE_{L_0}$,

$$H_0(\zeta) = \hat{P} \wedge u([\zeta u] \to P\{u\}),$$
$$H_1(\zeta) = \hat{P} \neg \vee u([\zeta u] \wedge P\{u\}),$$
$$H_2(\zeta) = \hat{P} \vee u(\wedge v[[v \equiv u] \equiv [\zeta v]] \wedge P\{u\}),$$
$$H_3(\zeta) = \hat{P} \vee u([\zeta u] \wedge P\{u\}),$$
$$H_4(\zeta) = \hat{P} P\{\zeta\},$$
$$H_5(\varphi) = {}^{\hat{}}\varphi,$$
$$H_6(\delta, \beta) = [\delta \beta],$$
$$H_7(\alpha, \zeta) = \lambda P[\lambda_e \alpha(P\{\alpha\} \wedge \zeta)],$$
$$H_8(\delta, \zeta) = [\delta {}^{\hat{}}\zeta],$$
$$H_9(\alpha, \delta) = [\delta \alpha],$$
$$H_{10}(\alpha, \delta) = \neg [\delta \alpha],$$

where u, v are $v_{0,e}$, $v_{2,e}$ respectively and P is $v_{0, \langle s, \langle e, t \rangle \rangle}$; (3) j is a function with $\bigcup_{\delta \in \Delta} X_\delta$ as its domain; (4) for every natural number n, $j(v_n) = v_{n,e}$; and (5) for every $\delta \in \{3, \ldots, 8\}$, every natural number n, and every ζ, if ζ is the nth member of X_δ (in, let us say, the standard lexicographic ordering of expressions of L_1), then $j(\zeta) = c_{n, g(\delta)}$.

For the remainder of this section let us assume that $\mathcal{T}_0$ has, as above, the form $\langle g, H_\gamma, j \rangle_{\gamma \in \Gamma}$.

We could, as in Montague [5], characterize directly the logically possible models for L_1; but a somewhat more perspicuous method is to proceed by way of translation into L_0. Indeed, we understand by K_1, or the class of *logically possible models for* L_1, the class of pairs $\langle \mathscr{B}, \langle i_0, j_0 \rangle \rangle$ such that, for some $\mathscr{B}'$, (1) $\langle \mathscr{B}', \langle i_0, j_0 \rangle \rangle \in K_0$; (2) $\mathscr{B}$ is the interpretation for L_1 induced by L_0, $\mathscr{B}'$, and $\mathscr{T}_0$; and (3) for all $\alpha \in \mathrm{BST}$, the expressions

$j(\mathbf{entity}) \equiv \lambda u[u \equiv u]$,
$j(\mathbf{be}) \equiv \lambda \mathscr{Q} \lambda \mathscr{P} \mathscr{P} \{\hat{u} \mathscr{Q} \{\hat{v}[u \equiv v]\}\}$,
$\mathrm{V}u(j(\alpha) \equiv \hat{P}P\{u\})$

are true sentences of L_0 with respect to $\langle \mathscr{B}', \langle i_0, j_0 \rangle \rangle$, where u, v, P, $\mathscr{P}$, $\mathscr{Q}$ are $v_{0,e}$, $v_{1,e}$, $v_{0,\langle s, \langle e, t \rangle \rangle}$, $v_{0,g(4)}$, $v_{1,g(4)}$ respectively.

Examples.[8]   (1) The expression **every man is a man** is K_1-valid in L_1.

(2) The expression **every man such that he loves a woman is a man** is K_1-valid in L_1.

(3) The expression **every alleged murderer is a murderer** is in DS_{L_1} but is not K_1-valid in L_1.

(4) The expression **every tall murderer is a murderer** is also in DS_{L_1} but is not K_1-valid in L_1.

(5) The expression **every big midget is a big entity** is in DS_{L_1} but is not K_1-valid in L_1.

(6) The expression **every unmarried midget is a(n) unmarried entity** is in DS_{L_1} but is not K_1-valid in L_1.

(7) **Jones seeks a horse such that it speaks** and **a horse such that it speaks is a(n) entity such that Jones seeks it** are in DS_{L_1}, but neither K_1-entails the other in L_1.

(8) **Jones finds a horse such that it speaks** and **a horse such that it speaks is a(n) entity such that Jones finds it** are in DS_{L_1}, but neither K_1-entails the other in L_1.

Parts (3) and (5) shows that our treatment of adjectives—which is essentially due to unpublished work of J. A. W. Kamp and Terence Parsons—is capable of accommodating so-called *non-intersective* adjectives; and part (7) that the present treatment of

[8] In these examples the notions of K_1-validity and K_1-entailment are applied to expressions of the *ambiguous* language L_1, while they were defined above only in connection with *unambiguous* languages. The extension of the notions to the ambiguous case (involving relativization to analyses) is, however, routine. Further, the examples given here involve no important ambiguities, in the sense that each has only one *natural* analysis; and it is with respect to this analysis that the assertions are meant to hold.

verbs can accommodate *intensional* verbs. The analogues (4), (6), and (8) may, however, seem strange. The sentences mentioned in (4) and (6) are certainly true in the standard or intended model for L_1—indeed, *necessarily* true in that model, in the sense of being true in every model like it except in the choice of a designated point of reference; and the two sentences mentioned in (8) are synonymous according to that model. One may wonder, however, whether natural notions of logical truth and logical equivalence could be found according to which the sentences in (4) and (6) would be logically true and those in (8) logically equivalent. As far as the sentences in (8) are concerned—and more generally sentences whose logical properties depend on the extensionality of certain verbs—the solution is provided by the notion of K_1'-equivalence, where K_1' is as characterized below. Adjectives can be dealt with in a related but simpler and more obvious way; indications may be found in Montague [5] and in unpublished work of Parsons.

Suppose that $\mathscr{M}$ is a model for intensional logic (L_0). If $\zeta \in \mathrm{Cat}_{g(8),L_0}$, then ζ is said to be (*first-order*) *reducible* in $\mathscr{M}$ if and only if the expression

$$\mathrm{V}R\wedge\mathscr{P}([\zeta\mathscr{P}] \equiv \mathscr{P}\{R\})$$

is a true sentence of L_0 with respect to $\mathscr{M}$, where R, $\mathscr{P}$ are the first variables of types $\langle s, \langle e, t\rangle\rangle$ and $g(4)$ respectively which do not occur in ζ. An expression $\zeta \in \mathrm{Cat}_{g(7),L_0}$ is said to be *first-order reducible with respect to its subject*, or simply *subject-reducible*, in $\mathscr{M}$ if and only if the expression

$$\wedge\mathscr{Q}\mathrm{V}R\wedge\mathscr{P}([[\zeta\mathscr{Q}]\mathscr{P}] \equiv \mathscr{P}\{R\})$$

is a true sentence of L_0 with respect to $\mathscr{M}$, and *fully* (*first-order*) *reducible* in $\mathscr{M}$ if and only if the expression

$$\mathrm{V}S\wedge\mathscr{P}\wedge\mathscr{Q}([[\zeta\mathscr{Q}]\mathscr{P}] \equiv \mathscr{P}\{\hat{u}\mathscr{Q}\{\hat{v}S\{u, v\}\}\})$$

is a true sentence of L_0 with respect to $\mathscr{M}$, where R, S, $\mathscr{P}$, $\mathscr{Q}$ are the first variables of types $\langle s, \langle e, t\rangle\rangle$, $\langle s, \langle e, \langle s, \langle e, t\rangle\rangle\rangle\rangle$, $g(4)$, and $g(4)$ respectively which do not occur in ζ.

We now distinguish a certain subset EIV, or the set of *extensional intransitive verbs*, of the set BIVP. (The other members of BIVP might be called *intensional intransitive verbs*.) In view of the finitude of BIVP, membership in EIV could be determined by simple enumeration of the positive or negative cases. (To be sure, one would be hard pressed to find *any* intransitive verb of English that should clearly qualify as intensional.) In a similar way we distinguish sets SETV and FETV such that FETV $\subseteq$ SETV $\subseteq$ BTVP. The members of SETV should be those verbs that one wishes to regard as *subject-extensional transitive verbs*, and the members of FETV those that one wishes to regard as *fully extensional transitive verbs*; for example, **love** and **find** are to be in FETV, and **seek, worship, conceive** and **see** (in the nonveridical sense, in which some men have seen dragons) in SETV–FETV.

By K'_1, or the class of *strongly logically possible models for L_1*, is understood the class of pairs $\langle \mathscr{B}, \langle i_0, j_0 \rangle \rangle$ such that, for some $\mathscr{B}'$, conditions (1)–(3) of the definition above of K_1 are satisfied, and in addition (4) for all $\alpha \in$ EIV, $j(\alpha)$ is first-order reducible in $\langle \mathscr{B}', \langle i_0, j_0 \rangle \rangle$; (5) for all $\alpha \in$ SETV, $j(\alpha)$ is subject-reducible in $\langle \mathscr{B}', \langle i_0, j_0 \rangle \rangle$; and (6) for all $\alpha \in$ FETV, $j(\alpha)$ is fully reducible in $\langle \mathscr{B}', \langle i_0, j_0 \rangle \rangle$.

Remark. (1) **Jones finds a horse such that it speaks** and **a horse such that it speaks is a(n) entity such that Jones finds it** are K'_1-equivalent in L_1.

(2) Neither of the expressions **Jones seeks a horse such that it speaks** and **a horse such that it speaks is a(n) entity such that Jones seeks it** K'_1-entails the other in L_1.

Quantification on multiple occurrences of variables is expressible in L_1 by **such that** locutions. Consider, for instance, the sentence **every man loves a woman such that she loves him.** Ordinary usage would endow this sentence with two readings. According to one, which is the only reading allowed in L_1, multiple reference does not occur. The pronoun **him** "dangles"; it has no antecedent within the sentence itself but refers to an object specified by the linguistic or extralinguistic context of utterance. According to a second and more natural reading, multiple reference occurs and **him** has **man** "as its antecedent." This assertion can be expressed in L_1, not by the original sentence, but by **every man is a(n) entity such that it loves a woman such that she loves it.**

Notice that the reduction of multiple reference to **such that** locutions has the consequence, in my opinion correct, that *multiple reference often necessitates transparency*. Thus, although **Jones seeks a unicorn** could be true even though there are no unicorns, the more natural reading of **a man such that he seeks a unicorn loves a woman such that she seeks it** (according to which **it** does not dangle but has **unicorn** as its antecedent) could not be; this reading would have to be expressed not by the original sentence but by **a unicorn**[9] **is a(n) entity such that a man such that he seeks it loves a woman such that she seeks it.**

The qualification 'often' appears in the dictum above in order to allow for such at least apparent exceptions as **Jones seeks a unicorn such that Robinson seeks it,** which has an interpretation in L_1 that involves neither a dangling pronoun nor the existence of unicorns.

REFERENCES

1. Frege, G. Über Sinn und Bedeutung. *Zeitschrift für Philosophie und philosophische Kritik* 100:25–50 (1892).
2. Montague, R. Pragmatics and Intensional Logic. *Synthèse* 22:68–94 (1970). Chap. 4 in this book.
3. —. Pragmatics. In R. Klibansky (ed.), *Contemporary Philosophy: A Survey*, vol. 1. Florence, 1968. Chap. 3 in this book.

[9] That is, **some unicorn.** I have made no attempt to capture the ambiguity, felt strongly in this sentence, according to which the indefinite article **a** may sometimes have the force of universal, as well as the more usual existential, quantification. By the way, no significance should be attached to the failure of L_1 to reflect the ambiguity of such sentences as **every man loves a woman such that she loves him** and **a man such that he seeks a unicorn loves a woman such that she seeks it.** It would be possible to represent this ambiguity formally at the expense of complicating the characterization of L_1—for instance, by altering the constituent R of L_1 so that each of the sentences above would be related by R to the disambiguated sentences underlying *both* (and not just one) of its paraphrases in L_1. The general characterization of R would then present some difficulty. It would have to account, for instance, for the 'multiple reference' reading of **every man such that he seeks a unicorn loves a woman such that she seeks it,** which is **every unicorn is a(n) entity such that every man such that he seeks it loves a woman such that she seeks it.** (In this case the singular term **a unicorn** *must* be treated universally and not existentially.)

4. —. On the Nature of Certain Philosophical Entities. *Monist* 53:161–94 (1969). Chap. 5 in this book.
5. —. English as a Formal Language. In B. Visentini et al., *Linguaggi nella Società e nella Tecnica*. Milan, 1970. Chap. 6 in this book.
6. Tarski, A. O Wyrazie Pierwotnym Logistyki (On the Primitive Term of Logistic). English translation in A. Tarski, *Logic, Semantics, Metamathematics*. Oxford, 1956.

8. The Proper Treatment of Quantification in Ordinary English

The aim of this paper is to present in a rigorous way the syntax and semantics of a certain fragment of a certain dialect of English. For expository purposes the fragment has been made as simple and restricted as it can be while accommodating all the more puzzling cases of quantification and reference with which I am acquainted.[1]

Patrick Suppes claims, in a paper prepared for the present workshop, that "at the present time the semantics of natural languages are less satisfactorily formulated than the grammars . . . [and] a complete grammar for any significant fragment of natural language is yet to be written." This claim would of course be accurate if restricted in its application to the attempts emanating from the Massachusetts Institute of Technology, but fails to take into account the syntactic and semantic treatments proposed in Montague [8 and 9]. Thus the present paper cannot claim to present the *first* complete syntax (or grammar, in Suppes'

Originally published in J. Hintikka, J. Moravcsik, and P. Suppes (eds.), *Approaches to Natural Language: Proceedings of the 1970 Stanford Workshop on Grammar and Semantics.* Dordrecht, D. Reidel Publishing Company, 1973, pp. 221–42. Reprinted with permission. Much of the content reported here was supported by United States National Science Foundation Grant GS-2785. I am indebted to Mr. Michael Bennett, Mr. Harry Deutsch, and Mr. Daniel Gallin for helpful comments. [Editor's note: The content of this chapter was presented in September 1970 at the 1970 Stanford Workshop on Grammar and Semantics.]

[1] The medieval and twentieth-century philosophical literature has pointed out a number of such difficulties, most of them involving so-called intensional contexts. I am indebted to Barbara Hall Partee for pointing out others, both in conversation and in her provocative paper Partee [10]. (This remark should not, however, be taken as implying agreement with any of Professor Partee's conclusions.)

terminology) and semantics for a significant fragment of natural language; and it is perhaps not inappropriate to sketch relations between the earlier proposals and the one given below.

Montague [9] contains a general theory of languages, their interpretations, and the inducing of interpretations by translation. The treatment given below, as well as that in Montague [8] and the treatment of a fragment of English proposed at the end of Montague [9], can all easily be construed as special cases of that general theory. The fragment in Montague [8] was considerably more restricted in scope than those in Montague [9] or the present paper, in that although it admitted indirect discourse, it failed to accommodate a number of more complex intensional locutions, for instance, those involving *intensional verbs* (that is, verbs like **seeks, worships, conceives**). The fragment in Montague [9] did indeed include intensional verbs but excluded certain intensional locutions involving pronouns (for instance, the sentence **John wishes to catch a fish and eat it,** to which a number of linguists have recently drawn attention). The present treatment is capable of accounting for such examples, as well as a number of other heretofore unattempted puzzles, for instance, Professor Partee's **the temperature is ninety but it is rising** and the problem of intensional prepositions. On the other hand, the present treatment, unlike that in Montague [9], will not directly accommodate such sentences as J. M. E. Moravcsik's **a unicorn appears to be approaching,** in which an indefinite term *in subject position* would have a nonreferential reading, but must treat them indirectly as paraphrases (of, in this case, **it appears that a unicorn is approaching** or **that a unicorn is approaching appears to be true**).

On their common domain of applicability the three treatments essentially agree in the truth and entailment conditions imposed on sentences.[2] Further, when only *declarative* sentences come into consideration, it is the construction of such conditions that (Suppes notwithstanding) should count as the central concern of syntax and semantics.[3] Nevertheless, the details of the present

---

[2] With the exception that in Montague [9] a number of intuitively plausible ambiguities were for simplicity ruled out.

[3] In connection with imperatives and interrogatives truth and entailment conditions are of course inappropriate, and would be replaced by fulfilment conditions and a characterization of the semantic content of a correct answer.

development possess certain aesthetic merits, of coherence and conceptual simplicity, not to be found in the treatment of English in Montague* [9]. (It is in order to preserve these merits that I here forego a direct account of such sentences as Moravcik's.)

1. THE SYNTAX OF A FRAGMENT OF ENGLISH

Let e and t be two fixed objects (0 and 1, say) that are distinct and neither ordered pairs nor ordered triples. Then *Cat*, or the set of *categories* of English, is to be the smallest set X such that (1) e and t are in X, and (2) whenever A and B are in X, A/B and $A//B$ (that is, $\langle 0, A, B \rangle$ and $\langle 1, A, B \rangle$ respectively) are also in X.

It should be pointed out that our categories are not sets of expressions but will instead serve as *indices* of such sets. We regard e and t as the categories of entity expressions (or individual expressions) and truth value expressions (or declarative sentences) respectively. We shall regard the categories A/B and $A//B$ as playing the same semantical but different syntactical roles. An expression of either category is to be such that when it is combined (in some as yet unspecified way, and indeed in different ways for the two categories) with an expression of category B, an expression of category A is produced. (The precise character of the categories A/B and $A//B$ is unimportant; we require only two different kinds of ordered pair.)

It will be observed that our syntactic categories diverge from those of Ajdukiewicz [1] only in our introduction of two compound categories (A/B and $A//B$) where Ajdukiewicz would have had just one. The fact that we need only two copies is merely an accident of English or perhaps of our limited fragment; in connection with other languages it is quite conceivable that a larger number would be required.[4]

Keeping in mind the intuitive roles described above, we may single out as follows certain traditional syntactic categories.

IV, or the category of intransitive verb phrases, is to be t/e.

T, or the category of terms, is to be t/IV.

[4] It was perhaps the failure to pursue the possibility of syntactically splitting categories originally conceived in semantic terms that accounts for the fact that Ajdukiewicz's proposals have not previously led to a successful syntax. They have, however, been employed semantically in Montague [8] and, in a modified version, in Lewis [4].

TV, or the category of transitive verb phrases, is to be IV/T.
IAV, or the category of IV-modifying adverbs, is to be
   IV/IV.
CN, or the category of common noun phrases, is to be t//e.

The following categories will also be exemplified in our fragment
although no special symbol will be introduced for them.

t/t is the category of sentence-modifying adverbs.
IAV/T is the category of IAV-making prepositions.
IV/t is the category of sentence-taking verb phrases.
IV//IV is the category of IV-taking verb phrases.

By B_A is understood the set of *basic expressions* of the category
A; the notion is characterized as follows.

B_{IV} = {**run, walk, talk, rise, change**}
B_T = {**John, Mary, Bill, ninety, he$_0$, he$_1$, he$_2$, ...**}
B_{TV} = {**find, lose, eat, love, date, be, seek, conceive**}
B_{IAV} = {**rapidly, slowly, voluntarily, allegedly**}
B_{CN} = {**man, woman, park, fish, pen, unicorn, price,
   temperature**}
$B_{t/t}$ = {**necessarily**}
$B_{IAV/T}$ = {**in, about**}
$B_{IV/t}$ = {**believe that, assert that**}
$B_{IV//IV}$ = {**try to, wish to**}
B_A = Λ (that is, the empty set) if A is any category
   other than those mentioned above. (In particular,
   the sets B_e of basic entity expressions and B_t of
   basic declarative sentences are empty.)

By a *basic expression* of the present fragment is understood a
member of $U_{A \in Cat} B_A$.
By P_A is understood the set of *phrases* of the category A. (We
may read 'P_{CN}', 'P_{TV}', and the like as 'the set of common noun
phrases', 'the set of transitive verb phrases', and so on.) These
sets are introduced, in a sense to be made precise below, by the
following rules, S1–S17.

SYNTACTIC RULES

Basic rules

S1. $B_A \subseteq P_A$ for every category A.

S2. If $\zeta \in P_{CN}$, then $F_0(\zeta)$, $F_1(\zeta)$, $F_2(\zeta) \in P_T$,
where $F_0(\zeta) =$ **every** ζ,
$\qquad F_1(\zeta) =$ **the** ζ,
$\qquad F_2(\zeta)$ is **a** ζ or **an** ζ according as the first word in ζ
takes **a** or **an**.

S3. If $\zeta \in P_{CN}$ and $\phi \in P_t$, then $F_{3,n}(\zeta,\phi) \in P_{CN}$, where
$F_{3,n}(\zeta,\phi) = \zeta$ **such that** ϕ'; and ϕ' comes from ϕ by

replacing each occurrence of **he**$_n$ or **him**$_n$ by $\left\{ \begin{array}{l} \textbf{he} \\ \textbf{she} \\ \textbf{it} \end{array} \right\}$

or $\left\{ \begin{array}{l} \textbf{him} \\ \textbf{her} \\ \textbf{it} \end{array} \right\}$ respectively, according as the first B_{CN} in ζ

is of $\left\{ \begin{array}{l} \text{masc.} \\ \text{fem.} \\ \text{neuter} \end{array} \right\}$ gender.

Rules of functional application.

S4. If $\alpha \in P_{t/IV}$ and $\delta \in P_{IV}$, then $F_4(\alpha,\delta) \in P_t$, where
$F_4(\alpha,\delta) = \alpha \delta'$ and δ' is the result of replacing the
first *verb* (i.e., member of B_{IV}, B_{TV}, $B_{IV/t}$, or $B_{IV//IV}$)
in δ by its third person singular present.

S5. If $\delta \in P_{IV/T}$ and $\beta \in P_T$, then $F_5(\delta,\beta) \in P_{IV}$, where
$F_5(\delta,\beta) = \delta \beta$ if β does not have the form **he**$_n$ and
$F_5(\delta,\textbf{he}_n) = \delta \textbf{ him}_n$.

S6. If $\delta \in P_{IAV/T}$ and $\beta \in P_T$, then $F_5(\delta,\beta) \in P_{IAV}$.

S7. If $\delta \in P_{IV/T}$ and $\beta \in P_t$, then $F_6(\delta,\beta) \in P_{IV}$, where
$F_6(\delta,\beta) = \delta \beta$.

S8. If $\delta \in P_{IV//IV}$ and $\beta \in P_{IV}$, then $F_6(\delta,\beta) \in P_{IV}$.

S9. If $\delta \in P_{t/t}$ and $\beta \in P_t$, then $F_6(\delta,\beta) \in P_t$.

S10. If $\delta \in P_{IV/IV}$ and $\beta \in P_{IV}$, then $F_7(\delta,\beta) \in P_{IV}$, where
$F_7(\delta,\beta) = \beta \delta$.

Rules of conjunction and disjunction.

S11. If ϕ, $\psi \in P_t$, then $F_8(\phi,\psi)$, $F_9(\phi,\psi) \in P_t$, where $F_8(\phi,\psi) = \phi$ **and** ψ, $F_9(\phi,\psi) = \phi$ **or** ψ.

S12. If γ, $\delta \in P_{IV}$, then $F_8(\gamma,\delta)$, $F_9(\gamma,\delta) \in P_{IV}$.

S13. If $\alpha,\beta \in P_T$, then $F_9(\alpha,\beta) \in P_T$.

Rules of quantification.

S14. If $\alpha \in P_T$ and $\phi \in P_t$, then $F_{10,n}(\alpha,\phi) \in P_t$, where either (i) α does not have the form $\mathbf{he}_k$, and $F_{10,n}(\alpha,\phi)$ comes from ϕ by replacing the first occurrence of $\mathbf{he}_n$ or $\mathbf{him}_n$ by α and all other occurrences of $\mathbf{he}_n$ or $\mathbf{him}_n$ by $\left\{ \begin{array}{c} \mathbf{he} \\ \mathbf{she} \\ \mathbf{it} \end{array} \right\}$ or $\left\{ \begin{array}{c} \mathbf{him} \\ \mathbf{her} \\ \mathbf{it} \end{array} \right\}$ respectively, according as the gender of the first B_{CN} or B_T in α is $\left\{ \begin{array}{c} \text{masc.} \\ \text{fem.} \\ \text{neuter} \end{array} \right\}$, or (ii) $\alpha = \mathbf{he}_k$, and $F_{10,n}(\alpha,\phi)$ comes from ϕ by replacing all occurrences of $\mathbf{he}_n$ or $\mathbf{him}_n$ by $\mathbf{he}_k$, or $\mathbf{him}_k$ respectively.

S15. If $\alpha \in P_T$ and $\zeta \in P_{CN}$, then $F_{10,n}(\alpha,\zeta) \in P_{CN}$.

S16. If $\alpha \in P_T$ and $\delta \in P_{IV}$, then $F_{10,n}(\alpha,\delta) \in P_{IV}$.

Rules of tense and sign.

S17. If $\alpha \in P_T$ and $\delta \in P_{IV}$, then $F_{11}(\alpha,\delta)$, $F_{12}(\alpha,\delta)$, $F_{13}(\alpha,\delta)$, $F_{14}(\alpha,\delta)$, $F_{15}(\alpha,\delta) \in P_t$, where:

$F_{11}(\alpha,\delta) = \alpha\,\delta'$ and δ' is the result of replacing the first verb in δ by its negative third person singular present;

$F_{12}(\alpha,\delta) = \alpha\,\delta''$ and δ'' is the result of replacing the first verb in δ by its third person singular future;

$F_{13}(\alpha,\delta) = \alpha\,\delta'''$ and δ''' is the result of replacing the first verb in δ by its negative third person singular future;

$F_{14}(\alpha,\delta) = \alpha\,\delta''''$ and δ'''' is the result of replacing the first verb in δ by its third person singular present perfect; and finally,

$F_{15}(\alpha,\delta) = \alpha\,\delta''''$ and δ'''' is the result of replacing the first verb in δ by its negative third person singular present perfect.

The precise characterization of the sets P_A, for A a category, is accomplished as follows. We first define the auxiliary notions occurring in the rules above in an obvious and traditional way: the *gender* of an arbitrary member of $B_T \cup B_{CN}$, the *indefinite article taken* by an arbitrary basic expression, and the *third person singular present*, the *negative third person singular present*, the *third person singular future*, the *negative third person singular future*, the *third person singular present perfect*, and the *negative third person singular present perfect* of an arbitrary verb. Then we may regard S1–S17 as constituting a simultaneous inductive definition of the sets P_A. Since, however, inductive definitions of this form are somewhat unusual, it is perhaps in order to state a corresponding explicit definition: the sets Γ_A (for A ∊ Cat) are the smallest sets satisfying S1–S17; that is to say, $\langle P_A \rangle_{A \in Cat}$ is the unique family of sets indexed by Cat such that (1) $\langle P_A \rangle_{A \in Cat}$ satisfies S1–S17, and (2) whenever $\langle P'_A \rangle_{A \in Cat}$ is a family of sets indexed by Cat, if $\langle P'_A \rangle_{A \in Cat}$ satisfies S1–S17, then $P_A \subseteq P'_A$ for all A ∊ Cat. (It is easily shown, using an idea I believe to have originated with Dr. Perry Smith, that there is exactly one family of sets satisfying these conditions.)

By a *meaningful expression* of the present fragment of English we may understand a member of any of the sets P_A for A ∊ Cat.

As an example, let us show that

every man loves a woman such that she loves him

is a declarative sentence (that is, member of P_t). By S1, **love** $\in P_{TV}$ and $\mathbf{he_0} \in P_T$. Hence, by S5, **loves $\mathbf{him_0}$** $\in P_{IV}$. Therefore, by S1 and S4, $\mathbf{he_1}$ **loves $\mathbf{him_0}$** $\in P_t$. Thus, by S1 and S3, **woman such that she loves $\mathbf{him_0}$** $\in P_{CN}$. Therefore, by S2, **a woman such that she loves $\mathbf{him_0}$** $\in P_T$. Hence, by S1 and S5, **love a woman such that she loves $\mathbf{him_0}$** $\in P_{IV}$. Therefore, by S1 and S4, $\mathbf{he_0}$ **loves a woman such that she loves $\mathbf{him_0}$** $\in P_t$. Also, by S1 and S2, **every man** $\in P_T$; and hence, by S14, **every man loves a woman such that she loves him** $\in P_t$.

We may indicate the way in which this sentence has just been constructed by means of the following *analysis tree:*

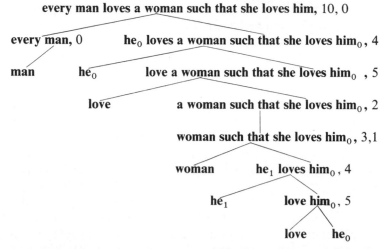

every man loves a woman such that she loves him, 10, 0

every man, 0   **he$_0$ loves a woman such that she loves him$_0$** , 4

man   **he$_0$**   **love a woman such that she loves him$_0$** , 5

love   **a woman such that she loves him$_0$**, 2

woman such that she loves him$_0$, 3,1

woman   **he$_1$ loves him$_0$** , 4

he$_1$ **love him$_0$** , 5

love   **he$_0$**

To each node we attach a meaningful expression, together, in case that expression is not basic, with the index of that structural operation among F_0–F_2, $F_{3,0}$, $F_{3,1}$, ..., F_4–F_9, $F_{10,0}$, $F_{10,1}$, ..., F_{11}–F_{15} (as characterized above, within S1–S17) which we understand as having been applied in obtaining the expression in question; the nodes dominated by any node are to be occupied by the expressions to which the structural operation is understood as having been applied in obtaining the expression occupying the superior node. (For example, the numbers 10,0 attached to the top node of the tree above indicate that the expression attached to that node is regarded as the value of the operation $F_{10,0}$ as applied to certain arguments; and the nodes beneath indicate that those arguments are understood to be the expressions **every man** and **he$_0$ loves a woman such that she loves him$_0$**.) A precise characterization of an *analysis tree* in the sense of these remarks would be routine and will not be given here; for such a characterization in an analogous content the reader might consult Montague [8].

Now there are other ways of constructing the sentence under consideration, and hence other analysis trees for it; indeed, it can be shown that every declarative sentence of our fragment has infinitely many analysis trees. But in the case considered, the various analyses will differ only inessentially; that is to say, they will all lead to the same semantical results.

There are other cases, however, of which this cannot be said. For instance, the sentence

John seeks a unicorn

has two essentially different analyses, represented by the following two trees:

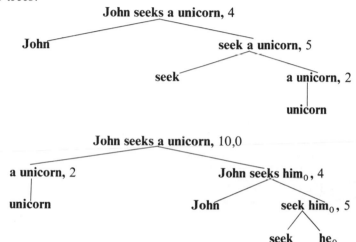

As we shall see, the first of these trees corresponds to the *de dicto* (or nonreferential) reading of the sentence, and the second to the *de re* (or referential) reading.

Thus our fragment admits genuinely (that is, semantically) ambiguous sentences. If it were desired to construct a corresponding unambiguous language, it would be convenient to take the analysis trees themselves as the expressions of that language; it would then be obvious how to characterize (in keeping with Montague [9]) the structural operations of that language and the correspondence relation between its expressions and those of ordinary English.[5] For present purposes, however, no such construction is necessary.

[5] This way of constructing an underlying unambiguous language, though convenient here, would be unsuitable in connection with fragments of natural language exhibiting greater syntactical complexities of certain sorts.

2. INTENSIONAL LOGIC

We could (as in Montague [8]) introduce the semantics of our fragment directly; but it is probably more perspicuous to proceed indirectly, by (1) setting up a certain simple artificial language, that of tensed intensional logic, (2) giving the semantics of that language, and (3) interpreting English indirectly by showing in a rigorous way how to translate it into the artificial language. This is the procedure we shall adopt; accordingly, I shall now present the syntax and semantics of a tensed variant of the intensional logic I have discussed on earlier occasions.[6]

Let s be a fixed object (2, say) distinct from e and t and not an ordered pair or triple. The *Type*, or the set of *types*, is the smallest set Y such that (1) $e,t \in Y$, (2) whenever $a,b \in Y$, $\langle a,b \rangle \in Y$, and (3) whenever $a \in Y$, $\langle s,a \rangle \in Y$.

We shall employ denumerably many variables and infinitely many constants of each type. In particular, if n is any natural number and $a \in Type$, we understand by $v_{n,a}$ the nth variable of type a, and by Con_a the set of constants of type a. (The precise cardinality of Con_a need not concern us, provided only that it be infinite.)

By ME_a is understood the set of *meaningful expressions* of type a; this notion has the following recursive definition:

(1) Every variable and constant of type a is in Me_a.
(2) If $\alpha \in ME_a$ and u is a variable of type b, then $\lambda u\alpha \in ME_{\langle b,a \rangle}$.
(3) If $\alpha \in ME_{\langle a,b \rangle}$ and $\beta \in ME_a$, then $\alpha(\beta) \in ME_b$.
(4) If $\alpha,\beta \in ME_a$, then $\alpha = \beta \in ME_t$.
(5) If $\phi,\psi \in ME_t$ and u is a variable, then $\neg\phi, [\phi \wedge \psi], [\phi \vee \psi], [\phi \rightarrow \psi], [\phi \leftrightarrow \psi], \vee u\phi, \wedge u\phi, \Box\phi, W\phi, H\phi \in ME_t$.
(6) If $\alpha \in ME_a$, then $[\hat{\ }\alpha] \in ME_{\langle s,a \rangle}$.

---

[6] In particular, in talks before the Southern California Logic Colloquium and the Association for Symbolic Logic in April and May of 1969, and in the paper Montague [9]. The addition of tenses is rather routine in the light of the discussion in Montague [6]; and it would be possible to replace the tense operators by predicates, thus preserving exactly the language in Montague [9], in the manner indicated in Montague [5].

(7) If $\alpha \in ME_{\langle s,a \rangle}$, then $[\check{}\alpha] \in ME_a$.

(8) Nothing is in any set ME_a except as required by (1)–(7).[7]

By a *meaningful expression* of intensional logic is understood a member of $\cup_{a \in Type} ME_a$.

If u is a variable of type a, then $\lambda u \alpha$ is understood as denoting that function from objects of type a which takes as value, for any such object x, the object denoted by α when u is understood as denoting x. The expression $\alpha(\beta)$ is as usual understood as denoting the value of the function denoted by α for the argument denoted by β. The equality symbol $=$, the negation symbol $\neg$, the conjunction symbol $\wedge$, the disjunction symbol $\vee$, the conditional symbol $\rightarrow$, the biconditional symbol $\leftrightarrow$, the existential quantifier $\vee$, and the universal quantifier $\wedge$ are all understood in the usual way. The symbols $\square$, W, H may be read "it is necessary that," "it will be the case that," "it has been the case that," respectively. The expression $[\hat{}\alpha]$ is regarded as denoting (or having as its *extension*) the *intension* of the expression α. The expression $[\check{}\alpha]$ is meaningful only if α is an expression that denotes an intension or sense; in such a case $[\check{}\alpha]$ denotes the corresponding extension.

We could have done with a much smaller stock of primitive symbols, as in Montague [9]; but there is no point in considering here the relevant reductions.

In the presentation of actual expressions of intensional logic square brackets will sometimes for perspicuity be omitted, and sometimes gratuitously inserted.

Let A, I, J be any sets, which we may for the moment regard as the set of entities (or individuals[8]), the set of possible worlds, and the set of moments of time respectively. In addition, let a be a type. Then $D_{a,A,I,J}$, or the set of *possible denotations* of type a corresponding to A, I, J, may be introduced by the following

---

[7] Clause (8) is of course vague but can be eliminated in a familiar way. To be exact, the recursive definition given above can be replaced by the following explicit definition: ME_a is the set of all objects α such that $\alpha R a$, where R is the smallest relation such that clauses (1)–(7) hold (with all parts of the form '$\beta \in ME_a$' replaced by '$\beta R a$').

[8] Or possible individuals. If there are individuals that are only possible but not actual, A is to contain them; but this is an issue on which it would be unethical for me as a logician (or linguist or grammarian or semanticist, for that matter) to take a stand.

recursive definition. (If X and Y are any sets, then as usual we understand by X^Y the set of all functions with domain Y and values in X, and by $X \times Y$ the *Cartesian product* of X and Y (that is, the set of all ordered pairs $\langle x, y \rangle$ such that $x \in X$ and $y \in Y$). Further, we identify the truth values falsehood and truth with the numbers 0 and 1 respectively.)

$$D_{e,A,I,J} = A,$$
$$D_{t,A,I,J} = \{0, 1\},$$
$$D_{\langle a,b \rangle,A,I,J} = \mathbf{D}_{b,A,I,J}{}^{D_{a,A,I,J}},$$
$$D_{\langle s,a \rangle,A,I,J} = D_{a,A,I,J}{}^{I \times J}.$$

By $S_{a,A,I,J}$, or the set of *senses* of type a corresponding to A, I, J, is understood $D_{\langle s,a \rangle,A,I,J}$, that is, $D_{a,A,I,J}^{I \times J}$.

By an *interpretation* (or intensional model) is understood a quintuple $\langle A, I, J, \leqslant, F \rangle$ such that (1) A, I, J are nonempty sets, (2) $\leqslant$ is a simple (that is, linear) ordering having J as its field, (3) F is a function having as its domain the set of all constants, and (4) whenever $a \in Type$ and $\alpha \in Con_a$, $F(\alpha) \in S_{a,A,I,J}$.

Suppose that $\mathfrak{A}$ is an interpretation having the form $\langle A, I, J, \leqslant, F \rangle$. Suppose also that g is an $\mathfrak{A}$-*assignment* (of values to variables), that is, a function having as its domain the set of all variables and such that $g(u) \in D_{a,A,I,J}$ whenever u is a variable of type a. If α is a meaningful expression, we shall understand by $\alpha^{\mathfrak{A},g}$ the *intension* of α with respect to $\mathfrak{A}$ and g; and if $\langle i, j \rangle \in I \times J$ then $\alpha^{\mathfrak{A},i,j,g}$ is to be the *extension* of α with respect to $\mathfrak{A}$, i, j, and g—that is, $\alpha^{\mathfrak{A},g}(\langle i, j \rangle)$ or the function value of the intension of α when applied to the point of reference $\langle i, j \rangle$. These notions may be introduced by the following recursive definition.

(1) If α is a constant, then $\alpha^{\mathfrak{A},g}$ is $F(\alpha)$.

(2) If α is a variable, then $\alpha^{\mathfrak{A},i,j,g}$ is $g(\alpha)$.

(3) If $\alpha \in ME_a$ and u is a variable of type b, then $[\lambda u \alpha]^{\mathfrak{A},i,j,g}$ is that function h with domain $D_{b,A,I,J}$ such that whenever x is in that domain, $h(x)$ is $\alpha^{\mathfrak{A},i,j,g'}$, where g' is the $\mathfrak{A}$-assignment like g except for the possible difference that $g'(u)$ is x.

(4) If $\alpha \in ME_{\langle a,b \rangle}$ and $\beta \in ME_a$, then $[\alpha(\beta)]^{\mathfrak{A},i,j,g}$ is $\alpha^{\mathfrak{A},i,j,g}(\beta^{\mathfrak{A},i,j,g})$ (that is, the value of the function $\alpha^{\mathfrak{A},i,j,g}$ for the argument $\beta^{\mathfrak{A},i,j,g}$).

(5) If $\alpha, \beta \in ME_a$, then $[\alpha = \beta]^{\mathfrak{A},i,j,g}$ is 1 if and only if $\alpha^{\mathfrak{A},i,j,g}$ is $\beta^{\mathfrak{A},i,j,g}$.

(6) If $\phi \in ME_t$, then $[\neg\phi]^{\mathfrak{A},i,j,g}$ is 1 if and only if $\phi^{\mathfrak{A},i,j,g}$ is 0; and similarly for $\wedge$, $\vee$, $\rightarrow$, $\leftrightarrow$.

(7) If $\phi \in ME_t$ and u is a variable of type a, then $[\bigvee u\phi]^{\mathfrak{A},i,j,g}$ is 1 if and only if there exists $x \in D_{a,A,I,J}$ such that $\phi^{\mathfrak{A},i,j,g'}$ is 1, where g' is as in (3); and similarly for $\bigwedge u\phi$.

(8) If $\phi \in ME_t$, then $[\square\phi]^{\mathfrak{A},i,j,g}$ is 1 if and only if $\phi^{\mathfrak{A},i',j',g}$ is 1 for all $i' \in I$ and $j' \in J$;[9] $[W\phi]^{\mathfrak{A},i,j,g}$ is 1 if and only if $\phi^{\mathfrak{A},i,j',g}$ is 1 for some j' such that $j \leqslant j'$ and $j \neq j'$; and $[H\phi]^{\mathfrak{A},i,j,g}$ is 1 if and only if $\phi^{\mathfrak{A},i,j',g}$ is 1 for some j' such that $j' \leqslant j$ and $j' \neq j$.

(9) If $\alpha \in ME_a$, then $[^\frown\alpha]^{\mathfrak{A},i,j,g}$ is $\alpha^{\mathfrak{A},g}$.[10]

(10) If $\alpha \in ME_{\langle s,a\rangle}$, then $[^\smile\alpha]^{\mathfrak{A},i,j,g}$ is $\alpha^{\mathfrak{A},i,j,g}(\langle i,j\rangle)$.

If ϕ is a *formula* (that is, member of ME_t), then ϕ is *true* with respect to $\mathfrak{A}$, i,j if and only if $\phi^{\mathfrak{A},i,j,g}$ is 1 for every $\mathfrak{A}$-assignment g.

It will be useful to call attention to some particular meaningful expressions of intensional logic. If $\gamma \in ME_{\langle a,t\rangle}$ and $\alpha \in ME_a$, then γ denotes (that is, has as its extension) a set (or really the characteristic function of a set) of objects of type a, and we may regard the formula $\gamma(\alpha)$, which denotes truth exactly in case the object denoted by α is a member of that set, as *asserting* that the object denoted by α is a member of the set denoted by γ. If $\gamma \in ME_{\langle a,\langle b,t\rangle\rangle}$, $\alpha \in ME_a$, and $\beta \in ME_b$, then γ may be regarded as denoting a (two-place) *relation*, and $\gamma(\beta,\alpha)$ is to be the expression $\gamma(\alpha)(\beta)$, which asserts that the objects denoted by β and α stand in that relation. If $\gamma \in ME_{\langle s,\langle a,t\rangle\rangle}$ and $\alpha \in ME_a$; then γ denotes a *property*, and $\gamma\{\alpha\}$ is to be the expression $[^\smile\gamma](\alpha)$, which asserts that the object denoted by α has that property. If $\gamma \in ME_{\langle s,\langle a,\langle b,t\rangle\rangle\rangle}$, $\alpha \in ME_a$, and $\beta \in ME_b$, then γ may be regarded as denoting a *relation-in-intension*, and $\gamma\{\beta,\alpha\}$ is to be the expression $[^\smile\gamma](\beta,\alpha)$, which asserts that the objects denoted by β and α stand in that

---

[9] [Editor's note: Here, $\square$ is interpreted in the sense of 'necessarily always.']

[10] [Editor's note: The form of this definition is not quite correct, since $\alpha^{\mathfrak{A},g}$ is undefined when α is not a constant. But the intention is clear; what is to be defined recursively is $\alpha^{\mathfrak{A},i,j,g}$. Clauses (1) and (9) should be revised to read as follows.

(1) If α is a constant then $\alpha^{\mathfrak{A},i,j,g}$ is $F(\alpha)(\langle i,j\rangle)$.

(9) If $\alpha \in ME_a$ then $[^\frown\alpha]^{\mathfrak{A},i,j,g}$ is that function h with domain $I \times J$ such that whenever $\langle i,j\rangle \in I \times J$, $h(\langle i,j\rangle) = \alpha^{\mathfrak{A},i,j,g}$.

The *intension* $\alpha^{\mathfrak{A},g}$ of α relative to $\mathfrak{A}$ and g is then defined explicitly:

$\alpha^{\mathfrak{A},g}$ is that function h with domain $I \times J$ such that whenever $\langle i,j\rangle \in I \times J$, $h(\langle i,j\rangle) = \alpha^{\mathfrak{A},i,j,g}$.

It then follows as a corollary that $[^\frown\alpha]^{\mathfrak{A},i,j,g} = \alpha^{\mathfrak{A},g}$ for all $\langle i,j\rangle \in I \times J$.]

relation-in-intension. If u is a variable of type a and $\phi \square a$ formula, then $\bar{u}\phi$ is to be $\lambda u\phi$, which denotes the set of all objects of type a that satisfy ϕ (with respect to the place marked by u), and $\hat{u}\phi$ is to be $[\hat{\ }u\phi]$, which denotes the property of objects of type a expressed by ϕ. If $\alpha \in \mathrm{ME}_e$, then α^* is to be $\hat{P}[P\{\hat{\ }\alpha\}]$, where P is $v_{0,\langle s,\langle\langle s,e\rangle,t\rangle\rangle}$.

3. TRANSLATING ENGLISH INTO INTENSIONAL LOGIC

We first introduce a mapping f from the categories of English to the types of intensional logic. Accordingly, f is to be a function having Cat as its domain and such that

$$f(e) = e,$$
$$f(t) = t,$$
$$f(A/B) = f(A/\!/B) = \langle\langle s, f(B)\rangle, f(A)\rangle \text{ whenever } A, B \in Cat.$$

The intention is that English expressions of any category A are to translate into expressions of type $f(A)$.[11]

In all that follows let g be a fixed biunique function such that (1) the domain of g is the set of basic expressions of our fragment of English other than **be, necessarily,** and the members of B_T, and (2) whenever $A \in Cat$, $\alpha \in B_A$, and α is in the domain of g, $g(\alpha) \in Con_{f(A)}$. Let j, m, b, n be particular distinct members of Con_e. (If we had introduced a definite well-ordering of the constants of intensional logic, we could at this point have explicitly defined g, j, m, b, and n. Such details would, however, be irrelevant to our present concerns.) Let u, v be the particular individual variables $v_{0,e}, v_{1,e}$ respectively; x, y, x_n be the particular individual-concept variables $v_{1,\langle s,e\rangle}$, $v_{3,\langle s,e\rangle}$, $v_{2n,\langle s,e\rangle}$ respectively (for any natural number n); p be the proposition variable $v_{0,\langle s,t\rangle}$; P, Q be the variables $v_{0,\langle s,\langle\langle s,e\rangle,t\rangle\rangle}$, $v_{1,\langle s,\langle\langle s,e\rangle,t\rangle\rangle}$, which range over properties of individual concepts; $\mathscr{P}$ be the variable $v_{0,\langle s,\langle\langle s,\langle\langle s,e\rangle,t\rangle\rangle,t\rangle\rangle}$, which ranges over properties of properties of individual concept; M be the variable $v_{0,\langle s,\langle e,t\rangle\rangle}$, which ranges over properties of

---

[11] The simplicity and uniformity of the present correspondence stands in remarkable contrast to the *ad hoc* character of the type assignment in Montague [9].

individuals; S be the variable $v_{0,\langle s,\langle e,\langle e,t\rangle\rangle\rangle}$, which ranges over two-place relations-in-intension between individuals; and G be the variable $v_{0,\langle s,\langle e,f(IAV)\rangle\rangle}$.

We shall now consider some rules of translation, T1–T17, which will be seen to correspond to the syntactic rules S1–S17 respectively and to constitute, in a sense to be made precise below, a definition of the translation relation.

TRANSLATION RULES

Basic rules.

T1. (a) If α is in the domain of g, then α translates into $g(\alpha)$.
   (b) **be** translates into $\lambda\mathscr{P}\lambda x\mathscr{P}\{\hat{y}[\check{}x = \check{}y]\}$.
   (c) **necessarily** translates into $\hat{p}[\Box\check{}p]$.
   (d) **John, Mary, Bill, ninety** translate into j^*, m^*, b^*, n^* respectively.
   (e) **he**$_n$ translates into $\hat{P}\,P\{x_n\}$.

T2. If $\zeta \in P_{CN}$ and ζ translates into ζ', then **every** ζ translates into $\hat{P}\Lambda x[\zeta'(x) \to P\{x\}]$, **the** ζ translates into $\hat{P}Vy\,[\Lambda x\,[\zeta'(x) \leftrightarrow x = y]\wedge P\{y\}]$, $F_2(\zeta)$ translates into $\hat{P}Vx[\zeta'(x) \wedge P\{x\}]$.

T3. If $\zeta \in P_{CN}$, $\phi \in P_t$, and ζ, ϕ translate into ζ', ϕ' respectively, then $F_{3,n}(\zeta, \phi)$ translates into $\hat{x}_n[\zeta'(x_n)\wedge \phi']$.[12]

Rules of functional application.

T4. If $\delta \in P_{t/IV}$, $\beta \in P_{IV}$, and δ, β translate into δ', β' respectively, then $F_4(\delta, \beta)$ translates into $\delta'(\check{}\beta')$.

T5. If $\delta \in P_{IV/T}$, $\beta \in P_T$, and δ, β translate into δ', β' respectively, then $F_5(\delta, \beta)$ translates into $\delta'(\check{}\beta')$.

T6. If $\delta \in P_{IAV/T}$, $\beta \in P_T$, and δ, β translate into δ', β' respectively, then $F_5(\delta, \beta)$ translates into $\delta'(\check{}\beta')$.

---

[12] [Editor's note: To avoid collision of variables, the translation must be $x_m[\zeta'(x_m) \wedge \psi]$, where ψ is the result of replacing all occurrences of x_n in φ' by occurrences of x_m, where m is the least even number such that x_m has no occurrences in either ζ' or φ'.]

T7. If $\delta \in P_{IV/t}$, $\beta \in P_t$, and δ, β translate into δ', β' respectively, then $F_6(\delta, \beta)$ translates into $\delta'(\hat{}\beta')$.

T8. If $\delta \in P_{IV//IV}$, $\beta \in P_{IV}$, and δ, β translate into δ', β' respectively, then $F_6(\delta, \beta)$ translates into $\delta'(\hat{}\beta')$.

T9. If $\delta \in P_{t/t}$, $\beta \in P_t$, and δ, β translate into δ', β' respectively, then $F_6(\delta, \beta)$ translates into $\delta'(\hat{}\beta')$.

T10. If $\delta \in P_{IV/IV}$, $\beta \in P_{IV}$, and δ, β translate into δ', β' respectively, then $F_7(\delta, \beta)$ translates into $\delta'(\hat{}\beta')$.

Rules of conjunction and disjunction.

T11. If $\phi, \psi \in P_t$ and ϕ, ψ translate into ϕ', ψ' respectively, then ϕ **and** ψ translates into $[\phi \wedge \psi]$, ϕ **or** ψ translates into $[\phi \vee \psi]$.

T12. If $\gamma, \delta \in P_{IV}$ and γ, δ translate into γ', δ' respectively, then γ **and** δ translates into $\hat{x}[\gamma'(x) \wedge \delta'(x)]$, γ **or** δ translates into $\hat{x}[\gamma'(x) \vee \delta'(x)]$.

T13. If $\alpha, \beta \in P_T$ and α, β translate into α', β' respectively, then α **or** β translates into $\hat{P}[\alpha'(P) \vee \beta'(P)]$.

Rules of quantification.

T14. If $\alpha \in P_T$, $\phi \in P_t$, and α, ϕ translate into α', ϕ' respectively, then $F_{10,n}(\alpha, \phi)$ translates into $\alpha'(\hat{x}_n\phi')$.

T15. If $\alpha \in P_T$, $\zeta \in P_{CN}$, and α, ζ translate into α', ζ' respectively, then $F_{10,n}(\alpha, \zeta)$ translates into $\hat{y}\alpha'(\hat{x}_n[\zeta'(y)])$.

T16. If $\alpha \in P_T$, $\delta \in P_{IV}$, and α, δ translate into α', δ' respectively, then $F_{10,n}(\alpha, \delta)$ translates into $\hat{y}\alpha'(\hat{x}_n[\delta'(y)])$.

Rules of tense and sign.

T17. If $\alpha \in P_T$, $\delta \in P_{IV}$, and α, δ translate into α', δ' respectively, then $F_{11}(\alpha, \delta)$ translates into $\neg \alpha'(\hat{}\delta')$,
$F_{12}(\alpha, \delta)$ translates into $W\alpha'(\hat{}\delta')$,
$F_{13}(\alpha, \delta)$ translates into $\neg W\alpha'(\hat{}\delta')$,
$F_{14}(\alpha, \delta)$ translates into $H\alpha'(\hat{}\delta')$,
$F_{15}(\alpha, \delta)$ translates into $\neg H\alpha'(\hat{}\delta')$.

The precise import of the rules T1–T17 is that the translation relation may be defined as the smallest binary relation satisfying them; that is to say, an expression ϕ is characterized as *translating into* an expression ϕ' if the pair $\langle\phi, \phi'\rangle$ is a member of every binary relation R such that T1–T17 hold (with the condition that one expression .translates into another replaced by the condition that the relation R holds between the two expressions).

The translation relation is of course not a function; a meaningful expression of English may translate into several different expressions of intensional logic. We could, however, speak of *the translation* of a given meaningful expression of English corresponding to any given analysis tree for that expression; the rather obvious definition of this notion will be omitted here. The interpretations of intensional logic may, by way of the translation relation, be made to play a second role as interpretations of English.[13] Not all interpretations of intensional logic, however, would be reasonable candidates for interpretations of English. In particular, it would be reasonable in this context to restrict attention to those interpretations of intensional logic in which the following formulas are true (with respect to all, or equivalently some, worlds and moments of time):

(1) $\text{V}u \,\square\, [u = \alpha]$, where α is j, m, b, or n,

(2) $\square\, [\delta(x) \rightarrow \text{V}u\, x = {}^{\wedge}u]$, where δ translates any member of B_{CN} other than **price** or **temperature**,

(3) $\text{V}M\wedge x \,\square\, [\delta(x) \leftrightarrow M\{{}^{\vee}x\}]$, where δ translates any member of B_{IV} other than **rise** or **change**,

(4) $\text{V}S\wedge x\wedge\mathscr{P} \,\square\, [\delta(x, \mathscr{P}) \leftrightarrow \mathscr{P}\{\hat{y}S\{{}^{\vee}x, {}^{\vee}y\}\}]$, where δ translates **find, lose, eat, love,** or **date,**

(5) $\wedge\mathscr{P}\text{V}M\wedge x \,\square\, [\delta(x, \mathscr{P}) \leftrightarrow M\{{}^{\vee}x\}]$, where δ translates **seek** or **conceive,**

(6) $\wedge p\text{V}M\wedge x \,\square\, [\delta(x, p) \leftrightarrow M\{{}^{\vee}x\}]$, where δ translates **believe that** or **assert that,**

(7) $\wedge P\text{V}M\wedge x \,\square\, [\delta(x, P) \leftrightarrow M\{{}^{\vee}x\}]$, where δ translates **try to** or **wish to,**

---

[13] Alternatives are possible. For instance, we could instead consider *direct* interpretations of English induced by interpretations of intensional logic in conjunction with our translation procedure; the precise general construction is given in Montague [9]. Though this would probably be the best approach from a general viewpoint, it would introduce slight complications that need not be considered in the present paper.

(8) $\vee G \wedge \mathscr{P} \wedge Q \wedge x \ \square \ [\delta(\mathscr{P})(Q)(x) \leftrightarrow \mathscr{P}\{\hat{y}[[^{\vee}G](^{\vee}y)(Q)(x)]\}]$, where
δ translates **in,**

(9) $\square \ [\textbf{seek}'(x, \mathscr{P}) \leftrightarrow \textbf{try-to}' \ (x, \ ^{\wedge}[\textbf{find}' \ (\mathscr{P})])]$, where **seek'**,
try-to', find' translate **seek, try to, find** respectively.

The truth of (1) guarantees that proper nouns will be "logically determinate" according to the interpretations under consideration, that is, will have extensions invariant with respect to possible worlds and moments of time. In view of (2), "ordinary" common nouns (for example, **horse**) will denote sets of *constant* individual concepts (for example, the set of constant functions on worlds and moments having horses as their values; from an intuitive viewpoint, this is no different from the set of horses). It would be unacceptable to impose this condition on such "extraordinary" common nouns as **price** or **temperature**; the individual concepts in their extensions would in the most natural cases be functions whose values vary with their temporal arguments. The truth of (3) is the natural requirement of *extensionality* for intransitive verbs, that of (4) the condition of extensionality (or extensional first-order reducibility) for transitive verbs, and that of (8) the condition of extensionality (or extensional first-order reducibility) for prepositions. The *intensional* (or nonextensional) transitive verbs **seek** and **conceive,** as well as the verbs **believe that, assert that, try to, wish to** of other categories, are nevertheless *extensional with respect to subject position*, and this is expressed by imposing conditions (5)–(7). Condition (9) is the natural definition of **seek** as **try to find.**

Several notions of a logically possible interpretation may reasonably come into consideration, depending on whether, and if so how many, conditions analogous to (1)–(9), stemming from our intended system of translation, are to be imposed. For present purposes we may perhaps resolve the matter as follows: by a *logically possible interpretation* understand an interpretation of intensional logic in which formulas (1)–(9) are true (with respect to all worlds and moments of time). Logical truth, logical consequence, and logical equivalence, for formulas of intensional logic, are to be characterized accordingly. For instance, a formula ϕ of intensional logic is construed as *logically true* if it is true in every logically possible interpretation, with respect to all worlds and moments of time of that interpretation; and two formulas ϕ and ψ of intensional logic are *logically equivalent* if and only if the biconditional $[\phi \leftrightarrow \psi]$ is logically true.

If δ is an expression of intensional logic of such type as to translate a transitive or intransitive verb, then δ_* is to be an expression designating the set of individuals or relation between individuals that naturally corresponds to the set or relation designated by δ. In particular, if $\delta \in ME_{f(IV)}$, then δ_* is to be the expression $\hat{u}\delta([^{\smallfrown}u])$; and if $\delta \in ME_{f(TV)}$, then δ_* is to be $\lambda v \hat{u}\delta([^{\smallfrown}u], [^{\smallfrown}v^*])$. Notice that since $f(CN) = f(TV)$, this characterization is also applicable in the case in which δ translates a common noun.

It is a consequence of principles (2), (3), (4) that if δ is among the constants involved in those principles (that is, constants translating "ordinary" common nouns or "extensional" transitive or intransitive verbs), then δ is definable in terms of δ_*. More exactly, the following formulas are logically true:

$\square[\delta(x) \leftrightarrow \delta_*(^{\smallfrown}x)]$, if δ translates any member of B_{CN} or B_{IV} other than **price, temperature, rise,** or **change**;

$\square[\delta(x, \mathscr{P}) \leftrightarrow \mathscr{P}\{\hat{y}\delta_*(^{\smallfrown}x, ^{\smallfrown}y)\}]$, if δ translates any member of B_{TV} other than **seek** or **conceive**.

Notice that although the verb **be** (or its translation) is not covered by principle (4), it is by the last principle above. The reason why the extensionality of **be** was not explicitly assumed is that it can be proved. (More precisely, the analogue of (4) in which δ is the expression translating **be** is true in all interpretations (with respect to all worlds and moments).)

4. EXAMPLES

The virtues of the present treatment can perhaps best be appreciated by considering particular English sentences and the precisely interpreted sentences of intensional logic that translate them. I shall give a list of such examples. It is understood that each English sentence listed below translates into some formula logically equivalent to each of the one or more formulas of intensional logic listed with it, and that every formula into which the English sentence translates is logically equivalent to one of those formulas. It should be emphasized that this is not a matter of vague intuition, as in elementary logic courses, but an assertion to which we have assigned exact significance in preceding sections and which can be rigorously proved. (The constants of intensional logic that translate various basic expressions of English are designated below by primed variants of those expressions.)

The first five examples indicate that in simple extensional cases symbolizations of the expected forms are obtained.

> **Bill walks: walk$'_*(b)$**
> **a man walks: $\mathsf{V}u[\mathbf{man}'_*(u) \wedge \mathbf{walk}'_*(u)]$**
> **every man walks: $\bigwedge u[\mathbf{man}'_*(u) \rightarrow \mathbf{walk}'_*(u)]$**
> **the man walks: $\mathsf{V}v\bigwedge u[[\mathbf{man}'_*(u) \leftrightarrow u = v] \wedge \mathbf{walk}'_*(v)]$**
> **John finds a unicorn: $\mathsf{V}u[\mathbf{unicorn}'_*(u) \wedge \mathbf{find}'_*(j, u)]$**

The next sentence, though superficially like the last, is ambiguous and has two essentially different symbolizations corresponding to the two analysis trees presented above; the first gives the *de dicto* reading; and the second the *de re*.

> **John seeks a unicorn:** $\begin{cases} \mathbf{seek}'(\,{}^\smallfrown j, \hat{\mathsf{P}}\mathsf{V}u[\mathbf{unicorn}'_*(u) \wedge \mathsf{P}\{{}^\smallfrown u\}]) \\ \mathsf{V}u[\mathbf{unicorn}'_*(u) \wedge \mathbf{seek}'_*(j, u)] \end{cases}$

The source of the ambiguity of **John seeks a unicorn** will perhaps be clarified if we compare that sentence with the intuitively synonymous **John tries to find a unicorn,** which contains no intensional verbs but only the extensional verb **find** and the 'higher-order' verb **try to.** Here, though perhaps not in **John seeks a unicorn,** the ambiguity is clearly a matter of scope, and indeed depends on the possibility of regarding either the component **find a unicorn** or the whole sentence as the scope of the existential quantification indicated by **a unicorn.**

> **John tries to find a unicorn:**
> $\begin{cases} \mathbf{try\text{-}to}'(\,{}^\smallfrown j, \hat{y}\mathsf{V}u[\mathbf{unicorn}'_*(u) \wedge \mathbf{find}'_*(\,{}^\smallsmile y, u)]) \\ \mathsf{V}u[\mathbf{unicorn}'_*(u) \wedge \mathbf{try\text{-}to}'(\,{}^\smallfrown j, \hat{y}\,\mathbf{find}'_*(\,{}^\smallsmile y, u))] \end{cases}$

It might be suggested, as in Quine [11] or Montague [7], that intensional verbs be allowed only as paraphrases of more tractable locutions (such as **try to find**).[14] Such a proposal, however, would not be naturally applicable, for want of a paraphrase, to such intensional verbs as **conceive** and such intensional prepositions as **about**; and I regard it as one of the principal virtues of the present treatment, as well as the one in Montague [9], that it enables us to deal directly with intensional locutions. The next example accordingly concerns **about** and gives us, as intuition demands, one reading of **John talks about a unicorn** that does not entail that there are unicorns.

John talks about a unicorn:
$$\begin{cases} \textbf{about}'(\hat{P}Vu[\textbf{unicorn}'_*(u) \wedge P\{^\smallfrown u\}])(^\smallfrown\textbf{talk}')(^\smallfrown j) \\ Vu[\textbf{unicorn}'_*(u) \wedge \textbf{about}'(^\smallfrown u^*)(^\smallfrown\textbf{talk}')(^\smallfrown j)] \end{cases}$$

The next two examples indicate that our uniform symbolization of **be** will adequately cover both the **is** of identity and the **is** of predication; views along this line, though not the rather complicated analysis of **be** given here, may be found in Quine [11].

Bill is Mary: $b = m$
Bill is a man: $\textbf{man}'_*(b)$

The next few examples concern an interesting puzzle due to Barbara Hall Partee involving a kind of intensionality not previously observed by philosophers. From the premises **the temperature is ninety** and **the temperature rises,** the conclusion **ninety rises** would appear to follow by normal principles of logic; yet there are occasions on which both premises are true, but none on which the conclusion is. According to the following symbolizations, however, the argument in question turns out not to be valid. (The reason, speaking very loosely, is this. **The temperature** "denotes" an individual concept, not an individual; and **rise**, unlike most verbs, depends for its applicability on

---

[14] Strictly speaking, this would mean, within the framework of the present paper, introducing a syntactic operation F such that, for example, F **(John tries to find a unicorn)** = **John seeks a unicorn,** a syntactic rule to the effect that $F(\phi) \in P_t$ whenever $\phi \in P_t$, and a corresponding translation rule that whenever $\phi \in P_t$ and ϕ translates into ϕ', $F(\phi)$ translates into ϕ'.

the full behavior of individual concepts, not just on their extensions with respect to the actual world and (what is more relevant
here) moment of time. Yet the sentence **the temperature is ninety**
asserts the identity not of two individual concepts but only of their
extensions.)

> **the temperature is ninety :** $\lor y[\land x[\textbf{temperature}'(x) \leftrightarrow x = y] \land$
> $[\check{}y] = n]$
> **the temperature rises:** $\lor y[\land x[\textbf{temperature}'(x) \leftrightarrow x = y] \land$
> $\textbf{rise}'(y)]$
> **ninety rises : rise**$'(\check{}n)$

We thus see the virtue of having intransitive verbs and common
nouns denote sets of individual concepts rather than sets of
individuals—a consequence of our general development that
might at first appear awkward and unnatural. It would be
possible to treat the Partee argument itself without introducing
this feature, but not certain analogous arguments involving
indefinite rather than definite terms. Notice, for instance, that
a price rises and **every price is a number** must not be allowed to
entail **a number rises.** Indeed they do not according to our
treatment; to see this, perhaps it is enough to consider the first
premise, which, unlike **a man walks,** requires individual-concept
variables (and not simply individual variables) for its symbolization.

> **a price rises :** $\lor x[\textbf{price}'(x) \land \textbf{rise}'(x)]$

The next example shows that ambiguity can arise even when
there is no element of intensionality, simply because quantifying
terms may be introduced in more than one order.

> **a woman loves every man :**
> $$\begin{cases} \lor u[\textbf{woman}'_*(u) \land \land v[\textbf{man}'_*(v) \rightarrow \textbf{love}'_*(u, v)]] \\ \land v[\textbf{man}'_*(v) \rightarrow \lor u[\textbf{woman}'_*(u) \land \textbf{love}'_*(u, v)]] \end{cases}$$

The next example indicates the necessity of allowing verb
phrases as well as sentences to be conjoined and quantified.
Without such provisions the sentence **John wishes to find a
unicorn and eat it** would (unacceptably, as several linguists have
pointed out in connection with parallel examples) have only a

"referential" reading, that is, one that entails that there are unicorns.

John wishes to find a unicorn and eat it :

$$\begin{cases} \vee u[\textbf{unicorn}'_*(u) \wedge \textbf{wish-to}'(\hat{}j, \, \hat{y}[\textbf{find}'_*(\check{}y, u) \wedge \textbf{eat}'_*(\check{}y, u)])] \\ \textbf{wish-to}'(\hat{}j, \, \hat{y}\vee u[\textbf{unicorn}'_*(u) \wedge \textbf{find}'_*(\check{}y, u) \wedge \textbf{eat}'_*(\check{}y, u)]) \end{cases}$$

The next example is somewhat simpler, in that it does not involve conjoining or quantifying verb phrases; but it also illustrates the possibility of a nonreferential reading in the presence of a pronoun.

Mary believes that John finds a unicorn and he eats it :

$$\begin{cases} \vee u[\textbf{unicorn}'_*(u) \wedge \textbf{believe-that}'(\hat{}m, \, \hat{}[\textbf{find}'_*(j, u) \wedge \textbf{eat}'_*(j, u)])] \\ \textbf{believe-that}'(\hat{}m, \, \hat{}\vee u[\textbf{unicorn}'_*(u) \wedge \textbf{find}'_*(j, u) \wedge \textbf{eat}'_*(j, u)]) \end{cases}$$

On the other hand, in each of the following examples only one reading is possible, and that the referential:

(1) **John seeks a unicorn and Mary seeks it,**
(2) **John tries to find a unicorn and wishes to eat it,**

$$\vee u[\textbf{unicorn}'_*(u) \wedge \textbf{believe-that}'(\hat{}m, \, \hat{}[\textbf{find}'_*(j, u)]) \wedge \textbf{eat}'_*(j, u)]$$

This is, according to my intuitions (and, if I guess correctly from remarks in Partee [10], those of Barbara Partee as well), as it should be; but David Kaplan would differ, at least as to (2). Let him, however, and those who might sympathize with him consider the following variant of (2) and attempt to make non-referential sense of it:

(2′) **John wishes to find a unicorn and tries to eat it.**

Of course there are other uses of pronouns than the ones treated in this paper—for instance, their use as what have been called in Geach [2 and 3] and Partee [10] *pronouns of laziness*, that is, as "standing for" longer terms bearing a somewhat indefinite relation to other expressions in the sentence in question (or preceding sentences within the discourse in question). For instance, it is not impossible to construe **it** in (2) as standing for **the unicorn he finds** (that is, **the unicorn such that he finds it**), **a unicorn he finds,** or **every unicorn he finds,** and in this way to obtain a nonreferential reading of that sentence; but this is not a reading with which David Kaplan would be content.

REFERENCES

1. Ajdukiewicz, K. *Język i Poznanie* (*Language and Knowledge*). Warsaw, 1960.
2. Geach, P. *Reference and Generality*. Ithaca, 1962.
3. —. Intentional Identity. *Journal of Philosophy* 64:627–32 (1967).
4. Lewis, D. General Semantics. *Synthèse* 22:18–67 (1970).
5. Montague, R. Pragmatics and Intensional Logic. *Synthèse* 22:68–94 (1970). Chap. 4 in this book.
6. —. Pragmatics. In R. Klibansky (ed.), *Contemporary Philosophy: A Survey*, vol. 1. Florence, 1968. Chap. 3 in this book.
7. —. On the Nature of Certain Philosophical Entities. *Monist* 53:161–94 (1969). Chap. 5 in this book.
8. —. English as a Formal Language. In B. Visentini et al., *Linguaggi nella Società e nella Tecnica*, Milan, 1970. Chap. 6 in this book.
9. —. Universal Grammar. *Theoria* 36:373–98 (1970). Chap. 7 in this book.
10. Partee, B. Opacity, Coreference, and Pronouns, *Synthèse* 21:359–85 (1970).
11. Quine, W. *Word and Object*. Cambridge, Mass., 1960.

9. A Paradox Regained (with David Kaplan)

Another attempt has recently been made (by R. Shaw, in [10]) to analyze a puzzle variously known as the Hangman (Quine [8]), the Class A Blackout (O'Conner [7], Alexander [1], and Cohen [3]), the Unexpected Egg (Scriven [9]), the Surprise Quiz, the Senior Sneak Week,[1] the Prediction Paradox (Weiss [13]), and the Unexpected Examination (Shaw, [10]). The following simple version of the paradox is sufficient to exhibit the essential features of all other versions. A judge decrees on Sunday that a prisoner shall be hanged on noon of the following Monday, Tuesday, or Wednesday, that he shall not be hanged more than once, and that he shall not know until the morning of the hanging the day on which it will occur. By familiar arguments it appears both that the decree cannot be fulfilled and that it can.

Treatments of the paradox have for the most part proceeded by explaining it away, that is, by offering formulations which can be shown not to be paradoxical. We feel, with Shaw, that the interesting problem in this domain is of a quite different character; it is to discover an exact formulation of the puzzle which is genuinely paradoxical. The Hangman might then take a place beside the Liar and the Richard paradox, and, not unthinkably, lead like them to important technical progress.

Before the appearance of Shaw's article, we had considered a form of the paradox essentially identical with his, and found it, contrary to his assertion, not to be paradoxical. At the same time

Originally published in *Notre Dame Journal of Formal Logic* 1:79–90 (1960). Reprinted with permission. The content of this article was presented before the Philosophy Club of the University of California at Los Angeles on March 14, 1958.
[1] Abraham Kaplan, in conversation.

we were successful in obtaining several versions which are indeed paradoxical. The present note is intended to report these observations.

It is perhaps advisable to begin with a simple treatment due to Quine. The judge's decree, D_1, delivered Sunday, is that one of the following three conditions will be fulfilled: (1) The prisoner K is hanged on Monday noon, but not on Tuesday or Wednesday noon, and K does not know on Sunday afternoon that 'K is hanged on Monday noon' is true; (2) K is hanged on Tuesday noon, but not on Monday or Wednesday noon, and K does not know on Monday afternoon that 'K is hanged on Tuesday noon' is true; or (3) K is hanged on Wednesday noon, but not on Monday or Tuesday noon, and K does not know on Tuesday afternoon that 'K is hanged on Wednesday noon' is true.

Let **M**, **T**, and **W** be the respective sentences 'K is hanged on Monday noon', 'K is hanged on Tuesday noon', and 'K is hanged on Wednesday noon'. Let K_s be the formula 'K knows the sentence x on Sunday afternoon' (regarded as synonymous with 'K knows on Sunday afternoon that the sentence x is true'), and let K_m and K_t be analogous, but referring to Monday and Tuesday respectively, rather than Sunday. Thus, in place of the phrase 'knows that', which requires indirect discourse, we use a locution which represents knowledge as a relation between persons and sentences. Our motive is to avoid the well-known difficulties associated with indirect discourse, and to preclude the suggestion that such difficulties may be held accountable for the paradox of the Hangman.[2]

In accordance with this usage, the variable 'x' in K_s, K_m, and K_t has names of sentences as its substituends. It is therefore desirable to introduce a system of names of expressions. Thus if E is any expression, $\bar{E}$ is to be the *standard name* of E, constructed according to one of several alternative conventions. We might, for instance, construe $\bar{E}$ as the result of enclosing E in quotes.

---

[2] In connection with this treatment of knowledge, see Carnap [2], in which, however, only the relation of belief is considered explicitly. We should mention as well another departure from ordinary usage. Judicial decrees would ordinarily not be construed as indicative sentences. To those who are bothered by our practice of identifying decrees with indicative sentences, we suggest reading 'the indicative corresponding to the decree' for 'the decree'.

Within technical literature a more common practice is to identify $\bar{E}$ with the numeral corresponding to the Gödel-number of E. As a third alternative, we could regard $\bar{E}$ as the structural-descriptive name of E (within some well-determined metamathematical theory).[3] A foundation for our later arguments could be erected on the basis of any one of these conventions.

If E is any expression, then $K_s(E)$ is to be the result of replacing 'x' by E in K_s; and analogously for $K_m(E)$ and $K_t(E)$. Thus, if we choose the first convention for forming standard names, $K_s(\bar{M})$ is the sentence 'K knows the sentence 'K is hanged on Monday noon' on Sunday afternoon'. The decree D_1 can now be expressed as follows:

$$[M \,\&\, \sim T \,\&\, \sim W \,\&\, \sim K_s(\bar{M}) \,\vee$$
$$[\sim M \,\&\, T \,\&\, \sim W \,\&\, \sim K_m(\bar{T})] \,\vee$$
$$[\sim M \,\&\, \sim T \,\&\, W \,\&\, \sim K_t(\bar{W})].$$

A few additional conventions will be useful. We shall employ the symbol '$\vdash$' for the logical relation of derivability within elementary syntax.[4] Thus if S_1 and S_2 are sentences, $S_1 \vdash S_2$ if and only if S_2 is derivable from S_1 in elementary syntax (or, as we shall sometimes say, S_1 logically implies S_2); similarly, we say that $\vdash S_2$ just in case S_2 is provable in elementary syntax. It is well known from work of Gödel that the relation of derivability within elementary syntax is itself expressible in elementary syntax. Accordingly, we let I be a formula of elementary syntax, containing 'x' and 'y' as its only free variables, which expresses in the 'natural way' that x logically implies y. If E_1 and E_2 are any expressions, then $I(E_1, E_2)$ is to be the result of replacing 'x' by E_1 and 'y' by

---

[3] The second convention was introduced in Gödel [4] and the third convention in Tarski [11].

[4] By *elementary syntax* we understand a first-order theory containing—in addition to the special formulas K_s, K_m, K_t, M, T, and W—all standard names (of expressions), means for expressing syntactical relations between, and operations on, expressions, and appropriate axioms involving these notions. The form of such a theory will of course depend on the convention adopted for the assignment of standard names. If the second convention is adopted, we could identify elementary syntax with Peano's arithmetic (the theory P of Tarski, Mostowski, Robinson, [12]) or even with the much weaker theory Q (of the same work)—in either case, however, supplemented by the special formulas mentioned above.

E_2 in **I**. Thus the assertion that $S_1 \vdash S_2$ is expressed in elementary syntax by the sentence $\mathbf{I}(\bar{S}_1, \bar{S}_2)$.

K reasons in the following way that D_1 cannot be fulfilled. For assume that it is. First, the hanging cannot take place on Wednesday noon; for if it did, the first two disjuncts of D_1 would fail, and the third would hold. But then K would know on Tuesday afternoon that $\sim M$ and $\sim T$ were true, and thus since $\sim M$ and $\sim T$ together imply $\mathbf{W}$, he would also know on Tuesday afternoon the truth of $\mathbf{W}$, which contradicts $\sim K_t(\overline{\mathbf{W}})$.

In this part of the argument K depends on two rather plausible assumptions concerning his knowledge:

(A_1) $[\sim M \,\&\, \sim T] \supset K_t(\overline{\sim M \,\&\, \sim T})$

(A_2) $[\mathbf{I}(\overline{\sim M \,\&\, \sim T}, \overline{\mathbf{W}}) \,\&\, K_t(\overline{\sim M \,\&\, \sim T})] \supset K_t(\overline{\mathbf{W}})$.

A_1 is a special case of the principle of knowledge by memory, and A_2 of the principle of the deductive closure of knowledge, that is, the principle that whatever is implied by one's knowledge is part of one's knowledge. Both principles may appear dubious in full generality, but we can hardly deny K the cases embodied in A_1 and A_2, especially after he has gone through the reasoning above.

By the foregoing argument, A_1 and A_2 together logically imply $\sim \mathbf{W}$. It is reasonable to assume that K knows A_1 and A_2 (again, after using them in the previous argument):

(A_3) $K_m(\overline{A_1 \,\&\, A_2})$.

Thus, by the following instance of the principle of the deductive closure of knowledge:

(A_4) $[\mathbf{I}(\overline{A_1 \,\&\, A_2}, \overline{\sim \mathbf{W}}) \,\&\, K_m(\overline{A_1 \,\&\, A_2})] \supset K_m(\overline{\sim \mathbf{W}})$,

K is able to establish not only that he cannot be hanged on Wednesday noon, but that he *knows* he cannot (that is, $K_m(\overline{\sim \mathbf{W}})$).

K proceeds to exclude Tuesday noon as follows. If he is to be hanged Tuesday noon, then, still assuming D_1, he infers that the second disjunct of D_1 must hold. It follows (by A_5 below) that K would know on Monday afternoon that $\sim M$ is true. But $\sim M$, together with $\sim \mathbf{W}$, implies $\mathbf{T}$. Thus $\mathbf{T}$ is a logical consequence of

K's knowledge, and hence K knows on Monday afternoon that
$\mathbf{T}$ is true. However, this contradicts $\sim K_m(\overline{\mathbf{T}})$.

In this part of the argument K depends on the following analogues to A_1 and A_2:

(A_5) $\sim\mathbf{M} \supset K_m(\overline{\sim\mathbf{M}})$,

(A_6) $[\mathbf{I}(\overline{\sim\mathbf{M}\ \&\ \sim\mathbf{W},\mathbf{T}})\ \&\ K_m(\overline{\sim\mathbf{M}})\ \&\ K_m(\overline{\sim\mathbf{W}})]\supset K_m(\overline{T})$.

By a similar argument, employing analogous assumptions, K
also excludes Monday noon as a possible time of execution and
concludes that D_1 cannot be fulfilled.

The hangman reasons, on the other hand, that the decree *can*
be fulfilled, and in fact on any of the days in question. Suppose,
for example, that K is hanged on Tuesday noon but not on Monday or Wednesday; this is clearly a possible state of affairs. Then
$\sim\mathbf{M}$, $\mathbf{T}$, and $\sim\mathbf{W}$ are true. Further, the sentence $\mathbf{T}$ is not *analytic*,
even in the broad sense of following logically from the general
epistemological principles whose instances are $A_1–A_6$. Appealing
to intuitive epistemological principles (whose precise formulation
is beyond the scope of the present paper), the hangman observes
that one cannot know a non-analytic sentence about the future.
In particular, K cannot know on Monday afternoon that he will be
hanged on Tuesday noon; thus we have $\sim K_m(\mathbf{T})$. But the second
disjunct of D_1 follows; thus D_1 is fulfilled.

As Quine points out, there is a fallacy of which K is guilty. The
fallacy, repeated several times, crops up quite early in the argument, in fact, when K applies A_2. This application requires that
$\sim\mathbf{M}\ \&\ \sim\mathbf{T}$ logically imply $\mathbf{W}$, when obviously it does not.
Indeed, $\sim\mathbf{M}\ \&\ \sim\mathbf{T}$ *together with* D_1 logically implies $\mathbf{W}$; but to
use this fact, we must replace A_2 by the following plausible
analogue:

(A_2') $[\mathbf{I}(\overline{\sim\mathbf{M}\ \&\ \sim\mathbf{T}\ \&\ D_1,\ \mathbf{W}})\ \&\ K_t(\overline{\sim\mathbf{M}\ \&\ \sim\mathbf{T}})$

$$\&\ K_t(\overline{D_1})]\supset K_t(\overline{\mathbf{W}}),$$

and add the assumption

$\qquad K_t(\overline{D_1})$.

But it is unreasonable to suppose that K knows that the decree will be fulfilled, especially in view of his attempt to prove the contrary.

As Shaw has remarked, the paradoxical flavor of the Hangman derives from a self-referential element in the decree which was not incorporated in Quine's formulation. The decree proposed by Shaw is essentially this: Either (1) K is hanged on Monday noon, but not on Tuesday or Wednesday noon, and on Sunday afternoon K does not know *on the basis of the present decree* that 'K is hanged on Monday noon' is true; (2) K is hanged on Tuesday noon, but not on Monday or Wednesday noon, and on Monday afternoon K does not know *on the basis of the present decree* that 'K is hanged on Tuesday noon' is true; or (3) K is hanged on Wednesday noon, but not on Monday or Tuesday noon, and on Tuesday afternoon K does not know *on the basis of the present decree* that 'K is hanged on Wednesday noon' is true.[5]

Two matters require clarification before a symbolic version of this decree can be given. First, we may ask what is meant by knowledge of one sentence on the basis of another. If A and B are sentences, then we understand the assertion that K knows B on the basis of A as meaning that K knows the conditional sentence whose antecedent is A and whose consequent is B. Other interpretations are possible, but those known to us would not materially alter our discussion. Secondly, we may question the propriety of self-reference. How shall we treat in our symbolic version the phrase 'the present decree'? It has been shown by Gödel (in [4]; see also Mostowski [6]) that to provide for self-reference we need have at our disposal only the apparatus of elementary syntax. Then, whenever we are given a formula F whose sole free variable is 'x', we can find a sentence S which is provably equivalent to $F(\bar{S})$, that is, the result of replacing in F the variable 'x' by the standard name of S. The sentence $F(\bar{S})$ makes a certain assertion *about* the sentence S. Since S is provably equivalent to $F(\bar{S})$, S makes the same assertion about S, and thus

---

[5] The only significant respect in which this version differs from Shaw's is in saying 'K does not know on the basis of the present decree' where Shaw would say 'K cannot deduce from the present decree'. But the latter version cannot be taken in its usual sense. On Tuesday afternoon, for instance, K's deduction will involve as premises not only the decree but also the *mnemonic knowledge* of not having been hanged on Monday or Tuesday noon.

is self-referential. Besides this method and its variants, no other precise ways of treating self-referential sentences are known to us.

In particular, we can find a sentence D_2 which is provably equivalent to the sentence

$$[M \& \sim T \& \sim W \& \sim K_s(\overline{D_2 \supset M})] \vee$$
$$[\sim M \& T \& \sim W \& \sim K_m(\overline{D_2 \supset T})] \vee$$
$$[\sim M \& \sim T \& W \& \sim K_t(\overline{D_2 \supset W})].$$

We may then not unreasonably identify D_2 with Shaw's decree.

All relevant features of D_2 are preserved if only two dates of execution are considered. Our analysis of Shaw's argument will therefore be focused on a decree D_3 such that

$$(1) \quad \vdash D_3 \equiv [[M \& \sim T \& \sim K_s(\overline{D_3 \supset M})] \vee$$
$$[\sim M \& T \& \sim K_m(\overline{D_3 \supset T})]].$$

K is now able to show that D_3 cannot be fulfilled. His argument is closely analogous to the earlier fallacious argument. He excludes first Tuesday and then Monday as possible dates of execution, and he employs as assumptions on knowledge the following analogues to A_1–A_4 ;

$(B_1) \quad \sim M \supset K_m(\overline{\sim M})$

$(B_2) \quad [I(\overline{\sim M, \; D_3 \supset T}) \& K_m(\overline{\sim M})] \supset K_m(\overline{D_3 \supset T})$

$(B_3) \quad K_s(\overline{B_1 \& B_2})$

$(B_4) \quad [I(\overline{B_1 \& B_2, \; D_3 \supset M}) \& K_s(\overline{B_1 \& B_2})] \supset K_s(\overline{D_3 \supset M}).$

The argument can be explicitly rendered as follows. First observe that, by (1) and the sentential calculus,

$(2) \quad \sim M \vdash [D_3 \supset T],$

$(3) \quad \vdash [D_3 \& T] \supset \sim K_m(\overline{D_3 \supset T}),$

$(4) \quad \vdash [D_3 \& T] \supset \sim M.$

By (4),

$(5) \quad B_1 \vdash [D_3 \& T] \supset K_m(\overline{\sim M}).$

It is known that whenever a relation of derivability holds in elementary syntax, we can prove in elementary syntax that it holds.[6] Thus, by (2),

(6) $\vdash \mathbf{I}(\overline{\sim \mathbf{M}}, \overline{D_3 \supset \mathbf{T}})$,

and hence

(7) $B_2 \vdash K_m(\overline{\sim \mathbf{M}}) \supset K_m(\overline{D_3 \supset \mathbf{T}})$.

By (3), (5), and (7),

$\qquad B_1 \& B_2 \vdash [D_3 \& \mathbf{T}] \supset [K_m(\overline{D_3 \supset \mathbf{T}}) \& \sim K_m(\overline{D_3 \supset \mathbf{T}})]$.

Thus

(8) $B_1 \& B_2 \vdash D_3 \supset \sim \mathbf{T}$.

By (1) and the sentential calculus,

(9) $\vdash [D_3 \& \sim \mathbf{T}] \supset \mathbf{M}$,

(10) $\vdash [D_3 \& K_s(\overline{D_3 \supset \mathbf{M}})] \supset \sim \mathbf{M}$.

By (8) and (9),

$\qquad B_1 \& B_2 \vdash D_3 \supset \mathbf{M}$.

Therefore, by the principle used to obtain (6).

$\qquad \vdash \mathbf{I}(\overline{B_1 \& B_2}, \overline{D_3 \supset \mathbf{M}})$.

Hence

$\qquad B_4 \vdash K_s(\overline{B_1 \& B_2}) \supset K_s(\overline{D_3 \supset \mathbf{M}})$.

Therefore

$\qquad B_3 \& B_4 \vdash K_s(\overline{D_3 \supset \mathbf{M}})$.

Thus, by (10),

$\qquad B_3 \& B_4 \vdash D_3 \supset \sim \mathbf{M}$

Hence, by (8),

(11) $B_1 \& B_2 \& B_3 \& B_4 \vdash D_3 \supset [\sim \mathbf{M} \& \sim \mathbf{T}]$.

---

[6] See, for example, Kleene [5].

But by (1) and sentential logic,

$$\vdash D_3 \supset [\mathbf{M} \vee \mathbf{T}],$$

and thus, by (11),

(12) $B_1 \& B_2 \& B_3 \& B_4 \vdash \sim D_3.$

We have shown, then, that under the (quite reasonable) assumptions B_1–B_4 the decree cannot be fulfilled.

Mr. Shaw considers his decree genuinely paradoxical, not merely incapable of fulfillment. There appears to us, however, no good reason for supposing it so. Let us attempt to show that D_3 can be fulfilled, using the hangman's earlier argument. Suppose as before that K is hanged on Tuesday noon and only then. In this possible state of affairs, $\sim \mathbf{M}$ and $\mathbf{T}$ are true. The hangman must now establish $\sim K_m(D_3 \supset \mathbf{T})$. To apply his earlier line of reasoning, he must show that $D_3 \supset \mathbf{T}$, considered on Monday afternoon, is a non-analytic sentence about the future. But $D_3 \supset \mathbf{T}$ is in fact analytic; for as K has shown, $\sim D_3$ follows logically from general epistemological principles, and hence so does $D_3 \supset \mathbf{T}$.

Now Mr. Shaw's judge, if it were suggested to him that K might be able to show his original decree (D_3) incapable of fulfillment, might attempt to avoid official embarrassment by reformulating his decree with an added stipulation, as follows. *Unless K knows on Sunday afternoon that the present decree is false*, one of the following conditions will be fulfilled: (1) K is hanged on Monday noon but not on Tuesday noon, and on Sunday afternoon K does not know on the basis of the present decree that 'K is hanged on Monday noon' is true; or (2) K is hanged on Tuesday noon but not on Monday noon, and on Monday afternoon K does not know on the basis of the present decree that 'K is hanged on Tuesday noon' is true.

But in avoiding official embarrassment the judge has plunged himself into contradiction. Now we have a genuinely paradoxical decree! To demonstrate this, it is best to give a symbolic version, and in so doing to treat self-reference just as before; that is, we find a sentence D_4 (regarded as expressing the decree) such that

(1) $\vdash D_4 \equiv [K_s(\overline{\sim D_4}) \vee [\mathbf{M} \,\&\, \sim\mathbf{T} \,\&\, \sim K_s(\overline{D_4 \supset \mathbf{M}})] \vee$

$$[\sim\mathbf{M} \,\&\, \mathbf{T} \,\&\, \sim K_m(\overline{D_4 \supset \mathbf{T}})]].$$

We shall employ the following plausible assumptions, of which C_1 is an instance of the principle that whatever is known is true, and C_2–C_8 are analogues to B_1–B_6 :

(C_1) $K_s(\overline{\sim D_4}) \supset \sim D_4$

(C_2) $\sim\mathbf{M} \supset K_m(\overline{\sim\mathbf{M}})$

(C_3) $K_m(\overline{C_1})$

(C_4) $[\mathbf{I}(\overline{C_1 \,\&\, \sim\mathbf{M}}, \overline{D_4 \supset \mathbf{T}}) \,\&\, K_m(\overline{C_1}) \,\&$

$$K_m(\overline{\sim\mathbf{M}})] \supset K_m(\overline{D_4 \supset \mathbf{T}})$$

(C_5) $K_s(\overline{C_1 \,\&\, C_2 \,\&\, C_3 \,\&\, C_4})$

(C_6) $[\mathbf{I}(\overline{C_1 \,\&\, \ldots \,\&\, C_4}, \overline{D_4 \supset \mathbf{M}}) \,\&$

$$K_s(\overline{C_1 \,\&\, \ldots \,\&\, C_4})] \supset K_s(\overline{D_4 \supset \mathbf{M}})$$

(C_7) $K_s(\overline{C_1 \,\&\, \ldots \,\&\, C_6})$

(C_8) $[\mathbf{I}(\overline{C_1 \,\&\, \ldots \,\&\, C_6}, \overline{\sim D_4}) \,\&\, K_s(\overline{C_1 \,\&\, \ldots \,\&\, C_6})] \supset K_s(\overline{\sim D_4})$.

First observe that, by (1),

(2) $C_1 \vdash D_4 \supset \sim K_s(\overline{\sim D_4})$.

By (1) and (2),

(3) $C_1 \,\&\, \sim\mathbf{M} \vdash D_4 \supset \mathbf{T}$,

(4) $C_1 \vdash [D_4 \,\&\, \mathbf{T}] \supset \sim K_m(\overline{D_4 \supset \mathbf{T}})$,

(5) $C_1 \vdash [D_4 \,\&\, \mathbf{T}] \supset \sim\mathbf{M}$.

By (5),

(6) $C_1 \,\&\, C_2 \vdash [D_4 \,\&\, \mathbf{T}] \supset K_m(\overline{\sim\mathbf{M}})$.

By (3) and the fact that whenever a relation of derivability holds, we can prove that it holds, we obtain:

(7) $\vdash \mathbf{I}(\overline{C_1 \,\&\, \sim\mathbf{M}}, \overline{D_4 \supset \mathbf{T}})$.

Hence

$$C_4 \vdash [K_m(\overline{C_1}) \,\&\, K_m(\overline{\sim M})] \supset K_m(\overline{D_4 \supset T}).$$

Therefore, by (6),

$$C_1 \,\&\, \ldots \,\&\, C_4 \vdash [D_4 \,\&\, T] \supset K_m(\overline{D_4 \supset T}).$$

Thus, by (4),

$$C_1 \,\&\, \ldots \,\&\, C_4 \vdash [D_4 \,\&\, T] \supset [K_m(\overline{D_4 \supset T}) \,\&$$
$$\sim K_m(\overline{D_4 \supset T})],$$

and therefore

(8) $C_1 \,\&\, \ldots \,\&\, C_4 \vdash D_4 \supset \,\sim T.$

By (1) and (2),

(9) $C_1 \vdash [D_4 \,\&\, \sim T] \supset M,$

(10) $C_1 \vdash [D_4 \,\&\, K_s(\overline{D_4 \supset M})] \supset \,\sim M.$

By (8) and (9),

$$C_1 \,\&\, \ldots \,\&\, C_4 \vdash D_4 \supset M,$$

and hence, by the principle invoked in connection with (7),

$$\vdash I(\overline{C_1 \,\&\, \ldots \,\&\, C_4}, \,\overline{D_4 \supset M}).$$

Therefore

$$C_6 \vdash K_s(\overline{C_1 \,\&\, \ldots \,\&\, C_4}) \supset K_s(\overline{D_4 \supset M}),$$

and thus

$$C_5 \,\&\, C_6 \vdash K_s(\overline{D_4 \supset M}).$$

Hence, by (2),

$$C_1 \,\&\, C_5 \,\&\, C_6 \vdash D_4 \supset \,\sim M.$$

Therefore, by (2) and (8),

(11) $C_1 \,\&\, \ldots \,\&\, C_6 \vdash D_4 \supset [\sim K_s(\overline{\sim D_4}) \,\&\, \sim M \,\&\, \sim T].$

But by (1),

$$\vdash D_4 \supset [K_s(\overline{\sim D_4}) \lor M \lor T],$$

and thus, by (11),

(12) $C_1 \& \ldots \& C_6 \vdash \sim D_4$.

We have shown, then, that under our assumptions the decree cannot be fulfilled.

But using (12) and the principle used to obtain (7), we obtain:

$$\vdash \mathbf{I}(\overline{C_1 \& \ldots \& C_6}, \overline{\sim D_4}).$$

Hence

$$C_8 \vdash K_s(\overline{C_1 \& \ldots \& C_6}) \supset K_s(\overline{\sim D_4}).$$

Therefore

(13) $C_7 \& C_8 \vdash K_s(\overline{\sim D_4})$.

But by (1),

$$\vdash K_s(\overline{\sim D_4}) \supset D_4,$$

and thus, by (13),

(14) $C_7 \& C_8 \vdash D_4$.

Under our assumptions, then, the decree necessarily will be fulfilled. Thus if the formulation D_4 is adopted, both K and the hangman are correct!

What we have shown is that the assumptions C_1–C_8 are incompatible with the principles of elementary syntax. The interest of the Hangman stems from this fact, together with the intuitive plausibility of the assumptions. Indeed, before discovering the present paradox, we should certainly have demanded of an adequate formalization of epistemology that it render the conjunction of C_1–C_8, if not necessary, at least not impossible. Thus the Hangman has certain philosophic consequences; but these can be made sharper by consideration of a simpler paradox, to which we were led by the Hangman.

First, it should be observed that if we consider only one possible date of execution, rather than two, a paradox can still be obtained. In this case the decree is formulated as follows. Unless K knows on Sunday afternoon that the present decree is false, the following condition will be fulfilled: K will be hanged on Monday noon, but on Sunday afternoon he will not know on the basis of the present decree that he will be hanged on Monday afternoon.

What is more important, however, is that the number of possible dates of execution can be reduced to zero. The judge's decree is now taken as asserting that the following single condition will be fulfilled: K knows on Sunday afternoon that the present decree is false. Thus we consider a sentence D_5 (regarded as expressing the decree) such that

(1) $\vdash D_5 \equiv K_s(\overline{\sim D_5})$.

The paradox rests on three simple assumptions which are analogous to C_1, C_3, and C_4:

(E_1) $K_s(\overline{\sim D_5}) \supset \sim D_5$

(E_2) $K_s(\overline{E_1})$

(E_3) $[\mathrm{I}(\overline{E_1}, \overline{\sim D_5}) \,\&\, K_s(\overline{E_1})] \supset K_s(\overline{\sim D_5})$.

By (1),

$$\vdash D_5 \supset K_s(\overline{\sim D_5}).$$

Hence

$$E_1 \vdash D_5 \supset \sim D_5,$$

and therefore

(2) $E_1 \vdash \sim D_5$.

By (2) and the fact that whenever a relation of derivability holds, we can prove that it holds, we obtain:

$$\vdash \mathrm{I}(\overline{E_1}, \overline{\sim D_5}).$$

Thus

$$E_3 \vdash K_s(\overline{E_1}) \supset K_s(\overline{\sim D_5}),$$

and therefore

$$E_2 \,\&\, E_3 \vdash K_s(\overline{\sim D_5}).$$

But then, by (1), we obtain:

(3) $E_2 \,\&\, E_3 \vdash D_5$.

We have shown, in (2) and (3), that the assumptions E_1-E_3 are incompatible with the principles of elementary syntax. But E_1-E_3 are even more plausible than C_1-C_8. Not only are E_1-E_3 simpler than their earlier counterparts, but they have the added advantage of containing no instance of the principle of knowledge by memory.

In view of certain obvious analogies with the well-known paradox of the Liar, we call the paradox connected with D_5 the Knower.

Let us now examine the epistemological consequences of the Knower. There are a number of restrictions which might be imposed on a formalized theory of knowledge in order to avoid the contradiction above. Of these, the simplest intuitively satisfactory course is to distinguish here as in semantics between an object language and a metalanguage, the first of which would be a proper part of the second. In particular, the predicate 'knows' would occur only in the metalanguage, and would significantly apply only to sentences of the object language. According to this proposal, a sentence like 'K knows 'K knows 'Snow is white''' or 'Socrates knows 'there are things which Socrates does not know'' would be construed as meaningless. A less restrictive course would involve a sequence of metalanguages, each containing a distinctive predicate of knowledge, which would meaningfully apply only to sentences of languages earlier in the sequence. A more drastic measure (which seems to us distinctly unreasonable) is to reject some part of elementary syntax, perhaps by denying the existence of self-referential sentences.

The assumptions (E_1)–(E_3) are instances of the following schemata:

(S_1) $K_s(\bar{\phi}) \supset \phi$,

(S_2) $K_s(\overline{K_s(\phi) \supset \phi})$,

(S_3) $[\mathbf{I}(\bar{\phi}, \bar{\psi}) \& K_s(\bar{\phi})] \supset K_s(\bar{\psi})$,

where ϕ and ψ are arbitrary sentences. Using the Knower, we can show that any formal system containing the apparatus of elementary syntax, and including among its theorems all instances of (S_1)–(S_3), is inconsistent. Using the Liar, Tarski has obtained a similar result: any formal system containing the apparatus of elementary syntax, and including among its theorems all sentences

$$T(\bar{\phi}) \equiv \phi,$$

where ϕ is a sentence of the formal system, is inconsistent; see Tarski [11]. The precise relations between Tarski's result and ours are not at present clear, but would appear to constitute an interesting subject of research.

It should be mentioned that if any one of S_1-S_3 is removed, it can be shown that the remaining schemata are compatible with the principles of elementary syntax.

REFERENCES

1. Alexander, P. Pragmatic Paradoxes. *Mind* 62: 65–67 (1953).
2. Carnap, R. On Belief Sentences. In R. Carnap, *Meaning and Necessity*, enlarged ed., Chicago, 1956.
3. Cohen, L. Mr. O'Connor's 'Pragmatic Paradoxes'. *Mind* 59: 85–87 (1950).
4. Gödel, K. Über formal unentscheidbare Sätze der *Principia Mathematica* und verwandter Systeme I. *Monatshefte für Mathematik und Physik* 38: 183–98 (1931).
5. Kleene, S. *Introduction to Metamathematics*. Princeton, 1952.
6. Mostowski, A. *Sentences Undecidable in Formalized Arithmetic*. Amsterdam, 1952.
7. O'Connor, D. Pragmatic Paradoxes. *Mind* 57: 358–59 (1948).
8. Quine, W. On a So-Called Paradox. *Mind* 62: 65–67 (1953).
9. Scriven, M. Paradoxical Announcements. *Mind* 60:403–07 (1951).
10. Shaw, R. The Paradox of the Unexpected Examination. *Mind* 67: 382–84 (1958).
11. Tarski, A. Der Wahrheitsbegriff in den formalisierten Sprachen. *Studia Philosophica* 1: 261–405 (1936).
12. Tarski, A., A. Mostowski, and R. Robinson. *Undecidable Theories*. Amsterdam, 1953.
13. Weiss, P. The Prediction Paradox. *Mind* 61:265–69 (1952).

10. Syntactical Treatments of Modality, with Corollaries on Reflexion Principles and Finite Axiomatizability

On several occasions it has been proposed that modal terms ('necessary', 'possible', and the like) be treated as predicates of expressions rather than as sentential operators.[1] According to this proposal, we should abandon such sentences as 'Necessarily man is rational' in favor of "Man is rational' is necessary' (or "Man is rational' is a necessary truth'). The proposal thus amounts to the following: to generate a meaningful context a modal term should be prefixed not to a sentence or formula but to a *name* of a sentence or formula (or perhaps a variable whose values are understood as including sentences).

The advantage of such a treatment is obvious: if modal terms becomes predicates, they will no longer give rise to non-extensional contexts, and the customary laws of predicate calculus with identity may be employed. The main purpose of the present paper is to consider to what extent within such a treatment the customary laws of modal logic can be maintained.

These considerations form the content of Section 2. Sections 3 and 4 use identical methods, but contain results unrelated to modal logic; Section 3 concerns the non-provability of certain

Originally published in *Acta Philosophica Fennica* 16:153–67 (1963). Reprinted with permission. This paper was written while the author held a United States National Science Foundation Grant, NSF G–19830. I wish to express gratitude also to my student, Mr. David Kaplan, and to Professor R. L. Vaught for helpful discussion and correspondence.

[1] Examples of such proposals may be found in [6], in which necessary truth is identified with provability in a certain system, as well as Carnap [1, pp. 233–60] and Quine [14].

arithmetical 'reflexion principles', and Section 4 contains general theorems on non-finite axiomatizability.[2]

1. PRELIMINARIES

The terminology of Tarski, Mostowski, and Robinson [17] will be adopted. A few additional notions will be employed, for instance, that of a *logical axiom* (for the first-order predicate calculus with identity). The logical axioms can be chosen in various ways; we impose only the following requirements: (1) the set of logical axioms is to be recursive; (2) all logical axioms are to be sentences (that is, formulas without free variables); (3) the logical axioms are to be complete under the rule of detachment (or *modus ponens*), in the sense that, for any theory T, the set of logically valid sentences of T is to be the smallest set closed under detachment and containing all logical axioms which are sentences of T.

Let φ be a formula whose only free variable is u. Then $\psi^{(\varphi)}$, or the *relativization* of ψ to φ, can be defined for an arbitrary formula ψ by the following recursion: if ψ is atomic, $\psi^{(\varphi)}$ is ψ; $(\sim\psi)^{(\varphi)}$ is $\sim\psi^{(\varphi)}$, $(\psi \to \chi)^{(\varphi)}$ is $\psi^{(\varphi)} \to \chi^{(\varphi)}$, and analogously for the other sentential connectives; $(\Lambda\alpha\,\psi)^{(\varphi)}$ is $\Lambda\alpha\,(\varphi(\alpha) \to \psi^{(\varphi)})$, and $(V\alpha\,\psi)^{(\varphi)}$ is $V\alpha\,(\varphi(\alpha) \wedge \psi^{(\varphi)})$.[3] If T is a theory, then $T^{(\varphi)}$, or the *relativization* of T to φ, is that theory whose constants are those of T together with those occurring in φ, and whose valid sentences are the logical consequences within this vocabulary of the set of sentences $\psi^{(\varphi)}$, where ψ is a valid sentence of T.

We shall be particularly interested in the theories P and Q of Tarski, Mostowski, and Robinson [17] (*Peano's arithmetic* and

---

[2] The results of this paper may be considered as applications of the Paradox of the Hangman, or rather the related Paradox of the Knower, in the sense that the proof of the basic lemma of the paper, Lemma 3, was partly suggested by the latter paradox. Both paradoxes were first exactly formulated in Kaplan and Montague [7], which contained the conjecture that they might, like the Liar, lend themselves to some sort of technical application.

[3] Thus the notation '$x(y)$' (as well as the notation '$x(y,z)$' in later passages) is used, as in Tarski [17], for proper substitution in a formula for the variable u (or the variables u, v). The same notation will also be used for the value of a function, but the context will always suffice to determine the intended sense.

Robinson's arithmetic respectively).[4] Both theories have as non-logical constants the symbols, $0, S, +, \cdot$; their possible realizations will consequently have the form $\langle A, z, s, p, t \rangle$, where $z \in A$, s is a function mapping A into A, and p, t are functions mapping the set of ordered pairs of elements of A into A. By the *standard realization* (of P or Q) is understood that realization $\langle A, z, s, p, t \rangle$ in which A is the set of natural numbers, z is the number zero, s is the successor function, and p, t are the respective operations of addition and multiplication of natural numbers. When we speak simply of *truth* or *definability* we mean truth or definability in the standard realization $\mathfrak{A}_0$. In other words, a sentence is said to be *true* if it is a sentence of Q and true in $\mathfrak{A}_0$, and a formula φ is said to *define* a set X of natural numbers if φ is a formula of Q whose only free variable is u, and φ is satisfied in $\mathfrak{A}_0$ by those and only those natural numbers which are members of X. Derivatively, we call a *set* of sentences *true* if all its members are true, and a *theory true* if its set of valid sentences is true; and we say that φ *defines* a set X of *expressions* if φ defines the set of Gödel numbers of members of X.[5]

If X is a set of natural numbers, T a theory, and φ a formula of T whose only free variable is u, then we say that φ *super-numerates* X in T if $\vdash_T \varphi(\Delta_n)$ whenever $n \in X$, and that φ *numerates* X in T if, for every natural number n, $n \in X$ if and only if $\vdash_T \varphi(\Delta_n)$. On the other hand, if X is a set of *expressions*, we say that φ *numerates* or *super-numerates* X in T if φ respectively numerates or super-numerates in T the set of Gödel numbers of members of X.

A function f mapping the set of natural numbers into itself is said to be *functionally numerable* in a theory T if there is a formula φ of T with free variables u, v such that, for all natural numbers n,

$$\vdash_T \varphi(\Delta_n, v) \leftrightarrow v = \Delta_{f(n)}.$$

[4] The only properties of Q used in this paper are that (i) the constants of Q are $0, S, +, \cdot$, (ii) Q is true (in the sense about to be explained), (iii) Q is finitely axiomatizable, and (iv) all one-place recursive functions of natural numbers are functionally numerable in Q (again in a sense which is about to be explained). Thus Q could be replaced everywhere by any other theory with these properties.

[5] To make these definitions (as well as those in the next paragraph) perfectly unambiguous we should have to make certain disjointness assumptions, for instance, that no natural number is an expression. Without such assumptions, however, the intended sense of truth and definability will in what follows be clearly determined by the context.

We can associate with each expression a term of Q which can be regarded as the standard name of that expression; to be specific, we associate with an expression σ the name $\Delta_{nr(\sigma)}$ (that is, the result of prefixing $nr(\sigma)$ occurrences of S to the individual constant 0, where $nr(\sigma)$ is the Gödel number of σ). Keeping this interpretation in mind, we can regard the following lemma as a principle of self-reference; it is implicit in many earlier publications, and proved in essentially the present form in Montague [12].

Lemma 1. If T is a theory in which all one-place recursive functions of natural numbers are functionally numerable, ψ is a formula of T whose only free variable is u, and E is a one-place recursive function of expressions, then there is a sentence φ of T such that

$$\vdash_T \varphi \leftrightarrow \psi(\Delta_{nr(E(\varphi))}).$$

Lemma 2. If T is a theory which is an extension of $Q^{(\beta)}$, for some formula β whose only free variable is u, then all one-place recursive functions of natural numbers are functionally numerable in T.

Proof. This is easily derived from the fact, proved in [17], that all recursive functions are functionally numerable in Q.

The next statement is the central lemma of the present paper, and forms the basis of most of the results of the following sections.

Lemma 3. Suppose that T is a theory and α a formula whose only free variable is u, and, for all sentences φ, ψ of T,

(i) $\vdash_T \alpha(\Delta_{nr(\varphi)}) \to \varphi$,
(ii) $\vdash_T \alpha(\Delta_{nr(\varphi)})$, if φ is $\alpha(\Delta_{nr(\psi)}) \to \psi$,
(iii) $\vdash_T \alpha(\Delta_{nr(\varphi)})$, if φ is a logical axiom,
(iv)   if $\vdash_T \alpha(\Delta_{nr(\varphi \to \psi)})$ and $\vdash_T \alpha(\Delta_{nr(\varphi)})$, then $\vdash_T \alpha(\Delta_{nr(\psi)})$,
(v) $Q^{(\beta)}$ is a subtheory of T, for some formula β whose only free variable is u.

Then T is inconsistent.

Proof. Since Q is finitely axiomatizable, so is $Q^{(\beta)}$. Let χ be a valid sentence of $Q^{(\beta)}$ from which all valid sentences of $Q^{(\beta)}$ are logically derivable, and let T' be that theory whose valid sentences are the sentences of T derivable from χ. By Lemmas 1 and 2, there is a sentence φ of T such that

(1) $\vdash_{T'} \varphi \leftrightarrow \alpha(\Delta_{nr(\chi \to \sim \varphi)})$.

If we let L be the theory whose valid sentences are the logically valid sentences of T, it follows by the Deduction Theorem that

$\vdash_L \chi \to (\varphi \leftrightarrow \alpha(\Delta_{nr(\chi \to \sim \varphi)}))$.

Hence, by sentential logic,

(2) $\vdash_L (\alpha(\Delta_{nr(\chi \to \sim \varphi)}) \to (\chi \to \sim \varphi)) \to (\chi \to \sim \varphi)$.

Let γ be the sentence $\alpha(\Delta_{nr(\chi \to \sim \varphi)}) \to (\chi \to \sim \varphi)$. It follows from (iii) and (iv) that if ψ is any logically valid sentence of T, then $\vdash_T \alpha(\Delta_{nr(\psi)})$. In particular, we have by (2) that

(3) $\vdash_T \alpha(\Delta_{nr(\gamma \to (\chi \to \sim \varphi))})$.

Therefore, by (iv) and (ii),

(4) $\vdash_T \alpha(\Delta_{nr(\chi \to \sim \varphi)})$,

and hence, by (1),

$\vdash_T \varphi$.

By (4) and (i),

$\vdash_T \chi \to \sim \varphi$,

and hence, by (v),

$\vdash_T \sim \varphi$,

and T is inconsistent.

Tarski's theorem on the undefinability of truth (proved in [16], using the Paradox of the Liar) can be formulated as follows: if T is a theory, α is a formula whose only free variable is u, condition (v) of Lemma 3 is satisfied, and in addition

(i′) $\vdash_T \alpha(\Delta_{nr(\varphi)}) \leftrightarrow \varphi$, for all sentences φ of T,

then T is inconsistent.

This theorem is an immediate consequence of Lemma 3. There seems, however, to be no direct implication in the opposite direction; indeed, Tarski's assumption (i') appears intuitively much stronger than the combination of (i)–(iv).

The following lemma, closely related to Lemma 3, will also be used.

Lemma 4. Suppose that T is a theory and α a formula whose only free variable is u, and that, for all sentences φ, ψ of T, conditions (i), (iii), (v) of Lemma 3 hold, together with the following:

(iv') if $\vdash_T \alpha(\Delta_{nr(\varphi \to \psi)})$, then $\vdash_T \alpha(\Delta_{nr(\varphi)}) \to \alpha(\Delta_{nr(\psi)})$.

Then $\vdash_T \sim \alpha(\Delta_{nr(\gamma)})$, for some sentence γ of T of the form $\alpha(\Delta_{nr(\delta)}) \to \delta$.

Proof. We form χ, φ, γ as in the proof of Lemma 3, and carry through that proof up to and including step (3). From (3) and (iv') we conclude that

$$\vdash_T \alpha(\Delta_{nr(\gamma)}) \to \alpha(\Delta_{nr(\chi \to \sim \varphi)}).$$

From this we conclude by (1) that

$$\vdash_T \alpha(\Delta_{nr(\gamma)}) \to \varphi,$$

and by (i) that

$$\vdash_T \alpha(\Delta_{nr(\gamma)}) \to (\chi \to \sim \varphi).$$

But $\vdash_T \chi$ by (v); hence, by the two assertions above,

$$\vdash_T \sim \alpha(\Delta_{nr(\gamma)}),$$

and γ has by its construction the required form.

2. MODALITY

According to the proposal mentioned at the beginning of this paper, modal statements will occur in a syntax language (or metalanguage). As was intimated in connection with Lemma 1, we suppose syntax to be arithmetized and use as syntax languages those languages which contain the symbols of arithmetic.[6] Thus

---

[6] This approach is by no means essential, and is adopted only to allow us to build on terminology and results already present in the literature. An equivalent and perhaps more natural approach would employ a syntax language (such as the one introduced in Tarski [16]) which speaks directly about expressions.

we assume throughout the present section that N is a formula whose only free variable is u; and, for any sentence φ, we set $N[\varphi]$ equal to the sentence

$$N(\Delta_{nr(\varphi)}),$$

that is, the proper substitution of what might be regarded as the name of φ for all free occurrences of u in N. We think of $N[\varphi]$ as expressing the assertion that φ is necessarily true, but we impose no special conditions on N. For example, N may be a complex formula of set theory, or simply an atomic formula πu, where π is a one-place predicate. In particular, we do not assume that N is in any sense equivalent to a formula of P.

The following remark concerning the limitations of syntactical interpretations of modal logic is due to Gödel [6]: if N is the standard formula of P defining the set of valid sentences of P, then $N[N[\varphi] \rightarrow \varphi]$ is untrue for some sentences φ of P.

Gödel's proof of this remark employs his earlier theorem (in [5]) to the effect that the consistency of P is not provable in P, and like the proof of that earlier theorem depends essentially on the exact structure of the formula N. Now it is easy to find formulas of P (other than the standard formula) which define the set of valid sentences of P and with respect to which the consistency of P is provable in P.[7] We might hope to use one of these more complex formulas to express necessity and still maintain the characteristic modal law

$$N[N[\varphi] \rightarrow \varphi].$$

But this hope is vain, as our investigations (in particular, Theorem 4, which is a generalization of Gödel's remark) will show. Stronger negative results are also obtainable, like the following.

Theorem 1. Suppose that T is any theory such that

(i) T is an extension of Q (or of $Q^{(a)}$, for some formula α whose only free variable is u),

---

[7] Examples may be found in Feferman [3], but simpler examples may be constructed in a rather obvious way. (Feferman's formulas were devised so as to satisfy certain additional conditions as well.)

and, for all sentences φ, ψ of T,

(ii) $\vdash_T N[\varphi] \to \varphi$,
(iii) $\vdash_T N[N[\varphi] \to \varphi]$,
(iv) $\vdash_T N[\varphi \to \psi] \to (N[\varphi] \to N[\psi])$,
(v) $\vdash_T N[\varphi]$, if φ is a logical axiom.

Then T is inconsistent.

Proof. By Lemma 3, taking N for α.

Notice that the assumptions of Theorem 1 concern only those expressions $N[\varphi]$ in which φ is without free variables. Thus the difficulties exhibited both here and below are seen to be independent of the familiar problems resulting from quantification into modal contexts.

It has been shown in joint work of Mr. David Kaplan and the author that none of the hypotheses (ii)–(v) can be dropped. Theorem 1 can, however, be slightly strengthened in view of Lemma 4:

Theorem 2. Suppose that T satisfies conditions (i), (ii), (iv), (v) above. Then there is a single sentence φ of T such that

$$\vdash_T \sim N[N[\varphi] \to \varphi].$$

The following assertion, which overlaps Theorem 1, can be obtained directly from Lemma 3.

Theorem 3. Suppose that T satisfies conditions (i) and (ii) of Theorem 1, and that

(vi) $\vdash_T N[\varphi]$ whenever φ is a sentence such that $\vdash_T \varphi$.

Then T is inconsistent.

The following generalization of Gödel's remark is a simple consequence of Theorem 1.

Theorem 4. Suppose that U is any true theory with the same constants as P, and that N is a formula of P defining the set of valid sentences of U. Then $N[N[\varphi] \to \varphi]$ is untrue for some sentences φ of P.

Proof.   Assume the hypothesis, and that $N[N[\varphi] \to \varphi]$ is true for all sentences φ of P. Let T be the theory whose valid sentences are the true sentences of P. Then T and N will satisfy conditions (i)–(v) of Theorem 1. Hence T is inconsistent, which is absurd.

Now what general conclusions can be drawn from Theorems 1–4? In the first place, observe that the schemata in conditions (ii)–(v) of Theorem 1 are provable in the well-known systems of first-order modal logic with identity, that is, the systems of Carnap [2] and Kripke [8]. These schemata would, moreover, be provable in any reasonable extension to predicate logic of S1, the weakest of the Lewis modal calculi.[8] Further, it is not un-natural to impose condition (i): modal logic, like ordinary logic, ought to be applicable to an arbitrary subject matter, including arithmetic. Condition (vi), though not needed in Theorem 1, is rather natural, and appears as an inference rule in many familiar systems.

Thus if necessity is to be treated syntactically, that is, as a predicate of sentences, as Carnap and Quine have urged, then virtually all of modal logic, even the weak system S1, must be sacrificed.

This is not to say that the Lewis systems have no natural inter-pretation. Indeed, if necessity is regarded as a sentential operator, then perfectly natural model-theoretic interpretations may be found, for instance in Kripke [8] and Montague [10], which satisfy all the Lewis systems S1–S5. It should be observed, however, that the *natural* model-theoretic interpretations (as opposed to *ad hoc* interpretations) provide no justification for any of S1–S4; for, though they satisfy the theorems of these systems, they satisfy additional modal principles as well, and indeed give all of S5, the strongest of the Lewis systems and the system whose quantified version was in a sense proved complete in Kripke [8].

Thus it seems at present doubtful that any philosophical interest can be attached to S1–S4. The natural model-theoretic treatment gives a system stronger than all of them, and no satisfactory syntactical treatment can be provided for any of them.

---

[8] For the Lewis calculi see Lewis and Langford [9, pp. 492 ff.]

3. ARITHMETICAL REFLEXION PRINCIPLES

Feferman has in [4] constructed 'recursive progressions of theories' in which the passage from a theory T to its successor consists in adding to T all instances of the schema

$$\alpha(\Delta_{nr(\varphi)}) \to \varphi,$$

where α is a rather special formula defining the set of valid sentences of T. In view of Gödel's theorem on non-demonstrable consistency (or rather the version of it given in Feferman [3]), it is clear that in the cases considered by Feferman the successor of a theory is always stronger than the theory itself. The theorems of the present section show this to be the case even in more general situations, when no limitation is placed on the structure of the formula α.

Lemma 5. Suppose that A, T are theories and α, β formulas whose only free variable is u, and that

(i) T is an extension of A,
(ii) T is an extension of $Q^{(\beta)}$,
(iii) the constants of A include those of $Q^{(\beta)}$,
(iv) α numerates in T the set of valid sentences of A,
(v) $\vdash_A \alpha(\Delta_{nr(\varphi)}) \to \varphi$, for each sentence φ of A.

Then T is inconsistent.

Proof. Let T' be the theory whose valid sentences are those sentences of A which are valid in T. Then T' and α satisfy the hypothesis of Lemma 3. Hence T' and therefore T are inconsistent.

Theorem 5. If A is a true theory with the same constants as Q, and α defines the set of valid sentences of A, then there is a sentence φ of A such that

$$\text{not } \vdash_A \alpha(\Delta_{nr(\varphi)}) \to \varphi.$$

Proof. Assume the hypothesis and that, for each sentence φ of A, $\vdash_A \alpha(\Delta_{nr(\varphi)}) \to \varphi$. Let T be the theory whose valid sentences are the true sentences of Q, and β the formula $u = u$. Then (i)–(v) of Lemma 5 hold, and hence T is inconsistent, which is absurd.

Theorem 5 can be strengthened; we may permit A to contain additional constants beyond those of Q.

Theorem 6. Suppose that

(i) A is a theory whose constants include those of Q,
(ii) all sentences of Q which are valid in A are true,
(iii) α defines the set of valid sentences of A.

Then there is a sentence φ of A such that

$$\text{not } \vdash_A \alpha(\Delta_{nr(\varphi)}) \to \varphi.$$

Proof. By Theorem 5, taking for A the theory whose valid sentences are those sentences of Q which are valid in A, and for α the formula $\alpha \wedge \beta$, where β is a formula of Q defining the set of sentences of Q.

A further extension is possible. Instead of requiring, as in Theorem 6, that the arithmetical part of A be true, we may require only that it be true in a certain relativized sense.

Theorem 7. Suppose that A is a theory and α, β formulas whose only free variable is u, and that

(i) the constants of A include those of $Q^{(\beta)}$,
(ii) φ is true, whenever φ is a sentence of Q and $\vdash_A \varphi^{(\beta)}$,
(iii) α defines the set of valid sentences of A.

Then there is a sentence φ of A such that

$$\text{not } \vdash_A \alpha^{(\beta)}(\Delta_{nr(\varphi)}) \to \varphi.$$

Proof. Assume (i)–(iii), and that, for every sentence φ of A, $\vdash_A \alpha^{(\varphi)}(\Delta_{nr(\varphi)}) \to \varphi$. Let T be the theory whose valid sentences are the sentences of A logically derivable from the valid sentences of A together with the sentences $\varphi^{(\beta)}$, where φ is a true sentence of Q.

Then T is consistent. For suppose otherwise. Then there would exist true sentences $\varphi_0, \ldots, \varphi_n$ such that $\vdash_A \sim (\varphi_0^{(\beta)} \wedge \ldots \wedge \varphi_n^{(\beta)})$. Hence $\vdash_A [\sim (\varphi_0 \wedge \ldots \wedge \varphi_n)]^{(\beta))}$, and thus, by (ii), $\sim (\varphi_0 \wedge \ldots \wedge \varphi_n)$ is true, which is impossible.

To show that $\alpha^{(\beta)}$ numerates in T the set of valid sentences of A, assume that $\vdash_A \varphi$. Then, by (iii), $\alpha(\Delta_{nr(\varphi)})$ is true, and hence

$\vdash_T [\alpha(\Delta_{nr(\varphi)})]^{(\beta)}$; that is, $\vdash_T \alpha^{(\beta)} (\Delta_{nr(\varphi)})$. For the converse, assume that $\vdash_T \alpha^{(\beta)}(\Delta_{nr(\varphi)})$ and it is not the case that $\vdash_A \varphi$. Then, by (iii), $\sim\alpha(\Delta_{nr(\varphi)})$ is true, and hence $\vdash_T \sim\alpha^{(\beta)}(\Delta_{nr(\varphi)})$, which is impossible by the consistency of T.

Thus A, T, $\alpha^{(\beta)}$ satisfy condition (iv) of Lemma 5. Condition (v) has been assumed, and it is easily seen that the remaining hypotheses of that lemma are also satisfied. It follows that T is inconsistent, contrary to what has been shown.

If we consider super-numerations rather than defining formulas, then the assumption of truth involved in Theorems 5–7 can be replaced by an assumption of consistency.

Theorem 8. Suppose that A is a consistent theory and α a formula such that

(i) A is an extension of $Q^{(\beta)}$, for some formula β whose only free variable is u,

(ii) α super-numerates in A the set of valid sentences of A.

Then there is a sentence φ of A such that

$$\text{not } \vdash_A \alpha(\Delta_{nr(\varphi)}) \to \varphi.$$

Proof. Assume the contrary, and apply Lemma 5, taking A for both A and T. (The verification of condition (iv) of Lemma 5 requires a small argument.) We conclude that A is inconsistent, contradicting the hypothesis of the theorem.

4. NON-FINITE AXIOMATIZABILITY

Theorem 8 yields some general theorems on non-finite axiomatizability. Observe that in these theorems we speak of formulas super-numerating the set of *logically* valid sentences of a theory, not as before the set of *all* valid sentences of the theory.

Theorem 9. Suppose that A is a theory such that, for some formula α,

(i) A is an extension of $Q^{(\beta)}$, for some formula β whose only free variable is u,

(ii) variable α super-numerates in A the set of logically valid sentences of A,

(iii) $\vdash_A \alpha(\Delta_{nr(\varphi)}) \to \varphi$, for each sentence φ of A.

Then A, if consistent, is not finitely axiomatizable.

Proof.   Assume the contrary, and let χ be a valid sentence of A from which all valid sentences of A are logically derivable. By (i) and Lemma 2, there is a formula γ of A whose only free variables are u, v, and such that, for each sentence φ of A,

(1) $\vdash_A \gamma(\Delta_{nr(\varphi)}, v) \leftrightarrow v = \Delta_{nr(\chi \to \varphi)}.$

Let δ be the formula $\lor v(\gamma(u, v) \land \alpha(v))$. Then it is easily deduced from (ii) that δ super-numerates in A the set of valid sentences of A. Hence, by Theorem 8, there is a sentence φ of A such that

   not $\vdash_A \delta(\Delta_{nr(\varphi)}) \to \varphi$.

But, by (1),

   $\vdash_A \delta(\Delta_{nr(\varphi)}) \to \lor v(v = \Delta_{nr(\chi \to \varphi)} \land \alpha(v))$; hence
   $\vdash_A \delta(\Delta_{nr(\varphi)}) \to \alpha(\Delta_{nr(\chi \to \varphi)})$; thus, by (iii),
   $\vdash_A \delta(\Delta_{nr(\varphi)}) \to (\chi \to \varphi)$; hence
   $\vdash_A \delta(\Delta_{nr(\varphi)}) \to \varphi$;

and we have arrived at contradiction.

Theorem 9 applies only to theories which explicitly contain arithmetic. In many situations, however, we consider theories which, like certain well-known systems of set theory, contain arithmetic only implicitly, by way of interpretability; the next theorem concerns non-finite axiomatizability in such situations.

We call a theory T' a *definitional extension* of a theory T if T' is an extension of T and there is a set D such that (i) D is a set of possible definitions[9] in T of non-logical constants of T' which are not constants of T, (ii) each non-logical constant of T' which is not a constant of T occurs in exactly one member of D, and (iii) a sentence of T' is valid in T' if and only if it is logically derivable from the union of D and the set of valid sentences of T.

---

[9] For the notion of a possible definition of a constant in a theory see Tarski, Mostowski, and Robinson [17].

Theorem 10. Suppose that A is a theory such that, for some A' and α,

(i) A' is a definitional extension of A,
(ii) A' is an extension of $Q^{(\beta)}$, for some formula β whose only free variable is u,
(iii) α super-numerates in A' the set of logically valid sentences of A,
(iv) $\vdash_{A'} \alpha(\Delta_{nr(\varphi)}) \to \varphi$, for each sentence φ of A.

Then A, if consistent, is not finitely axiomatizable.

Proof. Assume the contrary. Then there will clearly be a theory A' which satisfies (i)–(iv), as well as the following additional conditions:

(1) A' has only finitely many constants which are not constants of A,
(2) A' is finitely axiomatizable.

Using (i) and (1), it is not difficult to show the existence of a recursive function f of expressions such that, for each sentence φ of A',

(3) $f(\varphi)$ is a sentence of A,
(4) $\vdash_{A'} \varphi \leftrightarrow f(\varphi)$,
(5) if φ is logically valid, then so is $f(\varphi)$.

(Loosely speaking, we construct $f(\varphi)$ by first eliminating defined constants from φ, and then, if φ contains operation symbols, appending to the result an antecedent containing the existence and uniqueness conditions for the formulas used to define the operation symbols.)

By (ii) and Lemma 2, there is a formula γ of A' whose only free variables are u, v, and such that, for each sentence φ of A',

(6) $\vdash_{A'} \gamma(\Delta_{nr(\varphi)}, v) \leftrightarrow v = \Delta_{nr(f(\varphi))}$.

Let δ be the formula $Vv\,(\gamma(u, v) \wedge \alpha(v))$. By (iii), (3), and (5),

(7) δ super-numerates in A' the set of logically valid sentences of A'.

We show that, for each sentence φ of A',

(8) $\vdash_{A'} \delta(\Delta_{nr(\varphi)}) \rightarrow \varphi$.

Assume that φ is a sentence of A'. By (6),

$\vdash_{A'} \delta(\Delta_{nr(\varphi)}) \rightarrow \alpha(\Delta_{nr(f(\varphi))})$; hence, by (3) and (iv),
$\vdash_{A'} \delta(\Delta_{nr(\varphi)}) \rightarrow f(\varphi)$;

and (8) follows by (4).

Now A' is consistent, by (i) and the fact that A is consistent. Therefore, by (7), (8), (ii), and Theorem 9, A' is not finitely axiomatizable, which contradicts (2).

The conclusions of the last two theorems can be strengthened.

Theorem 11.   (i) If A satisfies the hypothesis of Theorem 9, then A is essentially non-finitizable (that is, no consistent extension of A having the same constants as A is finitely axiomatizable). (ii) If A satisfies the hypothesis of Theorem 10, then A is again essentially non-finitizable.

Proof.   It is easily seen that if A satisfies the hypothesis of one of the two theorems in question, then so does every consistent extension of A with the same constants as A.

Now Theorem 11 (i) can be applied to the theory P, and 11 (ii) to what in Montague [11] is called *general set theory*. Indeed, any theory which satisfies the condition, introduced in Definition 9 of [11], of being *strongly semantically closed* will also satisfy the hypothesis of Theorem 10 (or at least will be isomorphic to a theory satisfying the hypothesis of Theorem 10). This follows from Theorem 1 of [11]; we take for α (in Theorem 10) the standard formula of Q defining the set of logically valid sentences (in terms of derivability by detachment from the logical axioms).

These applications are not new; it was already shown in [11] that every strongly semantically closed theory is essentially non-finitizable. Theorem 11 (ii), however, leads to a much simpler proof of this conclusion than was previously available. In the first place, previous methods required as a lemma Gödel's theorem to the effect that the consistency of certain theories is not provable within the theories themselves; this is no longer required.

Secondly, the earlier methods required the verification of condition (iv) of Theorem 10 for one particular formula α, the 'standard' formula defining logical validity. But as Professor R. L. Vaught has observed and an inspection of the proof of Theorem 1 of [11] will reveal, the verification of (iv) becomes much easier if we take for α, as we may according to Theorem 11 (ii), the formula of Q which defines logical validity in terms of *genetic provability*[10] rather than in terms of derivability from the logical axioms; we thus avoid showing that the Herbrand theorem is, so to speak, 'provable in the object language'.

REFERENCES

1. Carnap, R. *The Logical Syntax of Language*. London, 1937.
2. —. Modalities and Quantification. *Journal of Symbolic Logic* 11:33–64 (1946).
3. Feferman, S. Arithmetization of Metamathematics in a General Setting. *Fundamenta Mathematicae* 49:35–92 (1960).
4. —. Transfinite Recursive Progressions of Axiomatic Theories. *Journal of Symbolic Logic* 27:259–316 (1962).
5. Gödel, K. Über formal unentscheidbare Sätze der *Principia Mathematica* und verwandter Systeme I. *Monatshefte für Mathematik und Physik* 38:173–98 (1931).
6. —. Eine Interpretation des intuitionistischen Aussagenkalküls. *Ergebnisse eines mathematischen Kolloquiums* 4:39–40 (1933).
7. Kaplan, D. and R. Montague. A Paradox Regained. *Notre Dame Journal of Formal Logic* 1:79–90 (1960). Chap. 9 in this book.
8. Kripke, S. A Completeness Theorem in Modal Logic. *Journal of Symbolic Logic* 24:1–14 (1959).
9. Lewis, C. and C. Langford. *Symbolic Logic*. New York and London, 1932.
10. Montague, R. Logical Necessity, Physical Necessity, Ethics, and Quantifiers. *Inquiry* 3:259–69 (1960). Chap. 1 in this book.
11. —. Semantical Closure and Non-Finite Axiomatizability I. In *Infinitistic Methods*, Warsaw, 1961.
12. —. Theories Incomparable with Respect to Relative Interpretability. *Journal of Symbolic Logic* 27:195–211 (1962).

[10] For an informal description of genetic provability see Montague [11, p. 51], and for an exact definition see Schütte [15].

13. Mostowski, A. On Models of Axiomatic Systems. *Fundamenta Mathematicae* 39:133–58 (1952).
14. Quine, W. Three Grades of Modal Involvement. *Proceedings of the XIth International Congress of Philosophy* 14:65–81 (Brussels, 1953).
15. Schütte, K. Schlussweisen-Kalküle der Prädikatenlogik. *Mathematische Annalen* 22:47–65 (1950).
16. Tarski, A. Der Wahrheitsbegriff in den formalisierten Sprachen. *Studia Philosophica* 1:261–405 (1935).
17. Tarski, A., A. Mostowski, and R. Robinson. *Undecidable Theories.* Amsterdam, 1953.

11. Deterministic Theories

1. INTRODUCTION

The purpose of this paper is to analyse the notions of a deterministic theory and of a deterministic history, and to investigate some of the properties of these notions. To Laplace is attributed the assertion that if we were given the positions and momenta of all particles at one particular time, we could deduce, using the laws of mechanics, the positions and momenta of all particles at any later time. Implicit in this assertion is an analysis of determinism as applied to theories. The analysis has been made more explicit by Nagel (in [20, p. 422]), who characterizes a theory as deterministic if it will "enable us given the state (of a system) . . . at one time to deduce the formulation of the state at any other time." (Derivatively, we might call a *history* deterministic if there is a deterministic *theory* which describes it.)

Now this definition cannot be taken quite literally. For let us suppose that classical mechanics is deterministic in the sense of Laplace and Nagel. It would follow, if we were to spell out the definition explicitly, that for any instants t_0 and t, there are sentences $\varphi(t_0)$ and $\varphi(t)$, expressing the state of the universe at

Originally published in *Decisions, Values and Groups* 2. Oxford, Pergamon Press, 1962; pp. 325–70. Reprinted with permission. This paper is based largely on work accomplished by the author while he was in attendance at the Interdisciplinary Behavioral Sciences Research Conference at the University of New Mexico, June–August, 1958. This work was supported by the Behavioral Sciences Division, Air Force Office of Scientific Research, under contract AF 49 (638)–33. The author wishes also to express his gratitude to Mr. David Kaplan, Professor Azriel Lévy and Mrs. Ruth Anna Mathers, who offered important suggestions and criticism.

t_0 and t respectively, such that $\varphi(t)$ is deducible from $\varphi(t_0)$ combined with the laws of classical mechanics. It seems unavoidable to suppose that if t and t_1 are any two distinct instants, and $\varphi(t)$ and $\varphi(t_1)$ are sentences expressing the state of the universe at t and t_1 respectively, then $\varphi(t)$ and $\varphi(t_1)$ are also distinct. It follows that there are at least as many sentences as there are instants, that is, real numbers. But there are only denumerably many sentences (in any standard language), and as Cantor has shown, there are more than denumerably many real numbers. We have thus arrived at contradiction, and Laplace's allegation has been shown to be quite trivially false.[1]

The investigations of the present paper will be conducted within metamathematics in the wider sense, construed as including the apparatus of set theory.[2] I shall employ the apparatus of syntax and set theory in an intuitive manner, making no attempt to trace it back to its theoretical foundations.

After some preliminary remarks of an expository nature, I shall offer definitions of the concept of a *deterministic theory*, the derivative concept of a *deterministic history*, and several related concepts. I shall then inquire whether two specific theories, often alleged to be deterministic, actually are so. In the remaining sections I shall present theorems relating determinism with various other concepts which at one time or another have been associated with it in the literature. Of particular importance is the discussion of explicit definability and determinism, in which the metamathematical methods employed are somewhat deeper than in the balance of the paper and which contains a contribution to the well-known n-body problem of physics.

I am acutely aware that much of what I have to say is trivial. For philosophical reasons, however, it ought perhaps to be said. Imprecision concerning the notion of determinism, besides being

---

[1] It is possible to do greater justice to Laplace by resorting to non-standard languages, to which arbitrarily many elementary expressions may be admitted, and which therefore may possess non-denumerably many sentences. Such an analysis, whose details are not entirely obvious, may be discussed in a later paper. Regardless of this possibility, it seems desirable to discover a definition which will not employ non-standard techniques.

[2] For an intuitive characterization of metamathematics in both the narrower and the wider senses, see Kleene [14].

traditional, continues to provide an amazingly ample source of philosophic confusion.[3]

2. PRELIMINARIES

The theories I shall consider are essentially *theories with standard formalization* in the sense of Tarski (See Tarski, Mostowski, and Robinson [27]), though for present purposes certain departures from Tarski's approach will be convenient. To be specific, the *symbols* to be employed are of four kinds:

(1) the *logical constants* of the first-order predicate calculus with identity, that is, the symbols

∨ (read "or"),
∧ (read "and"),
→ (read "if ... then"),
↔ (read "if and only if"),
∼ (read "not"),
⋀ (read "for all"),
⋁ (read "for some"),
= (read "is identical with");

(2) (individual) *variables*, that is, lower-case Roman letters with or without numerical subscripts (I assume that all variables have been arranged in a sequence, $v_0, \ldots, v_n, \ldots$);

(3) *individual constants* (these symbols are regarded as designating particular objects; examples from ordinary language are "three" and "Venus");

(4) *predicates* of an arbitrary number of places (if n is a positive integer, then an *n-place predicate* is a symbol which, when accompanied by n individual constants, generates a sentence; for example, in ordinary mathematical language the symbol " $<$ " is a two-place predicate);

---

[3] See, for instance, a recent symposium on determinism which appeared in *Journal of Philosophy* and to which two highly esteemed philosophers of science contributed. On the other hand, a brief but beautiful discussion of determinism, which appears in Carnap [1, 3, and 4], seems to have been ignored almost entirely by philosophers. Carnap's goal in this discussion is to analyze the principle of causation; for this reason, his contribution is not directly relevant to the present paper.

(5) *operation symbols* of an arbitrary number of places (if n is a positive integer, then an *n-place operation symbol* is a symbol which, when accompanied by n individual constants, generates a name; for example, " + " is a two-place operation symbol).

The symbols of categories (1) and (2) are utilized in common by all theories. Theories differ, however, in their supply of symbols from categories (3), (4) and (5). For brevity, the latter expressions will be called *non-logical* constants, or simply *constants*.

Since the languages of theories may differ only as to constants, we need specify only these when characterizing a *language*. In particular, it is convenient to regard a (scientific) language as an ordered pair $\langle l, m \rangle$, where l and m are sequences of constants, and in addition the first four terms of l are, in order, the one-place predicates R and N (regarded as denoting the class of real numbers and the class of natural numbers respectively) and the operation symbols + and $\cdot$. The terms of l are the *abstract constants* (theoretical constructs) of the language, and the terms of m are the *elementary constants* (observational terms or sometimes *state-variables*) of the language.

The literature of the philosophy of science contains many discussions of abstract and elementary constants,[4] usually accompanied by attempts to justify an absolute distinction between them. It is my opinion that such attempts, besides being fruitless, are unduly restrictive. We should permit the distinction to be drawn in an arbitrary way and in different ways for different purposes.

If L is a scientific language, then a *formula of L* is a syntactically correct combination of symbols, involving arbitrary logical constants and variables, but only those non-logical constants which are constants of L (either abstract or elementary). To be more precise, we should first introduce the notion of a *term*, as follows. The class of *terms of L* is the smallest class K satisfying the following conditions:

(1) All variables are members of K.

(2) All individual constants of L are members of K.

(3) For any members $\xi_1 \dots , \xi_n$ of K and any *n*-place operation

[4] See, for example, Carnap [2, pp. 56–69], or MacCorquodale, Meehl [16].

symbol δ of L, the expression

$$\delta\xi_1 \dots \xi_n$$

is a member of K.

Then the class of *formulas of L* is the smallest class F satisfying the following conditions:

(1) If ξ, η are terms of L, then $\xi = \eta$ is a member of F.

(2) For any terms $\xi_1, \dots, \xi_n$ of L and any n-place predicate π of L, the expression

$$\pi\xi_1 \dots \xi_n$$

is a member of F.

(3) For any members φ and ψ of F, the expressions

$(\varphi \wedge \psi)$,
$(\varphi \vee \psi)$,
$(\varphi \rightarrow \psi)$,
$(\varphi \leftrightarrow \psi)$,
$\sim \varphi$

are members of F.

(4) For any member φ of F and any variable α, the expressions

$\wedge\alpha\varphi$,
$\vee\alpha\varphi$

are members of F.

A *sentence of L* is a formula of L which contains no free variables, that is, all of whose occurrences of variables are "bound" by appropriate occurrences of "$\wedge$" and "$\vee$". For purposes of legibility, I shall often depart from the mode of writing terms and formulas which is prescribed by the definitions above. For instance, I shall write "$x + y$" and "$x \cdot y$" instead of "$+xy$" and "$\cdot xy$". Further, I shall deal rather freely with parentheses; in particular, peripheral parentheses will be dropped and the parentheses accompanying "$\vee$" and "$\wedge$" will sometimes be dropped, in accordance with the principle that "$\rightarrow$" and "$\leftrightarrow$" mark a greater break than "$\vee$" or "$\wedge$".

Given a formula φ and terms $\xi_0, \dots, \xi_n$, I understand by $\varphi(\xi_0, \dots, \xi_n)$ the formula obtained from φ by *proper simultaneous substitution* of $\xi_0, \ldots, \xi_n$ for the free occurrences of $v_0, \ldots, v_n$ respectively.[5]

A *theory* is characterized by two things, its language and its set of axioms; the latter may be an arbitrary set of formulas of the former. Thus we may regard a (*scientific*) *theory* as a couple $\langle L, V \rangle$, where L is a scientific language and V is a set of formulas of L. The *language of* the theory is L; a *term, formula, sentence of* the theory is respectively a term, formula, sentence of L. The *axioms of* the theory are the members of V.

We come now to some semantical notions, in particular those of a *model* and of *truth*. Let us suppose that L is a scientific language and L has the form $\langle \langle \varepsilon_1, \ldots, \varepsilon_k, \ldots \rangle, \langle \delta_1, \ldots, \delta_n, \ldots \rangle \rangle$. The purpose of a model for L is to provide an interpretation for each sentence of L. A *model for* L will have, then, the form $\langle D, \langle E_1, \ldots, E_k, \ldots \rangle, \langle D_1, \ldots, D_n \ldots \rangle \rangle$, where D is a non-empty set (the *domain of discourse* of the model), each E_i is an appropriate 'meaning' for the corresponding ε_i, and each D_i is an appropriate 'meaning' for the corresponding δ_i. For example, if δ_i or ε_i is an individual constant, then the corresponding D_i or E_i will be an element of D; the interpretation of a one-place predicate will be a subclass of D and of a two-place predicate will be a set of ordered pairs of elements of D; the interpretation of a one-place operation symbol will be a function, defined for all elements of D, whose value is always an element of D; and the interpretation of a two-place operation symbol will be a function, defined for all ordered pairs of elements of D, whose value for such an ordered pair is always an element of D. By a *standard model* for L is understood one according to which the mathematical symbols (that is, $R, N, +, \cdot$) receive their usual interpretation. To be more explicit, $\langle D, \langle E_1, \ldots, E_k, \ldots \rangle, \langle D_1, \ldots, D_n, \ldots \rangle \rangle$ is a *standard model* for L just in case it is a model for L, and in addition E_1 is the set R of real numbers, E_2 is the set N of natural numbers, E_3 and E_4 are functions such that for any real numbers x and y, $E_3(x, y) =$

---

[5] *Proper simultaneous substitution* may be defined in various ways. For example, let φ' be the first formula, in a fixed sequence of expressions, such that no variable free in any of $\xi_0, \ldots, \xi_n$ is bound in φ', and φ' is an alphabetic variant of φ (in the sense of Quine [21, pp. 109–15]), and let $\varphi(\xi_0, \ldots, \xi_n)$ be the result of replacing simultaneously in φ' each free occurrence of v_i bu ξ_i, for $i < n$.

$x + y$ and $E_4(x, y) = x \cdot y$, while if either x or y is not a real number, then $E_3(x, y) = E_4(x, y) = 0$.[6]

If φ is a formula of L whose free variables are among $v_0, \ldots, v_n$, M is a model for L, and $d_0, \ldots, d_n$ are elements of the domain of discourse of M, then φ is *satisfied in M by* the assignment $\langle d_0, \ldots, d_n \rangle$ if, loosely speaking, φ is true when its bound variables are construed as ranging over the domain of discourse of M, each of its free variables v_i is construed as referring to the corresponding constituent d_i of the assignment, its non-logical constants are interpreted in accordance with M, and its logical constants receive their usual interpretation.[7] The formula φ *holds* (or *is true*) *in M* (with respect to L) just in case φ is satisfied in M by every assignment $\langle d_0, \ldots, d_n \rangle$ whose constituents are elements of the domain of discourse of M. Thus a formula φ whose free variables are $\alpha_0, \ldots, \alpha_n$ will hold in M just in case the sentence

$$\wedge \alpha_0 \ldots \wedge \alpha_n \varphi$$

holds in M. A *class K* of formulas of L holds (or *is true*) *in M* (with respect to L) just in case every formula in K holds in M (with respect to L). A *theory* whose language is L holds *in M* if its class of axioms does so. If K is a class of formulas of L and φ a formula of L, then K *logically implies* φ or, in symbols, $K \vdash \varphi$, just in case φ holds in every model for L in which K holds. If T is a *theory* whose language is L, then $T \vdash \varphi$ under the same condition.[8]

It would perhaps be appropriate to comment on two decisions which are reflected in the definitions above. In the first place, our scientific languages contain only two levels of abstraction, represented by their abstract constants on the one hand and their

---

[6] If F is a function, then $F(x, y)$ is the value of F for the pair $\langle x, y \rangle$ of arguments. It should perhaps be pointed out that the models discussed here bear no relation to what psychologists call mathematical models, which are in our terminology theories of a certain kind. It will be noticed that " $+$ " and " $\cdot$ ", as well as " $=$ ", are used ambiguously, both in their usual mathematical sense and as names for certain symbols.

[7] For a precise characterization of this notion, see Tarski [25].

[8] In view of Gödel's completeness theorem for the predicate calculus with identity (Gödel [11]), an alternative definition of logical implication is available, which makes no reference to models but instead refers to axioms and inference rules, and derivations constructed by means of them. Certain consequences of Gödel's completeness theorem will be used later in the present paper.

elementary constants on the other. In certain contexts it might be desirable to consider more complex scientific languages involving three or more, perhaps infinitely many, levels of abstraction; but for present purposes such complexity is unnecessary. In the second place, the mathematical basis of our scientific theories (which employs only four symbols, R, N, $+$, and $\cdot$) may seem both arbitrary and excessively meager. Indeed, other mathematical bases, both more and less restrictive, are imaginable and for some purposes desirable. The present basis, however, is the natural choice in connection with Newtonian mechanics and is sufficiently rich for virtually all known psychological theories of a mathematical character.[9] Further, the present mathematical basis is less meager than it might superficially seem. Indeed, it is equivalent to what is classically described as differential and integral calculus.[10]

The following notions are of a rather special character and of greatest importance in connection with the philosophy of science. Let M be a model and let it have the form $\langle D, \langle E_1 \ldots, E_k, \ldots \rangle,$ $\langle D_1, \ldots, D_n, \ldots \rangle \rangle$. Then the *partial model corresponding to* M, or $Pm(M)$, is the sequence $\langle D_1, \ldots \ldots, D_n, \ldots \rangle$. S is a *history* if there is a standard model M for which $S = Pm(M)$. (In this definition the restriction to standard models has the following effect. If $S = \langle D_1, \ldots, D_n, \ldots \rangle$, S is a history and δ_n is an operation symbol, then the corresponding function D_n will be defined for all real numbers.) A history, then, provides interpretations not for all the constants of a language, but only for the elementary or observational constants. The consideration of histories presents one way of making precise Carnap's notion of a partially interpreted scientific theory (see Carnap [2, pp. 56–69]).

Because histories provide only a partial interpretation, the notion of truth is not appropriate in connection with them. Instead, I introduce the notion of *realization*. A formula φ of L is *realized by* a history S just in case there is a standard model M of

---

[9] An exception to this remark is decision theory, as developed, for instance, in Davidson, Suppes, and Segal [8], whose mathematical basis would most naturally include as well a part of the elementary calculus of classes.

[10] The precise sense of this remark, as well as its justification, is to be found in a forthcoming paper to be titled "The Undecidability of Integration Theory." [Editor's note: This paper was apparently never written.]

L such that $S = Pm(M)$ and φ is true in M. S *realizes a class of formulas* or *theory* K (in symbols, $S \in Rl(K)$) if there is a single standard model M such that $S = Pm(M)$ and K holds in M.[11]

3. TWO CLASSICAL THEORIES

In this section I introduce the theories PM, or classical particle mechanics, and CM, or Newtonian celestial mechanics. It is necessary, for metamathematical purposes, to provide precise axiomatic formalizations of these disciplines.

There exists at least one very clear treatment of the foundations of classical particle mechanics, which is due to McKinsey, Sugar and Suppes in [17]. But this treatment is not entirely adequate for our purposes. McKinsey, Sugar and Suppes do not provide axioms for a theory in standard formalization. Instead, they define a set-theoretical predicate, that of being an *n-dimensional system of particle mechanics*; their so-called "axioms" are only clauses in the definition.[12] Nonetheless, their treatment could rather easily be modified so as to yield an axiomatic theory. The theory so obtained, however, would require an extensive mathematical basis, considerably more comprehensive than our meager R, N, $+$, and $\cdot$.

For metamathematical purposes, it is desirable to employ a very simple mathematical basis; but to achieve simplicity in one direction, we must introduce complexity in another. Thus the following axiom system, while relying heavily on the earlier treatment of McKinsey, Sugar and Suppes in [17], will be found to be rather more complicated. In addition, I depart from their general approach in four ways. (1) My considerations will apply to a single spatial dimension, rather than an arbitrary number of dimensions. (2) I shall not admit arbitrary time-intervals as the duration of application of the theory; only one basic interval will be considered—the set of all real numbers. (3) I shall consider only those forces which are exerted by particles on particles.

---

[11] The symbol "$\in$" is used for class membership, so that, for example, "$x \in A$" is read "x is a member (or an element) of A."

[12] For a detailed discussion of these two approaches to axiomatization, see Suppes [24].

(4) I shall avoid the variable-binding operator "Σ" and the notion of the derivative of an arbitrary function, introducing instead a particular sum (the net force) and particular derivatives. The first three departures are motivated solely by considerations of simplicity. The fourth is required if we are to obtain a first-order theory in standard formalization and at the same time forego the apparatus of set theory.

The *elementary constants of PM* are (in standard order) P, f, m, s, v; here P is a one-place predicate, m, s, v are two-place operation symbols, and f is a three-place operation symbol. The *abstract constants of PM* comprise $R, N, +, \cdot$, together with the additional non-elementary constants which occur in the axioms below (in, say, the order of first appearance). The *axioms of PM* are the following formulas.

Conditional definitions of mathematical concepts[13]:

(1) $Rx \rightarrow [x = 0 \leftrightarrow x + x = x]$

(2) $Rx \rightarrow [x = 1 \leftrightarrow x \cdot x = x \wedge \sim x = 0]$

(3) $2 = 1 + 1$

(4) $9 = 2 + 2 + 2 + 2 + 1$

(5) $Rx \wedge Ry \rightarrow [x \leqslant y \leftrightarrow \vee z(Rz \wedge x + z \cdot z = y)]$

(6) $Rx \wedge Ry \rightarrow [x < y \leftrightarrow x \leqslant y \wedge \sim x = y]$

(7) $Rx \wedge Ry \rightarrow [z = x - y \leftrightarrow Rz \wedge z + y = x]$

(8) $Rx \wedge Ry \rightarrow \left[z = \dfrac{x}{y} \leftrightarrow Rz \wedge ([\sim y = 0 \wedge z \cdot y = x] \vee \right.$
$$\left. [y = 0 \wedge z = 0]) \right]$$

(9) $Rx \rightarrow [z = |x| \leftrightarrow (0 \leqslant x \wedge z = x) \vee (x < 0 \wedge z = 0 - x)]$

---

[13] It may seem strange that the only specifically mathematical axioms of *PM* are of a definitional character. In later derivations of physical theorems, we shall actually employ, beyond the axioms of *PM*, arbitrary true sentences involving our four mathematical primitives $R, N, +,$ and $\cdot$. This will be done in two ways. At times we shall introduce explicitly the class of such truths, and at other times we shall restrict our attention to standard models (in which all such truths will of course hold). Instead of conditional definitions, fully explicit definitions could have been introduced as axioms. The present procedure is adopted for the sake of Theorem 11.

(10) $Rx \rightarrow [x$ is integer $\leftrightarrow Nx \lor N(0 - x)]$.

The greatest integer which is at most equal to x:

(11) $Rx \rightarrow [z = [x] \leftrightarrow Rz \land z$ is integer $\land z \leqslant x \land \bigwedge w(w$ is integer
$$\land w \leqslant x \rightarrow w \leqslant z)].$$

The remainder after division of x by y:

(12) $Rx \land Ry \rightarrow rm(x, y) = x - y \cdot \left[\dfrac{x}{y}\right]$.

It is well known that the ordered pairs of natural numbers can be put into one-to-one correspondence with the natural numbers themselves. The operation J which is introduced in (13) below effects just such a correspondence. Thus if i and j are natural numbers, $J(i, j)$ is to be the natural number which represents the ordered pair $\langle i, j \rangle$. Further, $T_1(n)$ and $T_2(n)$, where n is a natural number, are to be respectively the first and the second term of the ordered pair represented by n.

(13) $Ni \land Nj \rightarrow J(i, j) = \dfrac{(i + j) \cdot (i + j + 1)}{2} + i$

(14) $Nn \rightarrow [i = T_1(n) \leftrightarrow Ni \land \bigvee j(Nj \land n = J(i, j))]$

(15) $Nn \rightarrow [j = T_2(n) \leftrightarrow Nj \land \bigvee i(Ni \land n = J(i, j))]$.

Now it is also possible to represent all finite sequences of natural numbers as natural numbers; that is, we can define an operation β such that, for any sequence $\langle a_0, \ldots, a_{n-1} \rangle$ of natural numbers, there will be a natural number g which 'represents' the sequence, in the sense that, for $i = 0, \ldots, n - 1, \beta(i, g) = a_i$. The particular operation which is introduced below is due to Gödel.[14] We may read '$\beta(i, g)$' as 'the ith term of the sequence (of natural numbers) represented by g'.

(16) $Ni \land Ng \rightarrow \beta(i, g) = rm(T_1(g), (i + 1) \cdot T_2(g) + 1)$.

We shall require a special case of the exponentiation function, in fact, the operation 10^k where k is a natural number. One would

[14] The operation is known as the Gödel β-function, and is discussed in Kleene [14].

expect to introduce the operation by means of a recursive definition, as follows: $10^0 = 1$; $10^{n+1} = 10^n \cdot (9 + 1)$. But this course is not available, unless we are willing to develop first a general method for justifying (or eliminating) recursive definitions—a procedure which, though not difficult at this point, since the principal requirement is the introduction of the β-function, would still lead us too far afield. We give instead an explicit (conditional) definition of 10^k. Its correctness, however, hinges on the general procedure for eliminating recursive definitions; the reader should see in this connection Kleene [14].

(17) $Nk \rightarrow [n = 10^k \leftrightarrow \bigvee g(Ng \wedge \beta(k, g) = n \wedge \beta(0, g) =$

$1 \wedge \bigwedge i[Ni \wedge i < k \rightarrow \beta(i + 1, g) = \beta(i, g) \cdot (9 + 1)])]$.

If x is a real number and n a natural number, then $D_n(x)$ is to be the nth digit in the decimal part of x. For example, if $x = 1.83666 \ldots$, then $D_0(x) = 8$, $D_1(x) = 3$, $D_2(x) = 6$, and so on. The appropriate definitional axiom is the following:

(18) $Nn \wedge Rx \rightarrow D_n(x) = [(x \cdot 10^n - [x \cdot 10^n]) \cdot 10^1]$.

Using the operation $D_n(x)$, we can represent each class of natural numbers as a real number. In particular, if K is such a class, we can represent K by that decimal $d_0 d_1 d_2 \ldots$ whose digits d_i are all either 0 or 1 and which contains 1 in just those places which are indexed by numbers i in K. For our purposes only the relation of *membership* in "pseudo-classes" of this kind is required. We read "$n\eta x$" as "n is a member of the class of natural numbers represented by x."

(19) $Nn \wedge Rx \rightarrow [n\eta x \leftrightarrow D_n(x) = 1]$.

A real number x represents a function on and to natural numbers just in case no two pairs $J(n, i)$ and $J(n, j)$ with $i \neq j$ are members of the class represented by x:

(20) $Rx \rightarrow [x \text{ is fun} \leftrightarrow \bigwedge n \bigwedge i \bigwedge j(Nn \wedge Ni \wedge Nj \wedge J(n, i)\eta x \wedge$

$J(n, j)\eta x \rightarrow i = j)]$.

A real number x represents an infinite sequence of infinite sequences of natural numbers just in case it represents a function which is defined for all pairs $J(i,j)$, where i,j are natural numbers; and the ith term of the jth sequence represented by x is the unique number n such that the pair $J(J(i,j), n)$ is a member of the class represented by x:

(21) $Rx \rightarrow [x$ is seq of seq $\leftrightarrow x$ is fun $\wedge$ $\wedge i \wedge j (Ni \wedge Nj \rightarrow$

$$Vn[Nn \wedge J(J(i,j), n)\eta x])]$$

(22) $Rx \wedge x$ is seq of seq $\wedge Ni \wedge Nj \rightarrow [n = T(i,j,x) \leftrightarrow$

$$Nn \wedge J(J(i,j), n)\eta x].$$

We may represent each infinite sequence S of real numbers as a real number in the following way. First, we represent each real number y in the sequence by that sequence of natural numbers whose 0th term is 0 or 1 according as y is negative or not, whose 1st term is the integral part of $|y|$, and whose remaining terms constitute the digits in the decimal part of $|y|$. Finally, we represent S by that real number which represents the sequence of those sequences of natural numbers which represent the terms of S.

(23) $Rx \rightarrow [x$ is seq of reals $\leftrightarrow x$ is seq of seq $\wedge$

$$\wedge j(Nj \rightarrow [T(0, j, x) = 0 \vee T(0, j, x) = 1] \wedge$$

$$0 \leqslant T(1, j, x) \wedge \wedge i[Ni \wedge 2 \leqslant i \rightarrow 0 \leqslant T(i, j, x) \wedge T(i, j, x) \leq 9]$$

$$\wedge \sim Vi_0[Ni_0 \wedge \wedge i(Ni \wedge i_0 \leqslant i \rightarrow T(i, j, x) = 9)])].$$

(The last clause is required because without it certain real numbers would have two distinct sequential representations; for instance, the number 1 would correspond both to $\langle 1, 1, 0, 0, 0, \ldots \rangle$ and to $\langle 1, 0, 9, 9, 9, \ldots \rangle$.) If x represents an infinite sequence of real numbers, we may characterize as follows the decimal part of the absolute value of the jth term of the sequence represented by x:

(24) $Rx \wedge x$ is seq of reals $\wedge Nj \rightarrow [y = \text{Dec}(j, x) \leftrightarrow Ry \wedge$
$$0 \leqslant y \wedge y < 1 \wedge \wedge n(Nn \rightarrow D_n(y) = T(n + 2, j, x))].$$

The jth term of the infinite sequence of real numbers represented by x:

(25) $Rx \wedge x$ is seq of reals $\wedge Nj \to [z = (x)_j \leftrightarrow (T(0, j, x) = 1 \wedge$
$$z = T(1, j, x) + \mathrm{Dec}\,(j, x)) \vee (T(0, j, x) = 0 \wedge$$
$$z = 0 - (T(1, j, x) + \mathrm{Dec}\,(j, x)))].$$

Kinematical axioms and definitions

In the following axioms, α is to denote the number of particles, p_n the nth particle and P the class of particles. Axiom (27) is purely definitional. Axioms (26) and (27) jointly imply that the class of particles is finite, and in fact has α elements.

(26) $N\alpha \wedge 0 < \alpha \wedge \Lambda i \Lambda j [Ni \wedge Nj \wedge i < \alpha \wedge j < \alpha \wedge p_i = p_j \to i = j]$

(27) $Px \leftrightarrow Vn[Nn \wedge n < \alpha \wedge x = p_n]$.

The terms $s(x, t)$, $v(x, t)$, and $a(x, t)$ are to denote respectively the position, the velocity and the acceleration of the particle x at the instant t. Axioms (29) and (30) serve to define v and a as the first and second derivatives, respectively, of s. These axioms are not, however, purely definitional; in addition, they imply the existence of $d/dt\, s(x, t)$ and $d^2/dt^2\, s(x, t)$, for each particle x and each real real number t.

(28) $Px \wedge Rt \to Rs(x, t)$

(29) $Px \wedge Rt \to \left[z = v(x, t) \leftrightarrow Rz \wedge \Lambda e \left(Re \wedge 0 < e \to \right.\right.$
$$Vd \left[Rd \wedge 0 < d \wedge \Lambda h \left(Rh \wedge 0 < |h| \wedge |h| < d \to \right.\right.$$
$$\left.\left.\left.\left. \left| \frac{s(x, t + h) - s(x, t)}{h} - z \right| < e \right) \right] \right) \right]$$

(30) $Px \wedge Rt \to \left[z = a(x, t) \leftrightarrow Rz \wedge \Lambda e \left(Re \wedge 0 < e \to \right.\right.$
$$Vd \left[Rd \wedge 0 < d \wedge \Lambda h \left(Rh \wedge 0 < |h| \wedge |h| < d \to \right.\right.$$
$$\left.\left.\left.\left. \left| \frac{v(x, t + h) - v(x, t)}{h} - z \right| < e \right) \right] \right) \right]$$

Dynamical axioms and definitions

In the following axioms, $f(x, y, t)$ is to be the force exerted by the particle x on the particle y at the instant t, and $m(x, t)$ is to be the mass of x at t. We might equally well have used (as is more customary) a one-place operation symbol for the mass of a particle, since according to Axiom (32) mass is constant in time. The convenience of the present procedure is that it maintains a certain grammatical uniformity among the elementary constants of *PM*.

(31) $Px \wedge Py \wedge Rt \rightarrow Rm(x, t) \wedge 0 < m(x, t) \wedge Rf(x, y, t)$

(32) $Px \wedge Rs \wedge Rt \rightarrow m(x, s) = m(x, t)$.

Axiom (33) is a definition of the net force operating on a particle x at an instant t. It turns out that $nf(x, t) = \sum_{n=0}^{a-1} f(p_n, x, t)$. This equality is not, however, available to us as a definition, because it involves the variable-binding operator 'Σ'. We must approach the net force circuitously, using the apparatus introduced above for the representation of sequences of real numbers.

(33) $Px \wedge Rt \rightarrow [z = nf(x, t) \leftrightarrow Vs(Rs \wedge s$ is seq of reals $\wedge$

$(s)_{a-1} = z \wedge (s)_0 = f(p_0, x, t) \wedge \wedge i[Ni \wedge i < \alpha - 1 \rightarrow$

$(s)_{i+1} = (s)_1 + f(p_{i+1}, x, t)])]$.

The next axiom is Newton's Second Law of Motion, which asserts that the net force operating on a particle is equal to the mass of the particle multiplied by its acceleration. It will be noticed that one component of the net force operating on x is the force exerted by x on itself, which need not be 0. In this way we accommodate the possibility of forces external to the system; all the external forces operating on x at t may be incorporated into $f(x, x, t)$. To say that the system of particles is *closed* then amounts to saying that, for each particle x and real number t, $(f(x, x, t) = 0$.

(34) $Px \wedge Rt \rightarrow nf(x, t) = m(x, t) \cdot a(x, t)$.

The final axiom is Newton's Third Law of Motion. (The First Law is, of course, superfluous.)

(35) $Px \wedge Py \wedge Rt \wedge \sim x = y \rightarrow f(x, y, t) = 0 - f(y, x, t)$.

The *elementary constants of* Newtonian celestial mechanics, or *CM*, are (in standard order) P, m, g, s, v; the only new constant is g, which is a two-place operation symbol. The *abstract constants* comprise those of *PM*, together with f. The axioms of *CM* are (1)–(35), together with the following three.

Gravitational axioms

In the following axiom, $g(x, t)$ is the gravitational constant for the particle x at the instant t. By Axiom (37) the value of $g(x, t)$ depends neither on x nor on t. Consequently, we could have introduced an individual constant rather than a two-place operation symbol; but, as in the case of the symbol for mass, the present choice has the advantage of maintaining a certain grammatical uniformity.

(36) $Px \wedge Rt \to Rg(x, t) \wedge 0 < g(x, t)$

(37) $Pw \wedge Px \wedge Rs \wedge Rt \to g(w, s) = g(x, t).$

Axiom (38) is Newton's Law of Gravitation, according to which the magnitude of the force exerted by one celestial particle on another is directly proportional to the product of the masses of the two particles and inversely proportional to the square of the distance between them. In the following formulation, $|d| \cdot d$ replaces d^2; this serves to indicate the direction of the gravitational force. By our definition of division, $z/0 = 0$; thus Axiom (38) implies that $f(x, x, t) = 0$, for each particle x and real number t. It is easy to see that (38) renders (35) superfluous.

(38) $Px \wedge Py \wedge Rt \to f(x, y, t) = g(x, t) \cdot$
$$\frac{m(x, t) \cdot m(y, t)}{|s(x, t) - s(y, t)| \cdot (s(x, t) - s(y, t))}.$$

It is not difficult to adapt *PM* and *CM* to space of more than one dimension. For example, in the case of three dimensions, we would replace the constant s by three constants, s_1, s_2 and s_3, representing positions with respect to each of three Cartesian axes and we would similarly replace each of the constants v, a, and f by three counterparts, representing the components of velocity, acceleration and force with respect to each of the three axes. Concomitant changes would, of course, be required in the axioms.

Now let us consider what sort of *histories* (in the sense of Section 2) correspond to the language of CM. If S is such a history, S will have the form $\langle P, m, g, s, v \rangle$, where P is a class and m, g, s, v are functions of two arguments which are defined at least for all real numbers and for the elements of P. We may regard P as a set of particles, and $m(x, t)$ as giving the mass of the particle x, $g(x, t)$ the gravitational constant, and $s(x, t)$ and $v(x, t)$ the position and velocity respectively of the particle x at the instant t. Thus the system S provides a complete *history* of the class P with respect to the state-variables m, g, s, and v, in the sense that S determines the value of each of these state-variables for every member of P at every possible instant. But this history may be very erratic indeed. It may not be a *physically possible* history, in any plausible sense of the term.

Suppose, however, that the system S *realizes* the theory CM. Then the history provided by S is compatible with Newtonian celestial mechanics, in the sense that *some* interpretation[15] can be found for the abstract constants of CM such that the axioms of CM are true when their abstract constants receive this interpretation and their elementary constants receive the interpretation supplied by S. It is useful in this case to regard S as a *physically possible history* (with respect to CM) of the class P.

4. NOTIONS OF DETERMINISM

Let us for the moment restrict our attention to a language $\langle \langle \varepsilon_1, \ldots, \varepsilon_k, \ldots \rangle, \langle \delta_1, \ldots, \delta_n \rangle \rangle$, whose elementary constants $\delta_1, \ldots, \delta_n$ are one-place operation symbols. When *models* and *histories* are mentioned, we shall have in mind models of this language and the partial models corresponding to them. Thus, for the present, a history will have the form $\langle D_1, \ldots, D_n \rangle$, where $D_1, \ldots, D_n$ are functions of one argument and are defined at least for all real numbers. We may regard such a sequence as providing a history with respect to certain state-variables whose only

---

[15] Subject only to the restrictions involved in the definition of a standard model.

argument is time. For instance, we might have in mind a structure consisting of n particles, and construe $D_i(t)$ (for $i = 1, \ldots, n$ and $t \in R$) as the position of the ith particle at the instant t. As another example, we may consider statistical learning theory[16] and construe $D_1(t), \ldots, D_k(t)$ as the probabilities of certain responses at time t, and $D_{k+1}(t), \ldots, D_n(t)$ as the probabilities, at time t, of certain reinforcing events. This example, if pursued through the definitions of the present section, would indicate that a theory possessing state-variables of an exclusively statistical character is not prevented by that fact alone from being deterministic.[17]

Let $S = \langle D_1, \ldots, D_n \rangle$, and let S be a history. Since S is a history of a certain structure, it is natural to be concerned with the state of that structure, according to S, at an arbitrary instant t. The relevant notion, what we shall call the *state of S at t*, or $st_s(t)$, is defined as follows, for any $t \in R$:

$$st_S(t) = \langle D_1(t), \ldots, D_n(t) \rangle.$$

It is now an easy matter, in the present special case, to analyse the notion of determinism discussed in Section 1. A theory with this property is such that, if we restrict our attention to those histories which are possible in the light of the theory, a given state will uniquely determine all *later* states; I call the property *futuristic determinism*.

Definition 1. A theory T (whose language is the given language $\langle\langle \varepsilon_1, \ldots, \varepsilon_k \rangle, \langle \delta_1, \ldots, \delta_n \rangle\rangle$) is *futuristically deterministic* just in case the following condition holds, for all S, S', t_0, and t:

If S, $S' \in Rl(T)$, t_0, $t \in R$,

$t_0 < t$, and $st_S(t_0) = st_{S'}(t_0)$,

then $st_S(t) = st_{S'}(t)$.

We may also consider a notion of *historical determinism*, according to which a given state uniquely determines all *earlier*

---

[16] In, for example, the formulation of Estes and Suppes [9].
[17] The same point has been made in Nagel [20].

states; such a notion would be appropriate in connection with such disciplines as archaeology.

Definition 2. A theory T (whose language is our given language) is *historically deterministic* just in case the following condition holds, for all S, S', t_c, and t:

If S, $S' \in Rl(T)$, t_0, $t \in R$,

$t < t_0$, and $st_S(t_0) = st_{S'}(t_0)$,

then $st_S(t) = st^{S'}(t)$.

A theory is (simply) *deterministic* if it is both futuristically and historically deterministic, that is, if the determination of states proceeds in both temporal directions.

Definition 3. A theory T (whose language is our given language) is *deterministic* just in case the following condition holds, for all S, S', t_0, and t:

If S, $S' \in Rl(T)$, t_0, $t \in R$, and $st_S(t_0) = st_{S'}(t_0)$, then

$$st_S(t) = st_{S'}(t).$$

Besides notions of categorical determinism, we may consider a kind of *conditional determinism*, according to which, if we are given not only an initial state but also the complete history of certain of the state variables, then the complete history of the remaining state variables is determined. In such a case, I shall say that the theory is *deterministic in* the given state-variables. It is perhaps this notion which psychologists have in mind when they speak of theories in which some variables (for instance, the stimulus-variable) are *independent* and others (for instance, the response-variable) are *dependent*. In our terminology, such theories will have as state-variables the combination of dependent and independent variables and will be *deterministic in* the independent variables. For convenience, I shall suppose in the following definition that, among $\delta_1, \ldots, \delta_n$, the "independent" state-variables are listed first, that is, are $\delta_1, \ldots, \delta_k$, for some $k < n$.

Definition 4.[18]   Let k be a natural number less than n. Then a theory T (whose language is our given language) is *deterministic in* $\delta_1, \ldots, \delta_k$ just in case the following condition holds, for all $S, S', D_1, \ldots, D_n, D'_1, \ldots, D'_n, t_0$, and t:

If $S, S' \in Rl(T)$, $S = \langle D_1, \ldots, D_n \rangle$,

$S' = \langle D'_1, \ldots, D'_n \rangle$, $D_1 = D'_1, \ldots,$

$D_k = D'_k$, $t_0, t \in \mathbf{R}$, and

$st_S(t_0) = st_{S'}(t_0)$, then $st_S(t) = st_{S'}(t)$.

It is obvious how to construct definitions of "futuristically deterministic in" and 'historically deterministic in', corresponding to Definitions 1 and 2.

Another notion, a kind of *partial determinism*, is sometimes important, particularly in connection with discussions of computability. Suppose that we wish to devise a theory which will describe the behavior of a calculating machine, and that we choose the state-variables δ_1 (which describes the internal state of the machine), δ_2 and δ_3 (which give the input), and δ_4 and δ_5 (which give the output).

We shall not wish to predict the values of δ_2 and δ_3, because these are imagined to be under the control of the operator of the machine. Nor is it necessary to predict the values of δ_1, for our interest lies only in the output or "answers" to the questions posed by the input, and the output is reported by δ_4 and δ_5. must, however, be given initial values of δ_1, δ_2, and δ_3 in order to predict later values of δ_4 and δ_5; thus δ_1, δ_2, and δ_3 cannot be entirely ignored.

Further, we should not expect to predict outputs on the basis of an *arbitrary* initial state. Instead, we should distinguish certain states as *active*, or as corresponding to the asking of a question,

---

[18] McKinsey, Sugar and Suppes in [17] rather indirectly suggest a definition of 'deterministic in' which is related to the present definition. Their suggestion is implicit in Theorem 2, p. 263, of [17]. The notion, however, which these authors seem to have in mind applies not to theories but, essentially, to classes of models. In particular, the authors consider the class of all *n-dimensional systems of particle mechanics*, in the sense which is explicated in their paper. General notions of determinism as applied to classes of models or histories seem to be of rather restricted interest. One such notion, however, will play a part in Section 5.

and expect to make predictions on the basis of active states alone. Otherwise the following situation might arise. Three states, S_1, S_2, and S_3, might occur in the order listed, such that S_1 is inactive, S_2 is active and the output of S_3 reports the answer to the question posed in S_2. If we could make predictions on the basis of inactive states, then we could predict the output in S_3 on the basis of S_1; but this output "depends on" the input in S_2, which is under the control of the operator and presumably not predictable on the basis of S_1.

In addition, we should not expect to predict *all* outputs subsequent to a given active state, but only those outputs leading up to the answer to the question posed in the given state. If the period of predictability extended further, we should again be predicting outputs which "depended" on later, unpredictable inputs. Thus we should distinguish certain states as *quiescent*, or as corresponding to the answering of a question, and expect to predict outputs on the basis of an active state only until a quiescent state is reached.

In constructing a definition of partial determinism, it is convenient to suppose that the state-variables $\delta_1, \ldots, \delta_n$ take only real numbers as values. Then a *state* will always be an n-tuple of real numbers. In the following definition, we regard A as the class of *active* states and Q as the class of *quiescent* states. For convenience, we suppose that the output variables are listed last among $\delta_1, \ldots, \delta_n$, and are indeed $\delta_{k+1}, \ldots, \delta_n$, for $k < n$.

Definition 5. Let k be a natural number less than n, and let A and Q be classes of n-tuples of real numbers. Then a theory T (whose language is our given language) is *partially deterministic* with respect to A, Q, and $\delta_{k+1}, \ldots, \delta_n$ just in case, for all S, S', $D_1, \ldots, D_n$, $D'_1, \ldots, D'_n$, t_0, and t, if the following conditions hold:

(i) $S, S' \in Rl(T)$,

(ii) $S = \langle D_1, \ldots, D_n \rangle$ and $S' = \langle D'_1, \ldots, D'_n \rangle$,

(iii) t_0, t are real numbers such that $t_0 < t$,

(iv) $st_S(t_0) = st_{S'}(t_0)$,

(v) $st_S(t_0) \in A$, and

(vi) for all real numbers t' such that $t_0 \leqslant t' < t$, either $st_S(t') \in Q$ or $st_{S'}(t') \in Q$, then the following equalities hold:

$$D_{k+1}(t) = D'_{k+1}(t),$$

.

.

.

$$D_n(t) = D'_n(t).$$

The preceding notions apply always to theories. We may also be interested in inquiring whether a certain *history*, for instance, the actual history of the universe, is deterministic. One notion is roughly the following. A *history* may be called *deterministic* if there is a deterministic theory which correctly describes it.

Definition 6. A *history S* (corresponding to our given language) is *deterministic* just in case there is a deterministic theory T such that $S \in Rl(T)$.

(Note that we do not require the language of T to be our given language $\langle\langle\varepsilon_1, \ldots, \varepsilon_k, \ldots\rangle, \langle\delta_1, \ldots, \delta_n\rangle\rangle$. The condition that $S \in Rl(T)$ implies only that T have exactly n elementary constants, all of which must be one-place operation symbols; for such theories T, the meaning of the assertion 'T is deterministic' is specified by Definition 3.)

Alternative definitions will immediately occur to the logician. In particular, we may impose on T the requirement that it be *recursively axiomatizable* or, more stringently, *finitely axiomatizable*.[19] The corresponding notions, whose interrelations, and relations with the notion of Definition 6, have not yet been investigated, I call respectively determinism$_R$ and determinism$_F$.

Definition 7. A *history S is deterministic$_R$* (*deterministic$_F$*) just in case there is a recursively axiomatizable (finitely axiomatizable) theory T such that $S \in Rl(T)$ and T is deterministic.

Counterparts to Definitions 1, 2, 4 and 5, involving histories rather than theories, are easy to construct.

---

[19] For the notions of recursive axiomatizability and finite axiomatizability, see Tarski, Mostowski, and Robinson [27].

Bertrand Russell has investigated, unsuccessfully, the notion of a deterministic history.[20] He considers essentially the following definition: A history S is "deterministic" if there is a function f such that, for any instants t_0 and t, we have:

$$st_S(t) = f(st_S(t_0), t_0, t).$$

This definition is inadequate, as Russell clearly points,[21] because it implies that *every* history is deterministic.[22] To amend the definition, Russell adds, we must impose some special condition on the function f; he arrives, however, at no adequate suggestion. The present treatment amounts, loosely speaking, to the requirement that the function f be capable of description by a theory (or, more stringently, by a recursively axiomatizable or finitely axiomatizable theory).

Having mentioned various notions of determinism, I shall proceed, in the balance of this paper, to ignore the greater part of them. In particular, when extending notions and proving theorems, I shall consider only "deterministic" and "deterministic in," that is, the notions introduced by Definitions 3, 4 and 6. It is clear that similar extensions and theorems could be devised for the other notions.

It is time now to extend our purview to languages of a more complex structure. In particular, let us shift our attention to a language $\langle\langle \varepsilon_1, \ldots, \varepsilon_k \rangle, \langle \pi, \delta_1, \ldots, \delta_n \rangle\rangle$, where π is a one-place predicate and $\delta_1, \ldots, \delta_n$ are two-place operation symbols. (The language of CM, for instance, satisfies this description.) A history will now have the form $\langle C, D_1, \ldots, D_n \rangle$, where C is a class and $D_1, \ldots, D_n$ are functions of two arguments, defined at least for all real numbers and all elements of C. We may regard C as the class of objects whose history is provided, and $D_1, \ldots, D_n$ as the histories of the state-variables $\delta_1, \ldots, \delta_n$ for the elements of C.

---

[20] In Russell [22].

[21] In the same selection, a few paragraphs later.

[22] The definition given by Russell is discussed at some length in Scriven [23]. Scriven too arrives at the conclusion that the definition is inadequate, but for reasons which are not clearly comprehensible to me. Scriven seems unaware that Russell has already arrived at this conclusion and for quite cogent reasons.

Suppose that $S = \langle C, D_1, \ldots, D_n \rangle$, S is a history, and $t \in R$. The notion of the state of S at t must be somewhat altered. First we must define the *state of x at t according to S*, for any $x \in C$, as follows:

$$st_S(x, t) = \langle D_1(x, t), \ldots, D_n(x, t) \rangle.$$

Then the *state of S at t*, or $st_S(t)$, is that function F whose domain is C such that, for each $x \in C$, $F(x) = st_S(x, t)$.[23]

Keeping in mind the revised notion of state, we may adopt Definition 3 without change.

Definition 8. A theory T (formulated in the present language) is *deterministic* just in case the following condition holds for all S, S', t_0, and t:

If S, $S' \in Rl(T)$, t_0, $t \in R$, and

$st_S(t_0) = st_{S'}(t_0)$, then $st_{S'}(t) = st_{S'}(t)$.

Another, seemingly more stringent, definition rather naturally suggests itself. We might call a theory deterministic if, whenever we have two histories $\langle C, D_1, \ldots, D_n \rangle$ and $\langle C', D_1', \ldots, D_n' \rangle$ which realize it, together with a biunique correspondence between the elements of C and C' such that at a given instant t_0 each element of C has the same state (according to S) as the corresponding element of C' (according to S'), then also at any other instant t each element of C will have the same state as the corresponding element of C'. (This definition, by the way, is related to a quite beautiful definition of Carnap,[24] which is not, however, directly applicable to theories.) The following theorem asserts the equivalence, at least under a certain assumption, between this definition and our Definition 8.

Theorem 1. If T is a theory (formulated in the present language) such that $T \vdash \pi x \rightarrow \sim Rx$, then the following two conditions are equivalent:

(i) T is deterministic,

---

[23] Nagel [20], gives a similar definition of the state of a system. He identifies the state of S at t with the *set* of all individual states at t. but this proposal is clearly inadequate.

[24] See Carnap [1, 3, and 4].

(ii)   for all $S, S', C, C', D_1, \ldots, D_n, D'_1, \ldots, D'_n, f, t_0$, and t, if

(1) $S, S' \in Rl(T)$,

(2) $S = \langle C, D_1, \ldots, D_n \rangle$ and $S' = \langle C', D'_1, \ldots, D'_n \rangle$,

(3) $t_0, t \in \mathbf{R}$,

(4) $C \underset{f}{\approx} C'$, that is, f is a biunique correspondence between C and C', and

(5)   for all $x \in C$, $st_S(x, t_0) = st_{S'}(f(x), t_0)$,
       then, for all $x \in C$, $st_S(x, t) = st_{S'}(f(x), t)$.

Proof.[25]   Assume condition (i), together with (1)–(5). Then there are standard models M and M' such that

(6) $S = Pm(M), S' = Pm(M')$,

and

(7) T holds in both M and M'.

Now there are a set D and a function g such that

(8) $C \underset{g}{\approx} D$

and

(9) D is disjoint from the domains of discourse both of M and of M'.

By (8) and (9), there are models P and P', and functions h and h' such that

(10) $M \underset{h}{\cong} P$ (that is, h is an isomorphism between M and P),

(11) $M' \underset{h'}{\cong} P'$,

(12) $h(x) = g(x)$, for each $x \in C$

(13) $h(x) = x$, for each x in the domain of discourse of M but not in C

(14) $h'(x) = g(f^{-1}(x))$, for each $x \in C'$, and

---

[25] The proof involves some notions and methods from abstract algebra. For explanations see, for example, Tarski [26].

(15) $h'(x) = x$, for each x in the domain of discourse of M' but not in C'.

By (2), (6), (7), and the hypothesis of the theorem, C and R are disjoint; thus, by (10), (13), and the fact that M is a standard model,

(16) P is a standard model.

Similarly,

(17) P' is a standard model.

It is well known that if two models are isomorphic, then every formula which holds in one also holds in the other. Hence, by (10), (11) and (7),

(18) T holds in both P and P'.

Now $Pm(P)$ has the form $\langle D, E_1, \ldots, E_n \rangle$, and $Pm(P')$ the form $\langle D, E'_1, \ldots, E'_n \rangle$. I shall show that

(19) $st_{Pm(P)}(t_0) = st_{Pm(P')}(t_0)$.

It is sufficient to show, for $x \in D$ and $i = 1, \ldots, n$, that $E_i(x, t_0) = E'_i(x, t_0)$. In fact, by (10), (12), and (13), $E_i(x, t_0) = D_i(g^{-1}(x), t_0)$. Further, $E'_i(x, t_0) =$ (by (11), (14), and (15)) $D'_i((gf^{-1})^{-1}(x), t_0) = D'_i(f(g^{-1}(x)), t_0) =$ (by (5)) $D_i(g^{-1}(x), t_0)$. Thus $E_i(x, t_0) = E'_i(x, t_0)$, and (19) is established.

By (3), (16), (17), (18), (19), and condition (i), we have:

(20) $st_{Pm(P)}(t) = st_{Pm(P')}(t)$.

To show the conclusion of condition (ii), it is sufficient to show, for $x \in C$ and $i = 1, \ldots, n$, that

(21) $D_i(x, t) = D'_i(f(x), t)$.

Indeed, $D_i(x, t) =$ (by (10) and (12)) $E_i(g(x), t) =$ (by (20)) $E'_i(g(x), t)$ and $D'_i(f(x), t) =$ (by (11) and (14)) $E'_i(g(f^{-1}(f(x))), t) = E'_i(g(x), t)$. Thus (21) is established, and with it condition (ii).

The proof that condition (ii) implies condition (i) is obvious.

The extension of Definition 4 to our present language is immediate.

Definition 9. Let k be a natural number less than n. Then a theory T (formulated in the language presently under consideration) is *deterministic in* $\delta_1, \ldots, \delta_k$ just in case the following condition holds, for all $S, S', C, C', D_1, \ldots, D_n, D'_1, \ldots, D'_n, t_0$, and t:

If $S, S' \in Rl(T)$, $S = \langle C, D_1, \ldots, D_n \rangle$,

$S' = \langle C', D'_1, \ldots, D'_n \rangle$, $D_1 = D'_1, \ldots, D_k = D'_k$,

$t_0, t \in R$, and $st_S(t_0) = st_{S'}(t_0)$, then $st_S(t) = st_{S'}(t)$.

Let us now relax assumptions on our language. In particular, let us consider a language $\langle\langle \varepsilon_1, \ldots, \varepsilon_k, \ldots \rangle, \langle \pi, \delta_1, \ldots, \delta_n \rangle\rangle$, where π is a one-place predicate and $\delta_1, \ldots, \delta_n$ are operation symbols of arbitrary numbers of places. (In the case of *PM*, for example, we have four state-variables—f, which is of three places, and m, s, v, each of which is of two places.)

Suppose that S is a history (corresponding to our present language), $S = \langle C, D_1, \ldots, D_n \rangle$, and $t \in R$. We can no longer speak of the state at t of an individual element of C. Instead, if we let $r + 1$ be the maximum number of places of the operation symbols $\delta_1, \ldots, \delta_n$, we must speak of the state at t of r-tuples of elements of C. Thus we define the *state of* $x_1, \ldots x_r$ *at* t *according to* S, for any $x_1, \ldots, x_r \in C$, as follows:

$st_S(x_1, \ldots, x_r, t) =$
$$\langle D_1(x_1, \ldots, x_{r_1}, t), \ldots, D_n(x_1, \ldots, x_{r_n}, t) \rangle,$$

where $r_1 + 1, \ldots, r_n + 1$ are the numbers of places of $\delta_1, \ldots, \delta_n$ respectively. (In connection with *PM*, $st_S(x, y, t)$ would be a quadruple $\langle D_1(x, y, t), D_2(x, t), D_3(x, t), D_4(x, t) \rangle$, in which $D_1(x, y, t)$ would be regarded as the force exerted by x on y at t, and $D_2(x, t), D_3(x, t)$, and $D_4(x, t)$ would be regarded respectively as the mass, position and velocity of x at t.) Then the *state of the history* S *at* t, or $st_S(t)$, is that function F whose domain is the set of all r-tuples of elements of C and which, for any such r-tuple $\langle x_1, \ldots, x_r \rangle$, satisfies the equality:

$F(x_1, \ldots, x_r) = st_S(x_1, \ldots, x_r, t)$.

Given this extended notion of the state of a system, the earlier definitions may be applied without change to our new language.

(The extended counterpart of Definition 6 indicates how to assign a precise sense to the question whether *the world* is deterministic (with respect to certain state-variables). Suppose, for instance, that we are interested in the state-variables of CM. Let C be the class of all particles, and, for each particle x and real number t, let $M(x, t)$, $G(x, t)$, $S(x, t)$ and $V(x, t)$ be respectively the mass of x, the gravitational constant, the position of x at t, and the velocity of x at t. Then to say that *the world* is deterministic with respect to (mass, the gravitational constant), position and velocity is to that the *history* $\langle C, M, G, S, V \rangle$ (that is, the actual history of the world in terms of the selected state-variables) is deterministic. (This example has been somewhat simplified by the fictitious assumption that the universe has only one spatial dimension.) Note, however, that in order to formulate the assertion that the world is deterministic, we must transcend the methodological standpoint indicated in the introduction to this paper. In particular, to specify the history $\langle C, M, G, S, V \rangle$, we have used the notions "particle", "mass", "gravitational constant", "position" and "velocity", none of which are available in metamathematics. But the necessary extension of our methodological standpoint is clear: we should need only to supplement metamathematics by the introduction of certain "empirical" notions; in fact, the notions listed above would suffice. Within such an extension of metamathematics, the assertion that the world is deterministic would possess a completely precise formulation.

We may now ask whether classical particle mechanics is deterministic, as is sometimes alleged. According to the following theorem, whose proof is too obvious to be included, the answer is negative.

Theorem 2.   PM is not deterministic.

Some authors[26] make the more cautious assertion that classical particle mechanics becomes deterministic once the force-function is specified. This can be understood in the sense of the following theorem.[27]

---

[26] For instance, Nagel [20].

[27] A theorem with very closely related constants has been stated by McKinsey, Sugar and Suppes [17], as Theorem 2.

Theorem 3. PM is deterministic in f.

Proof. Assume that $P, P' \in Rl(PM)$, $P = \langle C, F, M, S, V \rangle$, $P' = \langle C', F', M', S', V' \rangle$, $F = F'$, $t_0, t \in \mathbf{R}$, and

(1) $st_P(t_0) = st_{P'}(t_0)$.

By (1), $C = C'$; thus, in order to show that

(2) $st_P(t) = st_{P'}(t)$,

it is sufficient to show that, for each $x \in C$, $M(x, t) = M'(x, t)$, $S(x, t) = S'(x, t)$, and $V(x, t) = V'(x, t)$. Suppose, then, that $x \in C$. Now there are models R, R' such that

(3) R and R' are standard models,

(4) PM holds in both R and R',

(5) $P = Pm(R)$, and $P' = Pm(R')$.

By (3), (4), and (5), keeping in mind Axiom (32) of PM, we see that $M(x, t) = M(x, t_0)$ and $M'(x, t) = M'(x, t_0)$, for all $t \in \mathbf{R}$. Hence, by (1), we obtain:

(6) $M(x, t) = M'(x, t)$, for all $t \in \mathbf{R}$.

Now let N and N' be the interpretations, according to R and R' respectively, of the two-place operation symbol nf. By (3), (4) (referring to Axiom (33)), (5), and the fact that $F = F'$, we have:

(7) $N(x, t) = N'(x, t)$, for all $t \in \mathbf{R}$.

Let A and A' be the interpretations, according to R and R' respectively of the operation symbol a. Referring to Axiom (34), we see that $N(x, t) = M(x, t) \cdot A(x, t)$ and $N'(x, t) = M'(x, t) \cdot A'(x, t)$. Hence, by (6) and (7), together with Axiom (31), which guarantees that $M(x, t) > 0$,

(8) $A(x, t) = A'(x, t)$, for all $t \in \mathbf{R}$.

On the basis of Axiom (30), we see that V is everywhere differentiable with respect to its second argument, and that $d/dt\, V(x, t) = A(x, t)$. Hence, by the Fundamental Theorem of the Integral

Calculus,[28]

$$\int_{t_0}^{t} A(x, t)\, dt = V(x, t) - V(x, t_0).$$

Similarly,

$$\int_{t_0}^{t} A'(x, t)\, dt = V'(x, t) - V'(x, t_0).$$

Thus, by (1) and (8),

(9) $V(x, t) = V'(x, t).$

By an analogous method, referring this time to Axiom (29), we obtain:

(10) $S(x, t) = S'(x, t).$

By (6), (9), and (10), (2) is established, and with it the theorem.

Newton's Law of Gravitation affords one way of specifying the force-function of mechanics. Thus we might expect Newtonian celestial mechanics to be deterministic, and indeed this is often asserted to be the case. I am unable to say whether the assertion is true; I can only reduce the question to a straightforward problem in the theory of differential equations.

Theorem 4.   *CM* is deterministic if and only if, for all positive integers n, all real numbers $d_0, \ldots, d_{n-1}, e_0, \ldots, e_{n-1}, t_0$, and all positive real numbers $c_0, \ldots, c_{n-1}$, there is at most one n-tuple $\langle S_0, \ldots, S_{n-1} \rangle$ of functions on and to real numbers such that, for all $t \in R$ and $i = 0, \ldots, n - 1$, the following conditions hold:

(i) $\dfrac{d^2}{dt^2} S_i(t)$ exists,

(ii) $\dfrac{d^2}{dt^2} S_i(t) = \displaystyle\sum_{\substack{j=0 \\ j \neq i}}^{n-1} \dfrac{c_j}{|S_j(t) - S_i(t)| \cdot (S_j(t) - S_i(t))}$

(iii) $S_i(t_0) = d_i$

(iv) $\dfrac{d}{dt} S_i(t)|_{t = t_0} = e_i$

[28] See, for example, Landau [15].

Proof. Let us assume first the uniqueness property expressed in the theorem and show that CM is deterministic.

Suppose, then, that $P, P' \in Rl(CM)$, $P = \langle C, M, G, S, V \rangle$, $P' = \langle C', M', G', S', V' \rangle$, $t_0 \in R$, and

(1) $st_P(t_0) = st_{P'}(t_0)$.

Now there are standard models R, R' such that CM holds in both R and R', $P = Pm(R)$, and $P' = Pm(R')$. By (1), $C = C'$; thus, in order to show that

(2) $st_P(t) = st_{P'}, (t)$, for each $t \in R$,

it is sufficient to show that, for each $x \in C$ and $t \in R$,

(3) $M(x, t) = M'(x, t)$,

(4) $G(x, t) = G'(x, t)$,

(5) $V(x, t) = V'(x, t)$,

and

(6) $S(x, t) = S'(x, t)$.

But (3) and (4) are immediate, on the basis of (1), Axioms (32) and (37), and the fact that CM holds in both R and R'. Further, (5) follows from (6) on the basis of Axiom (29) and the fact that R, R' are standard models. It remains only to show (6).

In view of Axioms (26) and (27), there are a positive integer n and objects $x_0, \ldots, x_{n-1}$ such that $C = \{x_0, \ldots, x_{n-1}\}$.[29] By Axioms (29), (30), (33), (34), and (38), we have for each $t \in R$ and $i = 0, \ldots, n - 1$:

$$M(x_i, t) \cdot \frac{d^2}{dt^2} S(x_i, t)$$

$$= \sum_{j=0}^{n-1} \frac{G(x_j, t) \cdot M(x_j, t) \cdot M(x_i, t)}{|S(x_j, t) - S(x_i, t)| \cdot (S(x_j, t) - S(x_i, t))}$$

$$= \sum_{\substack{j=0 \\ j \neq i}}^{n-1} \frac{G(x_j, t) \cdot M(x_j, t) \cdot M(x_i, t)}{|S(x_j, t) - S(x_i, t)| \cdot (S(x_j, t) - S(x_i, t))}$$

[29] I denote thus the set whose only elements are $x_0, \ldots, x_{n-1}$.

Dividing by $M(x_i, t)$ (which we may do, since by Axiom (31) $M(x_i, t) \neq 0$) and setting $S_i(t) = S(x_i, t)$, we obtain (for each $t \in R$ and $i = 0, \ldots, n - 1$):

(7) $\quad \dfrac{d^2}{dt^2} S_i(t) = \displaystyle\sum_{\substack{j=0 \\ j \neq i}}^{n-1} \dfrac{G(x_j, t) \cdot M(x_j, t)}{|S_j(t) - S_i(t)| \cdot (S_j(t) - S_i(t))}.$

By Axioms (32) and (37), the products $G(x_j, t) \cdot M(x_j, t)$ are constant in time, and by Axioms (31) and (36), they are all positive; that is, there are positive real numbers $c_0, \ldots, c_{n-1}$ such that, for each $t \in R$ and $j = 0, \ldots, n - 1$,

(8) $\quad G(x_j, t) \cdot M(x_j, t) = c_j.$

Hence, by (7), we have (for each $t \in R$ and $i = 0, \ldots, n - 1$):

(9) $\quad \dfrac{d^2}{dt^2} S_i(t) = \displaystyle\sum_{\substack{j=0 \\ j \neq i}}^{n-1} \dfrac{c_j}{|S_j(t) - S_i(t)| \cdot (S_j(t) - S_i(t))}.$

By Axioms (29) and (30),

(10) $\quad \dfrac{d^2}{dt^2} S_i(t)$ exists (for each $t \in R$ and $i = 0, \ldots, n - 1$).

Let $d_0, \ldots, d_{n-1}$, $e_0, \ldots, e_{n-1}$, be numbers such that, for $i = 0, \ldots, n - 1$,

(11) $\quad S_i(t_0) = d_i,$

and

(12) $\quad \dfrac{d}{dt} S_i(t)|_{t=t_0} = V(x_i, t_0) = e_i.$

Now we turn to the system P'. Again referring to Axioms (31), (32), (36), and (37), we see that there are positive real numbers $c'_0, \ldots, c'_{n-1}$ such that, for each $t \in R$ and $j = 0, \ldots, n - 1$,

(13) $\quad G'(x_j, t) \cdot M'(x_j, t) = c'_j.$

Let us set $S'_i(t) = S'_i(x_i, t)$, for $t \in R$ and $i = 0, \ldots, n - 1$. By the procedure which led to (9), we obtain (for each $t \in R$ and

$i = 0, \ldots, n - 1)$:

(14) $\quad \dfrac{d^2}{dt^2} S_i'(t) = \displaystyle\sum_{\substack{j=0 \\ j \neq i}}^{n-1} \dfrac{c_j'}{|S_j'(t) - S_i'(t)| \cdot (S_j'(t) - S_i'(t))} \cdot$

But by (1), (8), and (13),

$\quad c_j = c_j'$

for $j = 0, \ldots, n - 1$. Hence, by (14),

(15) $\quad \dfrac{d^2}{dt^2} S_i'(t) = \displaystyle\sum_{\substack{j=0 \\ j \neq i}}^{n-1} \dfrac{c_j}{|S_j'(t) - S_i'(t)| \cdot (S_j'(t) - S_i'(t))},$

for each $t \in R$ and $i = 0, \ldots, n - 1$. Again, by Axioms (29) and (30),

(16) $\quad \dfrac{d^2}{dt^2} S_i'(t)$ exists (for each $t \in R$ and $i = 0, \ldots, n - 1$).

By (1) and (11),

(17) $\quad S_i'(t_0) = d_i,$

and by (1) and (12),

(18) $\quad \dfrac{d}{dt} S_i'(t)|_{t=t_0} = V'(x_i, t_0) = e_i,$

for $i = 0, \ldots, n - 1$. Applying our assumed uniqueness property, we obtain from (9)–(12) and (15)–(18) that $S_i = S_i'$, for $i = 0, \ldots, n - 1$. But from this, (6) follows, and with it the fact that CM is deterministic.

Assume, on the other hand, that CM is deterministic, $d_0, \ldots, d_{n-1}, e_0, \ldots, e_{n-1}, t_0$, are real numbers, $c_0, \ldots, c_{n-1}$ are positive real numbers, and that we have two n-tuples, $\langle S_0, \ldots, S_{n-1} \rangle$ and $\langle S_0', \ldots, S_{n-1}' \rangle$ (of functions on and to real numbers), which satisfy conditions (i)–(iv) for all $t \in R$ and $i = 0, \ldots, n - 1$. We must show that

(19) $\quad S_i = S_i'$, for $i = 0, \ldots, n - 1$.

Let $x_0, \ldots, x_{n-1}$ be arbitrary distinct objects,

(20) $C = \{x_0, \ldots, x_{n-1}\}$,

$\quad\quad G(x_j, t) = G'(x_j, t) = 1$,

(21) $M(x_j, t) = M'(x_j, t) = c_j$,

$\quad\quad S(x_j, t) = S_j(t)$,

$\quad\quad S'(x_j, t) = S'_j(t)$,

$\quad\quad V(x_j, t) = \dfrac{d}{dt} S_j(t)$,

$\quad\quad V'(x_j, t) = \dfrac{d}{dt} S'_j(t)$,

and let the domain of each of the functions G, G', M, M', S, S', V, V' be $C \cup R$ (that is, the union of C and R). It is then easy to verify that

(22) $\langle C, M, G, S, V \rangle, \langle C, M', G', S', V' \rangle \in Rl(CM)$.

By (20), (21), and conditions (iii) and (iv) (applied both to S_i and to S'_i), we see that

(23) $st_{\langle C,M,G,S,V \rangle}(t_0) = st_{\langle C',M',G',S',V' \rangle}(t_0)$.

By (22), (23), and the assumption that CM is deterministic,

$\quad\quad st_{\langle C,M,G,S,V \rangle}(t) = st_{\langle C,M',G',S',V' \rangle}(t)$, for all $t \in R$.

Hence $S_i(t) = S'_i(t)$, for all $t \in R$ and $i = 0, \ldots, n - 1$. But this implies (19), and the proof is complete.

5. PERIODICITY, RANDOMNESS, AND DETERMINISM

Throughout this section we shall have in mind a fixed language of one of the forms treated in Section 4; and the notions of history, state, and theory are to be understood as relativized to this language.

Determinism is sometimes associated with a property which we may call *periodicity*. We shall call a history S *periodic* if it satisfies the following description, which is due to Nagel (in [20, p. 421]):

"Suppose ... that at time t_0, S is in a state describable as P_0, Q_0, R_0, etc., that the state of S changes with time, and that at time t_1 S is in a state describable as P_1, Q_1, R_1, etc. Next imagine that S is brought back into the state it originally possessed at time t_0, that it is then permitted to change of its own accord .... After an interval $t_1 - t_0$ it once more exhibits the state describable as P_1, Q_1, R_1, that is, its state is once more what it was at time t_1." We have, accordingly, the following definition.[30]

Definition 10. A history S is *periodic* if and only if it satisfies the following condition, for all t_0, t_1, t_2, $t_3 \in R$:

If $st_S(t_2) = st_S(t_0)$ and $t_1 - t_0 = t_3 - t_2$, then $st_S(t_3) = st_S(t_1)$.

Nagel seems to suggest ([20, p. 422]) that periodicity is essential to determinism. Under our analysis, this is not the case. In fact, according to the following two theorems, there is no direct relation in either direction between determinism and periodicity.

Theorem 3. There are deterministic histories which are not periodic.

Proof. Let us for simplicity suppose that our fixed language contains only one elementary constant, a one-place operation symbol δ.

Let the function D be defined as follows, for all $t \in R$:

$$D(t) = \begin{cases} 0 \text{ if } t \in N \\ t \text{ if } t \notin N. \end{cases}$$

Let T be a theory whose only axiom is the formula

$$(Nt \wedge R\delta t \wedge \delta t + \delta t = \delta t) \vee (\sim Nt \wedge \delta t = t).$$

Then T is deterministic, and the history $\langle D \rangle \in Rl(T)$; hence $\langle D \rangle$ is deterministic. But $\langle D \rangle$ is clearly not periodic.

Theorem 6. There are periodic histories which are not deterministic.

---

[30] Nagel's description seems implicitly (because of such words as 'next', 'then') to refer to a notion of *futuristic periodicity*, which would correspond to futuristic determinism just as our notion of periodicity corresponds to determinism. It would be easy to construct a definition of futuristic periodicity by making slight changes in Definition 10.

Proof.   Again let us suppose that our fixed language contains only one elementary constant, a one-place operation symbol δ.

Let K be the class of all subsets of R of the power c (the power of the continuum), let L be the class of all subsets of the interval $[0, 1]$ (that is, the set of all real numbers x such that $0 \leqslant x \leqslant 1$), and let F be the function whose domain is K such that, for each $A \in K$, $F(A) = A \cap [0, 1]$. (Here, "$\cap$" is the symbol for the *intersection*, or *meet*, of two classes). For each $B \in L$, there is an $A \in K$ such that $F(A) = B$; thus the range of F is L. It follows that the cardinal number of K is at least as great as the cardinal number of L. But the latter cardinal is known to be 2^c.

Let M be the class of biunique functions whose domain is R and whose range is included in R. Now every member of K can be represented as the range of some function in M. Thus the cardinal of M is at least the cardinal of K, and hence is at least 2^c. But for each $D \in M$, the history $\langle D \rangle$ is periodic. Therefore

(1)   there are at least 2^c periodic histories $\langle D \rangle$ such that the domain of D is R and the range of D is included in R.

(It can easily be shown that there are also at most 2^c such histories, but this is unimportant for our present purposes.)

As a result of the definition of a deterministic theory, we observe that, for any deterministic theory T and any real number x, there is at most one history $\langle D \rangle$ such that the domain of D is R and the range of D is included in R, and which *corresponds to* $\langle T, x \rangle$ in the sense that $\langle D \rangle \in Rl(T)$ and $D(0) = x$. But every deterministic history $\langle D \rangle$ such that the domain of D is R and the range of D is included in R can be represented as the history corresponding to some pair $\langle T, x \rangle$, where T is a deterministic theory and $x \in R$. Thus the number of such histories is at most the number of such pairs, which in turn is at most the number of pairs $\langle T, x \rangle$, where T is an *arbitrary* theory and $x \in R$. But the number of theories is known to be c, and the cardinal number of R is by definition c. Thus the number of pairs $\langle T, x \rangle$, where T is a theory and $x \in R$, is $c \cdot c$, that is, c. Hence

(2)   there are at most c deterministic histories $\langle D \rangle$ such that the domain of D is R and the range of D is included in R.

Comparing (1) and (2), and recalling that $c < 2^c$, we see that there are histories $\langle D \rangle$ such that the domain of D is R and the range of D is included in R, and which are periodic but not deterministic. This completes the proof of the theorem.

Although there is no direct connection between determinism and periodicity, there is a certain indirect relation between the two notions, and this relation is reported in Theorem 7 below. Two additional notions must be introduced. First, we shall wish to speak of an arbitrary *class K of histories* as deterministic. We then regard K as consisting of all *possible histories:* we do not demand, as in our earlier discussion, that K have the form $Rl(T)$, for some theory T. Secondly, we shall require the notion of a class of histories which is *closed under temporal projection,* that is, such that if a history S is in the class, then so is any other history obtained from S by a rigid transformation of temporal coordinates.

Definition 11. A class K of histories is *deterministic* just in case the following condition holds, for all S, S', t_0, and t:

If $S, S' \in K, t_0, t \in R$, and $st_S(t_0) = st_{S'}(t_0)$, then $st_S(t) = st_{S'}(t)$.

Definition 12. Let $d \in R$. If $S(= \langle D_1, \ldots, D_n \rangle)$ is a history corresponding to a language whose only elementary constants are one-place operation symbols, then the *temporal projection of S by the distance d* (in symbols, proj (S, d)) is the unique history $\langle D'_1, \ldots, D'_n \rangle$ such that

(1) the common domain of the functions $D'_1, \ldots, D'_n$ is the same as that of the functions $D_1, \ldots, D_n$,

(2) if t is any element of this domain which is not a real number, then $D'_i(t) = D_i(t)$, for $i = 1, \ldots, n$, and

(3) for each $t \in R$, $D'_i(t) = D_i(t - d)$, for $i = 1, \ldots, n$.

Similarly, if $S(= \langle C, D_1, \ldots, D_n \rangle)$ is a history corresponding to a language whose elementary constants are (in order) π, $\delta_1, \ldots, \delta_n$, where π is a one-place predicate and $\delta_1, \ldots, \delta_n$ are operation symbols of $r_1, \ldots, r_n$ places respectively, then proj (S, d) is the unique history $\langle C, D'_1, \ldots, D'_n \rangle$ such that

(1) the common domain of $D'_1, \ldots, D'_n$ is the same as that of $D_1, \ldots, D_n$,

(2) for each $i = 1, \ldots, n$, if $x_1, \ldots, x_{r_i}$ are any elements of this domain for which either $x_{r_i} \in R$ or one of $x_1, \ldots, x_{r_i-1}$ is not in C, then $D_i'(x_1, \ldots, x_{r_i}) = D_i(x_1, \ldots, x_{r_i})$, and

(3) if $x_1, \ldots, x_{r_i-1} \in C$ and $t \in R$, then $D_i'(x_1, \ldots, x_{r_i-1}, t) = D_i'(x_1, \ldots, x_{r_i-1}, i - d)$, for $i = 1, \ldots, n$.

Thus if $S' = \text{proj}(S, d)$, then $st_{S'}(t) = st_S(t - d)$, for each $t \in R$.

Definition 13. If K is a class of histories, then K is *closed under temporal projection* just in case the following condition holds, for all S and d:

If $S \in K$ and $d \in R$, then $\text{proj}(S, d) \in K$.

Theorem 7. A history S is periodic if and only if there is a deterministic class of histories which is closed under temporal projection and of which S is a member.

Proof. Assume first that S is periodic. Let K be the class of all temporal) projections of S, that is, the class of all histories of the form $\text{proj}(S, d)$, where $d \in R$. Then $S \in K$, and it is easily shown that K is both deterministic and closed under temporal projection.

Assume on the other hand that there is a deterministic class K of histories which is closed under temporal projection and of which S is a member. To show that S is periodic, assume that $t_0, t_1, t_2, t_3 \in R$, $st_S(t_2) = st_S(t_0)$, and $t_1 - t_0 = t_3 - t_2$. Let $d = t_0 - t_2$, and let $S' = \text{proj}(S, d)$. Then

$$st_{S'}(t_0) = st_S(t_0 - d) = st_S(t_2) = st_S(t_0).$$

Further, $S, S' \in K$. Hence, since K is a deterministic class, $st_{S'}(t_1) = st_S(t_1)$. But $st_{S'}(t_1) = st_S(t_1 - (t_0 - t_2)) = st_S(t_1 - t_0 + t_2) = st_S(t_3 - t_2 + t_2) = st_S(t_3)$. Thus $st_S(t_3) = st_S(t_1)$, and the proof that S is periodic is complete.

Scriven, in [23], considers a definition of determinism which we may paraphrase as follows: a history S is deterministic if none of the functions which it comprises exhibits a random sequence of values. Unfortunately, Scriven immediately dismisses this definition, on the grounds that the concept of randomness has never been adequately defined.

Indeed, during the early development of von Mises' theory of probability, the notion of a random sequence was attended by a number of difficulties.[31] To all appearances, however, the difficulties were definitely resolved in 1940 by Alonzo Church,[32] at least with respect to those infinite sequences which have only finitely many distinct terms.

First, let us for simplicity confine our attention to *infinite binary sequences*, that is, functions whose domain is the class N of natural numbers and whose values are always either 0 or 1. I denote the nth term of the sequence s by s_n. The following definition of a random binary sequence is easily seen to be equivalent to Church's original definition. (For a justification of the definition, the reader is referred to Church's paper.)

If $s(= \langle s_0, \ldots, s_n, \ldots \rangle)$ is an infinite binary sequence and $n \in N$, then $s \upharpoonright n$ is to be the sequence consisting of the first n terms of s, that is, the finite sequence $\langle s_0, \ldots, s_{n-1} \rangle$, and $fr_n(s)$ is to be the frequency of 1's among the first n terms of s, that is k/n, where k is the number of 1's among $s_0, \ldots, s_{n-1}$. It is easy to define the notion of a *general recursive class of finite binary sequences*. For instance, if K is a class of finite binary sequences, we may consider the class K' of Gödel–numbers[33] of sequences in K; then we shall call K *general recursive* just in case K' is general recursive (in the familiar sense, as applied to classes of natural numbers[34]).

If $\tau(n)$ is any expression involving the variable "n", then I shall use the abbreviation "$\tau(n) \underset{n}{\Rightarrow} p$" to mean that $\tau(n)$ approaches the limit p as n approaches infinity.

If K is a subset of N and s is an infinite sequence, then I shall say that t *is the subsequence of s determined by K* (regarded as a class of indices) just in case there is an infinite sequence k such that (1) K is the set of terms of k, (2) k is strictly increasing (that is, for all $i, j \in N$ for which $i < j$, $k_i < k_j$), and (3) t is that infinite sequence for which $t_i = sk_i$, for all $i \in N$.

Finally, if s is an infinite binary sequence, then s is *random* if and only if there is a real number p such that, for all K and t, if

---

[31] For a detailed review of the early situation, see Mises [18].

[32] See Church [5].

[33] Obtained, for example, by methods used in Mostowski [19] or by the explicit procedure of Church [5].

[34] See, for instance, Kleene [14].

K is a general recursive class of finite binary sequences and t is the subsequence of s determined by the set of $n \in N$ such that $s \restriction n \in K$, then $fr_n(t) \underset{n}{\Rightarrow} p$. If we demand in this definition that $0 < p < 1$, then we obtain the notion of *strong randomness*, which seems to be the notion involved in Scriven's discussion.

A function D (which is defined for all real numbers) is said to *exhibit a random sequence of values* just in case the infinite sequence $\langle D(0), D(1), \ldots, D(n), \ldots \rangle$ is strongly random.

We may now ask whether there is a deterministic history $\langle D_1, \ldots, D_n \rangle$ (corresponding to a language in which the only elementary constants are one-place operation symbols) such that, for some $i \leqslant n$, D_i exhibits a random sequence of values.[35] It is my conjecture (though not yet confirmed) that by the methods of Wald [28] we can construct a strongly random infinite binary sequence which is definable in terms of $R, N, +$, and $\cdot$. Using such a sequence, we could easily find a deterministic history $\langle D \rangle$ such that D exhibits a random sequence of values.

6. EXPLICIT DEFINABILITY AND DETERMINISM

According to the definition discussed by Russell and mentioned in Section 4, a history is "deterministic" if there is a function f such that, for any instants t_0 and t,

$$st_S(t) = f(st_S(t_0), t_0, t).$$

It was pointed out earlier that this definition is inadequate and that if it is to be amended, some restriction must be imposed on the function f. We may investigate now the consequences of demanding, roughly, that f be *explicitly definable* in terms of $R, N, +$, and $\cdot$. More exactly, we shall turn to *theories* and ask under what conditions we can find, for each state–variable δ_i of a theory T (whose state–variables are the one-place operation symbols $\delta_1, \ldots, \delta_n$), a formula ψ involving no constants beyond

---

[35] The converse question, whether there is a non-deterministic system none of whose functions exhibits a random sequence of values, has an obviously affirmative answer. But this fact is of little interest; it stems from our decision to consider theories with a continuous, rather than a discrete, time-variable.

R, N, $+$, and $\cdot$ such that the formula

$$Rt_0 \wedge Rt \to [u = \delta_i t \leftrightarrow \psi(\delta_1 t_0, \ldots, \delta_n t_0, t_0, t, u)]$$

is derivable from T (on the basis of mathematics). We are thereby led to the notion of *provable determinism* (Definition 15), which is equivalent to the condition of explicit definability (Theorem 8), but, under a certain assumption, stronger than our original notion of determinism (Theorems 12 and 13).

We introduce first the *set of mathematical truths* corresponding to a theory T, and a notation for the set of axioms of T.

Definition 14. If T is a theory, then (i) M_T is the set of all formulas of T which are true in every standard model (for the language of T), and (ii) A_T is the set of axioms of T.

The set M_T provides a *mathematical basis* for the theory T. We shall usually be interested not in the notion of derivability from T alone, but derivability from the combination of T with M_T. The following theorem, whose proof is quite simple, establishes a connection between this kind of derivability and the notion of a standard model.

Theorem 8. If T is a theory whose class of axioms is finite and φ is a formula of T, then $M_T \cup A_T \vdash \varphi$ if and only if φ holds in every standard model in which T holds.

Let the language L_0 have the form $\langle\langle R, N, +, \cdot, \varepsilon_1, \ldots, \varepsilon_k\rangle, \langle\delta\rangle\rangle$, where δ is a one-place operation symbol. We shall for the moment consider primarily those theories which are formulated in L_0.

Definition 15. If T is a theory whose language is L_0, then T is *provably deterministic* if and only if there are constants $\varepsilon_1', \ldots, \varepsilon_k', \delta'$, and a theory T' such that

(1) $\varepsilon_1', \ldots, \varepsilon_k', \delta'$ are not constants of T, but have the same grammatical status as $\varepsilon_1, \ldots, \varepsilon_k, \delta$ respectively (for example, if ε_1 is an n-place predicate, an individual constant or an n-place operation symbol, then ε_1' is correspondingly an n-place predicate, an individual constant, or an n-place operation symbol),

(2) T' is obtained from T by replacing the constants $\varepsilon_1, \ldots, \varepsilon_k$,

δ by $\varepsilon'_1, \ldots, \varepsilon'_k, \delta'$ respectively, and

(3) $M_T \cup A_T \cup M_{T'} \cup A_{T'} \vdash Rt_0 \wedge Rt \wedge \delta t_0 = \delta' t_0 \rightarrow \delta t = \delta' t.$

Theorem 9. If T is a theory whose language is L_0, then the following conditions are equivalent:

(i) T is provably deterministic;

(ii) there is a formula ψ whose free variables are among $v_0, \ldots, v_3$, which contains no constants beyond R, N, $+$, and $\cdot$, and such that

$$M_T \cup A_T \vdash Rt_0 \wedge Rt \rightarrow [u = \delta t \leftrightarrow \psi(\delta t_0, t_0, t, u)].$$

Proof.[36] Assume condition (*i*), and let $\varepsilon'_1, \ldots, \varepsilon'_k, \delta', T'$ be as in Definition 15. Then

(1) $M_T \cup A_T \cup M_{T'} \cup A_{T'} \vdash Rt_0 \wedge Rt \wedge \delta t_0 = \delta' t_0 \rightarrow \delta t = \delta' t.$

It is well known that if a class K of formulas yields a formula, then some finite subclass of K also yields that formula; hence, by (1), there are sentences φ and φ' such that

(2) $\begin{array}{l} M_T \cup A_T \varphi, \\ M_{T'} \cup A_{T'} \varphi', \end{array}$

(3) $\{\varphi, \varphi'\} \vdash Rt_0 \wedge Rt \wedge \delta = \delta' t_0 \rightarrow \delta t = \delta' t$, and

(4) φ is a sentence of L_0.

Because of the special way in which T' was obtained from T, we may choose φ and φ' so that, in addition,

(5) φ' is obtained from φ by replacing the constants $\varepsilon_1, \ldots, \varepsilon_k$, δ by $\varepsilon'_1, \ldots, \varepsilon'_k, \delta'$ respectively.

By (3), we have

$\{\varphi, \varphi'\} \vdash Rt_0 \wedge Rt \wedge v = \delta t_0 \wedge v = \delta' t_0 \wedge u = \delta t \rightarrow u = \delta' t$, and

hence, by the Deduction Theorem and a few manipulations,

(6) $\Lambda \vdash Rt_0 \wedge \varphi \wedge v = \delta t_0 \wedge u = \delta t \rightarrow [Rt \wedge \varphi' \wedge v = \delta' t \rightarrow u = \delta' t].$

---

[36] The method used in the first half of this proof is closely akin to one employed by Craig; see Craig [7], in particular Section 3.

(Here Λ is the empty set.) According to (6), Λ yields a formula of the form $\chi \to \chi'$, where χ and χ' have the predicate R in common, the common constants of χ and χ' are (by (4) and (5)) among R, N, $+$, and $\cdot$, and the free variables of χ and χ' are v, t_0, t, and u. Hence, by a lemma of Craig,[37] there is a formula ψ such that

(7)   the free variables of ψ are among $v_0, \ldots, v_3$

(8) ψ contains no constants beyond R, N, $+$, and $\cdot$,

(9) $\Lambda \vdash Rt_0 \wedge \varphi \wedge v = \delta t_0 \wedge u = \delta t \to \psi(v, t_0, t, u)$, and

(10) $\Lambda \vdash \psi(v, t_0, t, u) \to [Rt \wedge \varphi' \wedge v = \delta't_0 \to u = \delta't]$.

By (9),

(11) $\{\varphi\} \vdash Rt_0 \wedge u = \delta t \to \psi(\delta t_0, t_0, t, u)$.

If Λ yields a formula χ, then Λ also yields the formula obtained from χ by replacing $\varepsilon'_1, \ldots, \varepsilon'_k, \delta'$ by $\varepsilon_1, \ldots, \varepsilon_k, \delta$ respectively. Hence, by (10), (5) and (8)

$$\Lambda \vdash \psi(v, t_0, t, u) \to [Rt \wedge \varphi \wedge v = \delta t_0 \to u = \delta t].$$

Therefore

(12) $\{\varphi\} \vdash Rt \wedge \psi(\delta t_0, t_0, t, u) \to u = \delta t$.

By (2), (11), and (12), we obtain:

$$M_T \cup A_T \vdash Rt_0 \wedge Rt \to [u = \delta t \leftrightarrow \psi(\delta t_0, t_0, t, u)],$$

and this, together with (7) and (8), completes the derivation of condition (ii).

Now assume (ii), and let ψ be as in (ii). Then

(13) $M_T \cup A_T \vdash Rt_0 \wedge Rt \to [u = \delta t \leftrightarrow \psi(\delta t_0, t_0, t, u)]$.

There are clearly $\varepsilon'_1, \ldots, \varepsilon'_k, \delta', T'$ satisfying conditions (1) and (2) of Definition 15. By (13), a general principle of substitution, and the fact that ψ contains none of the constants $\varepsilon_1, \ldots, \varepsilon_k, \delta$, we obtain:

(14) $M_{T'} \cup A_{T'} \vdash Rt_0 \wedge Rt \to [u = \delta't \leftrightarrow \psi(\delta't_0, t_0, t, u)]$.

[37] Craig [7], Lemma 1, pp. 270–71.

Combining (13) and (14), we have:

$$M_T \cup A_T \cup M_{T'} \cup A_{T'} \vdash Rt_0 \wedge Rt \wedge \delta t_0$$
$$= \delta' t_0 \to [u = \delta t \leftrightarrow u = \delta' t],$$

and hence

$$M_T \cup A_T \cup M_{T'} \cup A_{T'} \vdash Rt_0 \wedge Rt \wedge \delta t_0 = \delta' t_0 \to \delta t = \delta' t.$$

But this completes the derivation of condition (i).

Theorem 10. There are theories fromulated in L_0 which are provably deterministic but not deterministic.

Proof. Let T have as its only axiom the formula

$$\vee a \vee b (Ra \wedge Rb \wedge a + a = a \wedge b \cdot b = b \wedge \sim a = b \wedge \delta a = a \wedge \wedge x$$
$$[\sim x = a \to (\vee y \sim Ry \wedge \delta x = b) \vee (\wedge yRy \wedge \delta x = a)]).$$

It is rather easy to see that T is provably deterministic. To show that T is not deterministic, define standard models M, M' as follows:

$$M = \langle R, \langle R, N, +, \cdot, E_1, \ldots, E_k \rangle, \langle D \rangle \rangle,$$
$$M' = \langle R \cup \{x\}, \langle R, N, +, \cdot, E'_1, \ldots, E'_k \rangle, \langle D' \rangle \rangle,$$

where x is an arbitrary object which is not a real number, $E_1, \ldots, E_k, E'_1, \ldots, E'_k$ are arbitrary, and D, D' satisfy the following conditions:

$D(t) = 0$, for $t \in R$;

$D'(0) = 0$;

$D'(t) = 1$, for all $t \in R \cup \{x\}$ for which $t \neq 0$.

Then T holds in both M and M', $Pm(M) = \langle D \rangle$, and $Pm(M') = \langle D' \rangle$; hence $\langle D \rangle, \langle D' \rangle \in Rl(T)$. But

$$st_{\langle D \rangle}(0) = \langle 0 \rangle = st_{\langle D' \rangle}(0),$$

and

$$st_{\langle D \rangle}(1) = \langle 0 \rangle \neq st_{\langle D' \rangle}(1).$$

Therefore T is not deterministic.

If we consider only *predicative theories* (Definition 16), however, then provable determinism implies determinism (Theorem 12).

Definition 16. A theory T is *predicative* just in case there is a set K of sentences of T such that

(1) K is logically equivalent to A_T (that is, for all $\varphi \in K$ and $\psi \in A_T$, $A_T \varphi$ and $K \vdash \psi$),

(2) for each variable α and formula φ, if $\wedge \alpha\varphi$ is a subformula of a sentence in K, then φ has the form

$$(\pi\alpha \rightarrow \psi),$$

for some formula ψ and one-place predicate π, and

(3) for each variable α and formula φ, if $\vee \alpha\varphi$ is a subformula of a sentence in K, then φ has the form

$$(\pi\alpha \wedge \psi),$$

for some formula ψ and one-place predicate π.

Theorem 11. Both of the theories CM and PM are predicative.

Proof. By inspection, we see that each of the axioms of CM can be replaced by a 'predicative' sentence. The least obvious case is that of Axiom (27), but it can be replaced by the sentence

$$\wedge x(Px \rightarrow \vee n[Nn \wedge n < \alpha \wedge x = p_n]) \wedge \wedge n(Nn \rightarrow [n < \alpha \rightarrow P_n]).$$

If $M(= \langle D, \langle E_1, \ldots, E_n \rangle, \langle D_1, \ldots, D_m \rangle \rangle)$ and $M'(= \langle D', \langle E'_1, \ldots, E'_4 \rangle, \langle D'_1, \ldots, D'_m \rangle \rangle)$ are models corresponding to the same language L, then M is a *conservative extension* of M' just in case the following conditions hold, for each positive integer n, each constant ζ of L, and the corresponding interpretations Z and Z' (among $E_1, \ldots, E_h$, $D_1, \ldots, D_m$ and $E'_1, \ldots, E'_h, D'_1, \ldots, D'_m$ respectively):

(1) $D' \subseteq D$,

(2) if ζ is an individual constant, then $Z = Z'$,

(3) if ζ is a predicate (of any number of places), then $Z = Z'$, and

(4) if ζ is an n-place operation symbol and $x_1, \ldots, x_n$ are any elements of D', then $Z(x_1, \ldots, x_n) = Z'(x_1, \ldots, x_n)$.

(This notion differs from the usual notion of an extension only with respect to clause (3). Thus if L has no predicates, the two notions coincide.)

Lemma. If T is a predicative theory which holds in a model M', and M is a conservative extension of M', then T holds in M.

Proof. Let K be a class of sentences of T which satisfies conditions (1)–(3) of Definition 16. By (1),

(4) K holds in M'.

We can show that

(5)   for any subformula φ of a sentence in K, if the free variables of φ are among $v_0, \ldots, v_n$, and $d_0, \ldots, d_n$ are any elements of the domain of discourse of M', then $\langle d_0, \ldots, d_n \rangle$ satisfies φ in M if and only if $\langle d_0, \ldots, d_n \rangle$ satisfies

φ in M',

by a straightforward induction on the number of logical constants in φ. (In the induction step, we make essential use of (2) and (3).) It follows from (5) that if φ is any element of K, then φ holds in M if and only if φ holds in M'. Hence, by (4), K holds in M, and therefore, by (1), T holds in M.

Theorem 12. If T is a predicative theory (whose language is L_0) and T is provably deterministic, then T is deterministic.

Proof. Assume the hypothesis, and that $S, S' \in Rl(T)$, t_0, $t \in R$, and

(1) $st_S(t_0) = st_{S'}(t_0)$.

Then there are standard models M, M' such that T holds in both M and M', $S = Pm(M)$, and $S' = Pm(M')$. Let A be the domain of discourse of M, and A' that of M'. We can easily construct a conservative extension P of M and a conservative extension P' of M' such that the domain of discourse both of P and of P' is $A \cup A'$. By the preceding lemma,

(2) T holds in both P and P'.

Let $\varepsilon_1', \ldots, \varepsilon_k', \delta', T'$ be as in Definition 15, and introduce the language L as follows:

$$L = \langle\langle R, N, +, \cdot, \varepsilon_1, \ldots, \varepsilon_k, \varepsilon_1', \ldots, \varepsilon_k'\rangle, \langle\delta, \delta'\rangle\rangle.$$

Now P has the form $\langle A \cup A', \langle R, N, +, \cdot, E_1, \ldots, E_k\rangle\rangle, \langle D\rangle$, and P' the form $\langle A \cup A', \langle R, N, +, \cdot, E_1', \ldots, E_k'\rangle, \langle D'\rangle\rangle$. Let Q be the model for L determined as follows:

$$Q = \langle A \cup A', \langle R, N, +, \cdot, E_1, \ldots, E_k, E_1', \ldots, E_k'\rangle, \langle D, D'\rangle\rangle.$$

By (2),

(3) A_T and $A_{T'}$ both hold in Q (with respect to the language L).

Further, P and P' are clearly standard models; hence

(4) M_T and $M_{T'}$ both hold in Q (with respect to L).

According to Definition 15,

$$M_T \cup A_T \cup M_{T'} \cup A_{T'} \vdash Rt_0 \wedge Rt \wedge \delta t_0 = \delta' t_0 \rightarrow \delta t = \delta' t.$$

Hence, by (3) and (4), the formula

$$Rt_0 \wedge Rt \wedge \delta t_0 = \delta' t_0 \rightarrow \delta t = \delta' t$$

holds in Q (with respect to L). But t_0, $t \in R$, and, by (1), $D(t_0) = D'(t_0)$. Therefore $D(t) = D'(t)$, and consequently

$$st_S(t) = st_{S'}(t).$$

This completes the proof that T is deterministic.

Determinism does not imply provable determinism, even in the case of predicative theories.

Theorem 13.   There are predicative theories which are deterministic but not provably deterministic.

Proof. Let L be the language $\langle\langle R, N, +, \cdot, 0, 1\rangle, \Lambda\rangle$, where 0, 1 are individual constants, and let M_0 be the model $\langle R, \langle R, N, +, \cdot, 0, 1\rangle, \Lambda\rangle$. (I use '$\Lambda$' to denote the empty sequence as well as the empty set.) We may establish a *Gödel-numbering* of all sentences of L; that is, we may, in a known,[38] effective,

_____

[38] See Gödel [10].

biunique way, assign to each sentence φ of L a positive integer which we shall call the *Gödel-number* of φ. Further, we can find, for each natural number n, a corresponding term $\bar{n}$ of L which will 'denote' n with respect to any standard model; in particular, we give the following recursive definition:

$\bar{0}$ is the symbol 0.

If $n \in N$, then $\overline{n+1}$ is the expression $(\bar{n}+1)$.

Let the language of the theory T be $\langle\langle R, N, +, \cdot, 0, 1, Tr\rangle$, $\langle\delta\rangle\rangle$, where Tr is a one-place predicate and δ is a one-place operation symbol, and let the axioms of T be the following formulas:

(1) $Rx \rightarrow [x = 0 \leftrightarrow x + x = x]$;

(2) $Rx \rightarrow [x = 1 \leftrightarrow x \cdot x = x \wedge {\sim}x = 0]$;

(3) $Trx \rightarrow Nx$;

(4) $Tr\bar{n}$,

for each $n \in N$ such that n is the Gödel-number of a sentence of L which is true in M_0;

(5) ${\sim}Tr\bar{n}$,

for each $n \in N$ such that n is not the Gödel-number of a sentence of L which is true in M_0; and

(6) $Rt \rightarrow (Trt \wedge \delta t = 1) \vee ({\sim}Trt \wedge \delta t = 0)$.

Clearly,

(7) T is predicative.

To show that

(8) T is deterministic,

assume that $\langle D\rangle$, $\langle D'\rangle \in Rl(T)$ and $t \in R$. There are standard models M, M' such that $\langle D\rangle = Pm\langle M\rangle$, $\langle D'\rangle = Pm(M')$, and

(9) T holds in both M and M'.

Since M, M' are standard models, they will have, in view of (9) and the axioms (1) and (2), the respective forms $\langle A, \langle R, N, +, \cdot, 0, 1, K \rangle, \langle D \rangle \rangle$ and $\langle A', \langle R, N, +, \cdot, 0, 1, K' \rangle, \langle D' \rangle \rangle$.[39] To show that

(10) $D(t) = D'(t)$,

let us distinguish three cases. Case I: $t \in N$. By (9), together with axioms (3) and (6), we have, for all $x \in A$:

if $x \in K$, then $x \in N$,
if $x \in R$, then either $x \in K$ and $D(x) = 1$ or $x \in K$ and $D(x) = 0$.

Hence, since $t \in R$ but $t \in N$, $D(t) = 0$. By a similar argument $D'(t) = 0$, and (10) follows. Case II: $t \in N$, but t is not the Gödel-number of a sentence of L which is true in M_0. By (9) and (5), $t \in K$, and hence, by (9) and (6), $D(t) = 0$. By a similar argument, $D'(t) = 0$, and (10) follows. Case III: $t \in N$, and t is the Gödel-number of a sentence of L which is true in M_0. By (9) and (4), $t \in K$, and hence, by (9) and (6), $D(t) = 1$. By a similar argument, $D'(t) = 1$. This completes the proof of (10) and consequently of (8).

Let us now assume that T is provably deterministic. It follows by Theorem 9 (since the language of T satisfies the assumptions imposed on L_0) that there is a formula ψ such that the free variables of ψ are among $v_0, \ldots, v_3$,

(11) ψ contains no constants beyond R, N, $+$, and $\cdot$,

and

$$M_T \cup A_T \vdash Rt_0 \wedge Rt \rightarrow [u = \delta t \leftrightarrow \psi(\delta t_0, t_0, t, u)].$$

Hence

$$M_T \cup A_T \vdash Rt \rightarrow [1 = \delta t \leftrightarrow \psi(\delta 0, 0, t, 1)],$$

and therefore, by axiom (6),

(12) $M_T \cup A_T \vdash Rt \rightarrow [Trt \leftrightarrow \psi(\delta 0, 0, t, 1)].$

---

[39] Strictly speaking, we cannot assert that the interpretation of $+$ will be the same for the two models. Indeed, we may have, corresponding to $+$, two functions, $+'$ and $+''$, with different domains. No confusion, however, will arise from neglecting this possible difference, provided that we speak of the values of $+'$ and $+''$ only for arguments which are real numbers. Similar remarks apply to $\cdot$.

But 0 is the Gödel-number of no sentence. Thus, by (5), $M_T \cup A_T \vdash \sim Tr0$, and hence, by (6), $M_T \cup A_T \vdash \delta0 = 0$. Therefore, by (12),

(13) $M_T \cup A_T \vdash Rt \rightarrow [Trt \leftrightarrow \psi(0, 0, t, 1)]$.

By (11) there is a formula χ such that the only free variable of χ is v_0,

(14) χ is a formula of L,

and

$$M_T \cup A_T \vdash \psi(0, 0, t, 1) \leftrightarrow \chi(t).$$

Hence, by (13),

(15) $M_T \cup A_T \vdash Rt \rightarrow [Trt \leftrightarrow \chi(t)]$.

Now let M_1 be the model $\langle R, \langle R, N, +, \cdot, 0, 1, K \rangle, \langle D \rangle \rangle$, where K is the class of Gödel-numbers of sentences of L which are true in M_0, and, for all $t \in R$,

$$D(t) = \begin{cases} 1 \text{ if } t \in K \\ 0 \text{ if } t \notin K. \end{cases}$$

Clearly, A_T holds in M_1, and, since M_1 is a standard model, M_T holds in M_1. Hence, by (15), the formula

(16) $Rt \rightarrow [Trt \leftrightarrow \chi(t)]$

holds in M_1. Now if n is an arbitrary member of K, the formulas

$R\bar{n}$,

$Tr\bar{n}$

will hold in M_1, and therefore, by (16), so will

$\chi(\bar{n})$.

On the other hand, if n is an arbitrary natural number which is not in K, the formulas

$R\bar{n}$,

$Tr\bar{n}$

will hold in M_1, and hence, by (16), the formula

$$\chi(\bar{n})$$

will not hold in M_1. Thus

(17)   for all $n \in N$, n is the Gödel-number of a sentence of L which is true in M_0 if and only if the sentence $\chi(\bar{n})$ is true in M_1.

But $\chi(\bar{n})$ is a sentence of L (for each $n \in N$). Therefore $\chi(\bar{n})$ is true in M_1 (with respect to the language of T) if and only if $\chi(\bar{n})$ is true in M_0 (with respect to L). Hence, by (17).

> For all $n \in N$, n is the Gödel-number of a sentence of L which is true in M_0 if and only if the sentence $\chi(\bar{n})$ is true in M_0;

that is, speaking loosely, the notion of truth in the model M_0 is definable with respect to M_0. But this is impossible, according to a well-known theorem of Tarski; see Tarski [25]. We have thus arrived at contradiction, and consequently have shown that T is not provably deterministic. But from this, together with (7) and (8), the theorem follows.

Most of the notions and theorems presented so far in this section can be extended in an obvious way to languages of a more complex structure than L_0. For example, let L_1 be a language of the form $\langle\langle R, N, +, \cdot, \varepsilon_1, \ldots, \varepsilon_k \rangle\rangle, \langle \delta_1, \ldots, \delta_n \rangle\rangle$, where $\delta_1, \ldots, \delta_n$ are one-place operation symbols. Then, corresponding to Definition 15 and Theorem 9, we have the following definition and theorem.

Definition 17. If T is a theory whose language is L_1, then T is *provably deterministic* if and only if there are constants $\varepsilon'_1, \ldots, \varepsilon'_k, \delta'_1, \ldots, \delta'_n$, and a theory T' such that

(1) $\varepsilon'_1, \ldots, \varepsilon'_k, \delta'_1, \ldots, \delta'_n$ are not constants of T, but have the same grammatical status as $\varepsilon_1, \ldots, \varepsilon_k, \delta_1, \ldots, \delta_n$ respectively,

(2) T' is obtained from T by replacing the constants $\varepsilon_1, \ldots, \varepsilon_k$, $\delta_1, \ldots, \delta_n$ by $\varepsilon'_1, \ldots, \varepsilon'_k, \delta'_1, \ldots, \delta'_n$ respectively, and

(3) $M_T \cup A_T \cup M_{T'} \cup A_{T'} \vdash R t_0 \wedge R t \wedge \delta_1 t_0 = \delta'_1 t_0 \wedge \ldots \wedge \delta_n t_0 = \delta'_n t_0 \rightarrow \delta_1 t = \delta'_1 t \wedge \ldots \wedge \delta_n t = \delta'_n t$.

Theorem 14. If T is a theory whose language is L_1, then the following conditions are equivalent:

(i) T is provably deterministic;

(ii) for each $i = 1, \ldots, n$, there is a formula ψ_i whose free variables are among $v_0, \ldots, v_{n+2}$, which contains no constants beyond R, N, $+$, and $\cdot$, and such that

$$M_T \cup A_T \vdash Rt_0 \wedge Rt \rightarrow [u = \delta_i t \leftrightarrow \psi_i(\delta_1 t_0, \ldots, \delta_n t_0, t_0, t, u)].$$

Proof. Completely analogous to that of Theorem 9.

The situation becomes slightly more complicated when we pass to state-variables of more than one argument. Let L_2 be a language of the form $\langle\langle R, N, +, \cdot, \varepsilon_1, \ldots, \varepsilon_k\rangle, \langle\pi, \delta\rangle\rangle$, where π is a one-place predicate and δ is a two-place operation symbol, and let $\zeta_1, \ldots, \zeta_n$ be terms of L_2 without free variables. If T is a theory whose language is L_2, then T is said to *concern* $\zeta_1, \ldots, \zeta_n$ just in case $M_T \cup A_T \vdash \pi x \leftrightarrow x = \zeta_1 \vee \ldots \vee x = \zeta_n$.

Corresponding to Definition 15 and Theorem 9, we now have the following definition and theorem.

Definition 18. If T is a theory whose language is L_2 and which concerns $\zeta_1, \ldots, \zeta_n$, then T is *provably deterministic* (relative to $\zeta_1, \ldots, \zeta_n$) if and only if there are constants $\varepsilon'_1, \ldots, \varepsilon'_k$, π', δ', a theory T', and terms $\zeta'_1, \ldots, \zeta'_n$ such that

(1) $\varepsilon'_1, \ldots, \varepsilon'_k$, π', δ' are not constants of T, but have the same grammatical status as $\varepsilon_1, \ldots, \varepsilon_k$, π, δ respectively,

(2) T' is obtained from T by replacing the constants $\varepsilon_1, \ldots, \varepsilon_k$, π, δ by $\varepsilon'_1, \ldots, \varepsilon'_k$, π', δ' respectively, and, for each $i = 1, \ldots, n$, ζ'_i is obtained from ζ_i by the same replacement, and

(3) $M_T \cup A_T \cup M_{T'} \cup A_{T'} \vdash Rt_0 \wedge Rt \wedge \delta\zeta_1 t_0 = \delta'\zeta'_1 t_0 \wedge \ldots \wedge \delta\zeta_n t_0 = \delta'\zeta'_n t_0 \rightarrow \delta\zeta_1 t = \delta'\zeta'_1 t \wedge \ldots \wedge \delta\zeta_n t = \delta'\zeta'_n t$.

Theorem 15. If T is a theory whose language is L_2 and which concerns $\zeta_1, \ldots, \zeta_n$, then the following conditions are equivalent:

(i) T is provably deterministic (relative to $\zeta_1, \ldots, \zeta_n$);

(ii) for each $i = 1, \ldots, n$, there is a formula ψ_i whose free variables are among $v_0, \ldots, v_{n+2}$, which contains no constants beyond R, N, $+$, and $\cdot$, and such that

$$M_T \cup A_T \vdash Rt_0 \wedge Rt \rightarrow [u = \delta\zeta_i t \leftrightarrow \psi_i(\delta\zeta_1 t_0, \ldots, \delta\zeta_n t_0, t_0, t, u)].$$

Proof. Let $\delta_1, \ldots, \delta_n$ be one-place operation symbols which are not constants of L_2, and form the theory T_1 as follows. The language of T_1 is to be $\langle\langle R, N, +, \cdot, \varepsilon_1, \ldots, \varepsilon_k, \pi, \delta\rangle, \langle\delta_1, \ldots, \delta_n\rangle\rangle$, and the axioms of T_1 are to be those of T, together with the following identities:

(1) $\delta_1 t = \delta\zeta_1 t, \ldots,$

$\delta_n t = \delta\zeta_n t.$

Now assume condition (i), and that i is one of the numbers $1, \ldots, n$. It can then be shown in a straightforward way that T_1 is provably deterministic (in the sense of Definition 17). Hence, by Theorem 14, there is a formula ψ_i whose free variables are among $v_0, \ldots, v_{n+3}$, which contains no constants beyond $R, N, +,$ and $\cdot$, and such that

$$M_{T_1} \cup A_{T_1} \vdash Rt_0 \wedge Rt \to [u = \delta_i t \leftrightarrow \psi_i(\delta_1 t_0, \ldots, \delta_n t_0, t_0, t, u)].$$

Therefore, using the equalities (1), we have:

(2) $M_{T_1} \cup A_{T_1} \vdash \chi,$

where χ is the formula

$$Rt_0 \wedge Rt \to [u = \delta\zeta_i i \leftrightarrow \psi_i(\delta\zeta_1 t_0, \ldots, \delta\zeta_n t_0, t_0, t, u)].$$

It is easily seen that the theory whose set of axioms is $M_{T_1} \cup A_{T_1}$ is a *definitional extension* of the theory whose set of axioms is $M_T \cup A_T$; further, χ is a formula of T. Hence, by (2),

$$M_T \cup A_T \vdash \chi,$$

and condition (ii) is established.

The converse implication, from (ii) to (i), can be obtained by a similar argument, again passing through the theory T_1 and employing Theorem 14.

It should be pointed out that Theorem 12 no longer holds when we consider theories whose language is L_2. This fact, which was discovered by Mr. David Kaplan, detracts considerably from the interest of Theorem 11. In view of this situation, it would seem profitable, when considering theories formulated in L_2, to explore other definitions of provable determinism than the one provided by Definition 18. An interesting definition of this sort, for which Theorem 12 remains valid, has been suggested by Mr. Kaplan but will not be discussed here.

It is a completely automatic task to obtain analogues of Definition 18 and Theorem 15 for languages involving, in place of δ, several two-place operation symbols, $\delta_1, \ldots, \delta_m$. It is unnecessary to formulate explicitly the analogue of Definition 18; that of Theorem 15 follows.

Theorem 16. If T is a theory whose language has the form $\langle\langle R, N, +, \cdot, \varepsilon_1, \ldots, \varepsilon_k\rangle, \langle \pi, \delta_1, \ldots, \delta_m\rangle\rangle$ (where π is a one-place predicate and $\delta_1, \ldots, \delta_m$ are two-place operation symbols) and which concerns the terms $\zeta_1, \ldots, \zeta_n$ of this language, then the following conditions are equivalent:

(i) T is provably deterministic (relative to $\zeta_1, \ldots, \zeta_n$);

(ii) for each $i = 1, \ldots, m$ and each $j = 1, \ldots, n$, there is a formula ψ_{ij} whose free variables are among $v_0, \ldots, v_{m \cdot n + 2}$ which contains no constants beyond $R, N, +,$ and $\cdot$, and such that

$$M_T \cup A_T \vdash Rt_0 \wedge Rt \to [u = \delta_i \zeta_j t \leftrightarrow \psi_{ij}(\delta_1 \zeta_1 t_0, \ldots,$$

$$\delta_1 \zeta_n t_0, \ldots, \delta_m \zeta_1 t_0, \ldots, \delta_m \zeta_n t_0, t_0, t, u)].$$

Let us turn our attention once more to Newtonian celestial mechanics. In the manner briefly indicated at the end of Section 3, we may construct (in the style of CM) a theory of celestial mechanics for an arbitrary number of dimensions. If k is a positive integer, let CM_k be the theory thus obtained for k dimensions; then $CM = CM_1$.

As in the proof of Theorem 13, we may associate with each natural number n a term $\bar{n}$ of CM_k which will "denote" n with respect to any standard model. In particular, we may identify $\bar{n}$ with the term

$$\underbrace{0 + 1 + 1 + \ldots + 1}_{n \text{ times}}.$$

If n is any positive integer, we may add to the theory CM_k the axiom

$$\alpha = \bar{n},$$

which is understood as asserting that the number of particles is n. Let the theory so obtained be called $CM_{k,n}$. It is easily seen that

$$M_{CM_{k,n}} \cup A_{CM_{k,n}} \vdash Px \leftrightarrow x = p_0 \vee \ldots \vee x = p_{\overline{n-1}}.$$

Thus $CM_{k,n}$ is a theory which concerns the terms $p_0, \ldots, p_{\overline{n-1}}$, and we may apply Theorem 16 to it.

Now the famous *n-body problem for k dimensions* can be regarded as the task of finding formulas ψ_{ij} which satisfy condition (ii) of Theorem 16, taking $CM_{k,n}$ as T, $p_0, \ldots, p_{\overline{n-1}}$ as $\zeta_1, \ldots, \zeta_n$, and the elementary operation symbols of $CM_{k,n}$ as $\delta_1, \ldots, \delta_m$. (It is trivial to find such formulas for m and g, and consequently the problem is usually stated with reference to position and velocity alone.[40]) By Theorem 16, then, the n-body problem for k dimensions is soluble just in case the theory $CM_{k,n}$ is provably deterministic.

The methods of this paper not only provide a criterion for the solubility of the n-body problem for k dimensions but also, in cases where the theory $CM_{k,n}$ has been effectively shown to be provably deterministic, will lead to an actual solution of the problem. Clause (3) of the definition of provable determinism requires that a certain formula be *logically derivable* from a certain class of formulas. To *show effectively* that a theory is provably deterministic, we must actually exhibit a derivation of the required kind. Given such a derivation, we can construct, in an automatic way, formulas ψ_{ij} satisfying condition (ii) of Theorem 16. To carry out this task, we need only follow through the constructions used in proving Theorems 9 and 15, the antecedent constructions of Craig, and the constructions of Herbrand which are antecedent to those of Craig.[41]

There are several positive integers k and n such that, although no solution to the n-body problem for k dimensions is known, certain *special cases* of the problem (obtained by imposing added conditions on the behavior of the particles involved) have been solved. Each special case of the n-body problem for k dimensions corresponds to an *extension* of the theory $CM_{k,n}$,

[40] For a discussion of the n-body problem, together with various special cases of it, see, for example, Hamel [12].

[41] See Craig [6, 7], and Herbrand [13].

that is, a theory obtained from $CM_{k,n}$ by adding axioms but without altering the language. By Theorem 16, a special case of the n-body problem for k dimensions is soluble just in case it corresponds to a provably deterministic extension of $CM_{k,n}$. Further, by the remarks above, we shall be able to produce an actual solution to each special case which corresponds to an extension of $CM_{k,n}$ for which we have an effective proof of provable determinism.

REFERENCES

1. Carnap, R. *Abriss der Logistik*. Vienna, 1929.
2. —. Foundations of Logic and Mathematics. In *Encyclopedia of Unified Science*, Chicago, 1939.
3. —. *Einführung in die symbolische Logik*. Vienna, 1954.
4. —. *Introduction to Symbolic Logic and its Applications*. New York, 1958.
5. Church, A. On the Concept of a Random Sequence. *Bulletin of the American Mathematical Society* 46:130–35 (1940).
6. Craig, W. Linear Reasoning. A New Form of the Herbrand-Gentzen Theorem. *Journal of Symbolic Logic* 22:250–68 (1957).
7. —. Three Uses of the Herbrand-Gentzen Theorem in Relating Model Theory and Proof Theory. *Journal of Symbolic Logic* 22:269–85 (1957).
8. Davidson, D., P. Suppes, and S. Siegal. *Decision Making*. Stanford, 1951.
9. Estes, W. and P. Suppes. Foundations of Statistical Learning Theory I: The Linear Model for Simple Learning. Technical report, Office of Naval Research, Stanford, 1957.
10. Gödel, K. Über formal unentscheidbare Sätze der *Principia Mathematica* und verwandter Systeme I. *Monatshefte für Mathematik und Physik* 38:173–98 (1931).
11. —. Die Vollständigkeit der Axiome des logischen Funktionenkalküls. *Monatshefte für Mathematik und Physik* 37:349–60 (1940).
12. Hamel, G. *Theoretische Mechanik*. Berlin, 1949.
13. Herbrand, J. Recherches sur la Théorie de la Démonstration. In *Travaux de la Société des Sciences et des Lettres de Varsovie*, Classe III 33, Warsaw, 1930.
14. Kleene, S. *Introduction to Metamathematics*. Princeton, 1952.
15. Landau, E. *Differential and Integral Calculus*. New York, 1951.

16. MacCorquodale, K. and P. Meehl. Hypothetical Constructs and Intervening Variables. *Psychological Review* 55:95–107 (1948).
17. McKinsey, J., A. Sugar, and P. Suppes. Axiomatic Foundations of Classical Particle Mechanics. *Journal of Rational Mechanics and Analysis* 2:253–72 (1953).
18. Mises, R. *Probability, Statistics, and Truth.* New York, 1939.
19. Mostowski, A. *Sentences Undecidable in Formalized Arithmetic.* Amsterdam, 1952.
20. Nagel, E. The Causal Character of Modern Physical Theory. In H. Feigl and M. Brodbeck (eds.), *Readings in the Philosophy of Science.* New York, 1953.
21. Quine, W. *Mathematical Logic,* rev. ed. Cambridge, Mass., 1955.
22. Russell, B. On the Notion of Cause, with Applications to the Free-Will Problem. In H. Feigl and M. Brodbeck (eds.), *Readings in the Philosophy of Science.* New York, 1953.
23. Scriven, M. The Present Status of Determinism in Physics. *Journal of Philosophy* 54:727–41 (1957).
24. Suppes, P. *Introduction to Logic.* Princeton, 1957.
25. Tarski, A. Der Wahrheitsbegriff in den formalisierten Sprachen. *Studia Philosophica* 1:261–405 (1936).
26. —. Contributions to the Theory of Models. *Indagationes Mathematicae* 16:572–88 (1954) and 17:56–64 (1955).
27. Tarski, A., A. Mostowski, and R. Robinson. *Undecidable Theories.* Amsterdam, 1953.
28. Wald, A. Die Widerspruchsfreiheit des Kollektivbegriffes der Wahrscheinlichkeitsrechnung. *Ergebnisse eines mathematischen Kolloquiums* 8:38–72 (1935–36).

Works of Richard Montague, a Bibliography

All items except those indicated by * are on file in the Philosophy Reading Room, University of California at Los Angeles.

1. Montague and J. Tarski. On Bernstein's Self-Dual Set of Postulates for Boolean Algebras. *Proc. Am. Math. Soc.* 5:310–11 (1954).
2. Non-finitizable and Essentially Non-finitizable Theories. *Bull. Am. Math. Soc.* 61:172–73 (1955).
3. On the Paradox of Grounded Classes. *Journal of Symbolic Logic* 20:140 (1955).
4.* Well-founded Relations: Generalizations of Principles of Induction and Recursion. *Bull. Am. Math. Soc.* 61:443 (1955).
5. Zermelo-Fraenkel Set Theory Is Not a Finite Extension of Zermelo Set Theory. *Bull. Am. Math. Soc.* 62:260 (1956).
6. Montague and D. Kalish. A Simplification of Tarski's Formulation of the Predicate Calculus. *Bull. Am. Math. Soc.* 62:261 (1956).
7. —. An Extension of Tarski's Notion of Satisfaction. *Bull. Am. Math. Soc.* 62:261 (1956).
8. —. Formulations of the Predicate Calculus with Operation Symbols and Descriptive Phrases. *Bull. Am. Math. Soc.* 62:261 (1956).
9. Montague and L. Henkin. On the Definition of 'Formal Deduction'. *Journal of Symbolic Logic* 21:129–36 (1956).
10. Models of Set Theories. *Bull. Am. Math. Soc.* 62:599–600 (1956).
11. Review of Wang, Arithmetic Translations of Axiom Systems (*Trans. Am. Math. Soc.* 71:283–93 (1951)). *Journal of Symbolic Logic* 21:402–403 (1956).
12.* Independently Axiomatizable Theories. *Bull. Am. Math. Soc.* 63:26 (1957).
13. Review of Wang, Between Number Theory and Set Theory (*Math. Assn.* 126:385–409 (1953)). *Journal of Symbolic Logic* 22:82–83 (1957).
14. Montague and D. Kalish. Remarks on Descriptions and Natural Deduction, Part 1. *Archiv für mathematische Logik und Grundlagenforschung* 3:50–64 (1957).

15. Non-finite Axiomatizability. In *Summaries of Talks Presented at the Summer Institute of Symbolic Logic in 1957 at Cornell University Sponsored by the American Mathematical Society under a Grant from the National Science Foundation* 2:256–59. Mimeographed, Cornell, 1957.

16. Two Theorems on Relative Interpretability. *Ibid.* 2:263–65.

17. Montague and A. Tarski. Independent Recursive Axiomatizability. *Ibid.* 2:270–71.

18. Montague and R. Vaught. Models of Set Theory. *Ibid.* 3:353–55.

19.* An Extension of Gödel's Incompleteness Theorem. *Bull. Am. Math. Soc.* 63:399 (1957).

20. Review of Wang, Truth Definitions and Consistency Proofs (*Trans. Am. Math. Soc.* 73:243–75 (1952)). *Journal of Symbolic Logic* 22:365–67 (1957).

21. Montague and D. Kalish. Remarks on Descriptions and Natural Deduction, Part 2. *Archiv für math. Logik und Grundlagenforschung* 3:65–73 (1958).

22.* Incomparable Theories. *Notices of the Am. Math. Soc.* 6:362–63 (1958).

23. Montague and D. Kalish. 'That'. *Philosophical Studies* 10:54–61 (1959). Chapter 2 in this book.

24. The Continuum of Relative Interpretability Types. *Journal of Symbolic Logic* 23:460 (1958).

25. Montague and R. Vaught. Natural Models of Set Theories. *Fundamenta Mathematicae* 47:219–42 (1959).

26. —. A Note on Theories with Selectors. *Fundamenta Mathematicae* 47:243–47 (1959).

27. Review of Martin, *Truth and Denotation: A Study in Semantical Theory* (Chicago, 1958). *Journal of Symbolic Logic* 24:217–19 (1959).

28. D. Kaplan and Montague. A Paradox Regained. *Notre Dame Journal of Formal Logic* 1:79–90 (1960). Chapter 9 in this book.

29. Logical Necessity, Physical Necessity, Ethics, and Quantifiers. *Inquiry* 4:259–69 (1960). Chapter 1 in this book.

30. Review of Martin, On Inscriptions (*Philosophy and Phenomenological Research* 11:535–640 (1951)). *Journal of Symbolic Logic* 25:84–85 (1960).

31. Review of Martin, On Inscriptions and Concatenation (*Philosophy and Phenomenological Research* 12:418–21 (1952)). *Journal of Symbolic Logic* 25:85 (1960).

32. Review of Leblanc, Evidence Logique et Degré de Confirmation (*Revue Philosophique de Louvain* 52:619–25 (1954)). *Journal of Symbolic Logic* 25:86 (1960).

33. Review of Leblanc, On Logically False Evidence Statements (*Journal of Symbolic Logic* 22:345–59 (1957)). *Journal of Symbolic Logic* 25:86–87 (1960).

34. Review of Simon, Definable Terms and Primitives in Axiom Systems (in *The Axiomatic Method*, Amsterdam, 1959). *Journal of Symbolic Logic* 25:355–56 (1960).

35. Towards a General Theory of Computability. *Synthèse* 12:429–38 (1960).

36. Semantical Closure and Non-finite Axiomatizability I. In *Infinitistic Methods*. Warsaw, 1961.

37. R. Eberle, D. Kaplan, and Montague. Hempel and Oppenheim on Explanation. *Philosophy of Science* 28:418–28 (1961).

38. Fraenkel's Addition to the Axioms of Zermelo. In *Essays in the Foundations of Mathematics*. Jerusalem, 1961.

39. Two Contributions to the Foundations of Set Theory. In *Proceedings of the International Congress of Logic, Methodology and Philosophy of Science*. Stanford, 1962.

40. Deterministic Theories. In *Decisions, Values, and Groups* 2. Oxford, 1962. Chapter 11 in this book.

41. Theories Incomparable with Respect to Relative Interpretability. *Journal of Symbolic Logic* 27:195–211 (1962).

42. Syntactical Treatments of Modality, with Corollaries of Reflexion Principles and Finite Axiomatizability. *Acta Philosophica Fennica* 16:153–67 (1963). Chapter 10 in this book.

43. Set Theory and Higher-Order Logics (abstract). *Journal of Symbolic Logic* 28:266 (1963).

44. D. Kalish and Montague. *Logic: Techniques of Formal Reasoning*. New York, 1964.

45. —. On Tarski's Formalization of Predicate Logic with Identity. *Archiv für mathematische Logik und Grundlagenforschung* 7:81–101 (1965).

46. Set Theory and Higher-Order Logic. In *Formal Systems and Recursive Functions, Proceedings of the Eighth Logic Colloquium, Oxford, July 1963*. Amsterdam, 1965.

47. Interpretability in Terms of Models. *Indagationes Mathematicae* 27:467–76 (1965); and *Koninklijke Nederlandse Akademie van Wetenschappen, Amsterdam, Proceedings*, ser. A, 68:457–76 (1965).

48. D. Kaplan and Montague. Foundations of Higher-Order Logic. *Proceedings of the 1964 International Congress for Logic, Methodology, and Philosophy of Science, Jerusalem, August–September 1964*. Amsterdam, 1965.

49. Reductions of Higher-Order Logic. In *The Theory of Models: Proceedings of the 1963 Symposium at Berkeley*. Amsterdam, 1965.

50. Review of Martin, *Intension and Decision: A Philosophical Study* (Englewood Cliffs, N.J., 1963). *Journal of Symbolic Logic* 31:98–102 (1966).

51. R. Marcus, W. Boone, and Montague. Meeting of the Association for Symbolic Logic. *Journal of Symbolic Logic* 31:147 (1966).

52. Review of Tucker, The Formalization of Set Theory (*Mind* 72:500–18 (1963)). *Journal of Symbolic Logic* 31:676–77 (1966).

53. A generalization of Recursion Theory (abstract). *Journal of Symbolic Logic* 32:443–44 (1967).

54. General Formulations of Gödel's Second Underivability Theorem (abstract). *Journal of Symbolic Logic* 32:444 (1967).

55. Pragmatics. In R. Klibansky (ed.), *Contemporary Philosophy: A Survey* 1. Florence, 1968. Chapter 3 in this book.

56. Recursion Theory as a Branch of Model Theory. In van Rootselaar and Staal (eds.), *Logic, Methodology, and Philosophy of Science* 3. Amsterdam, 1968.

57. Pragmatics and Intensional Logic. *Synthèse* 22:68–94 (1970). Chapter 4 in this book.

58. On the Nature of Certain Philosophical Entities. *Monist* 53:159–94 (1969). Chapter 5 in this book.

59. Comments in Symposium on 'Formal Logic and Natural Languages'. *Foundations of Language* 5:256–84 (1969).

60.* On the Nature of Certain Philosophical Entities (summary). *Akten des 15. Internationalen Kongresses fur Philosophie, Vienna, September, 1968* 3:201–02 (1969).

61. On the Nature of Certain Philosophical Entities (abstract). *Review of Metaphysics* 23:165–66 (1969).

62. English as a Formal Language I. In B. Visentini et al., *Linguaggi nella Società e nella Tecnica*. Milan, 1970. Chapter 6 in this book.

63. Universal Grammar. *Theoria* 36:373–98 (1970). Chapter 7 in this book.

64. Universal Grammar. Reference materials for a talk, May, 1970.

65. The Proper Treatment of Quantification in Ordinary English. In J. Hintikka, J. Moravcsik, and P. Suppes (eds.), *Approaches to Natural Language*. Dordrecht, 1973. Chapter 8 in this book.

66. Quantification in Ordinary English. Reference materials, October 16, 1970.

67. Letter to D. Scott with comments on Scott's Advice on Modal Logic, June 21–30, 1968.

68. Universal Grammar. Mimeographed version marked 'to appear.'

69. Intensional Logic and Some of its Connections with Ordinary Language. Reference materials for a talk, April, 1969. Delivered at Southern California Logic Colloquium, Los Angeles, March 14, 1969; and at Association for Symbolic Logic, Cleveland, May 1, 1969.

Index